Perspectives on the Adirondacks

PERSPECTIVES
ON THE
ADIRONDACKS

A Thirty-Year Struggle by People Protecting Their Treasure

BARBARA McMARTIN

Syracuse University Press

Publication of this book is made possible by a grant from Furthermore, a program of the J. M. Kaplan Fund.

Library of Congress Cataloging-in-Publication Data

McMartin, Barbara.
Perspectives on the Adirondacks : a thirty-year struggle by people
Protecting their treasure / Barbara McMartin.—1st ed.
p. cm.
Includes bibliographical references (p.) and index.
ISBN 0-8156-0742-3 (cl. : alk. paper)
Adirondack Park (N.Y.)—History. 2. Adirondack Park
(N.Y.)—Management—History. 3. Adirondack Park (N.Y.)—Environmental
conditions. 4. Adirondack Mountains Region (N.Y.)—History. 5.
Adirondack Mountains Region (N.Y.)—Environmental conditions. I. Title.
F127.A2 M366 2002
974.7'5—dc21
2002003406

Contents

Illustrations

🌲 | Acknowledgments

SEVERAL INDIVIDUALS AGREED to read the book in manuscript. Their input helped me find a focus for the book that otherwise would have been missing. I found their advice and suggestions invaluable: Paul Bray, member of many environmental groups, formerly head of bill drafting for the New York State Assembly; James C. Dawson, New York State Regent and member or officer of many environmental groups; James Hotaling, Local Planning, Adirondack Park Agency; Peter Bauer, executive director, Residents' Committee to Protect the Adirondacks and staff member Commission on the Adirondacks in the 21st Century; Thomas Ulasewicz, former lawyer for DEC and executive director of Adirondack Park Agency; Philip G. Terrie, professor of English and American Culture Studies at Bowling Green State University, author of *Forever Wild: A Cultural History of Wilderness in the Adirondacks* and *Contested Terrain: A New History and People in the Park*.

My thanks to all of them for their comments. My book is richer for their help. I especially want to thank Betsy Folwell for editing this book. She has edited several of my earlier books, and each time her insight has helped me focus on what I want to accomplish. I am very fortunate to have her and all the others spend so much time working on this book.

I am also indebted to the New York State Archives, the Adirondack Research Library of the Association for the Protection of the Adirondacks, the Saranac Free Library, and the Johnstown Public Library. My most important resource proved to be the Adirondack Museum Library at Blue Mountain Lake, and I appreciate Jerold Pepper's help in using it.

This book is a compendium of memories, and a large number of individuals agreed to be interviewed. Not only did they contribute personal insights to the story, but many helped me shape my ideas and understanding of the events. I am indebted to all of them.

Writing a history that begins a mere three decades ago and ends in the present creates strange problems. Newspaper accounts, letters, faxes, and so on abound; in addition almost all of the participants are living and their memories become a part of the record. But memories are sometimes ephemeral or clouded with the perspective of personal desires, wishful thinking, roles in ongoing conflicts, and more recent events. Indeed, it has been challenging to sort out reality from recollection and to reconcile different memories. Many players remember certain events differently, especially those where emotions ran high or the issue was complex. I have tried to use only information that has been corroborated by more than one individual or to note where there are questions.

Even the newspaper accounts vary according to the perspectives of the papers or their correspondents, but they are a very valuable resource because they tell us what people in the Adirondacks knew as events were unfolding.

With these caveats, I could not have written this book without the interviews, notes, e-mails, and conversations with so many of the people who made things happen in the past thirty years. I thank them all for their help.

The following is an alphabetical list of those interviewed. The backgrounds of those quoted are mentioned in the text. Carol LaGrasse deserves special thanks for assisting my research on all aspects of the property rights movement in the Adirondacks. Harold Jerry, who died as I was finishing this book, was the first person I interviewed; I could have written an entire book about his accomplishments with respect to the Adirondacks, and I was honored to include his views.

Susan Allen
Howard Aubin
John Banta
Claire Barnett
Tim Barnett
Peter Bauer
Dick Beamish
Mary Arthur Beebe
Mark Behan
Frances Beinecke
Robert Bendick
Peter Berle
Peter Borelli
Paul Bray
Cali Brooks

Eleanor Brooks
Wayne Byrne
George Canon
Emily Haydon, CLEAR
Chuck Clusen
John Collins
Jim Cooper
Graham Cox
Arthur Crocker's papers
Bill Curran
Lou Curth
Donald Curtis
Karen Habla Daniels
George Davis
James C. Dawson

Mike DiNunzio

Roger Dziengelewski

Steve Erman

Senator Hugh Farley

Robert Flacke

Dale French

Jim Frenette

David Gibson

Barbara Glazer

Robert Glennon

Roger Gray

Evelyn Greene

Andy Halloran

Ken Hamm

Phil Hansen

Glenn Harris's papers

Jennifer Potter Hays

Ed Hood

Jim Hotaling

Ted Hullar

Harold Jerry

Robert Kafin

John Keating

William Kissel

Heidi Kretser

Judy LaBelle

Carol LaGrasse

Richard Lefebvre

Joe Martens

Terry DeFranco Martino

Bernard Melewski

Ann Melious

Per and Margaret Moberg

Carol Monroe

Charlie Morrison

Frank Murray

George Nagle

Dave Newhouse

Ralph Nyland

Peter S. Paine, Jr.

Jim Papero

Richard Persico

Clarence Petty

Dennis Phillips

Richard Purdue

Jean Raymond

Karyn Richards

Joe Rota

Ron Rybecki

Sam Sage

Neil Seymour

John Sheehan

Senator Ronald Stafford

Bob Stegemann

Philip Terrie

Liz Thorndike

Tom Ulasewicz

Vincent Vaccaro

Peter E. Van de Water

Abby Verner

Lee Wasserman

Christopher Westbrook

Ross Whaley

Neil Woodworth

| # Acronyms and Abbreviations

AARCH	Adirondack Architectural Heritage
AATV	Association of Adirondack Towns and Villages
ACC	Adirondack Conservation Council
ACT	Adirondack Community Trust
ADA	Americans with Disabilities
ADE	*Adirondack Daily Enterprise*
ADK	Adirondack Mountain Club; club
AEDC	Adirondack Economic Development Corporation
AJ	*Adirondack Journal*
ALA	Adirondack Landowners Association
AM	Adirondack Museum
ANC	Adirondack Nature Conservancy
ANCA	Adirondack North Country Association
APA	Adirondack Park Agency; the agency
APA Act	Adirondack Park Agency Act
APC	Adirondack Planning Commission
ARC	Adirondack Research Consortium
ARTC	Adirondack Regional Tourism Council
ASA	Adirondack Solidarity Alliance
ATIS	Adirondack Trail Improvement Society
ATU	*Albany Times Union*
ATV	all-terrain vehicles
BLC	Blue Line Council
CABR	Champlain-Adirondack Biosphere Reserve
CAC	Citizen's Advisory Committee
CCFP	Constitutional Council for the Forest Preserve
CFAM	Commission's Files at the Adirondack Museum
CLEAR	Clearinghouse on Environmental Advocacy and Research

Council	The Adirondack Council
CSAP	Citizens to Save the Adirondack Park
DEC	Department of Environmental Conservation; department
DED	Department of Economic Development
DLF	Division of Lands and Forests
DOH	Department of Health
DOS	Department of State
ECL	Environmental Conservation Law
ECO	Environmental Conservation Office
EIS	Environmental Impact Statement
EPF	Environmental Protection Fund
EPL	Environmental Planning Lobby
ESFPA	Empire State Forest Products Association
ETF	Environmental Trust Fund
FPAC	Forest Preserve Advisory Committee
GFPS	*Glens Falls Post Star*
GIS	Geographic Information System
HCN	*Hamilton County News*
HKH Foundation	Harold K. Hochschild Foundation
HPAC	High Peaks Advisory Committee
HPIC	High Peaks Information Center
HPUMP	High Peaks Unit Management Plan
HPWAUMP	High Peaks Wilderness Area Unit Management Plan
IDAs	Industrial Development Authorities
IP	International Paper [7]
ISTEA	Intermodal Surface Transportation Efficiency Act
LGA	Lake George Association
LGD	Local Government Day
LGRB	Local Government Review Board; review board
LPN	Lake Placid News
LWV	League of Women Voters
MOA	Memorandum of Agreement
MOU	Memorandum of Understanding
NBC	NYS Natural Beauty Commission
NCNE	*North Creek News Enterprise*
NCNST	North Country National Scenic Trail
NFLC	Northern Forest Lands Council
NGO	nongovernmental organization
NIMO	Niagara Mohawk Power Corporation

NPS EOO	National Park Service Equal Opportunity Office
NRA	National Rifle Association
NRDC	National Resources Defense Council
OIGs	Overall Intensity Guidelines
OPDPR	Office of Program Development, Planning and Research
OPRHP	Office of Parks, Recreation, and Historical Preservation
ORDA	Olympic Regional Development Authority
OSI	Open Space Institute
OSP	Open Space Plan
PAW	Protect Adirondack/Appalachian Wilderness
PLUDP	Private Land Use and Development Plan
PR	(Plattsburgh) Press Republican
PRFA	Property Rights Foundation of America, Inc.
PS	*Post Star*
RARE	Roadless Area Review and Evaluation
RCPA	Residents' Committee to Protect the Adirondacks
RC&D	Resource Conservation and Development
RM	Resource Management
RU	Rural Use
SDRs	structural development rights
SEQR	State Environmental Quality Review
Sierra	Adirondack Committee of the Atlantic Chapter of the Sierra Club
SLMP	State Land Master Plan
SROs	Special Revenue Other
SUNY ESF	State University of New York Syracuse College of Environmental Science and Forestry
TAC	The Adirondack Council
TDR	transferable development right
TFG	The Forestland Group
TLFP	*Tupper Lake Free Press*
TRP	Temporary Revocable Permit
TSC	Temporary Study Commission
U & I	Use and Information
UHEAC	Upper Hudson Environmental Action Committee
UMP	Unit Management Plan
UNESCO	United Nations Educational, Scientific and Cultural Organization
USF&G	U.S. Fidelity and Guaranty Corp.

USGS   U.S. Geological Survey
VICs   Visitors' Interpretive Centers
WCS   Wildlife Conservation Society
W-LGN   *Warrensburg–Lake George News,*
21st Century
   Commission   Commission on the Adirondacks in the 21st Century;
                the commission

Perspectives on the Adirondacks

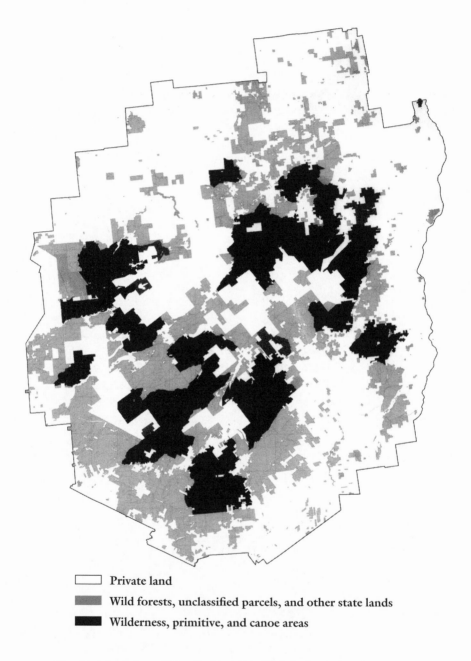

☐ Private land

■ Wild forests, unclassified parcels, and other state lands

■ Wilderness, primitive, and canoe areas

Blue Line boundary of New York's Adirondack Park showing the private lands and the major classifications of Forest Preserve lands.

1 | Introduction

Historical Introduction

HISTORY IS A LONG LINE of events, and the historian's role is to find out why events occurred, to elucidate their interconnectedness and influences, and to understand the role that individuals and groups or societies played in creating and reacting to those events. The flow of historical events is not smoothly linear; the proliferation of events corresponding to the world's increasing complexity is not a smooth expansion. There are short periods when multiple happenings are bunched together in times so momentous they are remembered as milestones of history. And sometimes it is the synergy of seemingly unrelated events that creates these clusters, and the results are true changes in direction.

In the history of the Adirondack Park, such a cluster occurred around 1890. Within a period of a few years loggers began to cut the region's softwoods more intensely than at any time before; they no longer harvested only the larger spruce for lumber but cut ever smaller trunks for pulp. The newly built railroad that traversed the Adirondacks from southwest to northeast allowed lumbermen to begin harvesting hardwoods for commercial use. It also allowed wealthy individuals and club members to reach the Adirondacks, where the beauty and remoteness inspired them to acquire huge private preserves. A growing tide of farsighted individuals saw aggressive timber cutting as a challenge to water preservation and the wild nature of the region. A movement, literary and artistic, philosophical and rhetorical, awakened the New York state legislature to the need for creating the Forest Preserve, the lands owned by the state that would be held forever as wild forest lands from which no trees could be removed (1885) and delineating the Adirondack Park (1892) with its blue-line boundary, which encompassed both the Forest Preserve and private lands. Both the legislature and the people of the state responded by giving the Forest

Preserve constitutional protection. The actions to accomplish this protection occurred in a decade or so centered on 1890.

One early action was the establishment of the Forest Commission, set up in 1885 to oversee the Forest Preserve. A series of commissions followed, culminating in 1911 in the creation of the state's Conservation Department. A group of landowners founded in 1901 the prototype of today's environmental organizations, the Association for the Protection of the Adirondacks, which adopted the motto "Watchdog of the Forest Preserve" in the late 1920s.

Many people have summarized and analyzed the Adirondack region's historical record prior to 1890 and from then to 1970. Frank Graham's book *The Adirondack Park, A Political History*[1] is perhaps the best and should be read as an added introduction to this book.

It is possible to describe in a single volume what happened before 1970 as Graham did, but I discovered that it was very difficult to condense into a single volume the events of the following thirty years with their complexity of philosophies, governments, regulations, bureaucracies, organizations, and people.

The 1970 Cluster

A second notable cluster of events, which occurred roughly eight decades after the birth of the Adirondack Park in 1892, began with the 1967 state constitutional convention. After much debate, the convention left unchanged the principle of the Forest Preserve and Article XIV, which states that all the lands owned or later acquired in eleven Adirondack counties "shall be forever kept as wild forest lands."

Modern challenges to the Forest Preserve had grown with the expanded use of motor vehicles. Modern highways brought increasing numbers of visitors to the Adirondack Park. The automobile provided middle-class vacationers the mobility to seek second homes adjacent to state lands and threatened to put camps along every shoreline within the park. The four-lane Adirondack Northway, completed in the 1960s, forever altered the park—not just by bringing more vacationers, but by making it possible to commute to cities outside the park from Adirondack hamlets and lakeshores.

After World War II, visitors sought to use jeeps on the old logging roads that had been cut through all but three or four hundred thousand acres of what had become the Forest Preserve. The introduction of snowmobiles and their owners' desires for trails in the Forest Preserve, the latter abetted by the Conservation Department, spawned a movement toward stricter controls of the Forest Preserve, controls that would address uses of the preserve that its creators never envisioned. By jeep and four-wheel-drive trucks people reached, or tried to reach, the remaining large tracts, of which a few were remnants of private preserves, but most were owned by forest-product industries or were public lands.

In the decades bracketing the mid-twentieth century, those using the park for recreation changed from primarily sportsmen, hunters, and fishermen to hikers and vacationers with motorboats, snowmobiles, and, ultimately, off-road vehicles. The nation's search for healthful recreation put more people in the backcountry than ever before. The new recreationists demanded developed campgrounds and well-marked trails. The numbers of visitors to the Adirondacks kept pace with the public's increasing wealth and leisure time.

The Joint Legislative Committee on Natural Resources had been looking at these new pressures on the park during the 1950s, in particular with respect to the way they affected the Forest Preserve. By 1960, the committee, now dubbed the Pomeroy Commission after R. Watson Pomeroy (New York state assemblyman, then New York state senator), considered the wilderness characteristics of the Forest Preserve, pushed legislation that would limit motorized use in the Forest Preserve, and tried to influence the Conservation Department to establish limits on the use of motors.

In 1967, Laurance S. Rockefeller, chairman of the State Council of Parks, and others proposed creating a 1.12-million-acre national park in the heart of the mountain region. The Adirondack Mountains National Park would include six hundred thousand acres of private land that the federal government would acquire in the next fifteen years. This proposal pleased no one, but it did unify the state in opposition to any federal presence in the Adirondacks. New Yorkers seemed determined to rely on the state constitution's Forever Wild clause to protect the Forest Preserve. At the same time, the need to deal with modern threats to the Forest Preserve became entwined with emerging concepts of wilderness and a desire that these be applied to the preserve. The proposal for a national park was quickly abandoned—but not before it had focused people's attention on the need to reform park management.

Ultimately it took Governor Nelson A. Rockefeller's political power to launch needed legislation. Rockefeller began by establishing the Temporary Study Commission on the Adirondacks, chaired by Harold Hochschild. Its recommendations and Rockefeller's commitment resulted in the passing of the Adirondack Park Agency (APA) Act in the spring of 1971. The act establishing the agency became effective in September 1971; within three years, the fledgling agency had written a State Land Master Plan to guide management of the Forest Preserve in the Adirondacks and a Private Land Use and Development

Plan to regulate development on private lands so that it would not threaten precious public lands. All this was none too soon, for, also in the early 1970s, Lake Placid won the right to begin planning for the 1980 Olympics with needed recreational facilities—wider ski trails, a ski jump, new roads, state-of-the-art telecommunications—more modern-day threats to the Forest Preserve. Infrastructure for the Olympics challenged the small-town character of nearby settlements.

Earth Day, April 23, 1970, marked the organization of an indigenous Adirondack environmental group,* the Upper Hudson Environmental Action Committee, based in North Creek. Growing rapidly, the environmental community had expanded in the decades leading up to 1970 to include the Adirondack Mountain Club (an uneasy alliance of recreation enthusiasts and conservationists) and the Constitutional Council for the Forest Preserve. Sierra Club members founded the Atlantic Chapter and its very active Adirondack Committee. Several of these groups joined together in 1974 to form the Adirondack Council as their litigating arm.

In the interval between 1890 and 1970, the period between the two milestone clusters, there were numerous threats to the Forest Preserve. Some, such as proposals for amendments to the state constitution that would have permitted the harvesting of trees for silviculture or for increasing deer herds, were relatively easy to defeat. Others, such as proposals to dam the region's free-flowing rivers and to flood wide swaths of forest to harness water for power were great challenges to the organizations that expanded to support the Forest Preserve. These groups included the Adirondack Mountain Club and the New York State Conservation Council.

The most effective leader in these struggles was Paul Schaefer, a member of the Association for the Protection of the Adirondacks. He used that organization, but often decided that it was more effective to found and mobilize special groups dedicated to specific issues. Among the nine different groups he founded were the Adirondack Moose River Committee (1945), which opposed the Higley and Panther mountain dams, and the Adirondack Hudson River Committee (1965), which fought the Gooley dam proposal. In 1945 he founded the Friends of the Forest Preserve, whose goals are found in the recommendations of the Temporary Study Commission.

---

* The term "environmental group" is used in this book to describe organizations concerned primarily with preserving or protecting the park. There is an enormous range of environmental groups, from those championing wilderness to those interested in recreational or economic values as well as natural resources.

The defense of Article XIV of the New York State constitution was the basis for every one of these actions to protect the Forest Preserve in the years before 1970. The blue line marking the park boundary had been expanded, more land was brought under Forest Preserve protection, and attorneys general had rendered opinions on the use of the Forest Preserve, but during the period between 1890 and the prelude to 1970, Article XIV remained the principal tool for protecting the growing Forest Preserve. No comprehensive additional protective legislation was considered until almost 1960, and none was passed until the APA Act.

Throughout the middle of the twentieth century, forest managers attached modern theories of biological and ecological protection to forest lands and began to theorize about the "wilderness" values of wild lands. The concept of wilderness emerged on the national level through the writings of John Muir, Aldo Leopold, and Bob Marshall among many others. Paul Schaefer's most important contribution in the 1920s and 1930s was his pursuit of the idea that the Forest Preserve is valuable for the land itself, not for any utilitarian values such as the water resources he worked to protect. In this way, he was one of the state's earliest wilderness voices.

On the national level, the concept of wilderness was codified in 1964 by Howard Zahniser[2] in the Federal Wilderness Act. According to that act "wilderness" was defined as an area where, in contrast to those areas where man and his own works dominate the landscape, the earth and its community of life are untrammeled by man—where man himself is a visitor who does not remain. Wilderness has primeval character, dominated by natural conditions, with the works of man substantially unnoticeable.

Threats to the Forest Preserve that climaxed before 1970 occurred because the concept of "forest preserve" was too unsubstantial to address the challenges of the late twentieth century; it proved difficult to translate "forever wild" into management and regulations. New York's form of forest preservation—never cutting trees—was remarkably adequate for the protection of flora and fauna, but it did not speak directly to wilderness concepts, nor did it address the changing world with its motors and mobility. Theorists in New York reflected on the ideas coming from the national scene, the need for biological and ecological protection of wild lands.

Influenced by discussions of wilderness at the national level, leaders in the state, both legislators and emerging environmentalists like Schaefer, began to imbue a part of the state's public lands with the emerging wilderness philosophy. The discussions of wilderness of the 1950s and 1960s created the intellectual foundation for the actions of 1970; they set the stage upon which the APA

Act was established. Thus, in significant ways, the concept of wilderness drove the establishment of the Adirondack Park Agency and the APA's State Land Master Plan.

However, the concept of wilderness circa 1970 was but one in a long line of interpretations. In the course of written history, wilderness has been depicted as a place of terror. Later it was seen as a spiritual place, imbued with romanticism. In the nineteenth century it was associated with a sense of the sublime and the country's frontiers. Wilderness became associated with uninhabited areas, places without human history. All these ideas of wilderness were creations of the culture at the time. The twentieth-century view placed humans outside the natural world, and according to William Cronon, "We leave ourselves little hope of discovering what an ethical, sustainable, honorable human place in nature might actually look like."[3] Cronon believes that the concept of wilderness has been misapplied and that at the end of the twentieth century it was only just becoming clear how humans fit into wilderness.

The failure for thirty years (1970 to 2001) to include humans in wilderness preservation philosophy has been the source of many governmental shortcomings. Only in the last decade of the twentieth century has concern for people become important. That concern has appeared in numerous small instances but not within the context of a much-needed philosophical discussion of the role of people in wilderness.

Something beyond theorizing on direct wild land protection was occurring around 1970. When the state established the blue-line boundary for the park, the expectation was that the state would acquire all the land within that boundary. Long before 1970 it was obvious that the state was not going to put all the land within the blue line in the Forest Preserve. (This recognition was not universal. An example, discussed later, was the Sierra Club Atlantic Chapter's opposition to the Perkins Clearing land exchange of 1979. Underlying this opposition was the group's failure to recognize the inevitable—that the park would always be a mix of public and private lands.) So, if all the land were not public, then conservationists began to believe that something had to be done to assure that the use of private lands complements the unique values associated with the public lands. The Adirondack Park Agency's Private Land Use and Development Plan established controls on private lands in order to protect the privately held forested tracts of the park from development. These controls included development limits on waterfronts and roadsides as well as large tracts devoted to forestry and private estates.

In other words, regulating development on private lands was driven primarily by concerns for public lands and for the undeveloped character of the private lands—commercial forests and farms—within the park, not by concerns for the park's residents. Political compromises, which permitted passage of the APA Act, left defects in the act that were so evident that attempts to strengthen the act began almost immediately. Some of the flaws were real, such as inadequate protection for waterfronts and roadsides. Others, like weak protection for open space, have turned out to be not as problematic. However, lack of concern for the citizens of the park, together with the intrinsic flaws in the APA Act, rendered this regulatory revolution imperfect. Nevertheless, despite its shortcomings, the act was monumental. At the time it was adopted, it embodied some of the strongest and broadest land use regulations in the country.

Contents of the Book

This book begins with two seminal events: the birth of the Department of Environmental Conservation (DEC), in part a reincarnation of the old Conservation Department, and the formative years of the Adirondack Park Agency, whose growing pains can be traced both to the inadequacies of the APA Act itself and to problems of its implementation. This book probes opposition to the private land use regulations of that act and the way that opposition subverted the desire of the act's creators to place some development controls within the purview of local government. It examines the Department of Environmental Conservation, the numerous changes in its leadership, and the opposition of its staff to relinquishing planning controls to the APA. It explores the resulting conflicts and the way they have forestalled some of the benefits that the APA Act might have brought to public lands.

During the last thirty years there have been many attempts to correct these deficiencies as well as to weaken the APA. The apex, or nadir, depending on the viewer's perspective, of the series of attempted corrections is another cluster of events, this one centered on 1990. That time could have been as important for the park and its people as the two previous clusters, but no suitable legislation resulted from the work of the Commission on the Adirondacks in the 21st Century. The commission was formed in 1989 to make recommendations on the future of the park, although a substantial number of its ideas were later realized without benefit of legislation. However, the immediate repercussions of the report produced one of the more negative periods in Adirondack history. It included confrontations, civil disobedience, destruction of property, and threats of violence against people. Actions by the driving forces behind the movement for change, combined with a groundswell for self-government among Adirondack residents and inadequate leadership by both the governor and the legislature, seemed to doom any attempt to improve the APA Act.

Despite the backlash against further impositions of governmental structures that originated outside the park, and sometimes because of the backlash, a number of positive things occurred in the last decade of the century. Public participation has been enhanced, and although the management of public input does not function as well as it might, local residents are becoming a constructive force for change in the park.

My Approach to the Book

The Adirondacks has spawned a literature of its own, one that rivals in volume as well as content that of any other natural region in the country. As extensive as it was before 1970, the number of articles, histories, promotional works, and reminiscences published since then has increased exponentially. The quantity of studies, analyses, regulations, technical reports, proposals, and drafts has been even more voluminous. Further, the number of pages in individual documents is huge. This volume makes dealing with what appears to be a relatively short period a daunting prospect. This excess, combined with the complexity of governmental layers and the plethora of groups supporting regulations affecting the park as well as groups opposed to such regulations, makes synthesizing the many parts into a comprehensive but readable whole a truly formidable endeavor. To meet this challenge it is obvious that I have had to make choices in material to be used. Although I have tried to make the reporting as objective as possible, I have not shied from expressing my opinions. The subjects that I cover in the greatest detail are the ones with which I was personally familiar and which I hope benefit from my perspective. In spite of all the sources I used, the book is partly autobiographical because it reflects events as I remember them.

The approach I have chosen relies not so much on analyzing the many reports and regulations, but on examining them through reactions to them by people living in the park as well as by those considered outsiders. Emphasis thus is directed toward the different organizations and agencies, for I have found that it has been individuals who have moved the organizations and agencies. This is partly the story of people trying to reduce governmental regulations or weaken the state's protection of wild lands. It is also the story of people trying to bring better governmental protection to the park, people trying to solve the overarching problems of dealing with the mix of public and private lands and to balance the concerns of local residents with those of people from all across the state.

Complicating the problem of telling the story of laws and regulations and the bureaucracies designed to enforce them—the institutions people have invented to solve the park's problems—is the fact that these elements are too cumbersome to describe. I have chosen certain issues that resonated with the public, others that created organizations either supporting or opposing those issues, and still others that reflect the work of individuals. The culture of the times and place has affected these individuals, but I see the effect people have had on events as the driving force in these decades. So participants tell the story through what they knew of events, how they reacted to them, how they altered them. The issues are seen through their eyes. It thus becomes a dynamic story. Because it represents different perceptions, it is not all fact, and does not cover all of the facts.

Some of the players in this thirty-year saga—those who have fled from the fray—have reminded me that this is a very small world we are talking about, the home of only 130,000 people. That number is so small it is easy to see how those in power statewide could ignore such a politically marginal pool of voters. I want readers to remember that this is the largest state park in the nation, the largest wilderness conglomerate outside Alaska. Its very importance elevates concerns for the lives of its residents to the level of its natural stature. These issues and concerns have significance worldwide, for most of the world's natural parks and biosphere reserves, many of which are inhabited like the park, are similarly complex.

Although the Adirondacks is a small world, it has problems far exceeding its size. Even the struggles among its people take on epic proportions. Violence in the park has been rare, but the polarization, the actual breach between people within such a small community, has been unsettling.

In the penultimate chapter I will discuss different attempts to involve the public in processes that led to environmental decision-making. Increased public participation reflected dramatic changes in management of the environment on the national level that occurred around 1970. Before that time government was represented by professional managers, and the public had little direct input. The decades after 1970 were marked by direct public involvement, which had its origin in early federal environmental acts from 1969 on and in such major events as Love Canal. Activists began to direct environmental discussions. In the last decade of the century involvement became even stronger because the public appeared to think of itself as decision makers.[4]

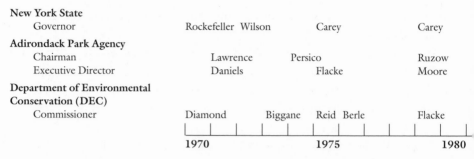

New York State					
Governor	Rockefeller	Wilson	Carey		Carey
Adirondack Park Agency					
Chairman		Lawrence	Persico		Ruzow
Executive Director		Daniels		Flacke	Moore
Department of Environmental Conservation (DEC)					
Commissioner	Diamond		Biggane	Reid Berle	Flacke

1970   1975   1980

Governors, Adirondack Park Agency chairmen and executive directors and Department of Environmental Conservation commissioners.

In the Adirondacks such involvement was essential to gain public support and acceptance for different programs, but it appears that many have failed in some way. Elizabeth (Liz) Thorndike, former APA member, believes that "most public participation processes had become outdated by 2000." Joe Rota, who became executive director of the Local Government Review Board, bemoans the complexity of the processes with respect to "people involvement," concluding that it has proven almost impossible to manage public participation effectively. Furthermore, public involvement in environmental issues in the park has not forestalled opposition that can stop majority decisions. As Graham Cox, an Audubon staffer, says, "One opposed individual can stop any consensus."

The three individuals quoted above will be reintroduced later; they are typical of the players on this complex stage and represent the breadth of ideas that shape the drama. And it is a sprawling and tangled drama with an enormous cast of diverse and lively characters.

In the 1990s, an additional divisive force appeared: instead of working out differences between groups and government over the use of the Forest Preserve, certain interests have increasingly taken their issues to the courts. But courts are places for settlement, not necessarily consensus; courts can easily make enemies of litigants by reinforcing positions of opposition, forcing people farther apart, destroying any possibility of consensus.

Former U.S. Senator Daniel Patrick Moynihan believes that democracy cannot work where ethnic differences are stronger than the sense of community or the ability of the community to come together. Similarly, I think a democratic process has not worked well in the Adirondacks because there is no sense of an Adirondack Park community to overcome the rampant individualism, the separateness of special interest groups, and the division of stakeholders into

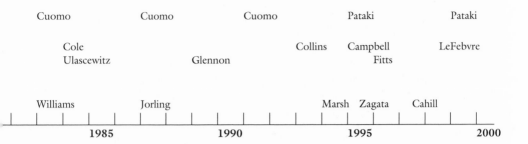

local and statewide interests. The numerous subregions of the park have vastly different characteristics, which often overshadow concepts of the park's identity. My book points to the absolute necessity to create an all-encompassing image of the park.

Leading to Conclusions

This work is arranged chronologically to emphasize the interconnectedness and synergism of themes, issues, and events. If I had written it topically, major subjects would include the creation and evolution of the DEC, the maturing of the APA, environmental groups, local Adirondack governments, groups opposed to additional regulation, backcountry and open space, economic development, forestry, the legislature and the Adirondack Park, Adirondack legislators, the Commission on the Adirondacks in the 21st Century, the Forest Preserve, land acquisition, and historic preservation. Perceptions or policies with respect to each of these themes have been dependent on the interactions between components. For example the desire to protect open space led to stronger environmental groups, which in turn led to the Commission, which resulted in a proliferation of groups opposed to regulation. The narrative exploring these relationships underscores the uniqueness and complexity of the park and highlights the turbulence of the times.

Over all these subjects is what I believe to be the major theme of those thirty years: integrating people with the park's natural resources. This process of integration has moved from recognizing the history of people in the park to concern for the people *of* the park, and ultimately to organizing public participation in the processes of governing and managing the park. My perspective has always been on process, so I will examine each theme for the processes at work—how they evolved and their level of success or failure. At heart this book focuses on the development of management tools for a "park of people and natural wonder."[5]

An introduction should anticipate conclusions. I shall disappoint: there are no sweeping conclusions, just analyses of things that helped, possibilities for the future, and many examples of paths taken that solved nothing.

I hope the reader will take away a sense of what has not worked as well as all the potentials. My conclusion will emphasize that we are on the right track, that during the past thirty years people have begun to work together to find ways to make the grand vision for the park a reality. Things have improved; many small steps are proving to be effective. But many things remain to be done because the pieces are not integrated into a structure that will effectively carry them into the future.

I conclude each example or description of events throughout the book with the message I believe it offers. I have found a common message: that it is essential to listen and learn from everyone and to remember that the people of the park are as important as its natural wonders. I will use that thought to hint at a structure to bring people and ideas together, but my conclusion will not flesh it out. I think the historical record points to such a structure, but others will have to develop it, or find another way.

PART ONE | *The 1970s and 1980s*

2

Formation of the Department of Environmental Conservation

IN PART TRIGGERED by the National Environmental Protection Act, several states began consolidating natural resources agencies around 1970. On July 1, 1970, New York State created the Department of Environmental Conservation (DEC or department) by integrating the old Conservation Department with the parts of the Department of Health (DOH) responsible for the environmental health of the whole state—clean air and water, pesticide use, waste management, pollution control, and so on.* From this merger grew DEC's huge bureaucratic structure, the behemoth to oversee all the modern environmental concerns.

Certainly the interconnectedness of so many environmental issues and programs warranted bringing them together with the creation of the modern DEC. However, the physical and administrative problems of combining five hundred air, water, and solid waste engineers from the Health Department with two thousand foresters, water resource engineers, geologists, and fish and wildlife biologists from the former Conservation Department and one individual from Governor Rockefeller's Office of Local Planning were difficult to solve.† Regional offices had to be integrated within the new organization

---

* At the same time, the Office of Parks, later Office of Parks, Recreation, and Historic Preservation, was split from the Conservation Department and made a separate entity. It retained responsibility for state parks, but not the Forest Preserve parks, although it manages two historic sites and the dispersal of snowmobile funds within the Adirondack and Catskill state parks.

† The one person was Charlie Morrison, who, in 1967, became director of the NYS Natural Beauty Commission (NBC), which comprised the heads of ten state agencies. NBC was housed with the Office of Local Government, whose commissioner chaired the NBC. When terms like "environmental quality" and "environmental conservation" replaced "natural beauty," NBC was folded into the newly created DEC.

housed at Wolf Road in Albany. The Division of Lands and Forests, which over-sees state lands, became but a small part of the new DEC.

A handful of states achieved such integrated programs at about the same time. Others, like Florida, retain several different governmental units, prompt-ing criticism that multiple agencies make it difficult to coordinate programs that involve both natural resources and aspects of environmental quality and health matters.[1]

In dividing the DEC into nine regions, both the Catskill and Adirondack parks were split into separate regions because county boundaries were used as building blocks for those regions, a carryover from the old Conservation De-partment. The ramifications of splitting the two Forest Preserve parks into sep-arate regions were debated within the department at the time and continue to be publicly debated.

Suggestions for regional planning groups within DEC have succeeded or failed depending on leadership within the department. In the early 1970s, DEC established an Office of Program Development, Planning and Research (OPDPR), which was abolished in 1978. Charlie Morrison, who was head of the Land Resources Bureau within OPDPR, saw his bureau chopped apart. Morrison was rescued and made a planner for the hydrology aspects of the statewide Wild, Scenic and Recreational Rivers Act, which placed controls on development of all the state's river corridors, as well as for other tasks. DEC later had a planning group working on acquisitions, but it was directed statewide and never focused on the Adirondacks. The result has been that no single entity within DEC has consistently been dedicated to planning for the Adirondack Park.

DEC may have been a new agency, but it was endowed—and encum-bered—with traditions and practices from the past. For decades after 1885, staff at the old forest commissions and at the Conservation Department be-lieved the Forest Preserve should be managed to produce timber.[2] These com-missions were "dominated by proponents of 'scientific forestry,' a concept espoused by Gifford Pinchot, chief forester of the United States Forest Ser-vice."[3] A Pinchot report for the Forest Commission in 1900 recommended that the "trees on state land be considered a renewable resource to be harvested periodically to produce income for the state and to 'improve the condition of the forest.' "[4] Commission staff not only believed in the economic values of harvesting Adirondack forests, they believed the forest could be improved to produce more softwoods.[5] They encouraged the federal government to con-duct a study in 1901 and again in 1903 to demonstrate the high value of trees in one of the most precious tracts of virgin forest in the Adirondacks, the four townships near and including Raquette Lake.[6] The Conservation Department worked hard to protect state forests by constructing a network of fire towers and the roads and trails that gave access to them.

Conservation Department staff later supported logging in the Adirondacks for various other reasons, game (deer) management among them.[7] Staff, educated in silviculture, fought for the right to cut timber after the 1950 blowdown and promoted jeep trails and fire truck trails in the 1950s. There were people within the Conservation Department who believed in harvesting the Forest Preserve right up until the time when DEC was formed in 1970. The department also embraced the use of motorized vehicles as eagerly as the public did. The Conservation Department promoted jeep trails, fire trails, snowmobiles; in later years the DEC was receptive to all-terrain-vehicle trails and snowmobile trail groomers.

Regional offices in the old Conservation Department had been at the beck and call of sportsmen. Staff responded by building campgrounds and establishing tree farms and reforestation projects, and by managing fish hatcheries, pheasant farms, and deer feeding areas. The department responded to the hiking public by taking over trails constructed by groups such as the Adirondack Mountain Club, but rarely initiated new trails. This failure to initiate trails accounted for the imbalance in the number of trails between the High Peaks Wilderness and the rest of the park. Further, it resulted for many years in DEC's abdicating responsibility for the High Peaks Wilderness to user groups, who built trails and set policies.*

These elements constituted the culture out of which the DEC was created. The philosophy was little different from the utilitarian view of wild lands that was pervasive in the United States in the twentieth century. Many department staff were either graduates of forestry schools or wildlife specialists. None was trained in recreation. This aspect of the department's culture was so pervasive that when DEC was established in 1970, almost no one embraced environmental or wilderness management.

At DEC the number of staff responsible for management of fish and wildlife has always exceeded those responsible for the forests and for people's access to

---

* Old-time guides and the Adirondack Mountain Club account for the construction, without thought to design, of trails in the High Peaks area. After a trail was built, its maintenance was handed over to the Conservation Department, which in later years financed Adirondack Mountain Club (ADK) and Adirondack Trail Improvement Society (ATIS) trail-crew work in the High Peaks. ADK owned the land from which emanated most trails into the High Peaks from the north. ATIS was an arm of the Ausable Club, which through its ownership of the Ausable Valley controlled all access to the High Peaks Great Range from the south.

them. Funding for fish and wildlife was greater than that for lands and forests, and this imbalance was institutionalized in DEC in 1982 by the creation of a dedicated fund, the Conservation Fund, for activities related to wildlife and sportsmen.

All this added up to a mindset that was not steeped in preservation. It was a culture in which staff may not have opposed environmental goals, but few were receptive to wilderness goals.

Here there are strong parallels to what was happening at the U.S. Forest Service. Although DEC and the U.S. Forest Service function in very different ways, their inherent cultures have many similarities. To acknowledge the basic difference, consider that parts of the Adirondack forests are as safe from harvest as human laws can make them. The state has saved and set aside so much that virtually no practices by the owners of industrial forest tracts affect the ecological values of our preserved forests.

DEC never had the opportunity to become a player in an economic culture as the Forest Service has, thanks to the Forever Wild clause. Historically, the U.S. Forest Service, a part of the Department of Agriculture, has permitted harvesting of trees on most lands under its protection. (It might have acted differently had it been part of the Department of the Interior.) Federal forests have been subject to a prolonged debate on what and how much to harvest. The Forest Service, like DEC's predecessors, was established in the late nineteenth century by men trained as foresters. While federal foresters were able to practice their calling, the state constitution prohibited managers of the Forest Preserve from doing the same. However, this prohibition did not prevent them from trying to change the laws. The Forest Service displayed a conspiracy of optimism that forests could be harvested at what proved to be unattainable levels. DEC displayed a similar air of optimism in believing it could address everyone's wishes and desires, no matter how conflicting.

DEC's structure—a central office with a small staff overseeing large regional offices*—has fostered another aspect of the department's culture—the independence of regional offices. This independence, too, was a heritage from the Conservation Department, which operated through many special commissions across the state. All but two of the commissions were integrated into the new DEC and became the basis for DEC's regional offices. The Tug Hill and the Lake George commissions remained separate.

---

* The Division of Lands and Forests has a handful of staff. The Bureau of Public Lands, which oversees all state public lands, has twelve staff members, one of whom is the Forest Preserve Specialist.

The regions can and have acted as independent fiefdoms. Where directors of regions are attuned to central office policy this independence has not been a problem. In fact, it has had its benefits, as those managers have been able to respond to their region's unique needs. However, the independence of regions has meant that DEC has often seemed to be headed in more than one direction at once. This was true even between regions, as this book will show: for example Regions 5 and 6 have contrasting approaches to land acquisition, planning, solid waste management, and other issues.

Even within the limited realm of recreation in the Forest Preserve, there have been many conflicts, both among user groups and between user groups and environmentalists. The most vocal user groups have often been hunters and proponents of motorized access to wild lands. Without strong central leadership, the DEC response to various groups has been inconsistent at best, favoring the most outspoken at worst. This response can be traced historically to the way the Conservation Department responded favorably to special interest groups.

At the time of the Rockefeller proposal to create a national park within the Adirondacks, the department claimed that it did a better job of managing public lands than the federal government did. I think this skewed sense of its abilities only demonstrates how little the department understood of the emerging concepts of wilderness and nonmotorized recreation and the department's role in balancing recreation and use with preservation.

The failure of the Conservation Department to develop a vision for the Forest Preserve was a major reason for the creation of the Adirondack Park Agency. In many areas DEC has never developed a strong policy of what was permitted or desirable. Even though the department was reined in and given direction by the APA Act and the State Land Master Plan (SLMP), some at DEC never admitted the yoke, never espoused the philosophies represented by the act and the SLMP. There has been no sense of vision for management, no sense that designated Wilderness Areas can be both preserved and used for appropriate recreation, no belief that in Wild Forest, areas that are virtual wilderness bordered with snowmobile trail corridors, many kinds of nonmotorized recreation could be developed. This book will show that although the SLMP was a major step, its implementation by DEC has been inadequate. Charlie Morrison, who served DEC from its inception until 1995, noted that "after thirty years of trying to work the bugs out of the organizational structure, the department again needs renewal."[8]

DEC's effectiveness has been plagued by much more than institutional and cultural problems. Until recent years there has been a new commissioner on the average of every two and a half years. Further, each commissioner has been able to shape the department and move it in directions different from those of his predecessor, often in response to the governor. Problems caused by changing political leaders and the department's turnover rate, along with its cultural inheritance, will be demonstrated in the following discussions. While these problems are endemic to DEC, they do not occur throughout all state government. For example, the New York State Regents oversee the Department of Education.

3 | Establishment of the
🌰 | Adirondack Park Agency

IT IS AMAZING the parallels we find in history. I remember being impressed by certain revelations of my research for *The Great Forest of the Adirondacks*. Threats to Adirondack forests had come from all sides before the establishment of the Forest Preserve and the Adirondack Park, but up until 1890, logging and forest destruction were remarkably benign except for farming and charcoal-making related to iron production. After 1890 it was a different story entirely. Railroads gave access to hardwood stands, paper plants devoured smaller and smaller diameter spruce, and private parks gobbled up enormous tracts of Adirondack land. The early 1890s marked the beginning of the most rapacious period of logging ever in the Adirondacks as well as the formal adoption of ways to protect Adirondack forests.

A similar parallel can be drawn about events culminating in 1970. In the late 1960s, threats from motorized access on public lands and the much more serious threat of development of private land kindled a movement toward strengthening the protection afforded both public and private lands within the park. In reality, only about sixty or so miles of snowmobile trails had been designated in areas being considered for Wilderness designation; and, even though the automobile brought more and more summer visitors, there were at the time few new cottages and little development. But the prospect of second-home development was very real. The threat was exacerbated by the fact that planning and zoning were almost nonexistent in the park. Just as a century before, all these problems came to a head in a period centered on one year. Within a year after DEC was launched in 1970, the Adirondack Park Agency Act was passed in response to threats to the integrity of both public and private lands within the park.

Above all, the Adirondack Park Agency Act was "an extension of the time-honored constitutional protections" [1] (and the land acquisition target created

by the blue-line boundary) that the people of the state have consistently upheld. Thus, the act was written to develop long-range Adirondack Park policy
that reflects statewide interests and concerns.

The APA Act outlined a comprehensive plan for Adirondack land use and
development and established an overseeing board with unpaid members, a
chairman, and a support staff. Staff created the Adirondack Park State Land
Master Plan (SLMP), which was adopted by the legislature in June 1972. The
State Wild, Scenic, and Recreational Rivers Systems Act was also adopted in
1972.* The Rivers Act called upon the agency to study the addition of many
miles of Adirondack rivers to the system. That study was completed, and in
1976 the APA adopted regulations for the private lands surrounding the 1,206
miles of Adirondack rivers added to the system. At the same time the agency
proposed studying ten more rivers for protection.

Staff completed the Adirondack Park Private Land Use and Development
Plan in time for hearings in late 1972, and it was adopted by the legislature in
early 1973.

The APA Act and Public Lands

According to the APA Act, DEC was to "provide for the care, custody, and control of the Forest Preserve," while the State Land Master Plan determined the
basic management guidelines DEC was to follow. State lands were divided into
categories:† Wilderness Areas were established to reflect the wilderness philosophy that was codified in the 1964 Federal Wilderness Act. Wild Forest Areas
were described as little different from Wilderness. The major differences were
that Wild Forests could accommodate trails for snowmobiles and that they were
often penetrated by roads.‡ This division had been emerging over a two-decade
period. Wilderness designations generally followed the geographic outline es-

---

* DEC manages a program fostered by the federal Wild and Scenic Rivers Program on rivers
within the state and in the Forest Preserve. APA manages the state's Wild, Scenic, and Recreational
Rivers Act on private lands within the park. The act requires management plans for river corridors,
blocks federally financed dams, and protects water quality.

† Wilderness; Wild Forest; Canoe; Primitive; Intensive Use; Historic; State Administrative;
Wild, Scenic and Recreational Rivers; and Travel Corridors. By far the greatest amount of state land
is in the first two categories.

‡ The APA Act specified a minimum size for Wilderness Areas; however, in many Wild Forests
there are contiguous tracts bounded by roads and snowmobile trails that exceed this minimum so
that they could be considered Wilderness Areas.

tablished by the Joint Legislative Committee on Natural Resources, headed by Senator Wheeler Milmoe from 1951 to 1959, at which time R. Watson Pomeroy became chairman. The Pomeroy Commission clearly intended that motorized access to all of the Forest Preserve would be curtailed.

In 1964 Pomeroy wrote: "To anyone who followed the proceedings of our Committee during those four years, it was axiomatic that we should have concluded in the statement that the one great threat to the preservation of natural conditions was the invasion which has taken place in recent years by individuals using forms of transportation unheard of at the time Article XIV was drafted." He also wrote that the committee would have recommended "That the Conservation Department take such action as may be necessary to regulate or, if necessary, prohibit the use of motorized equipment wherever the wilderness character of the Forest Preserve is threatened thereby."[2]

Pomeroy went on to describe how on October 3, 1964, "the blow fell," how the conservation commissioner announced an exception for snowmobiles, something Pomeroy felt was an "unconstitutional assumption of authority to permit a certain class of vehicles to travel anywhere in the preserve roads or no roads."[3] Discussions about snowmobiles continued through the 1960s, and the APA Act and the State Land Master Plan ultimately allowed their use in certain areas, but both the act and the plan clearly trace their origins back before Rockefeller's Temporary Study Commission that created the APA.

The division between Wilderness and Wild Forest had much to do with the adoption of the APA Act, and in this Paul Schaefer again played an important role in bringing together groups with opposing views. The New York State Conservation Council represented sportsmen who favored access and were opposed to Wilderness because it would eliminate vehicular use. Wild Forest designation appealed to them because town roads often penetrated the smaller tracts so classified. The Association for the Protection of the Adirondacks and the Friends of the Forest Preserve opposed the use of vehicles. In bringing the two sides together to support passage of the APA Act, this division into Wilderness and Wild Forest was pivotal in its appeal to both sides.

The APA Act was in part a response to the Conservation Department's failures with respect to creating a vision for the Forest Preserve and a management plan for it in the context of modern advances, in particular the rush to designate snowmobile trails. The APA Act itself, establishing the agency, and the basic planning document for public lands prepared by the agency, the State Land Master Plan, reflect not only the compromise to allow snowmobiles, but other compromises as well. APA's planning role for state lands should have been stronger and more specific in its guidelines for DEC's management role. But it is significant that the act established a regional public land-use planning agency for the Adirondacks outside the structure of DEC. This duality in turn caused a "tension" (word preferred by former APA member Arthur Savage) verging on actual conflict between DEC and APA that has never abated.

4 | Environmental Groups and the APA

THE APA ACT GAVE THE AGENCY POWER to review proposed private land development from March 1971 on, even before regulations to implement the Private Land Use and Development Plan were written and adopted, although no permits were issued until 1973. The greatest number of proposals for large-scale development in the park occurred in the late 1960s and through the seventies. Some were rushed so they could precede agency regulations; some produced court decisions that strengthened the APA Act; some were responsible for the start or reinvigoration of environmental support groups; and others were responsible for the establishment of organized opposition to the APA. In this interval, environmental groups began to play a strong role in the Adirondacks.

Sierra Club

Sierra Club, a national, grassroots organization that began on the West Coast in 1892, established its Atlantic Chapter in 1954 to address environmental issues concerning all the land east of the Mississippi. (That chapter was further divided so that the Atlantic Chapter now covers just New York State.) Sierra's national board established a permanent Adirondack Committee of the Atlantic Chapter in 1968.

Up to this time, the Conservation Department and the Department of Health had the responsibility for issuing permits within the park for water use and septic systems, typically engineering permits that addressed only water quality. (Septic systems were permitted as close as fifty feet to shorelines.) In response to a proposed development at Rainbow Lake in Franklin County in the late 1960s, Sierra Club, at the urging of member Al Forsythe and represented by Paul Bray, convinced the Department of Environmental Conservation to

27

hold public hearings in order to focus on the larger questions of the impact of development on the environment. (Bray, a lawyer and member of the Assembly's bill-drafting staff, was active for more than thirty years with numerous environmental causes and organizations, including the Sierra Club.) The Sierra Club argued that the department had the obligation to look at environmental impacts in deciding whether or not to issue permits, this long before the State Environmental Quality Review (SEQR) was established.* The old Conservation Department and the newly created DEC were both rudderless and somewhat incompetent, according to Bray and Ed Needleman and Bob Kafin, who became counsels to the Atlantic Chapter in 1971. Their work was financed by contributions to the Sierra Club Legal Defense Fund from people with deep pockets: William Rockefeller of Bay Pond; Ralph Friedman, owner of Kildare Club, the former Webb estate with 10,000 acres; Joe Cullman, CEO of Philip Morris, who married into the family that owned Kildare; and Wilhemena Dupont Ross, owner of what is now Brandon Park, a tract of 20,000 acres north of Bay Pond along the St. Regis River.

DEC had never had public hearings with evidence given by experts requiring the evaluation of potential environmental impacts. Its staff was not fully supportive of the process, an impediment that was typical of DEC's actions under the old Conservation Department lawyers, according to Kafin.[1] Sierra's Adirondack Committee considered that their insistence on public hearings and the balancing of economic benefits versus adverse environmental impact constituted holding actions to allow the Adirondack Park Agency to "get its act in place."[2]

Many large-scale developments were proposed in the late 1960s. Two of those that preceded the agency were abandoned for economic reasons. In 1967, the Great Northern Capital Corp. Ltd., a Canadian corporation, proposed a residential development consisting of three hundred parcels on 280 acres near Indian Lake. In 1970, the same group proposed five thousand half-acre residential lots on the ten-thousand-acre De Camp Tract along the North Branch of the Moose River in the Town of Webb.

Finch, Pruyn and Co. proposed the development of forty sites on 125 acres on the tract known as the Gooley Club, near the confluence of the Hudson and Indian rivers. The entire tract encompassed 1,125 acres, half in the Blue Ledge

---

* SEQR is a part of the Environmental Conservation Law Article 8, a body of law requiring preparation of environmental impact statements and substantive findings to be made from environmental impact statements (EIS).

area under study for inclusion in the Rivers Act. Pressures to have the state buy the tract went nowhere; however, the development was never pursued.

In the rush to begin work before the Adirondack Park Agency's regulations were complete, Ton-De-Lay Associates proposed a residential development of over four thousand parcels on 18,400 acres in the Town of Altamont. The project was so large that some suggested it would necessitate creation of a new township. Ton-De-Lay's proposal aroused opposition from both the Sierra Club and the Adirondack Mountain Club (ADK). Sierra Club believes it was responsible for convincing DEC Commissioner Henry Diamond to disapprove Ton-De-Lay's permit application on other than engineering grounds: that is, on the basis of environmental impact and cumulative development. (At this time water and sewer permits issued by DEC were the only permits needed for such a development.) The developer lost a suit that would have forced the DEC to issue the needed permits. That court case established the power of the commissioner to make general findings based on environmental impact, and the decision produced legal text that is significant today. Further, the decision of that court case became law in 1975 when the legislature codified the court's findings giving the DEC commissioner power to take into account cumulative environmental impact of a whole project when making a decision on any particular permit requirement for a given project.

Before this time the public could not be interveners, but a further outgrowth of Sierra's work on Ton-De-Lay established this public right. In addition this model used by DEC, with multiple interveners and trial-type hearings, was the origin of the model that APA established later for its hearings process. The state regulations codified statewide such judicial hearings presided over by an "administrative law judge."

Sierra Club played a significant role in the hearings APA held in late 1972 and early 1973 on its proposed Adirondack Park Private Land Use and Development Plan (PLUDP). Adirondack Committee members from that time recall being in a small group who worked well together and took strong stands.[3] Their positions were not necessarily radical but "principled ones," according to Ted Hullar, a member of Sierra Club who later became a deputy commissioner of DEC. Ted credits Dick Beamish, who was working for the Adirondack Park Agency at the time, with stimulating the Sierra Club and other organizations to participate in the PLUDP hearings. "He was out and about, with a missionary quality, yet professionally responsible, [inspiring] others to do the work of supporting APA."[4] Sierra's influence was strongly felt at the agency. William Kissel was employed as counsel for the agency through 1973 when he left, eventually taking a position with the Lake Placid Olympic Committee. (He became a member of the agency in 1998.) Kissel believes that the national environmental groups that became heavily involved in the agency's early days were extremist and well-moneyed, and may have made the agency more extremist.[5]

A footnote to the Ton-De-Lay proposals: In 1976 the APA through the attorney general's office sued the developer over a proposed 180-lot subdivision on 1,380 acres of the tract. Ton-De-Lay and its chief officer, Louis Paparazzo from Connecticut, responded by charging that the APA Act was unconstitutional. In a landmark case, the court found for the APA.

Adirondack Mountain Club

Sierra Club was not alone in these early struggles to define the Adirondack Park Agency. Dave Newhouse was very influential as chairman of the Adirondack Mountain Club's (ADK) Conservation Committee in the late 1960s through the 1970s. Newhouse had been a leader in the Constitutional Council for the Forest Preserve (CCFP), which was established to respond to the 1967 Constitutional Convention at which proposals to abolish Article XIV had surfaced. Both the CCFP and the ADK continued offering support for the APA Act, and Newhouse's role was pivotal. Since its inception ADK has been primarily concerned with recreation in the Adirondacks. Newhouse fought long and hard to establish the principles that served as the foundation of the club's environmental program.

Formed "in a log cabin on the roof of the original Abercrombie & Fitch building in New York City"[6] at the end of 1921 and incorporated in 1922, ADK adopted as a primary objective making the Forest Preserve more accessible to hikers and mountain climbers. To that end, the club also planned to construct open shelters and permanent camps on public lands in mountainous areas. During its first year, ADK began constructing the 132-mile Northville-Placid Trail and six lean-tos along its route. The club acquired Johns Brook Lodge in 1925, an interior cabin in the eastern High Peaks. Through its Loj chapter the club used the Lake Placid Club's facility at Heart Lake,[7] until ADK was able to acquire Adirondak Loj in 1957.[8] The property surrounding the Loj controls access to the High Peaks from the north.

Initially, conservation was not foremost among the Adirondack Mountain Club's objectives, but after 1928 the club adopted a policy that merged recreation and conservation. At this time, members tried to direct the club toward creating additional trails outside the High Peaks such as the Red Horse Trail in the Five Ponds area and Bob Marshall's trail that would stretch from Lake

George to Lake Placid. From the start the club was more concerned with trails in the High Peaks adjacent to its Adirondac Loj than elsewhere, and these trails were never completed.

In 1937 Conservation Department Commissioner Lithgow Osborne, who supported the building of trails, particularly ski trails, addressed ADK's annual dinner. His speech included the comment that "most hikers within the ADK have chosen to shut their eyes to the real need for more adequate trails in New York State. They are obsessed with the groundless fear that trails will bring crowds and that crowds will bring new auto roads into the wilderness."[9] By this time the trail network in the High Peaks was virtually complete, and ADK never did as much to push for trails in other areas of the park.

The club's conservation efforts included opposition to threats to harvest trees on the Forest Preserve, to cut trees to create game parks, and to build dams on Adirondack rivers. Given the dichotomy in the club's background, it is easy to understand why the club played a limited role in the development of Adirondack Park Agency in the early 1970s, despite Newhouse's efforts. By the late 1970s, Newhouse, slowly and deliberately, was able to overcome the problems of marshaling the Adirondack Mountain Club's large membership into a cohesive force for conservation. ADK's Conservation Committee, almost entirely Newhouse's creation, came up against the slow, ponderous, and often ill-informed ADK board of governors, on which the minority of at-large members was overwhelmed by the majority who represented individual chapters. The majority was more concerned with recreation and local chapter issues than with statewide issues. Newhouse persevered, and the club took on many issues, including support for APA.

ADK experienced several periods of growing pains that highlighted a prolonged adolescent phase. Membership, 2,550 in 1964, tripled by 1972; it remained stagnant and even declined through 1981 in a period when the club was plagued by deficits, especially at its lodges. The club recovered in the 1980s, especially after James C. Dawson became president and established committees overseeing ADK's lodges that were able put their operation in the black. Under Dawson, the club's budget went over a million dollars a year. The club's magazine was redesigned and its focus widened to include articles on Adirondack history, environment, and government.[10]

ADK membership increased through the rest of the eighties to 15,000 in 1988. By that time there was renewed emphasis on conservation and communication, and with the leadership of counsel Neil Woodworth, ADK had become one of the stronger forces for conservation with respect to the Forest Preserve. Woodworth's work as ADK's conservation director is discussed in part 3.

Upper Hudson Environmental Action Committee

Not all the support for Adirondack Park Agency came from outside the park. Earth Day, April 23, 1970, marked the official beginning of the Upper Hudson Environmental Action Committee, UHEAC. A true grassroots group, with founders from the Johnsburg-Chestertown area, UHEAC was initially more an outing group (it almost became a chapter of ADK). Through the early 1970s, UHEAC did support APA, but that was not its primary goal. However, it grew in the 1980s under the leadership of Don and Evelyn Greene, Dennis Conroy, and Louis Curth, at the time a DEC ranger from the area, and began to develop an environmental platform, representing mostly local concerns such as proposals by the Niagara Mohawk Power Corporation (NIMO) to string wires across the Hudson River. UHEAC favored important state acquisitions such as Kings Flow and for a while was a very active Adirondack-based environmental group, leading debates in nearby towns. It was at the forefront of opposition to aerial spraying for blackflies.

Citizens to Save the Adirondack Park

The one local group that did muster significant early support for Adirondack Park Agency was Citizens to Save the Adirondack Park (CSAP), which had its origins in its opposition to plans announced in 1972 by Horizon Adirondack Corporation, a subsidiary of Horizon Corporation of Tucson, Arizona, to develop upwards of nine thousand residential sites on 24,300 acres in the towns of Colton and Clare north of Cranberry Lake.

Citizens of the northwestern Adirondacks considered the Horizon threat so serious that they formed Citizens to Save the Adirondack Park the same year the project was announced. CSAP President Peter E. Van de Water, also a vice president of St. Lawrence University, led the group against the Horizon threat with a statewide press campaign. CSAP hired Dave Sive, considered at the time one of the country's foremost environmental lawyers. According to Van de Water, "it became obvious to everyone involved that success or failure of the Horizon 'test case' would depend on the private land use plan formulated by the APA and its passage by the legislature." [11]

Thus motivated, CSAP took an active role, along with the Sierra Club and the newly formed statewide Environmental Planning Lobby (EPL) in attending many of the fifteen hearings scheduled by APA on its draft Private Land Use and Development Plan. Van de Water credits the "tact and patience of APA Chairman Richard Lawrence [in keeping] the often stormy sessions orderly." [12]

These hearings were still exciting events. Adirondack author Philip Terrie recalls that he and William Verner, curator at the Adirondack Museum, attended the hearing at Indian Lake, where they were loudly booed for supporting the plan. Long Lake businessman John Hosley arrived carrying a spear and wearing an Indian headdress. Assemblyman Glenn Harris arrived by helicopter and announced his proposal for legislation to delay the plan for a year.[13] The circus in the Adirondacks had started.

Governor Rockefeller vetoed the bill to delay the Private Land Use and Development Plan for a year. It had been sponsored by Glenn Harris in the assembly and Ron Stafford in the senate. (Stafford's long tenure in the senate has given him power over virtually all Adirondack legislation that reaches the senate.) The enabling bill for the agency's land use program finally passed the legislature on May 14, 1973, but only after it had been much amended. Some eight hundred changes had been requested, five hundred changes were made, and some two hundred amendments were attached to the Private Land Use and Development Plan. Despite all the amendments, North Country legislators and supervisors, none of whom supported the APA Act, continued to oppose the plan. Increased state aid for local land use planning did nothing to make the plan acceptable to them.

Two of the more significant amendments were the establishment of the Local Government Review Board (LGRB) to monitor the APA and an expansion of agency membership to include an additional park resident as well as a representative of the Department of Commerce. With the passage of the APA Act, four park residents; three non-park residents; representatives of the Department of Economic Development (successor to Commerce), Department of State, and DEC; and the chairman constituted the membership of the agency.

Development Under the APA Act

According to Van de Water, local opposition to Horizon's plans and the newly adopted restrictive provisions of the APA were not the main reasons Horizon abandoned its plans: "The economy took a turn for the worse; energy costs curtailed travel; and the market for second-home development in general received considerable national exposure as a result of unscrupulous sales and marketing techniques."[14] Horizon's stock plummeted. In a major suit, which ultimately supported the APA Act, Horizon sought damages totaling $36 million on the charge that the state had unconstitutionally appropriated an interest in its holdings without compensation. Ironically, Horizon had paid only $2.3 million for the tract (the figure was $2.6 million by some newspaper accounts), and Horizon profits exceeded $2.1 million when the corporation sold the tract to Lyme Lumber Co. in 1977. Horizon's suit was dismissed in 1976, but before that time, the parent corporation had been charged with misrepresenting its properties sold in the Southwest.

The first proposal for development of the Sagamore Hotel property on Green Island, Lake George, was submitted to the agency in 1973. The developer tried to have the property reclassified as Hamlet (see definition below) to avoid Adirondack Park Agency jurisdiction. APA rejected this proposal, and the agency's decision was upheld by the courts. (In 1983, the agency did grant a part of the desired map amendment with the reclassification because it was included in the town's agency-approved land use program. Approvals were granted for 180 condominiums and improvements to the site.)

In 1974 Wambat Realty Corporation's proposed development of 850 residential sites on a portion of a 2,200-acre tract on the shores of Silver Lake in the Town of Black Brook was the catalyst for the formation of the Adirondack Council (see chap. 10). (Wambat Realty was a part of the Hammond Group of Wilmington, Delaware.) The town and the developer sued to compel APA approval for the project and rule on the constitutionality of the APA Act. The suit brought about the seminal decision on the primacy of the state's interests over local interests. The court ruled, "The preservation of the unique qualities of the Adirondacks has long been the state's concern."

A more modest proposal with origins in 1973 had much greater impact on the establishment of groups opposed to the APA. Anthony D'Elia, "Tony" to all, proposed to expand a golf course and a small existing community with up to 914 housing units on a 3,500-acre tract in the Town of Franklin. The agency directed D'Elia to hire an engineer to help him prepare his application, but as William Kissel later recalled, the engineer was not as helpful as he should have been.[15] As a result D'Elia's application was not adequately prepared to be considered under the temporary regulations. The APA and DEC held a joint hearing on D'Elia's Loon Lake Estates that lasted for twenty-eight days and granted conceptual approval, but with over sixty stipulations or conditions.[16] The most expensive and, in D'Elia's eyes, the most onerous called for constructing a sewage treatment plant. D'Elia sued, claiming that the conditions were illegal, but in 1975 the state court rejected his claim as untimely. This time the National Resources Defense Council (NRDC) joined local landowners as intervener in the suit. D'Elia claimed that he had enormous expenses related to the application to the agency in addition to the impossibility of fulfilling all the conditions.[17] Kissel believed that D'Elia's failure was a combination of problems with the project and Tony's personality: combative, abrupt to react, aggressive. Whatever the merit of his complaints, the episode seems to have colored D'Elia's approach to the agency and to government in general, and his frustration and anger at the agency carried over into the 1980s when he headed up the Local Government Review Board.[18]

5 🌰 Evolution of the Adirondack Park Agency

WHERE WAS THE FLEDGLING AGENCY as all this opposition was swirling around it? Philosophically, the agency was guided in those early years by the work of the Temporary Study Commission (TSC). More than that, the agency inherited personnel and members from the TSC:* Richard W. Lawrence Jr. became chairman and Peter S. Paine Jr. became a member. Other key members were Mary Prime, John Stock, and Richard A. Wiebe. George Davis, ecologist and director of planning, and Clarence Petty, Forest Preserve specialist, joined the staff, where Davis played a major role in agency planning. According to Bill Curran, agency staffer since the early days, it was these people who made it possible to create a working structure based on the APA Act.

The Private Land Use and Development Plan

The APA Act is a permissive statute; it does not prohibit types of development, but rather defines development and growth in terms of compatibility. Because of this the act is unique. The Private Land Use and Development Plan, as developed by the agency, is based on density zoning, not traditional use zoning. Private land is divided into six categories, four defined according to a guiding density of permissible development, based on the number of principle buildings allowed per square mile. A long list of compatible uses was established, and other uses could be permitted if they were found to be environmentally and aesthetically suitable for a specific site.

The density requirements—technically the Overall Intensity Guidelines, or

---

* APA is not a commission so its members are technically not commissioners; its members are called just that, "members," whose leader is designated chairman of the agency. I adhere to this convention throughout the book.

OIGs, number of buildings permitted per square mile in different categories—are approximate maximums. (The actual numbers used were educated guesses.) Translated into acres per principle building for the different land use categories, the minimum acreages per building range from 42.7 acres in Resource Management, to 8.5 acres in Rural Use, to 3.2 acres in Low Intensity, to 1.3 acres in Moderate Intensity Areas. There are no limits on the number of buildings per square mile in Hamlets. Permits are often granted by the agency for well below those maximum densities. Thus, from the start, the public found density zoning misleading and the agency's decisions subjective.[1] These elements of the APA plan were confusing to the public and have always seemed to be at the heart of the public's failure to understand—or accept—the Private Land Use and Development Plan.*

George Davis's views of land use controls, developed when he was a student at Cornell, carried much weight with the agency as it struggled to create both the State Land Master Plan and the Private Land Use and Development Plan. I have always been curious about where density zoning came from. In 1999 George Davis told me, "Temporary Study Commission discussed both density and use zoning, and it came down to proposing no development in Backcountry, in the most restrictive category." This prohibition would have been unacceptable to the public, and since that would essentially be use zoning, the commission did not deal with use zoning in other categories. The study commission invented density zoning on their own. They also discussed establishing "hard edges between villages and farmland or forests as in the European model, but ultimately rejected the use zoning that would create such hard edges."[2] Davis and the TSC were influenced by Ian McHarg's *Design with Nature*, in which McHarg recommended looking at the land and determining what it tells you before deciding what to put on it. Thirty years later Davis still believed this is the best approach.

The Cornell method, as it came to be known, had been used statewide by Governor Rockefeller's Office of Planning Coordination. It called for depicting resource information on Mylar overlays on existing U.S. Geological Survey (USGS) maps. (The scale of those 15-minute maps, the only maps available at the time for much of the central Adirondacks, was quite small.) The Mylars

---

* Tom Ulasewicz, former executive director of APA, does not agree that these characteristics were at the "heart" of the failure. He believes that public failure to accept the APA was caused by "subjective administration of permits by the agency and a failure to develop clear standards and criteria for agency actions, quantitative standards where possible, qualitative standards for noise, visual, and so on."

showed soil conditions, slope, water features, elevations, watersheds, forest cover, and so on. The information available was crude by today's standards but still provided a sophisticated composite that gave a remarkably clear picture of land suitable for development.

Because the APA Act encouraged future development in already settled areas, it was necessary to map existing development. Two teams drove all the roads in the Adirondacks assessing levels of development: Bill Curran and planner Richard Estes covered Franklin, St. Lawrence, Lewis, and part of Clinton counties. George Davis, his wife, Anita, and Gary Randorf covered the rest. Both teams were assisted by Clarence Petty and Greenleaf Chase, two of the most knowledgeable naturalists in the park.

The aggregate of all these factors expressed development suitability and is the basis of the agency's official map. The map determined the outlines of density categories, which are identified by different colors: green for Resource Management; yellow, Rural Use; orange, Low Intensity; red, Moderate Intensity; brown, Hamlets; and purple, Industrial Use Areas.[3]

The innovations present in the Private Land Use and Development Plan were weakened by the compromises needed to win legislative approval for both the APA Act and the plan. Shoreline restrictions were watered down four times in the process. The first weakening occurred within the Temporary Study Commission itself, in discussions where waterfront densities were separated into nondeveloped waterfronts (yellow) and those with some development (orange). Commission members feared legal challenges to restrictive zoning and, as a result, the initial proposals were changed to allow higher levels of development on the more valuable waterfront properties. Davis recalls the second weakening: "Once existing development was erased from the process, that is, not counted, density was watered down even more—the shift from yellow and orange to red, or the 'red spread.' "[4] The third weakening occurred with the application of clustering to development. "While clustering is normally a good thing," according to Davis, "it was permitted close to shorelines." Davis still believes that "there should have been bonuses to put clusters further set back from lakeshores." Finally, the legislature further reduced the density requirements by shifting the number of buildings permitted—a political necessity to get the act through the legislature.

Another aspect of the act and its application that has always puzzled observers is the concept of "open space" and methods for preserving it. Not only was the Forest Preserve key to the park, so were the huge tracts of private forests that could be logged and would complement state land if they remained largely protected from development. The report of the Temporary Study Commission speaks of the wild forest character of the park, but does not yet use the phrase "open space." Open space was an evolving concept that first appeared in an APA Open Space Report and in 1973 legislation that added the protection of open space and the open space character of the park to the APA Act.

The map designating the different density areas was challenged from the start, partly because it appeared to contain errors. There certainly were some errors, mostly minor technicalities.* Davis's methods of creating that map have been criticized. For those who wish to understand the APA Act, its acceptance, and its shortcomings in detail, I recommend the book *Protecting Open Space— Land Use Control in the Adirondack Park* by G. Gordon Davis and Richard A. Liroff.[5] The authors hired Roger Wells, an independent planner, to evaluate the map, and he found deficiencies in the use of standard cartographic procedures that would have assured accuracy. Wells was concerned with the absence of documentation and a lack of definition of the methodology.[6] He found that data collection was "thorough, rigorous and consistent," but lacking in documentation records that "would have proved an invaluable aid to those who must make the Plan work."[7] The book also criticizes George Davis's emphasis on existing development, but ignores the fact that doing so was essential to legislative passage of the APA Act.

The APA map was a massive undertaking. But John Banta, who served as APA's director of planning from 1979 through at least 2001, defends the map and the Private Land Use and Development Plan as the means of directing new development to places where it already existed. A later study by the Residents' Committee to Protect the Adirondacks (RCPA) shows that over the next three decades, new development generally followed the patterns established by the PLUDP, with most of it located in hamlets and built-up areas.[8] The RCPA study found that development was lightest in the valued "open space" of backcountry, just as the plan directed.

There were, however, two problems in the planning that continue to haunt a vision for the Adirondacks: the poor shoreline protection and the failure to adequately limit development along roadsides. These failures resulted from political decisions, not the guidelines that established the map. The RCPA report documents the results of these decisions. Privately owned waterfront in the Adirondacks continues to absorb the heaviest development pressure, even though private shorelines are almost completely built up. Gentrification—expanding and improving existing structures—is occurring along many previ-

---

* In the 1970s the agency discovered a number of technical errors in which land was mislabeled or ownership (state or private) improperly identified.

ously built-up shorelines. Building along roadsides sprawls out from almost every hamlet.*

Nevertheless, despite the compromises needed to achieve acceptance of the APA Act and the Private Land Use and Development Plan, major opposition appeared. According to Richard Persico, who became executive director of the Adirondack Park Agency in 1973 just in time to oversee the final approval of the Private Land Use and Development Plan, the young, inexperienced staff was really inventing procedures. There were too few people and limited financing. "Staff was young, enthusiastic, and dedicated, but they made mistakes," according to Persico. "They were green, and the agency act was over their heads, overwhelming, and in trying to establish an agency presence, staff were occasionally overbearing. Staff became so unpopular they did not want to drive cars with agency logos." [9]

Persico reacted by taking what he sees as a "pragmatic approach," focusing on what he considered "critical while easing up on the rest, and in the process giving something back to locals." To him, shorelines, wetlands, areas near the Forest Preserve were critical. But, he says, "the law was always too weak," and some staff members like George Davis were so frustrated by the limitations of the law that they tried to push it to extremes, "to go beyond the law without changing it. Staff resented the fact that the law did not protect adequately." Persico thought his job "was to be preservationist to the limit of the law, with respect for the law." He wanted to go after major problems but saw staff too often going after the trivial. He urged staff to be civil, to realize that "people were scared by the agency." Those approaches got him in trouble with the emerging environmental groups that were offering support for the agency. Further, Persico's restraint did nothing to improve his image with those opposed to the agency.

Organized Opposition to the Agency

Opposition to the agency occurred with the passage of the APA Act; it was galvanized during the writing of the Private Land Use and Development Plan. It

---

* Even though planners attempted to limit development to existing areas in order to create hard divisions between settled and open space areas, roadsides with scattered housing were given moderate intensity designation, so that a tremendous amount of building occurred along rural roadsides between 1970 and 2000, enough to fill most of the open spaces between dwellings that existed in 1970. To a certain extent the act and the Private Land Use and Development Plan are responsible for the visible sprawl.

was random at first, loads of manure dumped on the agency's steps, shots fired at the vehicles of agency staffers, letters to the editor disparaging agency staffers who had come from outside, mostly by name calling—commies, leftists, and so forth. Robert Glennon became APA counsel in 1974. In interviews he recalled the evening he went back to the agency for some papers and found a stranger inside dumping gasoline to torch the building.

The independence of North Country residents is at the heart of their opposition to the Adirondack Park Agency. In the early 1900s they had been just as opposed to limits on hunting as they were to the governmental interference and controls of the 1970s. The theme of opposition to "a big government that was telling them what to do" was a rallying point then and cropped up at every new proposal in the next thirty years. The power of big government made some residents fear they were victims of something they could not control. Added to this fear was the knowledge that people from outside, downstate, had pushed for the laws that now controlled the park and that created a new level of government. The feeling of being a victim precluded reaching out to government, even when governmental agencies tried to reach out to Adirondackers. Paul Bray believes that this sense of victimization caused North Country residents to ask for concessions, symbols, or tangible results in exchange for their acquiescence. Between 1970 and 1990 they went from asking that the agency be abolished to demanding representation of their own choice on the agency. But few went beyond to accept the inevitable while trying to work within the system to change its worst aspects. That shift does not appear until the early 1990s.

Opponents of APA abandoned scattered threats early in Persico's tenure and became very organized by the mid-1970s. They fed on examples of "victims" of agency wrongdoings. Tony D'Elia became the personification of a victim of the agency as well as a leader in organized opposition to it (see chapter 4). In 1974 D'Elia's experiences with the agency encouraged him to join forces with Ruth Newberry of Lake Placid to form the League for Adirondack Citizens' Rights. Newberry was a millionaire dime-store tycoon and developer of Ausable Acres. She became president of the league, whose motto was "The voice of the oppressed people of the Park." In the spring of 1975 the league planned a series of mass meetings across the park. Every one had the same theme: abolish the park agency. The league organized the "Adirondack Minutemen" as a protest group, and it held the first march on legislative offices in Albany in February 1976.

The league was greatly assisted by William Doolittle, editor and publisher of the *Adirondack Daily Enterprise,* published in Saranac Lake. That paper carried major inserts from the League for Adirondack Citizens' Rights. In January

1975, Doolittle, in a speech before the Ticonderoga Fish & Game Club, railed against the Private Land Use and Development Plan, focusing his opposition on the Fifth Amendment of the U.S. Constitution: "Nor shall private property be taken for public use without just compensation." This argument may have appeared in the Adirondacks earlier, but Doolittle seems to have been the first to express what was to become known as the "taking issue," and he did it eloquently if incorrectly: "Never in all of the challenges in all of the courts has severe zoning, which tends to exclude people and to appropriate the property of other people without compensation, been deemed legal."[10] (Numerous national court cases have supported zoning as a means of directing development.) He further embellished his speech with examples of a theme that continued to appear for years afterward—class struggle: "The men who have reaped the fortunes from polluting industries will send their minions and lackeys into these mountains to tell you that one house for every five acres is too crowded; the people who pollute the lakes with their huge luxury boats will call your snowmobiles foul and dirty; legal decisions too often follow money, and the richest men hire the best lawyers."[11]

In June 1975, the league launched a newsletter using their new logo of clasped hands and their new motto, "Hands Across the Mountains." The newsletter claimed that membership in the League for Adirondack Citizens' Rights surpassed sixteen thousand within eleven months.[12] Its first issue contained an editorial by Doolittle on the pitfalls of town planning according to APA standards. Doolittle reciprocated by printing a speech by Mrs. Newberry in his paper on the need for residents to be the protectors of the environment: "we must become faithful stewards of our beautiful mountains."[13] She talked of Adirondackers doing this with dignity, responsibility, and nobility. According to the league, Adirondackers "are desperate about conditions in the Adirondacks. But we do not want to resort to violence."[14]

D'Elia wrote of his early struggles with the agency in a book called *The Adirondack Rebellion*, published at the end of 1979.[15] His book has fascinating details of the people in his group and how it organized civil rebellion and rallied towns and villages to a cause.

Adirondack papers took up the protest. The *Ticonderoga Sentinel* editorialized that APA "regulations would tend to indicate that the majority of New York State residents would like to paddle canoes down uninhabited, uncivilized waters and ne'er pass any signs of life. At a time when the issue of caging animals for display in zoos is being raised, we are personally being 'caged' in the Adirondacks."[16]

To further publicize the protest against the agency, North Country businessmen Frank Casier and Bob Hunsiker began publishing the *Adirondack De-fender* in March 1976. Billed as "The Freedom Fighter's News," the first issue compared its mission to that of Thomas Paine two hundred years before.[17] It said Adirondackers wanted an Adirondack Park Local Government Planning and Control Board. A feature "Know the Enemy" described how numerous individuals had overlapping and multiple roles in the different environmental groups. It listed people like Ted Hullar of Sierra's Atlantic Chapter; Courtney Jones of Adirondack Council; lawyers such as Peter S. Paine Jr. and Arthur Savage; Dave Newhouse of Adirondack Mountain Club; and members of the 1975 legislative Task Force on the Environment, all of whom represented several organizations. Later issues reported that the Catholic Priest's Senate of Ogdensburg had joined the move to abolish the agency. Senator Stafford wrote that he was "overwhelmed by evidence of the failure of the political process to deal equitably with citizens of the Park."[18] Lists of agency decisions that the Freedom Fighters believed were wrong were featured in every issue of the paper, but they were never very detailed and always repetitive.

A winter 1976 issue of the *Adirondack Defender* printed a sample resolution for towns to call for abolition of the agency. Within months, eighty-six towns and eleven counties asked that the agency be abolished. The *Adirondack De-fender* grew in size (many ads were sold) and content, but its theme never changed. It helped spark Operation Survival, in which a blizzard of 327 applications was sent to the agency in an effort to tie up the agency and expose its inexact and often undefined permitting procedures.

In November 1975, Governor Hugh Carey appointed Robert Flacke, Lake George businessman and local Democratic official, to the APA chairmanship. Carey challenged Flacke to develop improved relations with local governments and a more humane way of working with people who came before the agency.[19] Flacke was brought in, many believed, to save the agency, and according to Persico, "Flacke did save APA from being gutted" by the legislature. To do this Carey gave Flacke considerable support. Persico believes Flacke had great rapport with towns and was very close to people in the park. "Flacke did not want to weaken the law, but he wanted to be more accommodating," according to Persico, and "that only made him suspect by the environmentalists." Within six months of his appointment as chairman, Flacke had the staff review cases that had come before the agency in which decisions were close and against applicants. When a couple of decisions were reversed, the growing environmental movement became convinced that Flacke was not on their side.

But Flacke was consistent throughout his tenure at APA and later at DEC. He summed up the philosophy of his career in a speech to the Environmental

Section of the New York State Bar Association in October 1992. He talked of managing and improving regulatory systems according to the rule of law and about how he expected his staff, including lawyers, to bring him all the facts, pro and con, and all aspects of the applicable laws. He invented the name "The Octopus Principle" for his way of viewing the many sides of an issue as multidimensional.*

Local Planning

All kinds of exceptions and qualifications apply to the APA Act, but they do not change the basic concepts, so the description in the box of its relationship to local planning should suffice for the discussion of how the towns and the agency reacted to the need for local planning to create an approvable program. In the early to mid-1970s the agency encouraged towns to create planning boards, and a quarter of a million dollars a year was distributed by the agency to towns for local planning. The agency had as many as six people on its local planning staff whose primary function was to assist town planning boards.

In 1977 Indian Lake was the first to adopt an agency-approved plan, followed the next year by Hague, Horicon, and Lake George. A handful of towns had engaged in local planning before 1970. Some, like Caroga (1980), went on to redo their plans and zoning codes and have them accepted by the agency. Queensbury and Colton completed their approved plans in 1982, Arietta in 1983, Lake George Village in 1985.

A few towns created approvable plans that were never submitted to the agency. Lake Placid received considerable money and assistance from the agency to create a locally approved plan, but it has not been submitted to the agency for approval. North Elba has a zoning code that is even stronger than APA regulations, especially with respect to shorefront development, although it is not stronger with respect to density guidelines. But North Elba decided it did not want agency approval so the town did not submit its plan to the agency. Of the original 107 towns and villages in the park, more than 90 used local planning assistance money in the early 1970s.

In the 1970s, the "box score" of towns with completed plans was noted, and as opposition to the agency coalesced, opponents found a focus for their

* Robert Flacke, "The Octopus Principle," comments submitted to the Environmental Section of the New York State Bar Association, October 1992. He also said that the APA "is administered by staff and lawyers who have visions that go far beyond the 'rule of Law.' They want to create law, selecting what facts to present."

Local Planning and the APA Act

Basic to the way the APA Act and the Adirondack Park Private Land Use and Development Plan were constructed was the idea that the agency should be concerned with development that would have regional impact, defined as Class A projects, and that local governments should control "smaller developments" and those less likely to adversely affect the environment—that is, Class B projects. Within the different categories of land use, corresponding thresholds of development were defined for Class A and Class B projects. For instance, in the most protected Resource Management Areas, a two-lot subdivision is Class A and requires an agency permit. However, a subdivision of ten to thirty-five lots in a Low Intensity Area is considered a Class B project, and a permit for it could be issued by the town, if the town had an "approved land use program." Non-regional subdivisions, (for instance two to fourteen lots in a Moderate Intensity area) do not require an agency permit unless they involve substandard lot sizes, wetlands, or other critical environmental areas.

From the start it was intended and anticipated that local governments would take over jurisdiction of the Class B projects and that they would create the necessary *approvable* (by the agency) land use and development program to do so. An approved program has to reasonably apply the APA Act's overall intensity guidelines, meaning the town can mix densities to suit local conditions so long as the town program approximates the guidelines.

Many other factors beside the density thresholds determine whether a project needs an agency permit: The act defines critical environmental areas by proximity to state land and in particular Wilderness areas; proximity to Wild, Scenic, or Recreational Rivers; existence of wetlands; proximity to certain travel corridors; or elevation of site. Other factors that determine whether an agency permit is required include the height of the project and so on. Such factors could mean that a project might need agency approval even if a town had an approved plan.

attacks by encouraging towns not to work toward approvable plans. The *Adirondack Defender* urged that towns not work with the APA to enact agency-approved local land use programs; one writer found fault with the condition that a local government could not approve a project if it would have "an undue adverse impact upon the natural, scenic, aesthetic, ecological, wildlife, historic, recreational or open space resources of the Park."[20] This clause, of course, is central to the APA Act itself. Acceptance of an approved plan was seen as an endorsement of the regional land use plan and thus politically incorrect in the

North Country. Locals saw it in terms of giving in to the agency. Local planning of any kind became a symbol of submission to the dreaded APA control.

Local Government Review Board

The Local Government Review Board (LGRB) had been created in 1970 as a part of the APA Act to relieve the fears of Adirondack towns that they would be overwhelmed by the establishment of the APA. Consisting of twelve members, one representative from each county wholly or partially in the park, the board was supposed to advise and assist the APA and give voice to local people. Initially given no state funding, the LGRB had to rely on money from Adirondack counties. Dick Purdue, Indian Lake developer, former mayor of Ossining, and long-time supervisor of Indian Lake, served as LGRB chairman in 1974. He presented memoranda to the agency in early 1974 that contained a number of suggestions for improving the APA Act.[21] While some of his suggestions would weaken the APA, his papers were moderate and constructive in tone. He concluded that the LGRB is convinced "that only a partnership [with APA] will work" for the APA to find its rightful place in land use controls for the Adirondacks. In general, LGRB's early years focused on calling attention to small issues, areas where the board believed the agency had erred. Gradually the LGRB took on a more active role in opposing the APA, perhaps because of shifts in its leadership, perhaps because it began to reflect what it felt was widespread Adirondack sentiment. In any event, by 1975 it had become one of the more vocal groups among those antagonistic to APA.

In 1975, the LGRB board scheduled ten public meetings, "Citizen Speakouts," where people who felt their rights had been threatened by the APA could be heard. LGRB's intent was to "offer ideas on how APA is functioning and [make] some recommendations for changes in the APA law."[22] The League for Adirondack Citizens' Rights joined in the speak-outs, and as the anti-APA rhetoric reached all the local newspapers, more and more residents of the park began to believe the rumors and accusations against the agency as well as the few evidential stories.

An assembly minority task force on the APA, created by Perry Duryea in the fall of 1975, held hearings in the North Country. Dick Purdue, speaking for the LGRB at one of the meetings, presented a long list of recommendations to the task force, but most other speakers demanded that APA be abolished. Of the nearly three hundred who attended the hearing at Lake George, half the speakers favored the agency but were overwhelmed by APA opponents. Those opponents supported by the League orchestrated protests that prompted the *Lake Placid News* to editorialize: "Tuesday's hearing left a great deal to be desired. Many first-time speakers who backed the agency were not treated fairly. And the League's recruitment posters, displayed on the platform behind the Task Force, did not give the impression of objectivity."[23] What the newspaper reports demonstrate is that while the League's work was visible and its positions on the APA were clear, there were park residents who had positive opinions of the APA in 1975.

APA had reviewed six hundred projects by 1975; fourteen were cited by the task force as examples of APA wrongdoing. The agency acknowledged that in three cases it had caused undue delays. In one case the agency admitted negligence in failing to send out a written notice; in another the agency agreed that permit conditions were more detailed than they should have been. APA offered evidence that the other allegations were not justified.

In 1976 the Local Government Review Board shifted from criticizing the APA's dealings with private landowners and local governments and began emphasizing what it saw as the APA Act's relationship to the park's social and economic ills.[24]

Opposition to APA became so vehement that North Country legislators could not ignore it. In January 1976, Senator Stafford and Assemblymen Harris, Ryan, and Solomon introduced a bill in the legislature that would abolish APA. This one drew attention away from bills, largely based on recommendations from the LGRB, that would have corrected some of the problems in the APA Act. A question lingers today: Why didn't Stafford pursue the LGRB's recommendations?

At the end of 1976, Dick Purdue, LGRB director from Hamilton County and a moderate voice on its board, withdrew from the Review Board because of what he saw as the LGRB's "high degree of responsiveness to highly organized pressure groups."[25] Ruth Newberry called his resignation "a victory for the real people of the Park." His resignation was precipitated by LGRB's vote in favor of the proposal to abolish APA. Richard Evans, one of Purdue's successors as chair of LGRB, was quoted as saying, "If a true partnership could be developed, many of the problems experienced with APA in recent years could have been avoided."[26] He, too, was unable to bring about that partnership.

Court decisions backing the APA in 1975 and 1976 confirmed the APA's right to reject the construction of boathouses on a development proposed for Lake Oseetah on aesthetic grounds. In 1975 and 1976 there was an attempt to develop 340 units on Last Chance Ranch on Adirondack Loj Road in North

Elba by reclassifying the land to increase the allowable density. APA denial of the map amendment went unchallenged.

Somehow developers seem to have been getting the message that large, undeveloped tracts were intended to remain intact or have development very limited in scale as determined by this new regional land use plan for the Adirondacks. An attempt to create a lakeshore community at Butler Lakes near West Canada Creek, a proposal for a campground at Harrisburg Lake, and a plan for a large residential development near North Creek, called Oven Mountain, have come before the agency in the last twenty years, but none, except proposals to rebuild the Lake Placid Club (see discussion of Gleneagles in chap. 17), has been of the scale of the early seventies' proposals. This trend to smaller developments demonstrates that only lakefront properties are deemed desirable and that only a few private lakeshore holdings remained that might admit large-scale developments. Economics were part of the reason, but the court decisions also clearly slowed large-scale proposals. The decisions did not, however, limit protests against agency controls. Nor did they successfully address the problems of the impact of cumulative development, which the agency was just beginning to see as a problem for the park.

In 1976 George Davis, as his tenure at the agency was ending, presented a paper on the need for greater emphasis on long-range planning. He wrote, "Decisions have been made for political expediency or fear of local public outcry. These decisions may have made the Park as it will exist in the future a bit less than it could have been. The flexibility available to the agency in its day-to-day decision making process is of value in insuring both human justice and protection of the Park. Unfortunately, it also contains the seed for potential damage when used to avoid some possible or even probably short-term public outcries."[27] Unfortunately for Davis, newspapers, and particularly the *Adirondack Defender*, picked up one paragraph in his paper and ignored his well-reasoned analysis of agency needs. His red flag: "It would appear that the state has two basic alternatives . . . 1) the purchase of all or most of the private land in the Adirondack Park, or 2) the use of governmental laws, rules, regulations and programs to achieve the goal."[28]

Embellishments of those points overshadowed any mention of his real message: Davis believed that the emphasis on *approvable* land use programs was the greatest obstacle to reaching good land use planning. "That complex package of documents which equates to an approvable land use program has somehow been set on a pedestal. Both the agency and local governments seem to have lost track of the intent of the law and become engulfed in the letter of the law."

Perhaps it was time to revisit what "approvable" means. "Does it meet the simple test?" Davis wrote, "If all parties accept good land use planning as a reasonable objective, then an administrative process can be set up that will meet the intent of the law."

In light of what happened in following years, I believe that Davis's suggestions should have been explored. As it was, opposition to the agency became so focused through organizations like D'Elia's League for Adirondack Citizens' Rights, the Freedom Fighters, and even the Local Government Review Board that this key element of the APA Act that allowed locals to take charge of some projects was doomed.

Despite agency efforts, opposition to APA in the late 1970s essentially stopped towns from submitting plans for approval. Local planning money began to dry up, decreasing to less than $200,000 after 1978. APA Chairman Ted Ruzow (1979–84) believed that regulation was the agency's primary role, and during his tenure help to towns declined significantly.[29] New York State's fiscal problems were part of the reason local planning assistance was not restored under Governor Cuomo. However, Tom Ulasewicz, executive director from 1984 to 1988, said that one of his charges had been to get towns back on track with planning.[30] Under him, the agency began a multi-town approach with not only planning assistance but computer sources, GIS capabilities, and a contractual approach to enhance local cooperation. This approach was very successful in the Lake George Basin.

While much local planning was accomplished, producing many local ordinances that meet the needs of local towns, no one has revisited the concept of "approvable." Persico had questioned the role of local towns in a different way, arguing for a redefinition of the A and B categories, perhaps even eliminating Class B and giving residents responsibility for everything in Hamlets, leaving the rest to the agency.

Overshadowing all this controversy is the APA Act's basic problem—it can only deal with new development. Towns and villages have a vital role in dealing with what has already been built, such as existing septic systems or eyesores such as junk cars, things that are not dealt with by agency regulations except as they relate to new development.

Underlying all the problems with encouraging local planning was a lingering discord within the agency. Early on there was concern that towns could not do a good enough job of regulating Class B projects. Some members actively delayed approval of town plans because they feared the towns had neither the resources nor the personnel. An even greater concern was the way towns lacked enforcement capability. Peter Paine spoke frequently in public meetings about these problems. This skepticism with regard to the ability of towns to take control of Class B projects persisted into the 1990s.

Summing Up the Early Years at Adirondack Park Agency

Despite the storms of public opinion, with Flacke and Persico at the helm the agency achieved many things: The APA prepared a model zoning and project review ordinance. The agency tackled the problem of review procedures and reduced the time to process routine permits to fifteen days. It established a coordinated review process with Department of Environmental Conservation and Department of Health. Public outreach was expanded with information sessions held across the park.

Persico faced calls for his resignation in 1976 from Assemblyman Daniel Haley of St. Lawrence County. In a twist, Persico was supported by Assemblyman Harris, but only because Harris believed the real threat to Adirondackers came from the APA Act itself, not from Persico.

Under Flacke and Persico, the agency worked for a legislative package of reforms that would simplify and expedite the permitting process. They convinced Glenn Harris to support measures that would correct some of the APA's more egregious problems such as replacing criminal proceedings in enforcement cases with civil ones and establishing criteria for amending the official map. (Before these changes individuals charged with wrongdoings under the APA Act actually faced criminal proceedings.) Persico believes that achieving this 1976 legislation was the agency's single most important accomplishment during his time as executive director.

In the years when Persico was executive director, the APA was strengthened by several court decisions. Persico made the statement that "the APA cannot lose in court. Our opponents know we'll win in court every time." D'Elia responded, "Mr. Persico has his judges and courts. Mr. Flacke [then chairman of APA] has his governor and Mr. Koppell [assemblyman] has his Environmental Committee. But we've got the towns, the counties, and the people of the Adirondacks . . . and we know your high and mighty APA will never work without the cooperation of local governments and people." [31] History seems to have proven that Persico, D'Elia, and George Davis were all correct in their assessments: Persico in the resolve of the courts; Davis in the need to redefine "approvable"; and D'Elia in the persistence of opposition from the towns. A letter to the editor in the mid-1970s summed up North Country feelings with the threat "our only defense is united passive resistance. If no town accepts APA dictatorship, Albany must eventually get sick of pouring money down a rat hole."[32]

In 1977 Beverly Sawaya Harris (wife of Glenn Harris) testified before the agency in her role as Local Government Review Board's executive director. Her recommendations for improving the agency ranged from the oft-stated (there should be locally chosen members in the agency) to a long list of what the review board saw as "glaring deficiencies" in existing APA rules and regulations, which resulted from the fact that statutory amendments to the APA Act and court decisions had not been integrated into the rules and regulations.[33] Despite her reasoned tone, the Review Board's efforts to abolish the agency continued to escalate. They seemed to peak as Robert Purdy from Keene replaced Beverly S. Harris.

On the other side, environmental groups stepped up their criticisms of Flacke and Persico on the grounds they were weakening the APA Act by appeasing Adirondack residents. They used as evidence the reversal of agency decisions. Adirondack Mountain Club attempted to understand why the agency was drawing so much antagonism in the North Country. In 1977 the club appointed a subcommittee of the club's Conservation Committee consisting of Erwin Miller, Peggy O'Brien, and myself. The subcommittee interviewed Persico, Flacke, and APA's counsel, Robert Glennon, and their extensive report indicated strong support for the way the agency was trying to make its operations more responsive to the public.

As a way of reaching out to communities, the agency held a series of meetings around the park in 1977 and 1978 on hamlet revitalization. The report of the APA-appointed Citizen's Advisory Task Force on Adirondack Hamlet Restoration and Development was a practical document.[34] It contained appendices with information on reaching arts, historical, preservation, small business, and other avenues of help and funding from state and federal sources. Fruits from that long-ago program took more than twenty years to ripen, but some of the nine towns where task force meetings were held now have significant hamlet restoration or development projects, among them Northville, North Creek, Old Forge, Lake George, Tupper Lake, and Keeseville. In the late seventies people saw the Adirondack railroads as a vital component of regional development and railroad redevelopment was finally becoming a reality in 2000. Paul Bray believes that the agency's failure to pursue these hamlet studies for nearly twenty years after 1978 is at the top of the list of the agency's deficiencies.

Open Space

Environmentalists began criticizing the agency for not acting strongly enough, but their rebukes were not entirely fair. For instance, in 1978, the agency, under Flacke and Persico, appointed a ten-member Citizen's Advisory Task Force on Open Space. Flacke was supportive of the task force, but its genesis was within the staff, with backing from other agency members. The agency had gradually realized the importance of the undefined term "open space," and that open space protection was of paramount importance to the agency's mission. The APA Act was believed inadequate to protect open space.[35] Environmentalists were beginning to see this flaw in the act as more important than all of its other deficiencies.

Bill Verner chaired the task force, and eight of its ten members were park residents.* The group acknowledged considerable APA staff support from planner George Nagle. Even before the Task Force on Open Space was appointed, APA's planners had been doing a lot of thinking about ways to improve the agency. A paper by George Nagle completed in early 1979 talked about what the agency could do to "establish a park," by formulating a vision statement to guide agency programs.†

George Nagle recalled the origins of the task force: "APA staff (primarily Glennon, Persico, and Nagle) kept stumbling across references to 'open space' in project reviews and local plans. Some really strong agency actions were based on open space considerations. Others on staff thought it was a fuzzy concept; everyone felt there was a need for specificity in defining open space in order to have regulatory significance."[36]

Nagle believed the task force was a splendid and diverse group who worked hard, with the result that their report did not simply represent a narrow preservationist perspective. Verner, according to Nagle, was urbane, generous, and

---

* Members were Verner, Long Lake; Timothy Barnett, director of Adirondack Nature Conservancy; Arthur Crocker, president of the Association for the Protection of the Adirondacks, New York City; Robert Eastment, Queensbury; Robert Kafin, lawyer, Glens Falls; George List, newspaper editor, Lake Pleasant; Henry Parnass, Saranac Lake; Mary Prime, Lake Placid; William Roden, Trout Lake; David Vanderwalker, St. Regis Falls.

† George O. Nagle, "The Adirondacks and the Adirondack Park Agency," Feb. 19, 1979. His vision statement: "To establish a Park in which the present open space character is preserved and enhanced, where man exists in equilibrium with nature and which, consistent with the foregoing, provides opportunities for recreation and refreshment, a continuing supply of timber and of high quality water, a basis for economic well being of its residents, and excellence in the cooperation of local, state and federal governments."

gracious as a task force leader and the kind of farsighted planner who was capable of reflecting on such parkwide issues.

The report of the task force, presented to the agency in April 1980, contained 131 recommendations intended to preserve and enhance the park's open space character. The task force noted that it tried to be "particularly sensitive to public concern relative to further regulation and imposition of further costs upon government. Nevertheless," Verner said, "it was equally aware that some degree of further regulation on a selective basis . . . is essential." [37] The group identified five categories of "primary and crucial importance": Controls on scenic county and state highways to preserve open space vistas and to maintain and enhance the demarcation between settled areas and Adirondack backcountry; a lake study to see how the quality of park lakes and lakeshores may best be preserved; maintenance and enhancement of the demarcation between settled areas and backcountry; help for settlements to maintain local parks and open space; and revisions of land acquisition policies. The report found unregulated sprawl the greatest threat to open space but argued for improving scenic vistas and highway views even if it meant cutting trees on state land. The recommendations to allow shore owners or local governments to control water use and prepare management plans for lakes remained just as important two decades after the report was released. The recommendation to use equitable taxation to encourage owners of private tracts to preserve open space was later partially addressed by the use of easements.

As defined by the task force "open space constitutes lands and waters that are unbuilt upon or predominantly unbuilt upon, where natural characteristics predominate over evidence of human occupation, activity, or presence, or where such human activity is directly dependent upon, or shaped by, those natural characteristics." [38]

Nagle believes that the concept of open space as defined in the report remains essential for preserving the Adirondacks. But defining open space was difficult. "Open space," Nagle believes, "is an intuitively understood concept (when I see it, I know it), but turning it into the nuts and bolts of regulation is difficult." Still, for all the task force's efforts, the report was unenthusiastically received by incoming APA chairman Theodore Ruzow and executive director Vince Moore. They had different agendas and were not inclined to use the report. Staff suffered from not having the tools to emphasize the importance of open space until their efforts were bolstered by later precedent-setting actions by the agency in the 1990s.

6 | Environmental Groups New and Old

Adirondack Council

DURING THESE TUMULTUOUS 1970S, another environmental voice had emerged in the form of a new organization—The Adirondack Council (TAC or Council or Adirondack Council for short; the organization has used "The" in its publications inconsistently over the years, so this book omits it). By 1977, after just a few short years, it had become a significant voice in the environmental movement, and it would grow to become the strongest environmental organization in the Adirondacks in the late 1980s and through 1990s. The Adirondack Council had its beginning in a specific challenge to the Adirondack Park Agency: In the agency's fledgling years, challenges to the APA Act by local developers were overshadowed by Wambat Realty Company's plans, announced in 1974, to subdivide and develop 2,200 acres on the shores of Silver Lake. Opposition to Wambat led summer resident William T. Hord to convene a meeting of the National Resources Defense Council (NRDC), Association for the Protection of the Adirondacks, Adirondack Mountain Club, ADK Foundation, Atlantic Chapter of the Sierra Club, Adirondack Conservancy, and Hawkeye Property Owners Association, of which Hord was a member. All of these groups were worried about the costs of bringing legal action to promote their environmental interests. Collectively, they became the founders of the Adirondack Council. Winning the lawsuit against Wambat in 1977 not only gave stature to the APA Act, but it established the Adirondack Council as a force in the park.

Adirondack Council also had its beginnings in a proposal by Dick Beamish to create a "Coalition to Safeguard the Adirondack Park"; an idea he says he discussed with Harold Jerry, who had been executive secretary of the Temporary Study Commission; Peter Berle, assemblyman who later became commissioner of DEC; Ted Hullar; and others, some of whom were active in Adirondack Council early on. According to Beamish, his fundraising proposal, dated April 3, 1975, was "the genesis of the Adirondack Council," but that idea was picked up by R. Courtney Jones, who became the council's first official leader. Jones was severely injured in an automobile accident, however, and his tenure at the council ended after only a few months.

Harold Jerry was instrumental in defining Council's role as a legal arm for other environmental organizations. Paul Bray believed Council had the potential to become a bureaucratic monster, and he remembers confronting Jerry with this and his (Bray's) belief that the council would become independent and self-sustaining. Jerry denied it and claimed the council would stay narrow, and events have proven him wrong.

Whatever its origins were, the organization quickly moved on to a new issue, the planning for the 1980 Olympics at Lake Placid. The organization opposed certain changes necessary to host the Olympics at Lake Placid, primarily the widening of NY Route 73 and the building of two new ski jumps at Intervale, on Route 73 south of Lake Placid. Actually, it was the Atlantic Chapter of the Sierra Club that mustered the strongest environmental challenges to the planning for the Olympics. Besides taking action on NY Route 73 and the ski jump, Sierra Club also questioned the refrigeration leaks on the bobsled runs and skating rinks and deals with NIMO to run a new transmission line.

A proposal to place the ski jump on Bassett Mountain in Jay had no local support, in part because the alternate site was so far from Lake Placid. By the time the agency held hearings on the ski jump, the state, under Governor Carey's name, had published a brochure stating that ski jumping at the 1980 Olympic Games would be held at Intervale.

Sierra Club remained opposed to the Intervale site. The arguments over the ski jump precipitated a split within the emerging environmental community and among the original members of the Adirondack Council. Council under Jones needed the Adirondack Mountain Club to object to the ski jump and failed to obtain the club's permission for that opposition. Even ADK was split. ADK's President Glenn Fish and Ed Ketchledge were involved with the Lake Placid Olympic Organizing Committee. Ketchledge, a naturalist and long-time ADK conservationist, was at the time a professor of botany at State University of New York Syracuse College of Environmental Science and Forestry, chairman of ADK's Olympic Committee, and ADK's liaison to the Olympics. He did not believe the jumps would affect views from the High Peaks. Fish and Ketchledge backed a movement to have the club withdraw from the Adirondack Council, and they wanted to publicize that separation.[1] High drama at the club's annual meeting in Niagara Falls culminated in a delayed vote by Adirondack Mountain Club's board, Ketchledge's late arrival, and a vote to withdraw. According to Dave Newhouse this was done without the consent of the club's conservation committee, and the withdrawal created a huge turmoil. Newhouse and others felt that "we had been betrayed" and that the issue was handled dishonestly, without open discussion within the club.[2] Ironically, within a year Ketchledge tried to get the club to rejoin the Adirondack Council, but the council demurred, believing that ADK had acted irresponsibly.

Sierra Club also had problems with the Adirondack Council and withdrew over the ski jump and other issues. Newhouse believes that while the Association for the Protection of the Adirondacks was a part of the Adirondack Council early on, it was not "organically a part of it." By the late 1990s member organizations in council were predominantly national environmental groups such as National Resources Defense Council, National Audubon Society, National Parks and Conservation Association, and the Wilderness Society.

The Association for the Protection of the Adirondacks

If this book adhered strictly to time sequences, then the Association for the Protection of the Adirondacks would have been introduced earlier. It is the oldest of the environmental groups supporting the Adirondacks. Association founders were worried that despite the work of scientific foresters, huge tracts of private land were threatened with destructive logging practices around 1900 so that Adirondack water resources continued to be threatened. With the object of protecting both their own interests and what they perceived to be the best interests of the Forest Preserve, a group of Adirondack property owners led by Lt. Governor Timothy L. Woodruff met on December 12, 1900, in New York City. Joining him in forming the association early in 1901 were Hon. Warren Higley of the Adirondack League Club, J. P. Morgan, William Rockefeller, Whitelaw Reid, F. Brandreth, Edward Litchfield, Alfred G. Vanderbilt, William Seward Webb, William C. Whitney, and others, who issued invitations to "all true sportsmen and lovers of nature throughout the state."[3]

The association styled itself "Watchdog of the Forest Preserve," and it figured strongly in many significant struggles and decisions through the first half of the century, but it never attracted substantial new membership. It was, from the 1960s to the early 1980s, a small, poorly funded group, led by Arthur Crocker. Crocker's realization that the association would be unable to undertake the lawsuits necessary to support the agency in its early years was one of the reasons he became a founding director of the Adirondack Council and led the association into the council. During Crocker's tenure (1964–82),[4] the association's annual reports were simple summaries of events ranging over such topics as the establishment of APA, open space, acid rain (the special report in 1979 on acid rain was a very early recognition of the problem, prompted by Crocker's attendance at one of the first Canadian forums on the subject), wilderness, motorized access to the Forest Preserve, and the Sagamore amendment to increase that historic site through an exchange of Forest Preserve land. Their format and style of writing were designed to appeal to its wealthy membership, which, although concerned with the Adirondacks and often able to influence state policy behind the scenes, was above the fray. Meetings of the board of trustees and annual meetings were social gatherings of the elite. The Adirondackers on its board were mostly wealthy summer residents. The association never reached out to year-round residents or even the summer residents who were members of lake associations.

With the founding and expansion of the Adirondack Council, there was a subtle shift in the environmental movement. No longer were environmentalists strongly supportive of Adirondack Park Agency; they began to question and find fault with its decisions and its leaders. By the late 1970s, the environmental movement began to take stronger stands than even the APA. As a result North Country opposition to APA expanded to opposition to the environmental movement in general.

7 | DEC under the Adirondack Park Agency Act

IN THE EARLY THROUGH MID-SEVENTIES, while so much attention was focused on the Adirondack Park Agency, the Department of Environmental Conservation continued to suffer growing pains. Many of its problems stemmed from characteristics of its commissioners. These ranged from ineffective managers to overzealous and independent leaders. Ogden Reid, appointed at the beginning of Governor Hugh Carey's first term (1975), came with high expectations from environmentalists. At first Reid's appointments met those expectations: Carol Ash, Ted Hullar, and Paul Elston were members of a group dubbed the "ecology kids" for their youth and enthusiasm, but "one would be hard-pressed to find a better group of public officials assembled in a single state agency,"[1] according to Rosemary Nichols, editor of *New York Environmental News*. Later she wrote that "Reid did not know what to do with his fine staff; he would not or could not make firm decisions from which departmental policy could reliably flow." Combined with the budget cuts necessitated by poor economic times, Reid's inability to manage such an organization became obvious. (Nichols faulted Reid's predecessor Henry Diamond for lack of management skills, but felt this did not hamper his tenure because he had Jim Biggane—"a past master at the art of managing. [Diamond] related to the public; Biggane minded the store.")[2]

Peter Berle

Nichols's complaints must have been common knowledge, for Governor Carey replaced Reid with Peter Berle in May 1976. Berle had been in the New York State Assembly, where he helped push the APA Act through the legislature. His two-and-a-half-year tenure at DEC was marked by strong leadership and an absolute desire to comply with the State Land Master Plan (SLMP). On his watch, wilderness lakes were closed to airplanes, tent platforms were removed from the Forest Preserve lakeshores, and all but one of the wilderness cabins (nonconforming-use structures according to the SLMP) were burned. (The 1972 SLMP called for the removal by 1975 of four cabins, all in Wilderness Areas.) Berle was well aware that "most people at DEC were committed to the cabins." However, he agreed with the SLMP's directive to remove them. In a later interview he recalled that "at Duck Hole, for instance, when the cabin was there, people packed in; when it was removed, people scattered."[3]

The three cabins burned on Berle's watch (near the end of 1978) also fueled a storm of protests from Adirondackers who wanted them kept and who opposed the State Land Master Plan in general. According to Per Moberg, Sierra Club activist and DEC staffer, Berle had ordered them burned without alerting Governor Carey, just one of Berle's missteps that resulted in his departure. (More important to Carey's replacing Berle were Berle's environmental stands against the rebuilding of part of Manhattan's West Side Highway below ground level and the closing of a newly built salmon hatchery at Pulaski, both projects dear to the governor. Berle's removal was accompanied by the replacement of his three top deputies, Langdon Marsh, Ted Hullar, and Philip Gitlin. Those who worked with Berle remember that he was never an insider in Carey's administration and that he broke a cardinal political rule by generating bad press for the governor.

The burning of the fourth cabin at West Canada Lakes Wilderness occurred later, but its story concludes the saga of the cabins. The fourth cabin remained standing until 1987, when commissioner Hank Williams determined to have it removed before he left office. Local rangers opposed the burning and it was rumored that every time the cabin was scheduled for removal, someone, quite possibly a DEC employee, alerted Senator Stafford so that the destruction was put off. Without telling the local rangers, Williams arranged to helicopter in a DEC crew from the Catskills to burn the cabin.[4]

The burning of the cabins is a symbol of the problems DEC faced in complying with the State Land Master Plan. It is a story not only of determination on the part of commissioners Berle and Williams, but of the strange culture they had to manage at DEC. That culture, of control by an administration rather than professionals, and the way staff can attempt to circumvent management will surface as problems in several instances.

Robert (Bob) Flacke

Governor Carey appointed Bob Flacke as DEC commissioner to replace Berle. The appointment was effective January 1979, and Flacke convinced Persico to follow him to Albany to serve as DEC's counsel and deputy commissioner. Persico left the Adirondack Park Agency with great reluctance, believing that DEC was a nightmare.

In a 1999 interview, Flacke recalled two thoughts he had regarding DEC from his time as commissioner. Both observations illuminate basic problems at DEC. During his third year Flacke wrote a paper in which he advocated separating the natural resources component from the department.[5] He also was quite critical of staff, saying "you can't hire good people for natural resources departments, there are no rewards in civil service; and it is hard to move them to Albany because you cannot finance moves as private industry can."

Land Acquisition and Perkins Clearing

Over the years, one of DEC's most important functions has been to acquire land for the Forest Preserve. In the past, the legislature has appropriated funds for acquisitions, but most of the money for many decades has come from bond acts, and in the intervals between bond acts, the state has often been unable to buy key tracts that have come on the market. After 1975, when the funds from the 1972 Bond Act were committed, the state had almost no money for land acquisition until the passage of the 1986 Environmental Bond Act. The State Land Master Plan had recommended a land swap along the eastern edge of the West Canada Lakes Wilderness Area, and in the late 1970s completing this swap seemed to be a good way to get around the shortage of funds. So both DEC and International Paper Company advanced the exchange and proposed a constitutional amendment to accomplish it.

Land swaps were always considered suspect by environmental groups, but only one group opposed the Perkins Clearing deal outright: Sierra Club. The Task Force on Open Space under Bill Verner had discussed the ultimate ownership of land within the park and concluded that the state would never purchase the "center of the park," although Verner strongly believed in providing the park with a totally protected core. (Verner referred to his idea as a "donut" theory, with the core surrounded by a buffer of lands with mixed ownership.) Most environmental groups concurred with the task force, all but Sierra Club. According to Sam Sage, Sierra Club opposed the Perkins Clearing swap primarily because "it marked the end of an era, the end of expectations that the park would ultimately be mostly publicly owned."[6]

The constitutional amendment permitting the exchange passed in November 1979 by a very small margin. Controversy over the exchange was exacerbated by DEC's attempts to comply with the SLMP by closing lakes in the West Canadas to airplanes and motorboats. This debate continued through the 1983 hearings on classifying land the state obtained in the exchange.

International Paper (IP) held a checkerboard of lots west of Perkins Clearing, making it difficult to build roads to access and log its lots. State lots, largely in Totten and Crossfield Township Number 3, had been acquired through nonpayment of taxes in 1871 and 1877 at a time when there had never been any logging in the area. Thus, many of the lots acquired by IP had virgin stands of timber.* The exchange was originally planned to involve giving 8,500 acres of Forest Preserve land to IP for 8,500 acres of cut-over IP land. Because the timber on state land was more valuable than that on the IP lots, IP was to pay an additional $200,000 in the exchange.[7] However, a survey of the timber on the tract and further appraisals and negotiations gave the state 10,344 acres and IP 7,133 acres. The state parcel consolidated the Forest Preserve into a contiguous tract that added six lakes to state ownership. IP gained the desired regular boundaries for its land. But the debate within the environmental community over land exchanges, even within the groups that did not actively oppose the Perkins Clearing swap, raised so many issues, among them the equity of the exchange and giving up a substantial tract of Forest Preserve, that no other large exchange has since been proposed.†

The debate over classification of the new state land proved even more controversial than the swap. An agency subcommittee and the staff had recommended that the acquired land and the interspersed lots that had previously been classified as Primitive should all be classified as Wilderness. Disputes over the classification culminated in a marathon three-day agency debate in January 1984. Agency members were deadlocked. DEC commissioner Hank Williams and DEC staff wanted the entire parcel classified as Wild Forest, thus permitting continued floatplane use at Whitney Lake. Williams appeared to be sup-

---

* I cannot find any evidence that the environmental groups that considered the exchange favorably were concerned with or even knew that the state land to be exchanged contained old-growth timber.

† Constitutional amendments permitting smaller exchanges for additions to the Piseco airport, cemeteries, and so forth have passed, but even these have generated considerable opposition.

porting the sportsmen's position as expressed by the Adirondack Conservation Council: ACC wanted road access to the Pillsbury Lake junction and to Otter Lake and Little Moose Pond as well as floatplane access to Whitney Lake.

Whitney Lake became a bargaining chip in the settlement. Finally Williams agreed to Wilderness designation for Whitney, and he proposed a compromise that designated as Wild Forest a nearly 2,000-acre triangle with its apex at Pillsbury Mountain. This compromise permitted motorized access for an additional mile to the Pillsbury Mountain Trail. It did nothing for sportsmen, despite Williams's desire to placate them. The agency approved the compromise by a vote of seven to three; two of the three negative voters, John Stock and Donald Wadsworth, favored the Wild Forest classification for the entire parcel, while Chairman Ted Ruzow voted negatively as a protest against the principle of exchange. Ruzow feared that exchange compromised the integrity of the Forest Preserve and the constitution.[8]

The story does not end there, however, for Adirondack Park Agency erred in the maps it sent out for public hearing, omitting some 2,200 acres that were part of the Jessup River Wild Forest.[9] Because of the mistake, the Local Government Review Board called for APA Executive Director Vince Moore's resignation, which happened anyway a few months later with the appointment of Herman (Woody) Cole as chairman.

The State Land Master Plan and Unit Management Plans

Williams's rocky tenure at DEC is as good a place as any to introduce DEC's greatest shortcoming in the years after 1972, the year the agency adopted the Adirondack Park State Land Master Plan. The SLMP defined several categories of which Wilderness and Wild Forest comprised the bulk of the Forest Preserve. Definitions of both categories were accompanied by descriptions of how to bring the land units defined into compliance with the definitions. Wilderness areas were to have little impact by man, so there was a substantial list of nonconforming structures and activities that were to be eliminated. These included removal of fire towers, closing of ranger cabins, and elimination of motorboat and floatplane use, all of which actions were opposed by many, if not most, people in the Adirondacks.* While giving a timetable for removing nonconforming

---

* One of my readers questioned my generalizations about people in the Adirondacks. It is true I have conducted no formal survey. It is also true that many who supported both APA and the SLMP were afraid to express themselves publicly. However, I have found many letters to the editor that substantiate my points. In addition, many people have expressed these ideas to me, enough so

uses, the 1972 State Land Master Plan contains no specifics on how the DEC was to manage or plan for managing the Forest Preserve, other than by following the broad definitions and descriptions. In fact, the 1972 SLMP does not even allude to section 816 of the APA Act that directs the DEC "to develop, in consultation with the agency, individual unit management plans for each unit of land under its jurisdiction." The 1972 plan does, however, recommend that the SLMP be periodically reviewed every five years and that there should be "greater public involvement in the whole process of acquisition, revision, and review."[10] Because no specific guidelines were provided for DEC's planning or management of state lands, DEC did little more than discuss how and when to remove some of the nonconforming uses.

The omissions in the 1972 SLMP with respect to methods for preparing unit management plans (UMPs) are difficult to understand. As part of his work for the Temporary Study Commission, George Davis had prepared sample UMPs for three areas: Pharaoh Lake as representative of Wilderness Areas, Hudson River Gorge as a Primitive Area, and Shaker Mountain as a Wild Forest Area. These plans were all written by the beginning of 1971 and along with a draft for an Adirondack Park plan were available to the agency as it began work on the State Land Master Plan.[11]

Several aspects of Davis's work point up two more of DEC's shortcomings that show up in later years. First, of Davis's three sample plans, only the Pharaoh Lake plan has been written and approved by the agency. Second, his Shaker Mountain plan included many new opportunities for recreation for a broad spectrum of users that included hunters, fishermen, and snowmobilers. His plan identified sixteen trailheads that would serve the area and some acquisitions that would enhance public access. Within DEC, as of 2000, Region 5, which covers more than two-thirds of the park, has not produced a single Wild Forest plan that included enhanced recreational opportunities.

From the time the State Land Master Plan was finished in 1972 until 1977 when the agency began working on a revision, DEC did not produce a single unit management plan. Under APA Chairman Ted Ruzow, but with considerable work from the agency's SLMP Committee and especially its chairman, Peter S. Paine Jr., the agency issued a revised State Land Master Plan in October 1979. Undoubtedly as a reaction to DEC's lack of response to the APA Act,

---

that I found them pervasive. With respect to the removal of the cabins, almost every time I talked to an old-time park resident about the West Canadas, I was reminded of the horror of the cabin removal. The symbols I noted here are remembered by many of those I encountered.

the 1979 plan specifically reminds the DEC that section 816 of the APA Act "directs DEC to develop, in consultation with the agency, individual unit management plans for each unit of land under its jurisdiction classified in the master plan." The revision goes on to list guidelines and criteria for the unit management plans. They should include an inventory of natural resources and an analysis of the area's ecosystem; an inventory of existing facilities for public and administrative use; an inventory of the actual and projected public use of the area; an assessment of the impact of that use on resources, ecosystems, and public enjoyment of the area with particular attention to portions of the area threatened by overuse; and an assessment of the physical, biological, and social carrying capacity of the area, again with attention to threats of overuse. The revised SLMP additionally requires that each UMP contain a statement of management objectives for protection and rehabilitation of the area's resources. In the long list that follows, giving objectives to be addressed on a site-specific basis, only two items can be considered forward-looking and use-oriented. They call for the identification of needed additions or improvements and for plans for providing further appropriate public use and improvement of access by the physically handicapped in Wild Forest areas accessible by automobile or in Intensive Use areas. The rest is preservation-oriented.*

The unit management plans were also required to consider the unit's relation to adjacent public and private lands, to have schedules for achieving the objectives, and to recommend future acquisitions as appropriate. DEC was supposed to submit an initial draft, with alternative management objectives where appropriate, to the agency for review and comment prior to the preparation of the final draft plan for public review. The public was to be given the opportunity to review and comment on the drafts. Revisions of the UMPs could only be made following the same procedures as spelled out for the SLMP. The 1979 SLMP ends with the admonition to DEC to complete all the plans before the next scheduled revision of the SLMP, which was to occur in 1984.

A sidebar to the 1979 revisions is that an item in a draft would have delayed closing floatplane access to Whitney Lake, gradually phasing it out with final closure in 1993. A suit by environmental groups eliminated the delay, thus upholding this Wilderness component of the SLMP.

---

* The rest requires removal of nonconforming uses; preservation of special-interest areas such as habitats of rare species; preservation of lakes, ponds, rivers, and streams; preservation of fish and wildlife, and aquatic and terrestrial habitats; regulation of public use so that the carrying capacity is not exceeded; rehabilitation of overused areas; and actions to minimize adverse impacts on the resource.

The State Land Master Plan called for unit management plans to be written for each Wilderness, Wild Forest, Primitive, Canoe, and Intensive Use area in the park. No new construction of facilities or major rehabilitation of existing facilities was to be done in any area by the DEC unless authorized by a completed UMP. It was anticipated that within a few years the most important UMPs would be written, ensuring wilderness protection as well as providing for recreational development of the Forest Preserve. It is amazing how little of this work was done before Williams became DEC commissioner. What is even more inconceivable is that, at least in DEC's Region 5, so little more was accomplished in the next two decades.[12]

For most New Yorkers, the unit management plan concept was and is a weird beast, a bureaucratic exercise, devoid of anything that might make such plans appealing to the public. UMPs are only slightly less difficult for the public to understand than APA private land regulations. For all their lack of public appeal, they are utterly essential. Unit management planning is a concept that had its origins in federal land management acts (for the Forest Service, Bureau of Land Management, and National Park Service, and under a different nomenclature for federal wilderness areas). UMPs are essentially the planning tools that were missing from the Conservation Department.

The Conservation Department and DEC turned old roads, routes to fire towers, old carriage roads, or trails built by individuals or groups like Adirondack Mountain Club into a trail network, but designed or built almost no hiking trails of its own. The Conservation Department never developed a comprehensive recreation plan, even though directed to do so by the legislature. DEC never put together a plan for land acquisition focused on the needs of the Forest Preserve. So, there were many good reasons for developing a plan such as the State Land Master Plan and including in it a means of requiring DEC to focus on just what its lands could do for the public as well as how they should be preserved. The early versions of the SLMP are long on prohibitions with respect to wilderness, short on prescriptions for recreation. It was hoped that DEC, with its knowledge of the lands it maintained, could supply the details. The reasons why this approach did not work are legion: DEC found it difficult to comprehend what the plans should include; the department had no complete inventory of its trails; and DEC had not solved the problem of integrating public input into the plans, a subject that will be explored in chapter 17. The Forest Preserve Advisory Committee had its origins in the first of three High Peaks advisory committees. The evolution of this committee chronicles DEC's attempts to establish a role for much-needed public participation. And tracing that evolution reveals the progress, or lack thereof, of the unit management plan process because the advisory committee's role included overseeing the UMPs, chronicling the slow pace of preparing them, and fighting to get them done.

For nearly thirty years, through serving on numerous boards of not-for-profits and special task forces and writing many books and articles, the one constant has been my membership in the Forest Preserve Advisory Committee to DEC. I evaluate its effectiveness in chapter 17; I recount its activities as if writing an autobiography.

High Peaks Advisory Committee

Overuse of the High Peaks and DEC's failure to manage the area as a wilderness were among the reasons for the creation of the Adirondack Park Agency and the implementation of the State Land Master Plan. Commissioner James Biggane of DEC appointed a High Peaks Advisory Committee in the summer of 1974. It reported directly to the Division of Lands and Forests and met quarterly beginning in 1974, with Jerome Jensen of DEC and a committee member as co-chairs. It should be recognized that Biggane took very seriously the problems of the High Peaks at that early date. The original members were "citizens known for their long interest and experience in the High Peaks area"; almost all were members of Adirondack Mountain Club. I met Biggane in mid-1974 and convinced him that the charge of looking only at the High Peaks would not solve the problem of overuse there and that the committee needed to address measures of directing use elsewhere in the park to relieve the pressures on the High Peaks. I was able to substantiate my claim that DEC had not provided trails for hikers throughout most of the southern Adirondacks. He agreed and asked me to join the committee in time for its second meeting in November 1974.

My nostalgia for those early days is fueled by the way the committee worked, the intelligence of its members, and the scope of issues addressed. Through 1975 and 1976 discussions ranged from carrying capacity, the condition of the trails, how to measure the number of hikers, and what to do about such things as trail erosion and overuse.[13] My role, since most members were narrowly focused on the High Peaks, developed into the task of writing introductory material and, with Jensen, compiling the final report, which synthesized the papers on different issues written by various members. The quality of the papers is apparent twenty-five years later: Bill Adriance wrote on the carrying capacity of different zones; Almy Coggeshell figured out ways of measuring the number of hikers. Others assessed the condition of trails in the High Peaks;

Ed Ketchledge reviewed the destruction of flora on the summits, particularly the alpine summits, which he found were gravely threatened.

According to the final report of 1977,[14] the committee determined that 14 percent or thirty miles of trails in the eastern High Peaks were in critical condition; that the deterioration was mostly due to the unplanned origin of the trails and their steepness as well as to mountain soils and water; that DEC's budget for the region was never adequate; that backpackers cause most of the human damage; that ADK's Ridge Runner program was an effective educational tool; that groups should not exceed ten campers or hikers; that problems of overuse are not found outside the eastern High Peaks; that campfires contribute to a considerable loss of vegetation; that cleanup efforts by volunteer groups, started in 1974, had reduced litter significantly; that permit systems such as those used in federally managed wilderness areas throughout the United States have been accepted and have worked effectively; and that winter hikers and campers are generally inexperienced.

The committee recommended completing the High Peaks Unit Management Plan as called for in the State Land Master Plan; evaluating the entire trail system in a comprehensive fashion; determining the carrying capacity for specific parts of the area; determining the best relocations for badly eroded trails; finding better ways to record use; limiting some or all camping to designated sites; and assuring that trailhead parking facilities are commensurate with appropriate hiking use. There were recommendations for educating the public; maintaining trails; rehabilitating specific trails, specifically to Mt. Marcy and Algonquin; eliminating the multiple herdpaths on trailless peaks by retaining one best route with minimal marking; redistributing hiking within and outside the area; prohibiting all camping above 4,000 feet and limiting camping to specific sites at elevations between 3,500 and 4,000 feet; encouraging the use of cooking stoves; prohibiting fires above 3,500 feet; limiting user groups to ten individuals; prohibiting camping within 100 feet of lakes, streams, or trails; and addressing the issue of crowded camping areas such as Marcy Dam, Indian Falls, Lake Colden, and Johns Brook Valley. To accomplish the latter, the report suggested, "should the Department find a permit system necessary *for control purposes,* the committee recommends gradual, limited use of permits rather than immediate, general use permits." The committee, though reluctant to recommend "a limiting permit system until all other means of solving the area's problems are exhausted, [agreed that] permits may be inevitable in specific areas or in sections of the Adirondack Park." The final report included a brief analysis of different types of permits and a note that "continued study of permit system[s] is necessary."

The committee approved special High Peaks signs, brochures, and other educational means of introducing the recommendations. Despite the fact that the recommendations were never codified into regulations, many did in fact become accepted in the High Peaks. DEC began to limit camping, especially at Lake Colden. It closed some sites, telling campers they had to go elsewhere. Even thirty years ago, the need for this protocol for High Peaks use was so great that most campers and hikers accepted it.

To those of us who have been following the progress of plans for the High Peaks, this is, in retrospect, an amazing document. Members planned and carried out research and studies on issues ranging from trail conditions to carrying capacity. With the exception of addressing problems that were unforeseen at the time, their recommendations do everything that is in the High Peaks Wilderness Area (var. Complex) Unit Management Plan (HPWAUMP) adopted in 1999 for the High Peaks *and more*. The twenty-two-year history of the advocacy needed to bring about the completion of the plan for the High Peaks involved a number of people who put pressure on DEC, and as James C. Dawson, member of many Adirondack committees, noted, "many of the players had their bedside copies of the 1977 report readily available to push DEC to the 1999 result."[15]

I dwell on the contents of the plan because the plan is symptomatic of DEC's actions over the years: Something good is accomplished, then discarded or buried, and ultimately reinvented with enormous duplication of effort and little forward motion. Therefore, it is appropriate to interrupt the story of the advisory committee here to tell the next chapter in the High Peaks saga. It is a mystery how DEC regressed from the committee's 1977 report to a draft High Peaks Unit Management Plan, issued at the end of 1978. That document, which caused something of a furor, especially at Adirondack Mountain Club, was deemed so unacceptable that it was withdrawn in spring 1979 with an announcement that DEC would prepare several other plans first to gain experience. The HPUMP was little more than a simplistic inventory of possible ways to deal with perceived problems. Its format was undoubtedly influenced by the new and poorly understood State Environmental Quality Review (SEQR) requirements. SEQR requires that for a given problem all possible actions be evaluated so that a best course of action can be determined. DEC's plan was an unprioritized list of alternatives for solving the problems already addressed by the High Peaks Advisory Committee,[16] instead of a set of recommendations based on an analysis of those alternatives. However, in including alternatives that could be considered by APA, it did reflect what the State Land Master Plan called for. It was obvious that DEC did not know what was required to write a

UMP and that its planning capabilities were severely limited. Nothing more happened to the HPUMP until the late 1980s.

The Formation of the Forest Preserve Advisory Committee

The High Peaks Advisory Committee continued to meet, though less regularly, gradually shifting its focus to the issues of diverting use from that region. I helped propose studies to discover those opportunities parkwide. Faced with severe cuts in DEC staff and knowing that "there is no money for anything new, certainly not new trails," the committee picked up the idea of "marked footpaths," a way of designating the numerous informal footpaths worn over the decades by fishermen, hunters, and others. It became apparent that a committee was needed that could address parkwide issues. With the appointment of Norm VanValkenburgh as director of the Division of Lands and Forests, the Forest Preserve Advisory Committee (FPAC) was established in 1980, an outgrowth of the High Peaks Committee but with a new charter and charge. Its mission was directed toward the entire Forest Preserve, the Catskills as well as the Adirondacks.

Of the twelve members, five were at-large and seven represented specific groups, either hiking clubs or organizations like Adirondack Council. Several members were holdovers from the old High Peaks group.* DEC invited a broad range of groups to nominate representatives, but no sportsmen's organizations did at first, so that both DEC and the committee were worried that the FPAC was not more broadly representative. DEC continued to mail minutes and information to a long list of organizations. For a time George Fuge represented the education sector, but he was primarily associated with the New York State Conservation Council and the sportsmen's perspective. In the latter role, he became frustrated because he was such an isolated minority, although several others were oriented toward the interests of sportsmen. However, membership of the FPAC was dominated by individuals with strong protectionist philosophies until the 1990s, when many new groups sent representatives, and especially at the end of the decade when the number of group representatives was increased to twelve, making it easier to broaden membership.

Dave Newhouse was elected co-chair with VanValkenburgh (Dave remained co-chair until 1997). DEC commissioner Robert Flacke welcomed the

* For the first two years, I represented ADK, then I was off for about a year and then reappointed as an at-large member, which I still am in 2001. I have chaired the committee since April 1997.

group and talked about its new direction. Among the subjects discussed at the first meeting were the planning process, wilderness designation, the range of attributes of various wilderness areas, and the development of wilderness recreational resources as well as true wilderness areas. The committee's future role was strongly tied to reviewing unit management plans. In an article detailing the beginning of the new committee I wrote, "Perhaps the most important result of this first meeting is that it marks DEC's acceptance of public review and advice." [17]

For years, alternate meetings were two-day affairs held at frugal but scenic locations such as Newcomb's Huntington Forest, Mountain Gate Lodge in the Catskills, and Paul Smith's College. Meetings were generally dominated by information on DEC activities, new regulations, problems, and progress, or lack thereof, on unit management plans. The revision of the State Land Master Plan in 1979, calling for prompt completion of the UMPs, generated little progress. [18]

The committee determined that in addition to the lack of funds and trained personnel that slowed work on UMPs, progress was hampered by lack of DEC policies. Almost all the plans involved DEC policies that were either out-of-date, incomplete, or nonexistent. It was amazing to discover that important policies such as trail construction and motorized use—thirty-seven major topics in all—did not exist or existed in very outdated forms and therefore were not available to the planners. Lack of policies threatened to create an anarchic situation in which each UMP could reinvent policy, creating a multitude of different approaches, a situation which would be unmanageable and which could not be made into regulations.

It seemed as if the problem came from the fact no one at DEC had time to write even the first draft of these policies; the problem of just getting something down on paper was an impediment to progress. So members and subcommittees began to draft policies, knowing that anything produced had to go through endless departmental review. This was at least a step in the right direction, and the committee did a great job. A few policies were written, for instance a bicycle policy that closed access to Wilderness areas, but even that was not implemented for several years. DEC actually reviewed only a few of the committee drafts, and several of those reviewed fell into the black hole of incompletion. Worse yet, such vital policies as snowmobile regulations and snowmobile trail standards or staff use of motor vehicles were not tackled by DEC until the 1990s. Making policies comply with the State Land Master Plan seemed to elude the department. A number of policies were completed or revised in the 1970s and early 1980s, but more than four times that number had never been updated as of 2001.

Over the years, the Forest Preserve Advisory Committee passed few resolutions spelling out recommendations to DEC. The committee's positions, detailed in the minutes, were often in opposition to DEC's activities or plans. The FPAC called for the removal of Camp Santanoni after the site was properly documented and parts preserved;[19] the creation of a better policy for DEC's removal of trees from state land (this policy was later rewritten); and limits on timber cutting reservations (the length of time an owner can still cut timber on land he has sold to the state) on lands acquired for the Forest Preserve. The committee discussed and occasionally made recommendations on a wide range of other topics: all-terrain-vehicle (ATV) use; limiting horsepower at fishing access sites; easements; Bond Acts; bicycle use in the Forest Preserve; unit management plans; work on trails in areas without UMPs;* Temporary Revocable Permits (TRPs); the Adirondack Park Centennial; the Catskill Interpretive Center; eminent domain; the Diamond/Lassiter acquisition; navigation rights; user fees for state lands (as proposed by Commissioner Tom Jorling in 1989); fees for camping; the perennial problems of DEC's budgets; liming to reduce the effects of acid rain (a political question with respect to Wilderness lakes); summit stewards; leasing Gore and Belleayre ski centers to private groups; Department of Corrections supervision of prisoners doing trail construction and maintenance; search and rescue; the Remsen-Placid railroad; limits on the size of camping group; excessive use of helicopters by staff; retirements from the department and the resulting unfilled positions, layoffs, and bumping; the need for corridor UMPs for long trails, such as canoe routes or realignments of the Northville-Placid trail; and restoration of fire towers on Wild Forest lands.

The committee opposed the fragmentation of units to facilitate special UMPs, such as separating the plan for the Black Mountain section of the Lake George Wild Forest from a comprehensive plan for the lake's east shore. This division was done to accommodate a state police tower and was counter to plans to consolidate areas.

Members brought to the department's attention acts that should not be oc-

---

* This discussion went on over several years in an ever-tightening noose of Catch-22: DEC argued that use levels forced them to cut trees, build bridges, and so on in the High Peaks as maintenance acceptable within a Memorandum of Understanding (MOU) with the Park Agency. DEC argued that resource protection was of paramount concern, yet all their steps to improve trails brought more and more use.

curring: illegal trail marking or camping by the public, or unlawful tree cutting, or use of motorized vehicles by both the public and staff. The department's responses, now mostly delivered by Garry Ives, chief of the Bureau of Preserve, Protection and Management, were that the department would look into the matters—a classic bureaucratic reaction that usually implies "file and forget." Ives's assignment to the committee was a hint that its importance to DEC was declining. In reading the minutes of the late 1980s and early 1990s, I am appalled at the number of problems raised by committee members that DEC never reacted to, failed to look into until they finally faded away unsolved, or— as in some cases to be discussed in the last chapter—until they blew up into major crises. One glaring example was the department's ignoring of campers who had turned a canoe launch site off NY Route 10 beside a bridge over the West Branch of the Sacandaga River into a de facto campground. This was at a spot where regulations clearly prohibited camping. It took photographs, numerous entreaties, and ten years before Albany finally directed the recalcitrant Region 5 to act.

Throughout, the committee was concerned with purchasing land for the Forest Preserve and made many recommendations to improve DEC's process of land acquisition.

If there was a common theme to the FPAC's recommendations, it was that DEC needed to improve stewardship of and planning for state lands in the Adirondacks and Catskills. Appearing at every meeting like the chorus of a bad song was an endless series of status reports on writing UMPs, an unbelievable exercise in dereliction that will be discussed further in part 3.

It was becoming obvious that DEC, and Region 5 in particular, were having difficulties determining how to write a plan. According to the July 1983 minutes of the FPAC, "[T]he present feeling is that there is a lack of structure in the planning process and a lack of understanding by people on [the advisory] committees of what goes into a plan. A good wilderness plan is needed now to serve as an example for others. In order to progress through the planning process, it may be desirable to get work done by contract." [20] (The threat of having to write plans under contract will figure strongly in unit management plan work as revived by Governor Pataki in 1999.)

After the aborted attempt to write a High Peaks UMP and spurred on by the 1979 revision of the State Land Master Plan, DEC began to focus on just how the department should write plans. Norm VanValkenburgh, director of the Division of Lands and Forests, prepared a detailed outline for UMPs that became DEC policy in 1980 and was followed by a paper on "Unit Planning for Wilderness Management" in 1982.

But the failure to complete plans was not universal. As early as 1986 it was obvious that Region 6 was doing a job of creating unit management plans far superior to Region 5, and this fact was noted at many succeeding FPAC meetings. The Catskill Regions 3 and 4 were completing plans through the 1980s at a great rate. Region 6 under Tom Brown had always been moved by a "can-do" philosophy, despite budget shortfalls and staff cutbacks.[21] Region 6 may have been more inclined to allow for motorized use, but it used good judgment in opening up the Independence River Wild Forest for horseback riding while keeping key hiking opportunities separate. The Five Ponds Wilderness UMP, twice revised, has proven a good tool for management, even when challenged by the blowdown of 1995. The Ha-de-ron-dah Wilderness UMP was completed in record time (published 1986). The Black River UMP is a balanced plan for a Wild Forest area, with some new opportunities for recreation. The Pepperbox Wilderness is preserved as a totally trailless wilderness. On balance, Region 6 has done a good job, so rather than focus on its efforts with respect to UMPs, most of the examples in this book are taken from Region 5 because they exemplify the problems Wolf Road (DEC's headquarters) has had in reaching and directing some of DEC's regions.*

For many years, while Region 5 made little progress on UMPs, it was curious that Wolf Road was unable to prod the region to greater productivity. Region 5 did begin work on two major plans: the Siamese Ponds Wilderness Area plan and the Pharaoh Lake Wilderness plan. The Siamese Ponds Wilderness Area plan was started in 1981. A Citizen's Advisory Committee (CAC) appointed to begin work on the plan spent a long time hashing out details. In fact, the committee's work was used as an example of the need for time limits for such committees and for better leadership on the part of DEC staff. Still, a draft of the plan for public consideration was completed in 1984. It did set aside a large chunk of the wilderness to be trailless, something championed by Erwin Miller. The committee did recommend a bridge or bridges for access across the East Branch of the Sacandaga River, but nothing came of the latter. It did not deal with the problems created by the fact that the beginning of some trails was on private lands, problems that persisted. It was very weak in recommending new trails and opportunities for hikers, generally holding to the status quo of

---

* Catskill Regions 3 and 4 have done a remarkable job of completing UMPs with vision, putting in place some of the new work called for in the UMPs, and revising UMPs almost on schedule. The plans guided the Catskill State Land Master Plan, which was developed by DEC, in contrast to the Adirondack SLMP, which was developed by APA. The Catskill plans observe the same distinctions between Wilderness and Wild Forest.

the limited existing trail network, with two exceptions that were retrenchments called for by the State Land Master Plan. According to the SLMP both John Pond Road and Old Farm Clearing Road were to be closed at the Wilderness boundaries. When the plan recommended that those closings be implemented, the storm of protest by residents was so great that it was a miracle the final draft of the plan was completed as quickly as it was. Old Farm Clearing was closed at the end of private land; John Pond Road was kept open past the Wilderness boundary because of an old cemetery.

The Pharaoh Lake Wilderness UMP was started in 1980, became dormant, and was then given new life in 1982. The UMP was supposed to incorporate plans for three adjacent primitive areas: Bald Ledge, Gooseneck, and Crane Pond. The State Land Master Plan directed the unit management plan to remove nonconformances in those areas so that they could become part of the Wilderness Area. It took five years (until April 1987) to complete a draft of the plan and another five years (until April 1992) before the plan was approved by APA and released by DEC. The final version incorporated two additional primitive areas, Hague Brook and First Brother, but omitted any plan for the contentious Crane Pond Primitive Area. Again, inept management of the advisory committee helped prolong the process, but the closing of Crane Pond Road, as called for in the SLMP, created so much opposition from both sportsmen and locals that it almost stopped the process. Controversy surrounding that road closing figures in the next chapter, but two things should be observed: the road has never been closed at the Wilderness boundary because DEC backed away, and APA's ability to require fulfillment of conditions in the SLMP was seriously compromised.

Region 5's intransigence and inability to produce unit management plans may be attributed to its director during this period, Tom Monroe. The independence of Region 5 under Monroe had a cultural basis in the days of the Conservation Department and in Region 5's first director, Bill Petty. Monroe used his independence to call together an advisory group of sportsmen and area residents who wanted to keep Crane Pond Road open. They kept talking and talking while nothing was being done, prolonging any decisions to act. Further, DEC ducked from the confrontations that developed, but more of that also in the next chapter.

In 1983 I represented Adirondack Mountain Club on the Forest Preserve Advisory Committee when that committee spent most of its time trying to urge DEC to get on with the required planning. It was a very depressing time. Mario Cuomo was elected governor in 1982, only to face enormous budget problems that would require cutbacks at many levels of government. The threat of cutbacks at DEC would hurt already underfunded programs. This pattern of underfunding was well documented the following year by an Assembly Ways and Means Committee's report.[22] The committee prepared an excellent analysis of DEC's budget from 1970 to 1984, and the analysis confirmed what DEC had been saying all along. It documented DEC's increasing responsibilities without sufficient funding. It showed how the Division of Lands and Forests had had its budgets decreased, forcing it to shift manpower and resources. The division literally had no staff for any planning work; already there was a twenty—to thirty-year backlog in boundary survey work, so that surveillance of trespass by loggers or by people on motor vehicles was almost impossible; little or no maintenance had been done on trails, lean-tos, and so forth since Civilian Conservation Corps days in the 1930s. And Cuomo proposed more cuts in DEC's budget.

Because I believed that DEC's ability to do any planning was already compromised, I arranged to make a presentation to the agency to tell the members just how little work DEC was doing to carry out the State Land Master Plan. I really criticized DEC commissioner Hank Williams—my notes for my talk are well reasoned but I remember being very forceful. It worked. He convened a group of representatives of various organizations, mostly environmentalists, to discuss the planning problems. The meeting, scheduled for May 2, 1983, was very productive; those attending understood DEC's problems. After several months, DEC issued a report on the meeting, complete with Commissioner Williams's comments on how he would respond to recommendations or why he or the DEC could not, mostly because of budget problems.

Williams's final report, written by VanValkenburgh and issued December 23, 1983 (more than seven months for a report!), was the most positive thing any of us had seen. It summarized the major suggestions from the May meeting and from letters submitted in response to the interim draft of his report. It gave a list of specific issues and told what Williams proposed to do to address them. It included a plan for expanded staffing for UMPs, a single manager for UMP planning, the combining of adjacent and related areas to reduce the number of plans needed, the completion of DEC policies to give consistency to the UMPs, with the list of facilities and activities to be addressed, and training for the staff that would create and carry out the plans.

Here I have to stop and wonder again how so much could possibly go wrong, when things for a brief moment seemed to be improving. The documents I have from this period might be just as applicable to Governor Pataki's initiative to complete the UMPs, as announced in 1999. Instead of a steady stream of plans following Williams's promises, my files contain a jumble of plans to plan, nothing more than attempts to figure out what to do. The first result, issued in September 1984, was an announcement of a "fast track" process,[23] a detailed outline for writing the plans that was supposed to make things simpler.

The 1984 assignment of foresters to work on unit management plans amounted to little since they were not relieved of their other responsibilities. In Williams's tenure the only other plans that were completed in Region 5 were those for smaller areas that were needed to permit special activities such as putting communication towers on Black Mountain, improving the Mt. Van Hoevenburg Recreation Area, and adding ski trails and other improvements to Whiteface and Gore Mountain ski areas.

In 1985 APA reprinted the State Land Master Plan to celebrate the Forest Preserve Centennial, but it was done without the required five-year revisions. The agency began work on those revisions in 1986. DEC wanted the agency to reconsider the closing of the contentious roads that were holding up UMPs: Old Farm Clearing, John Pond, and South Meadow roads. There were rumors of a real internal DEC fight between Tom Monroe and Norm VanValkenburgh on the issue. VanValkenburgh, as always, supported the State Land Master Plan, though he often seemed to be the only one in DEC fighting for its principles. Peter Paine, speaking for the agency, countered DEC's request by proposing that the Crane Pond Road should be upgraded from Primitive to Wilderness classification, thus requiring its closure. The agency voted to close the roads, and Williams, voting as DEC representative to the agency, was among those in the majority.

Governor Cuomo appointed Thomas Jorling as DEC commissioner in June 1987, and the department under Jorling issued a new draft handbook for unit management plans on January 13, 1988. This "Policy and Procedure for Forest Preserve Unit Management Planning" became policy on April 1, 1988, and the final draft included a timetable for completing the plans. With one exception, it is the same list issued under the Pataki administration in 1999—that is if you add fourteen years to the projected completion dates.

8 | Other Issues and Events in the 1980s

Adirondack Freedom Fighters

SHORTLY AFTER 1980, a new cast of Adirondack Park Agency opponents emerged. Funeral director Maynard Baker of Warrensburg, later supervisor of that town, organized a meeting attended by about seventy people.[1] Its purpose was "to find a legal means to abolish the agency in its entirety. . . . We're living on occupied land right now,"[2] Baker said, comparing the fight to our war for independence. Among those attending were Robert Purdy of Essex County (he was one of the leading opponents of APA in its formative years and later served for many years as supervisor of the Town of Keene), Joseph Rota of Local Government Review Board, and Andrew Halloran, counsel for LGRB. The review board was on record as calling for abolishing the agency, an action that still had the support of Senator Stafford and Assemblyman Harris. Halloran praised the new group, saying that the review board could not concentrate on the agency's abolition—"It would take time away from doing what we have to do." (He did not note that the review board could not technically call for the end of the agency.) Tony D'Elia, who was also present, told the group that the legislature would not help them—"New York City controls this state." He claimed the "only remaining avenue is a suit in federal courts, based on the 'taking issue.' " The group chose to be called the Adirondack Inholders Association and announced plans to raise a $100,000 war chest. Baker asked that each landowner post his property with blue flags to show outsiders just how much of the park is private land. "If they want a blue line, we'll give them a blue line."[3]

From this beginning emerged the Adirondack Freedom Fighters, which a year later was pursuing a lawsuit in federal court based on several parts of the U.S. Constitution.[4] They chose to fight the taking issue on grounds of the Fifth Amendment. They believed that the agency was constituted as court, judge,

and jury, contrary to the Seventh Amendment, and that people were being de-
prived of life, liberty, and the pursuit of happiness, counter to the Fourteenth
Amendment. In 1983, the Freedom Fighters claimed seven hundred members.
Attorney Fred Monroe said that the group needed $150,000 to mount a law-
suit, that it was still seeking not-for-profit status, and that lack of funding was its
biggest problem. That suit was never mounted, but similar suits were pursued
by other organizations in succeeding years.

Among the issues that energized the Freedom Fighters was the closing of
lakes to airplanes, which they saw as discrimination against disabled veterans,
and this theme, discrimination against the disabled, remained a rallying cry for
Baker and others through the 1990s.

Governor Cuomo and the Adirondack Park Agency

In 1983, his first year as governor, Cuomo visited Elizabethtown and listened
to many criticisms of the agency.[5] He was undeterred by a threat against him
personally that was phoned into the school where five hundred people waited
for him.[6] He "promised to investigate APA's 43-acre zoning, and learn its history and rationale."[7] He also lectured on the values of zoning ("you are not
unique, unequally burdened, every zoning law does it") and the fact that the
park is the concern of the whole state. Ed Hale of the *Watertown Daily Times*
wrote of Cuomo's dialogue with some of the fifty speakers, "Call it a draw."[8]

D'Elia followed up that meeting with a number of letters to the governor
on APA representation, red tape, rules and regulations, and excessive zoning.
D'Elia pinned his hopes for change on the governor's appointing Herman
(Woody) Cole to chair the agency in 1984, replacing Ruzow.

Ruzow had been something of a maverick during his five years as chairman
(1979–84). He thought that the APA Act had written off hamlets, thereby allowing them to go downhill. He moved the agency toward controlling pesti-
cides and herbicides, was one of the first to speak out about the threat of acid
rain, and opposed building prisons in the park.[9] In 1982 updated definitions for
the regulations, prepared by Ruzow and the agency, were accepted, but no
changes were made to the regulations themselves. At Governor Cuomo's Elizabethtown meeting, Ruzow's daughter talked of the way people had come to
accept the new [after 1979] agency under her father.[10]

Although Vince Moore served as executive director under Ruzow, they
were never a team. Moore, who had been with the agency under Persico, was
known for his strengths as a planner. Moore held semiannual retreats for agency
staff that were impressive in their planning scope.[11] Originally, Moore worked

as a consultant to Governor Rockefeller's Office of Planning Coordination. That office or its predecessor offices were fertile incubators for some of the people associated with the Adirondacks in succeeding years.* The group included Richard Estes (APA planner), Dick Persico, Robert Crowder (Department of Commerce representative to APA), Roger Swanson (Department of State representative to APA), and the star of the group, DEC commissioner Hank Williams, who had been the Office of Planning Coordination associate director.

During the administration changeover and through Cuomo's new appointments, the agency staff kept searching for ways to achieve better public acceptance.[12] In the latter half of 1983 and early 1984, four park-oriented organizations—Adirondack Mountain Club, Adirondack North Country Association, Adirondack Council, and the Adirondack Conservation Council—teamed up with the agency in holding a series of workshops, eleven scattered around the park, seven more throughout the rest of the state. The workshops were designed to develop goals for the Adirondacks. Those attending worked together to identify issues and then broke into smaller groups to focus on such aspects as the economy, environment, and so forth. There was significant overlap of issues among the different workshops, with a great range of views on the same issues.

Agency staff synthesized a final list of goals, which was issued in July 1984 (as the *Adirondack Goals Program*). It is an awesome wish list, a set of goals as applicable in 2001 as when it was created, even though the final report identified a number of goals that were starting to be addressed.[13] The list covered a wide range of topics: environment and recreation, economic development, governmental operations, communications and transportation, education, and

* State planning had existed on several levels since the 1930s. In 1960, Rockefeller consolidated planners from the Commerce Department (predecessor of Department of Economic Development) with planners from his office into the Office of Planning Coordination.

The Office of Planning Coordination succumbed to budget shortfalls in 1971, when it was abolished by the legislature. Lost were its function of coordination between state agencies, its comprehensive planning function, and its public information function. The only one of its functions that was retained was its role of providing technical assistance to local planning agencies. At that time, the Office of Planning Coordination became the Office of Planning Services.

There have been other planning efforts statewide such as coastal zone planning and a land use and housing unit funded by the U.S. Department of Housing and Urban Development. Even these functions were for a time farmed out to different state agencies, although coastal management is now within the Department of State. There have been regional planning efforts for areas such as the Capitol region, the Southern Tier, Erie-Niagara, and a very significant private-sector effort for the New York City area, but no central state planning agency for land use and development such as other states have.

energy. For each of the numerous subtopics within these broad categories the final report gave an issue summary and a list of solutions. The report was designed for action. Ed Hood, the agency staffer responsible for managing the workshops, believes the workshops themselves did help build public trust and confidence in the agency.

As with many agency initiatives, there was little follow-through, primarily because of the change in administration. According to Hood, the goals program as such "drifted into oblivion" as the agency became focused elsewhere.[14] However, the need to establish communication with the public surfaced in many different forms in the following years and the goals are still there. The agency continues to respond to the goals, although they are no longer specifically identified with this mid-1980s effort.

Cuomo took his time replacing Ted Ruzow at Adirondack Park Agency, and when he did there was considerable apprehension about his choice of Herman (Woody) Cole. That appointment in 1984 did not sit well with most environmentalists.[15] Even Cole's predecessor spoke out against the appointment, suggesting it was partisan politics. "The governor does not set the policy, the commissioners do. The chair does not take orders from the governor. Politicizing it, as it seems, is a grave mistake."[16]

Cole served through 1991. Despite Cole's openness and willingness to talk to Adirondack groups and his announced plans to involve APA in economic development in the park, locals were none too supportive of him either. Cole had many ideas about making APA more friendly, such as making the permit application process simpler, but many of those ideas, such as easing permit requirements, could not be achieved without changes to either the Adirondack Park Agency Act or to the regulations it generated.

When Tom Ulasewicz became executive director in 1984 the agency entered a fairly productive phase.* Ulasewicz believed that education was critical to the

---

* The author applied for the position of APA executive director and was one of three finalists interviewed. Cole seemed impressed with my thoughts on making the agency more easily understood by the public, but it was Ulasewicz, the agency's choice for executive director, who was responsible for the agency's contracting with me to write a series of brochures and booklets explaining aspects of the APA Act and its regulations. My first charge was to write a booklet explaining when a landowner needed to come to the agency for a permit and what he could expect when bringing an application before the agency. At first I demurred, feeling that the act and the regulations were so Byzantine and difficult that there might be no way to make them accessible. I wrote several flyers and five booklets in the *Citizen's Guide Series to Adirondack Lakes, Wetlands, Forest Preserve, Forestry, Rivers and Roads, Community Planning.* When I finally felt I had enough experience to write the *Citizen's Guide to Land Use Requirements,* I ran up against a stone wall: APA

expectation that park residents would accept the agency. To that end he championed the *Citizen's Guides* and arranged for the APA to add public relations and education specialists. He felt that educating the young was vital, that it was important to help the next generation understand the need for the agency. The Visitors Interpretive Centers were planned with this in mind and constructed during his tenure, and he believed that they would have an important educational role. For instance, he saw the Paul Smiths site as a place to teach about the value of wetlands. The agency conducted citizens planning meetings in different locations throughout the park so that top staff could help locals understand the agency law, policies, wetland mapping, and the permit process.

Two park residents were appointed at the same time as Cole: John Collins was a teacher from Long Lake who had been chairman of the Indian Lake Planning Board for sixteen years. Bill Roden from Warren County had strong connections to Adirondack sportsmen's organizations. All along, opponents of APA had been clamoring for more representation for Adirondack residents on the agency. Cuomo's move was in response to this, but it did not stop North Country groups from asking for increased representation of their choosing. The legislature approved Cuomo's choices at that time, but later in his term the legislature did not act on such nominations as that of Edwin Ketchledge. And, as his term wore on and as the terms of more agency members expired, Cuomo stopped making new appointments, mostly because his choices would probably not have met with legislative approval. By 1991, seven members were serving on expired terms. This issue of members serving on expired terms became one more source of contention in following years.

The problem of outdated APA rules and regulations grew worse during the time Ulasewicz served as executive director (1984–88). Some problems can be traced to the original APA Act, but many appeared because the agency was asked to consider things that had never been anticipated before 1970. An example is the need for communication or microwave towers. When confronted with new things, agency staff, without guidelines, were sometimes inconsistent in dealing with permit applications. Ulasewicz's solution was to develop poli-

---

Counsel Robert Glennon was adamantly opposed to a "user friendly" explanation of APA laws. I fought him for months, trying to get permission to paraphrase the laws in plain English. When I had finished the booklet, Glennon was supposed to do a final proofread for correctness. He delayed, and Ulasewicz, frustrated with the delay, said he would split the task with Glennon. When the booklet went to the printer it contained one numerical error, which probably could have been corrected by the insertion of an errata sheet or a reprint, but the process stopped and existing copies were mostly destroyed. A few people have closely guarded copies and find them very helpful.

cies or guidelines, to let everybody (including staff) know what the agency was doing in discretionary situations. These guidelines were of course not binding as regulations were, but they did address the permissiveness of the APA Act with consistency. (Recall that in the APA Act, almost everything is permitted, with qualifications.) Dealing with submerged wetlands is another topic that required such an approach.[17]

Tony D'Elia became paid director of the Local Government Review Board in 1983. In 1984, LGRB was promised state funds, which Cuomo included in his budget. Despite the fact that the funds were approved by the legislature, they were removed from the final budget. (Cuomo asked the legislature for funds for LGRB in 1988 but because of the state's fiscal problems vetoed the appropriation made by the legislature.)[18] That year—1984—might have been a turning point in the relations between the review board and the agency because the Adirondack Park Agency, under Woody Cole, began emphasizing economic development, local decision-making, and red-tape-cutting. D'Elia had a brief moment of acceptance by the agency. The latter happened when APA member John Stock invited D'Elia to participate in the deliberations of the APA's new committee on economic development. D'Elia's many ideas for an improved economic climate in the park were the subject of an article by Ed Hale, who wrote that D'Elia's participation was "a small victory for the watchdog board, but it's a real one."[19] Hale noted D'Elia's "intent eyes under black hair combed straight back, [and the way] he bristles like a porcupine."[20] It did not take long for D'Elia to become disenchanted with the agency's limited ability to focus on economic concern, and his behavior began more and more to reflect his bristly appearance.

D'Elia began to lead LGRB farther from its designated role as watchdog of the agency, and his attacks on the agency became increasingly vicious. He became increasingly disturbed as he pursued what seemed to be a vendetta against the agency, which he saw as the cause of his financial downfall. In 1985 he claimed that the agency was "trying to erase man from the Adirondack Park by the year 2000."[21] D'Elia expressed many of his diatribes through LGRB's *Newsletter* in the years 1983 through 1985. (The periodical took on the name *The Blue Line Review* in 1985. Its masthead and content downplayed its relation to the LGRB, but its Onchiota mailing permit remained the same.)

The LGRB protested the fact that state agencies had taken actions without APA permits and felt this double standard ought to be dealt with by returning fines levied on private individuals whom the agency deemed were in violation of the APA Act. D'Elia sided with APA's efforts to expand its powers over state agencies. The *Adirondack Daily Enterprise* equated D'Elia's stand with a betrayal of the people of the park.[22] Within a little more than a year, D'Elia charged that his phones were tapped.[23]

Land Acquisition and Bond Acts

Under Cuomo, the state, suffering from the poor economic climate that gripped the country and pinched as ever for funds to acquire public land, began to make plans for the 1986 Environmental Bond Act. Because of legislation passed in 1984 the state would finally be in a much better position to acquire conservation easements as well as fee acquisitions.[24] Prior to 1984 only adjacent landowners could enforce such restrictive covenants that "ran with the lands." A statutorily created conservation easement not only allowed the state to enforce the easement, it allowed the state as purchaser to apportion the real property tax, thus assuring a reduction for the landowner.

Cutbacks affecting all departments of government in the early 1980s dealt especially severely with the Department of Environmental Conservation. Funds from the 1972 Bond Act had long before been committed. DEC was failing to acquire important pieces of land that came on the market. The most egregious example was the Kings Flow property, west of Indian Lake, which was owned by a Boy Scout council. The state negotiated for the property at the snail's pace that accompanied all their acquisitions (DEC had to obtain at least two appraisals, sometimes a third, in order to make sure the state did not pay more than a property was worth). The state offered what it thought was reasonable based on the appraisals, but a private group was able to offer more and quickly acquired the parcel. Even though the new owners allowed access across the parcel to Chimney Mountain and Puffer Pond, the purchase blocked access to a large section of the Siamese Ponds Wilderness to the south.

A bond act was the only practical way to obtain funds for acquisitions and for the environmental infrastructure that had been so long neglected. Adirondack Council led environmental support for the bond act, whose passage was perceived as a suitable celebration for the 1985 centennial of the creation of the Forest Preserve. Despite the fact that downstaters voted for the bond act and had supported the Forest Preserve through many constitutional challenges, the Forest Preserve remained poorly understood by many downstaters. As a result celebrations of its centennial had little support beyond trying to make the public aware of its origins and values. The major function was a conference at Union College in Schenectady, sponsored in part by the Association for the Protection of the Adirondacks, where many important papers were aired to a relatively small audience. DEC's debate over how to celebrate the centennial is summarized in a strategic planning document prepared by Charlie Morrison. He intended the plan to guide goals and policies with respect to the Forest Preserve for the next one hundred years. I include his plan as a footnote because it was so complete and important and because its goals eluded DEC policy so totally in the following fifteen years.*

The 1986 Environmental Quality Bond Act would provide one hundred million dollars for Forest Preserve acquisitions as well as for many projects for the environment. Needless to say, there was strong and growing opposition to the state's acquiring more land in the Adirondacks. The LGRB was opposed, but Frank Casier, an opponent of state acquisitions, was chided for selling acreage near the Saranac River to the state. (He justified the sale as being small.) Once again, downstate support for the Forest Preserve proved decisive in the vote for the bond act, and its funds were quickly applied to the backlog of Forest Preserve acquisitions.

In preparation for the 1992 Bond Act, which, unlike the 1986 Bond Act, failed to be approved by the voters, DEC published a booklet detailing expenditures under the 1972 and 1986 Bond Acts. The total for Forest Preserve acquisitions under both bond acts was $35,794,000. In 1989, Langdon Marsh, then deputy commissioner at DEC, noted that it took only three years to commit funds from the 1986 Bond Act.

Adirondack Conservation Council

Among other groups that led the opposition to the APA was the Adirondack Conservation Council. The ACC is the regional arm of the New York State Conservation Council and has about three thousand members in Adirondack counties. In the 1960s, mostly through the efforts of Paul Schaefer, ACC's policies closely paralleled the statewide group and in particular strongly supported Article XIV and its prohibition of commercial lumbering on the Forest Preserve. It opposed the construction of reservoirs for power. It supported the

---

* Overall acquisition strategy instead of "piecemeal" approach. 2. Boundary and survey marking completed. 3. Improve enforcement on trespass cases. 4. Updating the deteriorating condition of Forest Preserve deed records and survey information. 5. Revise, with APA, the SLMP. 6. Provide accelerated and high quality Unit Management Plans. 7. Improve operational response capability to immediate situational problems such as site overuse. 8. Adequate maintenance of trails and facilities. 9. Strengthen ranger, ECO [environmental conservation officer], and forester educational and enforcement activities. 10. Improve coordination with planning for private land use. 11. Add central office core program staff assigned to Forest Preserve Bureau. 12. Add central office staffing for TRPs, on-site inspections, development of regulations, etc.

establishment of large wilderness areas from which motorized vehicles would be prohibited. ACC advocated motorized access to deer ranges, but not in areas proposed for wilderness designation, and endorsed habitat improvement for deer, but only where it could be done within the framework of Article XIV.

Between the late 1960s and the adoption of the Adirondack Park Agency Act, ACC developed in ways far removed from its beginnings and from the statewide organization. By the 1980s the group championed "strong conservation measures as opposed to the preservationist approach of no use" (conservation meaning balancing use and protection of the resource);[25] wider designation of Wild Forest Areas as opposed to Wilderness designation and reclassification of Wilderness lands to Wild Forest; access to all lands by existing roads using motor vehicles, motorboats, and aircraft; liming of ponds including those in Wilderness; and habitat management in Wilderness areas. ACC opposed public right of passage on most Adirondack rivers, wanting landowner agreements or easements instead.

ACC always has been a loose confederation of hunting and fishing clubs whose primary concerns were often local matters, including hunter education. ACC has not always functioned as a cohesive group, but its many representatives from local clubs could be overwhelmed by a few strong leaders, as began to happen in the late 1980s under Ed Morette and Don Sage. However, the larger group has always been concerned with issues of motorized access. It supported Herb Helms, a Long Lake floatplane pilot, in his suit to retain floatplane access to lakes in the West Canadas and opposed wilderness classification in the Perkins Clearing land exchange. It was only logical that ACC lead the opposition to the 1986 Bond Act.

In his efforts to garner support for the 1986 Bond Act, George Davis, at this time program director of Adirondack Council, worked to improve the state's methods of acquiring land.[26] Davis also tried through Paul Schaefer to bring about a rapprochement with the Adirondack Conservation Council. An ACC newsletter had charged Adirondack Council with promoting wilderness policies that were "trying to freeze sportsmen out of the Adirondack Park."[27] Davis drafted a letter for Adirondack Council's chairman Kim Elliman to the New York State Conservation Council that pointed out that acquiring lands for hunting and fishing was part of the bond act and that the two groups should work together for its passage. An April 1987 meeting attended by Davis and representatives of ACC, Adirondack Mountain Club, and the Association for the Protection of the Adirondacks considered Davis's proposals for acquisitions, some of which he tailored to ACC's Wild Forest interests. The effort failed, and ACC countered with an even stronger set of positions that included preserving motorized access on all acquisitions, timber harvesting, and habitat management. In other words ACC not only opposed any wilderness additions to the Forest Preserve, the organization was championing policies contrary to the state constitution's prohibition on cutting timber on the preserve. ACC's positions were hardening, and shortly afterward the organization entered a fourteen-year phase in which extremists dominated its activities.

Local Government Review Board

By 1987 the LGRB had stopped sending representatives to Adirondack Park Agency meetings in order to concentrate on the taking issue as a means of restricting the APA. According to Jim Frenette, who was then on the Franklin County Board of Legislators, D'Elia was making a "public spectacle" of himself and was not adding any credibility to the review board. Another legislator claimed that review board members had an "abrasive attitude" and were "inclined to be very, very strident." The LGRB had moved so far away from its original mission that it was able to retain its funding from Franklin County only by the narrowest of votes.[28] The LGRB protested APA's attempts to curb development along county roads and objected to fines levied against the owner of a Lake Placid boathouse that contained living quarters.[29] (This was the first of many boathouse decisions that plagued the agency because the act's definition of and prohibitions against living quarters in boathouses have proved inadequate.)

But D'Elia's efforts to pursue the taking issue were paying off. Eleven Adirondack counties anted up $55,000 to hire a Washington, D.C., law firm, which advised that the LGRB could not launch a suit against the park agency. The firm suggested instead that individuals or municipalities should sue individual members of the APA in federal court, claiming their rights had been violated under the Federal Civil Rights Act.

APA's response, according to Ulasewicz, was to outwardly ignore the LGRB, with the premise that "if we gave them enough rope, they would hang themselves. We deliberately did not deal with them."[30] Further, the agency, through chief planner John Banta's contacts and the attorney general's office, "watched the LGRB's legal plans very, very carefully."[31]

However, also in 1987, Franklin County almost withdrew funds from the LGRB over what the county saw as lack of progress in dealing with the APA.[32] The same year the Town of Saranac increased its funding for the LGRB. That town wanted to secede from the Adirondacks over its efforts to amend the APA map for the township.

In 1988, Maynard Baker through the LGRB challenged restrictions on motorized access in wilderness areas, particularly for handicapped individuals. This issue exploded in the mid-1990s, and it will figure prominently in this book's last section.

Another hint of the rebellion that was to come was an incident in Hamilton County in 1988. The county sold a parcel taken for nonpayment of taxes to a private group, contrary to the understanding that counties have to first offer land taken for back taxes to the state. Also stirring things up, albeit behind the scenes, were hints that Adirondack Council and Governor Cuomo might try to do something to revise the APA Act.

Attorney James Cooper

Local Government Review Board's attempts to generate lawsuits against the agency were finally stopped, not by the advice of county attorneys or by a broad effort by environmental groups, but by the actions of one man, Warrensburg attorney Jim Cooper. With almost no help, he challenged the right of counties to give funds to the LGRB defense fund since those moneys were to be used to challenge the constitutionality of APA. Cooper's initial suit was lost, but the court of appeals reversed the decision, stating that LGRB cannot use counties' moneys to help lawsuits filed by others against APA and cannot "research challenges to the APA."

The outcome of Cooper's suit justifies exploring it in detail, and it is very informative with respect to the participants. During 1985, the Local Government Review Board had obtained agreements from Franklin, St. Lawrence, Washington, Fulton, and Clinton counties to contribute to a fund to hire the Pacific Legal Foundation, a national legal group that took on property rights cases. It had previously agreed to represent a Hamilton County couple in federal court on the "taking issue." In April 1985 Warren County set aside $6,000 for the LGRB to "pay for technical witnesses, filing fees and other expenses that might come up during a court battle planned to fight the APA."[33] Warren County attorney Thomas Lawson informed the Board of Supervisors that the county could not legally contribute to such a fund.[34] Attorney Cooper agreed with Lawson, saying that the New York Constitution prohibits the use of public funds for private litigation.

The LGRB rephrased its request to Warren County, asking for funds to study APA's impact on the region. In a letter to the Warren County Board of Supervisors, Cooper wrote on ADK stationery: "We think that your board should resent the unskilled and unlawful first request of the LGRB for this $6000 and be, therefore, skeptical about their present comments that this same amount of money is required to duplicate services performed by state employees (civil service protected) with no ties to APA or DEC."[35] When Cooper protested in person at a meeting of the Board of Supervisors that it was contrary to the state constitution to give money to private litigants, the board "rewarded [him] by increasing the amount they had previously given the LGRB." For Cooper this was a slap in the face, and he recalls that it may have been the beginning of what became a private vendetta. Cooper researched and filed his suit in N.Y. State Supreme Court, knowing that it would be heard by Judge John G. Dier, who had a reputation for supporting local governments. Cooper predicted that he would lose the first round, but win in the appellate court, and that is exactly what happened. But the case was not settled until 1990, and between 1987 and 1990 the LGRB continued to talk about ways of opposing the APA.

In the unanimous decision of the appellate court, Judge Norman L. Harvey wrote:

> We reverse. We find that no material questions of fact have been presented herein and that plaintiff's summary judgment motion should have been granted as a matter of law. Plaintiff correctly alleges that Warren County's expenditure of county funds to pay for efforts to research a challenge against the agency was a use of public funds for improper purpose. . . . As the record shows, the county was aware that $6,000 of its $14,000 annual appropriation to the Review Board was earmarked to assist in a contemplated lawsuit against the agency. Although the Review Board clearly has no capacity to sue or be sued . . . the Review Board has nonetheless apparently taken steps to circumvent this mandate and still achieve its purpose by recruiting the assistance of law firms to undertake legal research and making the results of this research available to any entity willing to commence an action. Such expenditures by Warren County to the Review Board's legal research firm for use in private litigation clearly violates the NY Constitution.[36]

In answer to the original suit, both Joe Rota and Tony D'Elia had sworn that "it is not and never has been the intent of the LGRB to institute or commence litigation in any court for any reason, including an action to establish the unconstitutionality of the APLUDP."[37] This despite what D'Elia had told the LGRB and had written many times in his newsletters.[38] Further, in filing his original suit, Cooper deposed both Tony D'Elia and Joe Rota. In his deposition, D'Elia admitted that he had conferred with attorneys in Washington in connection with "the illegality and unconstitutionality of the APA Act."[39]

While the case was winding its way through the courts, the review board continued trying to retain a law firm. It took more than a year for the review board to retain a Washington, D.C., firm, by which time eleven counties had appropriated more than $60,000 toward the suit. But in order to continue fighting the agency D'Elia changed tactics: he chose to sue agency members and staff under the federal Civil Rights Law, adding that the LGRB board would supply legal research to any individual who wanted to press a suit to abolish the agency.[40]

In 1988 the LGRB saw the state "on the verge of taking more control in the Adirondacks," and claimed the state owned enough land. Frustrated on every front and stymied in its efforts to foment suits against the APA Act, the LGRB hired a Boston group to produce a booklet on how to challenge the APA,[41] but nothing came of it. In fact, after completing an initial survey of the issues, a representative of the firm wrote to the LGRB that the board should work with the shortly-to-be-formed Commission on the Adirondacks in the 21st Century, saying "there is a great opportunity . . . to engage in the dialogue to shape the future." The LGRB cancelled the contract; D'Elia said the group did not need to spend $15,000 of taxpayers' money for that advice."[42]

There was much dissension within LGRB in 1988, and Adirondack counties were not happy with its direction. Joe Rota decreed that the LGRB would "change its image from 'radical' group" to moderate,[43] and once again LGRB members returned to monitor agency meetings.

The review board had asked for a study to show that the APA had an adverse effect on Adirondack land values. When such a report was completed by the state Board of Equalization and Assessment,[44] D'Elia "lashed out" in disagreement with its findings, which showed that there was no decline in land values that could be attributed to the APA Act. He claimed the study had missed the point, that owners of strictly zoned land were unable to sell it at a price they considered adequate.[45] The 100-page, very technical report was based on analysis of over 4,300 sales in a twenty-year period. Rota complained that the study focused on the less restrictive land use categories. (The study had found few sales in the more restrictive areas.) Both D'Elia and Rota missed the point: resource management land, whose prices had risen more slowly than developable waterfronts, was just that, a resource for timber production, not to be judged for its development potential.* The study also found inaccuracies on the

---

* By the 1990s, this was no longer the case as wealthy individuals were again seeking large parcels in Resource Management limited to one residence.

part of local assessors who did not always take land use categories into account when determining the taxable value of a parcel.

The Vaccaro Case

An incident involving the DEC, which became one of the most inflammatory episodes of the next few years, had its origins in 1988, and again it was partly the attention drawn to the case by the Local Government Review Board and D'Elia that made it so pivotal. Dr. Vincent Vaccaro, a dermatologist from Utica, purchased from Syracuse China Corporation the thousand-acre Pine Lakes property just south of the border of the West Canada Lakes Wilderness in the Town of Morehouse. The property had rustic buildings used by the company owners. It was surrounded by state land and could only be reached by fording the West Canada Creek, a designated river. The state had been in negotiations with that company for years, at least as early as 1976, and some at DEC thought they had an agreement for the sale.

However, the state and Syracuse China had not settled on a purchase price for the land. In cases like this DEC could start condemnation through eminent domain, thereby allowing a court to decide the sale price. This "friendly" eminent domain was only used when price, not willingness to sell, was the issue with the landowner.

On March 14, 1988, the state offered Syracuse China $340,000 for the property, noting that this figure reflected "current Fair Market Value." The department still hoped to reach a negotiated settlement, but the offer was not accepted, so on April 1, 1988, DEC notified representatives of Syracuse China of the department's decision "to commence the Eminent Domain process in order to acquire the property." The letter added that the department would soon schedule a Notice of Public Hearing regarding this acquisition. This step would be the formal beginning of the procedure, and, as far as can be determined, DEC issued no formal notice and no public announcement at this time.

Out of the blue, DEC received a letter, dated July 11, from Syracuse China's parent corporation stating that the land had been sold to Dr. Vincent Vaccaro (the date of sale was July 8). The date on the DEC notice of public hearing was July 12, and the hearing was scheduled for August 11. On July 22, Dale Huyck, regional supervisor of DEC's real property office, wrote Vaccaro offering the same amount of money as DEC had offered to Syracuse China and on July 27 notified Vaccaro that the public hearing would proceed. Director of Lands and Forests Robert Bathrick wrote DEC Commissioner Tom Jorling on August 3, telling him about some of these events and stating "that he [Vaccaro] was aware that we had initiated eminent domain before he acquired it." Vaccaro succeeded in buying the property out from under the state. He may have been aware, but the dates and notices show that DEC had not given the formal notice before Vaccaro acted.[46] Some have called Vaccaro's actions unethical. That is stretching what happened. His actions certainly were in his own interests, not the state's, but a free market exists. He paid $440,000 for the property.

According to a legal notice in the *Hamilton County News* of January 1989, DEC proposed taking fee title to the property to "eliminate administrative and environmental problems."[47] In other words the state continued trying to take the parcel from Vaccaro by eminent domain. Vaccaro claimed that he had offered to sell the state logging and development rights, but the state, at the urging of all the environmental groups, especially Adirondack Council, proceeded to hearings on its right to obtain the parcel through eminent domain. A member of DEC staff, who insisted on not being identified, told me that at least one individual in the Division of Lands and Forests was so incensed that Vaccaro was taking the land out from under the state that the individual pursued obtaining the land for the state as if it were a personal vendetta. The Local Government Review Board called for a moratorium on state acquisition of land and took up Vaccaro's fight. In 1990 the LGRB lost on a challenge of DEC's right to acquire land through eminent domain, but the Vaccaro case became a cause célèbre for those opposed to the state's attempts to acquire additional Forest Preserve land or to strengthen the APA Act and Vaccaro himself became the symbolic victim of the evils of government. The role of the case will be interwoven in chapter 12 into the narrative of events surrounding the Commission on the Adirondacks in the 21st Century. It was unfortunate that the state did not acquire the Pine Ponds property, but it was only one of many the state failed to acquire at other times for lack of money, and it was not nearly as serious a loss to the public as the Kings Flow property.

The End of the Decade

In April 1990, D'Elia stepped down due to illness. He died within five months, and his obituary hailed him as "the father of Adirondack rebellion" and noted D'Elia's accomplishments: "He established a newspaper, *The Defender,* and the Adirondack Minutemen, a network of Adirondackers who responded to calls to protect citizen's property rights they believed threatened by APA. Crushed and nearly bankrupt by APA requirements for his proposed development of Loon Lake, he began a crusade against APA and crusaded across the park to discourage towns from creating APA approved zoning plans."[48]

Joe Rota became executive director of Local Government Review Board in January 1991. Changes in LGRB's direction were immediately evident: the LGRB joined APA in protesting proposed cuts in APA's staff. But LGRB did oppose Cuomo's legislative program.

In 1992, Senator Stafford again introduced a bill to abolish the APA. In the spring of 1992 there was a rare formal meeting of APA and LGRB. LGRB wanted voting rights at agency meetings. Voting rights were not granted, but Rota did refocus LGRB's activities toward a role of ombudsman for park residents.

9 | Forestry in the Park

THE TIMBER INDUSTRY has had a varied experience in the Adirondacks. Heavy logging practices on private tracts before the turn of the century depleted the sought-after softwoods from many of those forests. By 1915, desirable species were exhausted except on the Forest Preserve, and the industry went into a period of doldrums because there were only limited markets for the vast Adirondack privately owned hardwood stands. The slow period lasted until World War II, and even then there was only a small resurgence until the few remaining paper mills began using hardwoods. From the 1960s to the present, regrowth has far exceeded harvest on privately owned Adirondack forests, although that regrowth has not necessarily been of the most desired species.[1]

Adirondack forests are not universally healthy and they have not all been well managed. Loosely controlled by DEC, which in its better-funded days was able to provide professional foresters who could advise private landholders, New York forests are not particularly regulated. The park agency tried to change that, partly to fill the void left by DEC's declining help, partly because of a fear of clearcutting. With a minimal staff and expertise, the agency was never in a position to oversee the forest products industry. However, in the early 1980s, under Theodore Ruzow, the agency attempted to add regulations, particularly with respect to clearcutting.

There has been an endless argument over shelterwood cutting, where all but a few seed trees are harvested initially, and then the seed trees are removed after an interval in which regeneration of the stand was supposed to occur. Clearcutting as a means of changing species composition has been little understood and much opposed in the Northeast.

For all that foresters claim, not enough is known about regeneration: selective cutting works in the Adirondacks unless it becomes high-grading, which it usually does. (High-grading is the repeated removal of the best trees on a stand in a way that reduces the quality of what is left.)

The extent to which some tracts have been poorly treated is remarkable. There is no better example of poor practices than Brandreth Park. It was logged first in the late 1890s and again just before 1914 when a small portion was burned. Several more episodes of logging occurred, especially on part of a tract that was sold to International Paper. Large parts of both International Paper's and Brandreth's holdings were devastated by the blowdown of 1995. The logging practices have left a preponderance of less valuable trees. The percentages Don Potter quoted for the amount of softwoods (15 percent to 40 percent) seemed suspiciously high from the perspective of a tour of the tract's roads. According to Potter, one of the descendents of the first Brandreths and a property owner at Brandreth, even the hardwoods have been so altered that there is barely one hard maple left; red or soft maples dominate.

On other repeatedly logged stands throughout the park, beech dominate because they had no economic use. Where they dominated, beech die-back killed mature trees, leaving forests of beech sprouts and thickets of no commercial value.

On the other hand, there are many good managers of private forests in the park. Roger Dziengeleski, woodlands manager for Finch-Pruyn, claims that his corporation is among the best. The APA Act with its limits on harvesting in wetlands and restrictions on clearcutting is not sufficient to guarantee good forestry practices. These come from trained foresters and from good owners and managers of forest tracts.

The region's lumber industry is not healthy either. Even though regeneration exceeds harvests, there are insufficient mills to turn trees into wood products. Further, there is an inadequate amount of the desired species. Little is known about future markets. The decline in secondary industries, paper mills and sawmills, and manufacturers of wood products, log homes, flooring, and so on has been severe. The state's tax laws make it less desirable to improve stands. The problems confronting the industry are probably too technical for this book, but suffice it to say that problems exist.

In 1988 Mario Cuomo appointed a Governor's Task Force on Forest Industry, chaired by Ross Whaley, president of SUNY Syracuse College of Environmental Science and Forestry. Several individuals who have compared the task force's "1988 Report of the Governor's Task Force on the Forest Industry" with the many reports on the forest industry written before and after it[2] mentioned in interviews that this one was the best and simplest analysis of the forest products industry. The report's succinctly stated recommendations, substantiated by appendices, give a good analysis of the forest products industry at the time. These same recommendations and analyses have appeared in subsequent studies such as the one for the Commission on the Adirondacks in the 21st Century and the Northern Forest Lands Study, and none of the succeeding studies has added significantly to descriptions of the problems or suggestions for their solutions.

The task force led by Whaley had an impressive membership and group of advisors representing many different backgrounds, as well as DEC staff assistance from Karyn Richards. Its report, issued in 1989, outlined ways of stabilizing land use and ownership through easements and tax programs; of improving the health of the state's forests through research, monitoring, and planning; and of enhancing public awareness of the importance of New York's forests through education. It also called for new leadership within the governor's office and a development council to promote and coordinate government activities so they enhance the business climate for the forest industry.

The first three sets of recommendations are waiting to be acted on. The governor did act on part of the last mentioned—appointing a council. The council met and gradually faded away. It has not been deactivated; it just no longer meets.

Bob Stegemann, at the time with Empire State Forest Products Association (ESFPA) and now with International Paper Company, has many good things to say about the Whaley report. He feels it was an eye-opener in placing the forest products industry in the state's economic picture and in demonstrating the industry's importance in the Adirondack environment, especially for its value to open space. He feels that the energy and spirit generated by this effort became balkanized by various groups as environmental concerns were emphasized and economic concerns were downgraded, so that the results of the study were ultimately "disappointing." No succeeding studies have had a better result.

10 | The Adirondack Council

ADIRONDACK COUNCIL'S GROWTH through the 1980s was spectacular, but like other organizations it experienced growing pains. Harold Jerry followed R. Courtney Jones as chairman, with Gary Randorf at first as half-time secretary, then as executive director from 1977 to 1990 with interruptions: George Davis was acting director in 1983–84 in Randorf's absence and executive director briefly in 1987. Chuck Clusen was executive director in 1987–89.

When Harold Jerry became chairman in 1977 he was able to restore the council's fiscal standing, which had been depleted by legal expenses. Council began to add individual members in 1977, but Jerry did not recognize Council's potential as a membership organization, and as a result Adirondack Council remained fairly small until the late 1980s.

Through these years, a strong preservationist theme marked Council's stands. Council appeared to be everywhere, influencing the vote for the 1986 Environmental Quality Bond Act and worrying about state land acquisition. In 1988 Council's newsletters began to talk about the threat of development posed by the Patten Corporation. Its *State of the Park 1988* focused on all tracts that were or might be threatened by development: Adirondack Mountain Properties on the west shore of Tupper Lake, Otterbrook Timber Company's land between Lows and Cranberry lakes, Diamond International's land sold to Lassiter Properties, Yorkshire Timber Company acreage that could be sold to a developer if an easement were not obtained, Paul Smith's College land, and Whitney Industries' tracts on the north side of Forked Lake, as well as many other shoreline parcels.

As Adirondack Council gained strength in individual members, at least one chink appeared in its coalition of supporting groups. The Association for the Protection of the Adirondacks had been a part of Adirondack Council from the beginning and still perceived that "Council was to be the legal arm for Association [and other organization] court battles."[1] The association became concerned that its name appeared on Council's press releases on issues where the association had not taken a stand and which were not part of association policy. In the late 1980s, it was agreed that the association's name would not be used in press releases that implied association endorsement.

In 1986 George Davis proposed a six-volume work detailing land and easement acquisitions necessary to maximize the potential of the Adirondack Park. The series, called *2020 Vision, Fulfilling the Promise of the Adirondack Park*, was launched in 1988 with volume 1, *Biological Diversity—Saving All the Pieces*. In it Davis expanded on themes he had developed for the Temporary Study Commission. It was followed in 1990 by Davis's volume 2, *Completing the Adirondack Wilderness System*, and volume 3, *Realizing the Recreational Potential of Adirondack Wild Forests*, which I wrote.* The next three volumes, *River Corridors, Travel Corridors, and Lakes and Lakeshores*, were to be completed in 1992 so that a boxed set would be available for the park centennial. They were never written. The published documents played a large role in Davis's vision for the Commission on the 21st Century, and although they received a fair distribution, their proposals were never widely discussed. For many years, Davis's vision for wilderness—the creation of the Bob Marshall, Boreal, and Wild Rivers wilderness areas—remained a Council project. The Adirondack Mountain Club later adopted the rivers proposals, and at the end of the 1990s Sierra Club reinvented, renamed, and expanded the Bob Marshall concept.

Council was able to take on all these tasks because of the way it grew in the late 1980s in both membership and ability to raise funds. Much of the credit for this growth can be attributed to Dick Beamish, who was Adirondack Council's communications director from 1987 to 1989. He hired Lynn Poteau as director of development, and in just three years, through their efforts, membership grew from 2,500 to 15,000. (In 1995, Johns Hopkins University Press published Beamish's book, *Getting the Word Out in the Fight to Save the Earth*. It is

---

* By 1989, Davis was already focused on his proposals for the Commission on the Adirondacks in the 21st Century. It appeared that the Wilderness volume might be the last, and I lobbied Council strenuously to encourage the group to quickly publish the Wild Forest volume to minimize criticisms that Council was only interested in wilderness preservation. Council contracted with me to produce the volume, but the task proved very frustrating because Davis had included six key Wild Forest tracts in his Wilderness vision, all added to "round out" Wilderness boundaries. I argued and mustered a lot of evidence to show that making these parcels Wilderness would be a red flag to locals in that it would upset the existing pattern of recreation. I lost in all but one instance. I also argued that smaller acquisitions would achieve the desired results for recreation, but I was encouraged to up the acreage to balance Council's (Davis's) proposed Wilderness additions.

a great handbook for anyone associated with not-for-profit organizations; it is concise, simple, full of commonsense ideas illustrated by numerous examples, many of which came from Beamish's work at the Adirondack Council.)

Chuck Clusen became Council's executive director in June 1987 at a time when the country's good economy was finally reaching the Adirondacks, bringing with it several new proposals for developments on large tracts, more or less devised to stay within APA's density thresholds. Clusen remembers that, "Council went after them pretty hard. Council had some support from local communities. . . . It seemed as if the locals had gotten over earlier history because development [on this scale] threatened their life style." Clusen had three main concerns (lakeshore development, big-lot development, and an anti-speculation or land-transfer tax such as had been used in Vermont). Clusen approached Governor Cuomo with an idea for which he gives credit to Council staffer Dan Plumley and to Dick Beamish's support. The idea was to somehow get Cuomo to take action against the new development threats to the Adirondacks, but Clusen not did not suggest a specific action as others did when they proposed the Commission on the Adirondacks in the 21st Century (see chapter 12).

Clusen told me that he still does not understand what happened next. He believed that the Adirondack Council had the potential to grow and to become politically powerful but that he never had board support, something he credits in part to his differences with Dick Beamish. Clusen was asked to leave in early 1989. Beamish left shortly after.

People associated with these years speak of the difficulties caused by a transition from a board-driven organization to a staff-driven one. The transition away from a board-driven organization was complete when Clusen left. After a long search, Tim Burke was hired to replace Clusen. (Bernard Melewski, who continued as counsel and lobbyist, had served as acting director but did not want to take the job permanently.)

In the year just preceding Burke's arrival, membership growth had slowed, staff had increased, and Adirondack Council was again on shaky financial ground. Burke made several staff changes, and the Albany contingent became increasingly important as Council emphasized state and national issues like acid rain. It is interesting that when Council celebrated its twenty-fifth anniversary in 2000, the reasons for the organization's creation (opposition to Wambat, the need to create a litigating arm representing Adirondack environmental groups), which occurred a year before the celebrated birth date—1975—were not recalled. Council chose to reinvent itself as a partner with Adirondack communities, towns, and legislators as well as with statewide interests. This evolution came about as a response to the Commission on the Adirondack in the 21st Century, but we are getting ahead of the story. And, as we will see, there is no question but that Adirondack Council was the only group to call for a commission.

11 | The End of Act One

WHAT HAPPENED BETWEEN 1970 AND 1989? The Adirondack Park Agency defined itself and gradually increased its effectiveness with respect to regulating land use in the park. The term "open space" was more clearly defined. Numerous attempts were made to reach out to the disaffected residents of the park. The agency tried with limited success to be accepted in the North Country. Environmental groups grew and generated support for the agency, but opposition groups faded only slightly. Violence against the agency abated. The Local Government Review Board had not yet begun to play a constructive role in agency matters. None of the groups seemed to be talking to each other.

There were almost no successful attempts to address the flaws in the APA Act. APA was unable to exert real leadership with respect to the Department of Environmental Conservation's planning for the Forest Preserve.

If this section of the book has seemed fragmented, that is because it is. It is a narrative of events that have no discernible direction. Act One in this drama was little more than a tableau with players or groups of players strung out across a stage, talking but not listening to each other and almost never interacting. Because the actors were talking to themselves no clear pattern emerged; the drama never developed.

But the scene was changing, threats of increased development appeared, and the flaws of the agency act to deal with them became more problematical. Several visionary players were poised to lead the others into action in a dramatic Act Two.

PART TWO | *1989–1993*

12 | The Commission on the Adirondacks
🌰 | in the 21st Century

A NEW TWIST IN ADIRONDACK LAND SALES appeared in the late 1980s to remind environmentalists that the backcountry was not safe from development. Dan Christmas, of the well-financed Patten Corporation Northeast, began buying up old farms, moderate-sized forest patches, and riverfront tracts at fair prices. The corporation subdivided these into large lots, averaging a hundred acres, above the thresholds of subdivision density and lot size allowed by the agency, but in large enough developments that would require an APA permit. This speculative surge, fueled by prosperity and the breakup of large, private landholdings such as Diamond International's forest tracts, put new pressures on the park's remote places.

Patten acquired nearly fourteen thousand acres of Adirondack woodlands between 1985 and 1988. For fiscal year 1986–87 the corporation's revenues climbed 33 percent.[1] With quick turnover and aggressive acquisition, Patten's activities caught the attention of conservationists. And Patten was not the only one to profit: S. Curtis (Sandy) Hayes, a realtor in the northern Adirondacks, sold a million dollars worth of raw land in the Bloomingdale area in just one year.[2] Hard-pressed timber companies began to dabble in second-home development. International Paper sold building lots from 370 acres of shorefront on Raquette Pond and Tupper Lake. Otterbrook Timber announced plans to subdivide nine thousand acres on the eastern edge of the Five Ponds Wilderness.[3] Finch, Pruyn had proposals to build South Pond Estates near Long Lake,[4] a development that later went through several iterations and was never started. Adirondack Park Agency permit applications rose nearly 60 percent from the previous year during 1987. The 1987 precipitous decline in the stock market drove more investors into the real-estate market, and the lure of owning a piece of wilderness was real.

Patten came to the Adirondacks with a reputation of hit-and-run speculation in northeastern states and the Catskills, in particular in areas with little or no land use regulations. Attorneys general in several states had investigated its sales practices. To counter criticism of its Adirondack activities and to demonstrate that sales practices had changed, Patten in 1988 declared a one-year, self-imposed moratorium on backcountry development, particularly on sales (though not on purchases) in the park's Resource Management Areas.

Adirondack Council led the way in calling for an anti-speculation tax similar to Vermont's, with a proposal for a real-estate transfer tax to provide a steady source of income for state acquisition of Adirondack land and a one-year moratorium on all subdivisions of more than three lots and of 250 or more acres.[5] The council also called for a one-year study, commissioned by the governor, to assess the full implications of development within the park. Among environmental groups there was a feeling that opposition to Adirondack Park Agency was subsiding, that the next few years might be a time to reconsider the APA Act's shortcomings. The agency had become more open and responsive, but there had been no real letup in opposition to APA. Opposition might not have been as vociferous because there was no glaring issue around which to rally anti-APA feelings, but it was there nevertheless. So, with Adirondack Council's call for a one-year study began the most contentious and explosive series of events in Adirondack history.

"Adirondack Issues Top Cuomo Agenda" was the headline given Governor Cuomo's 1989 State of the State address by the *Adirondack Daily Enterprise*. He announced the formation of a new Commission on the Adirondacks in the 21st Century. (This will be referred to simply as "the commission"; all other commissions will be additionally identified.) At the same time Cuomo issued an executive order that would require that state agencies undergo the same level of agency review as private developers. He also proposed an anti-speculation tax on large land sales and increased shoreline protection, both of which, along with funding for the commission, would require legislative approval. North Country legislators, Ron Stafford in the senate and Tony Casale and Chris Ortloff in the assembly, were pleased that Cuomo was focusing on the Adirondacks but immediately voiced opposition to the anti-speculation tax and concern for the makeup of the commission.[6]

This book examines only a few of the major issues studied by the commission; it incorporates many comments from members of the commission in writings or as quoted at the time or in recollections gleaned from interviews between 1998 and 2001. It relies most heavily, however, on newspaper accounts of reactions to the commission's work: articles of this sort were the principal ways North Country residents learned about it.

Robert Glennon, who had become executive director of the Adirondack Park Agency in 1989, had warned that, "neither the present APA nor the present state acquisition program is going to preserve the Adirondack Park as we know it today."[7] The land sales of the late 1980s suggested that the Adirondacks were "entering a new period . . . an era of unbridled land speculation and unwarranted development that may threaten the unique open space and wilderness character of the region."[8] There is no question that a broad study of the Adirondacks was needed, but today there is a lingering question as to whether the time was ripe for a commission of the sort appointed by Governor Cuomo. All the environmental groups believed something had to be done. There were few dissenting notes; one came from Richard Booth, then an associate professor and director of regional and urban planning studies at Cornell. He feared that the time frame for the commission was too short and that setting up a commission might harm the park agency. He wrote Governor Cuomo, "Your action will send a very clear signal to all interested constituencies that the Agency is not the forum through which the state will examine and consider the park's future."[9] Booth believed that the agency had not fulfilled the planning and policy roles assigned to it by the APA Act.

Some at the agency voiced their objections privately to Frank Murray, Governor Cuomo's deputy for the environment. According to Tom Ulasewicz they believed they were being deceived by the way the environmentalists were directing the process in favor of their issues.[10]

Commission Members and Staff

Despite these objections to the commission Governor Cuomo proceeded with its establishment, and by the end of January Cuomo had announced its members. Peter A. A. Berle, then head of National Audubon Society, was appointed chairman and George Davis, leading Adirondack visionary, who formerly had been an APA planner and executive director of Adirondack Council, was named executive director. Their appointments and those of the rest of the commission were made from the governor's office through Frank Murray. Davis had been one of the most active among Council's staff and board in pushing for such a commission, but several individuals were concerned about Davis's suitability as executive director. Robert Kafin, an attorney with much experience of agency operations, wrote Berle, "The agency has become a tragically flawed institution. However, its problems are not those that I suspect George sees, nor those expressed in the conventional wisdom of the preservationist community or the outspoken opposition."[11]

Five members of the commission were Adirondack residents, people concerned with different regional issues: Claire Barnett of Westport had focused on social welfare and local communities. Sally Rockefeller Bogdanovich of Lake Clear Junction was a professional forester. Craig Gilborn, director of the Adirondack Museum, was chosen for his knowledge of education and tourism. Two of the five had directly served APA: Richard Lawrence of Elizabethtown had been its first chairman and Bob Flacke of Lake George had been chairman of APA as well as commissioner of DEC. Only Flacke had been a local government representative, but these five were concerned with balancing people's needs with land preservation. According to Frank Murray, Cuomo wanted Flacke on the commission because of his background but also because Cuomo hoped Flacke would be a moderator.[12]

Four nonresidents had impeccable environmental credentials: In addition to Berle they were Read Kingsbury, a newspaper editor from Rochester, a member of ADK and a staunch environmentalist; John Oakes, a former editorial page editor of the *New York Times,* who often wrote editorials supporting environmental causes; and Harold Jerry, who claimed park residency although he maintained a home and worked in Albany. Jerry had been executive director of the Temporary Study Commission, whose recommendations were realized in the APA Act, and was currently a commissioner on the NYS Public Service Commission. Ross Whaley, president of the SUNY College of Environmental Science and Forestry in Syracuse, was chosen for his forestry knowledge.

Robert Boice was a Watertown sportsman, and the three others were probably political choices but they all had strong business backgrounds: James E. Smith was chairman and CEO of Orange and Rockland Utilities; Harvey C. Russell was a public relations consultant with Pepsico; and John Bierworth was former chairman and CEO of Grumman Corp.

Cuomo's Charge to the Commission

Cuomo's charge to the commission was very broad. Members were to discover "What kind of Adirondack Park do we envision in the 21st century? Are existing state programs and policies inadequate to achieve that kind of park? What, if any, new programs or modifications in programs are necessary to achieve this kind of park? How can a strong economic base, compatible with the park being envisioned, be maintained, particularly with respect to tourism, outdoor recreation, forestry production and secondary wood products, and hamlet development and preservation?[13]" The group was given just over a year to answer all these questions.

From the start Davis saw this board as working much as the Temporary Study Commission had functioned: technical reports prepared by experts, members taking familiarization tours throughout the park, discussions of the issues leading to consensus recommendations, legislation written to implement the recommendations, and a huge push by the governor to see that the legislation was passed. But this was a whole new era, and Davis's failure to recognize the changes in the past two decades may have doomed the new commission from its inception. Several members, Barnett among them, believe that those organizing the commission's work had no insight at all into political reality.[14]

The two decades between the Temporary Study Commission and the Commission on the Adirondacks in the 21st Century had created another critical difference: the public had become accustomed to being consulted on environmental issues. The U.S. Environmental Protection Agency and N.Y. State Environmental Quality Review (SEQR) had mandates that the public be consulted on federal and state programs respectively. APA and DEC had held numerous public hearings and established precedents for asking for public input. Yet an early internal memo on the way the commission would deal with public information stated, "I see nothing in the governor's charge to the commission that says we should have a full blown public participation program. . . . If the goal of public involvement is to get broad public support, both north and south, we may be biting off more than we can chew. . . . If the goal is more limited to identifying key interests who will support and/or oppose . . . the recommendations, [then we need to] work with them to keep them informed and involved. . . . In the short time we have we must make the best use of the advisors, . . .choose the points of most crucial public involvement and keep up a steady drumbeat of positive messages."[15] Public involvement was a one-way street from the beginning, to sell the commission's concepts. This attitude plus the makeup of the commission may have doomed the commission's final report from the start, even without the fierce opposition that flared later.

Davis's renown as a visionary contrasted starkly with his lack of concern for or ability to interpret public input. His response to criticisms that there were not enough Adirondack residents on the commission was "hogwash . . . six is an adequate number when you consider that local residents own twenty-four percent of the private land in the park."[16] To the lack of locally elected officials on the commission, Davis observed that the members would have their own discussions, make their recommendations, and then let the "political process take its course."[17] Berle saw public input as providing what the commission thought it needed. He later said that it was possible "ideas were not properly processed, but they were not ignored."[18]

Another major difference between the commissions was in political leadership in the state. Cuomo was a Democrat and the senate was controlled by Republicans. Cuomo could not push through his programs as Nelson Rockefeller had been able to do. Rockefeller had had the benefit of Republican-controlled assembly and senate, and if he found that he could not push something through with Republican support, he reached out to the Democrats for help. Peter Berle is an example of a Democrat who offered help when Rockefeller needed support to secure passage of the APA Act.

Although opposition to the agency had ebbed in the two decades, it still simmered in the park. Peter Bauer, then working for *Adirondack Life*, believed not only that in the few years before 1989 local support for APA had increased, but that residents actually feared the development proposals of people like Dan Christmas of Patten Corp.; Roger Jacubowski, Tupper Lake developer and owner of Topridge; and others.

Public participation in all aspects of government within the park had grown; Adirondackers were finding their voice. Many towns were actively engaged in planning and adopting local zoning regulations, even though no additional towns had adopted APA-approved plans.

Outside the Adirondacks there was a growing movement toward property rights and an anti-environmental backlash. Just how much those movements had penetrated the North Country is an unanswered question. I suspect that before the formation of the commission they had not been strong, but the speed with which they were marshaled to oppose the commission indicates they were close at hand.

The commission's report was due on April 1, 1990, an unbelievably short time; the $250,000 appropriation for the commission's work was woefully inadequate given the size of the staff needed to prepare the technical reports that Davis felt were needed to substantiate the recommendations that would be the foundation of the answers to the governor's questions. (At its third meeting, Davis outlined the staff's goals—fifty papers, some of which would require "extensive research.")[19] In contrast, Berle believed the technical reports were designed for the work of the commission, to inform the commissioners and generate debate among them. He saw no direct link between the material in the reports and the final recommendations; debate among the commission members would create the final recommendations.[20] Berle approached the commission's work from his experience with legislative commissions: he was impressed by their capacity to last forever. He thought he could "do the task and bring it in on time and within budget."[21]

Even the loan of staffers from other government agencies could not make up the funding shortfall. This shortfall was a considerable distraction to the executive director: more than half of Davis's personal papers from the commission, which are archived at the Adirondack Museum, are letters to individuals and foundations requesting funds. While members were not paid, Davis's salary was nearly a quarter of the initial appropriation for the commission. His fundraising was quite successful, ultimately adding up to the half-million dollars needed for the commission's work by obtaining $163,000 in grants and $80,000 in in-kind services from various foundations, almost all of which were known supporters of conservation efforts, and several corporations.*

Commission Meetings

The commission's first meeting was guided by a letter from Cuomo to Berle that contained specific directions: Study and report on the amount of development and subdivision occurring within the park, particularly along shorelines and river corridors and within timber tracts and other remote areas. Analyze whether the APA Act is adequate to preserve the park's character and natural resources. Evaluate the adequacy of state financing to assure stewardship of state lands. Study and report on the forestry industry and the potential for breakup of forestry tracts and determine whether additional state action is needed to assure a healthy forest industry. Study the state's easement program. Determine how best to finance and manage all phases of park administration. Determine whether tax policies can be used to complement regulations in preserving the character of the park. Cuomo wanted facts as backup for the commission's findings.[22]

Davis came away from his first meeting with the governor believing that he wanted a complete look at the future, a vision for the next century, and that the governor did not care whether the commission's recommendations would be accepted or not. Later, Davis came to believe that, in retrospect, the report would have been politically better if the recommendations had been broken into long-term and short-term priorities, making it clearer that some of them would not be accomplished for several decades.[23]

No matter, Davis set about being comprehensive in his approach to what he thought the governor had asked for. And Cuomo's list was not just astonishing; it quickly became evident that time and financial constraints would limit the

---

* *Adirondack Daily Enterprise,* Oct. 24, 1989; these donors included the HKH Foundation, The J. M. Kaplan Fund; W. Alton Jones Foundation, Champion International Corp., International Paper Company, and General Electric.

commission staff's work to reviewing existing material. No new studies were possible. It turned out that it was not even possible to determine the number of subdivisions or the amount of new building since 1970 because existing data were located in many disparate sources that were presented with inconsistent parameters. This was particularly problematic because much of the commission's work was based on claims that the backcountry was being destroyed through development, or by the threat of development. Former APA member John Stock termed the threat "A solution in search of a problem."[24] He compared an APA development report that showed tremendous growth in single-family dwellings with the census and concluded that the growth was primarily in second-home development, which the TSC had termed "an appropriate use of private land in the park."

Berle said he never felt that the commission was responding to a development crisis; he believed that the term "crisis" was invented by others.[25] (That term appeared on the first page of the commission's Adirondack Park "Update." It certainly appeared in many newspaper accounts and in several letters written by Berle after the release of the commission report.[26]) It is strange that the understanding of the true amount of backcountry development was not achieved for another decade, despite the fact that the amount of development in backcountry is still one of the primary concerns of all the environmental groups.[27]

By the beginning of February 1990 Senator Stafford voiced the first of North Country's objections to the commission. He "had very severe problems with people from without coming in and telling us how to lead our lives." The *Adirondack Daily Enterprise* editorialized that the commission was a further erosion of home rule. Editor Doolittle predicted, "There will probably be 'public hearings' and forums. These are for allowing the local residents to speak before the hammer falls. The entire matter has already been arranged, just as it was 20 years ago. What lies ahead is the fraud of public participation." He was correct in that prediction, but not in his observation that "in the end the people of the Adirondacks will acquiesce, and that will be taken for agreement with the aims of the state takeover, when, in fact, it only indicates massive political disenfranchisement and exhaustion." How wrong he was in this, for Stafford's opposition had ignited a firestorm by giving voice to his constituents' discontent.

Despite the huge agenda, meetings were to be held only once a month, although they usually lasted for two or more days. A significant part of the schedule of early meetings was taken up by tours of different regions of the park.

The commission focused on two major themes. It struggled with methods of protecting open space and limits on development. According to Davis, all the commission members pushed for strong "open space protection." However, unlike the earlier commission, this one addressed questions of quality of life and economics in the park, how best to meld land preservation with concerns for the welfare of residents. Still, social concerns were of primary import to only a few of the members—who had to fight to ensure that their recommendations were adopted.[28]

Bob Glennon's emotional appeal—"do not compromise on any environmental issue"—highlighted the commission's first public meeting. Ross Whaley emphasized that there were additional issues beyond the environmental perspective, "all of which are rights. How do you balance a whole series of rights?" Woody Cole's stressed his view that some Adirondackers had "suffered from the misfortune of poverty for too long, and that hamlet restoration projects must be more important than 'paint up and fix up' efforts."[29]

Harold Jerry recalled that the earlier commission, the TSC, had considered traditional zoning, but had rejected that method of land use regulation because of a fear that its application on such a large scale would not meet court challenges.[30] George Davis, in an interview, described his fear that the APA Act's density zoning was inadequate to protect the backcountry and open space. In saying this he appeared to question the effectiveness of the methodology developed by Ian McHarg at Cornell, which was the basis of the TSC's zoning.

Harold Jerry raised the possibility of reconsidering use zoning, which had survived court challenges in other areas of the country. Thus he launched the battle that was to embroil much of the commission's work. It ultimately resulted in a compromise that many commission members felt would prove unworkable and that turned out to be a significant factor in the ultimate defeat of the commission's report.

It has always puzzled me why the commission was so focused on open space and backcountry protection in light of the way the APA Act had failed to solve the problems of roadside and waterfront development. Davis said he believed that "just about everybody" agreed on the need to focus on open space. The members were able to make several flights over the Adirondacks, and Davis recalled, "it was apparent to all that open spaces were islands within developed corridors [and that] these islands were what was unique about the Adirondacks, more characteristic even than the mountains and the lakes."[31] Stopping the breakup and development of large tracts owned by the forest industry was essential to protecting open space. Davis said, "There was some concern to protect the forest industry, but that was not the primary thrust" of open space protection.[32]

Davis talked about the need for information centers at major entrances to the park, although not on the scale of the destination center about to be opened at Paul Smiths. Such facilities and the placement of interpretive signs along highways were proposals recycled from the Temporary Study Commission. Like many other such old ideas, they were quickly adopted for consideration as part of the new commission's final report.

DEC's analysis of the problems confronting the park was the subject of the April meeting. DEC commissioner Thomas Jorling's call for more state land acquisition focused on inholdings and recreational waterways, but he noted that he thought the commission "is to make what I consider to be the final allocation of the landscape . . . within the Park." [33] He espoused expanded easements to protect the forest products industry. Langdon Marsh outlined ways of improving DEC's acquisition policies, for instance by giving the state the ability to negotiate for rights of first refusal and land exchanges. Basically, however, his report was a long summary of DEC's accomplishments with mostly technical suggestions for future work, certainly not a vision for the future. [34]

By April also, Davis began to respond to the lack of resident participation on the commission by expanding the role and makeup of an advisory group to include, possibly, members of the Local Government Review Board, county legislators, and other "local people with expertise in various aspects of Adirondack life." [35] Former APA Executive Director Tom Ulasewicz believed that staff and advisors had an environmental bent. He objected strongly to members of the commission that no past leaders at APA were asked to participate. [36]

The April meeting at Lake George also scheduled flights so that commission members would have an aerial view of the park, a bus tour of the Lake George region, a raft trip down the Hudson, and summaries of technical reports on development trends and wages and jobs opportunities. The latter, by economist James Dunne, pointed out that population in the park had been growing at a rate faster than the rest of the state, but that most of the growth occurred in peripheral towns where residents commuted to capital district jobs. APA further refined these economic figures in June to show that 21,000 single-family homes had been built in the park between 1967 and 1987 and 6,500 vacant residential lots had been created by subdivision.

The May meeting at Tupper Lake had a fiery session at which commission members grilled Ned Harkness of the Olympic Regional Development Authority (ORDA). John Oakes charged that Harkness was turning "Lake Placid into a glorified Coney Island." [37] Harkness's glowing report on activities at Lake Placid and Gore Mountain drew commission concerns that ORDA was fueling unwarranted expansion. Housing ORDA's employees (1,200 at peak) underscored the problems commission members saw with the level of affordable housing, which had been exacerbated in many areas by gradual gentrification.

The members toured a forest management site and heard a discussion of forestry problems from International Paper's Pat Flood. They also toured APA's new visitor interpretive center at Paul Smiths and heard presentations on the property tax base, lake and pond surface management, and land acquisition policies, the latter by James C. Dawson. (Dawson was Forest Preserve specialist for the commission on loan from State University of New York at Plattsburgh, where he was a professor of environmental studies.) The overly full agenda also included a talk by James Frenette, representing local government, on the perceived problem of an eroding tax base. (Town government concern for that was heightened by the state's policy of not paying local taxes on state land while the state was protesting local assessments it deemed too high.) Despite his concerns, Frenette was upbeat on the commission's activities: "You couldn't do anything better than getting out and talking to the people who are going to be affected by your decisions later on." [38]

Commission members attended the St. Lawrence Conference on the Adirondacks as part of their June meeting, where they also heard discussions on ways of preserving the forest industry by Assistant Commission Director Judy LaBelle and staff member Dan McGough, who came to the commission from Lyons Falls Pulp and Paper Co.

Also in June, Chairman Berle announced the appointment of sixty-nine advisors to the commission. Several were from the forest products industry and only a few represented local governments. Known environmentalists like Paul Schaefer, Norm VanValkenburgh, Dave Newhouse, Kim Elliman, and Peter Borrelli constituted the largest category. (All received letters of invitation to serve; I did not.[39] My name was not on the announced list, but it did appear on the final report, probably because I critiqued several papers dealing with state land.)

Berle also announced a series of public meetings to be held in October and November. Davis assumed that the advisors and the public hearings would fulfill the need for public input to the commission's work. Some commission members were upset that there was no real public input, not even a plan for it.[40] Berle assumed the data gathering would be completed in October and that with the completion of the hearings, members could begin to develop their recommendations. The frantic pace was keeping the commission's work on schedule.

A late June meeting at Blue Mountain Lake featured a protest by Indian Lake Supervisor Richard Purdue that Adirondackers were "relatively powerless . . . [and bore] the excessive and unfair burden of preserving open space." [41]

Purdue, former chairman of Local Government Review Board, also took that group to task for "being too hostile toward the APA, [thus] hampering communications between local residents and the state."[42]

Tom Cobb, staff member on loan from the Office of Parks, Recreation, and Historic Preservation (OPRHP), presented his report on recreation, noting that "there is no comprehensive [recreation] plan for the Adirondack Park, no coordination of planning."[43] Like many of the other shortcomings pointed out to the commission, this one has not been addressed more than a decade later. Chuck Scrafford, APA Forest Preserve specialist, talked about land classification, primarily the differences between Wilderness and Wild Forest. He noted the recent court decision, in the case concerning handicapped access brought by Maynard Baker, that declared, "the park is accessible in a meaningful way."[44] In the late afternoon Peter Berle led commission members on a climb to Blue Mountain's fire tower.

Also in June, the MacArthur Foundation announced that George Davis was the recipient of one of its fellowships. This award precipitated a change in Davis's correspondence, which had up to this time focused on fundraising and the appointment of advisors to the commission. In more than a dozen letters Davis began to explore opportunities to become an environmental consultant in foreign countries, among them several in South and Central America.[45]

Members juggled outings and discussions at the August meeting in Westport: a visit to Elizabethtown's Adirondack Center Museum, a bus trip to sites that demonstrated agriculture and economic development issues, and technical reports dealing with greenways, conflicts among water-based recreational users, fish and wildlife resources, and the role of nonprofit organizations in state land acquisitions. The economics paper in particular left some members disappointed. Claire Barnett sent Davis a letter detailing its shortcomings and real errors and outlining ways it should be strengthened. (Barnett was also director for special projects at SUNY Plattsburgh's Economic Development and Technical Assistance Center.)[46]

The August meeting's strenuous agenda apparently tired commission members so that by the time the last item appeared there were only seven members left to discuss the thorny question of a possible role for the federal government in the Adirondacks. Robert Boice, member from Watertown, vehemently opposed any such role, even if it would bring needed funds to the region.

The discussion of water-based recreation focused on excessive speed of motorboats, and several members castigated DEC for encouraging unwarranted use by construction of boat launch sites, particularly those not called for in the SLMP. The presentation on economic development stressed the overlap of state agencies, particularly those for tourism and economic development. The region's dependence on single, large employers suggested the need for many small enterprises.

A late August meeting was held at Old Forge and, although it was open to the public as all meetings since the first organization meeting had been, there were few attendees. Nevertheless, the commission's decision, at this meeting, to hold an executive session to discuss issues of land acquisition precipitated concern over the propriety of a closed meeting.

Technical reports at this meeting included those on large private forest tracts, forest land management, economic development, conservation easements, contemporary land use regulations, the effectiveness of the APA statute, and education in the park.

"Update"

In September, North Country newspapers featured a report on the fall conference held by the Association for the Protection of the Adirondacks at St. Huberts. The meeting coincided with the release of the commission's interim report, "Adirondack Park Update." The report contains a bland presentation of Davis's perspective on the park, basically what all the environmental groups had been saying, without as much hype as many had been using. It reflects almost no concern for local residents and gives little of the flavor of the material being developed in the technical reports. According to Claire Barnett, the tabloid was presented to commission members as a fait accomplis, ready to be mailed out. (It was offered to environmental groups to send to their membership, but the Adirondack Nature Conservancy thought it was so inadequate it refused to do so.[47] Most other groups did send it to their members.)

DEC Commissioner Jorling objected to "Update" because of the weight given such issues as "fragmentation of state agencies, glitches in the land acquisition process, forest preserve management problems . . . minor administrative issues . . . when compared with the more critical vision issues."[48]

Jorling's comments were and are typical of DEC's defensive attitude toward the APA. Few—less than twenty—of the commission's final recommendations deal with these DEC issues, and these mostly suggest reconstituting DEC's functions within a proposed Adirondack Park Service. The issues behind these recommendations reflect problems that persist through 2000.

A comment paper from longtime DEC forester Tom Shearer criticized the fact that "Update" did not suggest that there would be adequate analysis of the use of the Forest Preserve, that planning for such use was inadequate, and that planning for land acquisition had not been integrated into questions of recreation. And in fact, the commission draft is woefully short in these areas. He questioned whether the "commission is plotting a course of sound land use or dashing forward based on ideology."[49]

A larger than normal audience at St. Hubert's heard George Davis predict that the commission's final recommendations would be "bold, imaginative, and equitable. . . . It is important to be radical."[50] Davis was eloquent in describing threats to the park, particularly its backcountry, for which he used statistics developed by Glennon and APA staff to justify his concern. Without making specific recommendations, Davis implied that a new superagency might be needed. In a related interview, Harold Jerry talked of a park service, integrating several different agencies. Richard Lawrence later called for a major overhaul of the Adirondack Park Agency.

Davis's talks, after the release of "Update," included themes that would appear in the final report: low impact, or the "right kind" of tourism; hamlet-based development that creates a "sharply defined edge between urban and rural land use"; additional funds for land acquisition; transfer of development rights as a means of preserving open space; and taxation based on current use. His criticism of the way state agencies manage the park brought swift reaction from those agencies, which prompted a press release in which the commission stated that "the report is merely a thought-provoking item, not a paper designed to create adversarial positions among the agencies that should be working together."[51] Commission criticism of an Olympic Regional Development Authority-sponsored rock concert brought a swift reaction from the Olympic authority that it was only doing what the legislature directed it to do—utilize the Olympic facilities.

"Update" provoked nowhere near the reaction accorded Davis's speech and commission member interviews. At this juncture, comments on the commission's work became sharply critical. An *Adirondack Daily Enterprise* editorial headlined the commission as "same old song and dance," and the lead was an invitation from the commission to "watch the trees grow (the only form of legal entertainment for residents of the Adirondack Park.)"[52]

The Commission and the DEC

At the first of two meetings held in October, commission members went into executive session to consider Peter Borrelli's report on DEC. Borrelli, editor of *Amicus Journal* and former special assistant to the commissioner at DEC, had written a scathing analysis of DEC. He summarized his report for commission members: "DEC is still groping for a park definition. Part of the cause for this is their insistence on sticking with rigid non-ecological regional boundaries. . . . Internally the Division of Lands and Forests and the Division of Fish and Wildlife have varying philosophies that have not been successfully bridged. . . . While it is good to have concern for all [people], it is impossible to do so unless you have careful planning and an inventory of carrying capacities. . . . The APA/DEC relationship could not get any worse. . . . The commission should re-delegate responsibilities between APA and DEC."[53]

Jorling's reaction and his defense of the department were so strong that Borrelli's paper was never published as part of the commission technical reports.[54] The fact that it was kept out may have much to do with Jorling's strong role in promoting the commission's recommendations.

Commission Hearings

Two of the fourteen scheduled fall hearings were to be held in the park.* The first, on October 10, was held in Glens Falls. In press releases announcing the meetings, Davis stressed the failure of the Temporary Study Commission in its inability to protect shorelines and river corridors. He stated that after the meetings the commission would come up with a "vision statement" to give guidelines for the recommendations that were due the following spring. As the hearings began, Hamilton County supervisors prepared to draw up a response to the commission's interim report.

That first, well-attended (three hundred people, of whom about fifty spoke) meeting drew many park residents, and the speakers were surprisingly positive according to Sally Bogdanovich. She noted that, "there is a change in the feeling of a lot of people in the area."[55] Harold Jerry felt that the comments were less hostile and more keyed into environmental issues. The major objection seemed to be the fact that only two meetings were scheduled for inside the park. Even at one of the in-park meetings, the one at Old Forge, many speakers shared an environmental theme—the need for careful environmental planning.

The hearings at Rochester (250 in attendance) and Syracuse (60) heard many similar testimonies—limit development and protect the fragile mountain

---

* In a brief Graham Cox prepared for Cuomo to use when the report was announced, Cox gives the statistic that six hearings were held in and around the park, with 4,190 people attending, 600 speaking, and 900 sending written comments to the commission.

environment. Utica's hearing brought a mix of comments ranging from strong preservation and a three- to five-year moratorium on development to Assemblyman Anthony Casale's concern that a compromise be achieved between conservation and the economic health of the park's residents.[56] Plattsburgh's hearing (three hundred in attendance) was similarly varied, but marked by strong opposition to the state's use of eminent domain in land acquisition and concern that the commission's deadline did not give it ample time to address issues and make balanced recommendations.

Saranac Lake hosted twelve hundred people (two hundred registered to speak). There, eminent domain was tied to the Vaccaro case. The recent purchase (1988) of the Lassiter lands brought one of the most emotional appeals—a lumberman lamented the loss of his leased hunting camp and equated that with other rights whose loss he feared. Overall, the Saranac Lake meeting gave one attendee the impression that there was positive support for the agency.[57] Many expressed concern for the park, but a only few observed that more regulations were needed. Donald McIntyre, supervisor of Westport, said, "This land is just as special to us, if not more so, than to those so-called visionary environmentalists out there." A local attorney said, "It's an insult that the governor thinks we need more government, more restrictions."[58] One of the leaders in the rebellion against the Adirondack Park Agency in the early 1970s, Sandy Hayes, who with others dumped the load of manure at agency headquarters, admitted that there was "a bit of truth in the assertion . . . that Adirondackers have mellowed toward land-use regulations designed to protect their beloved mountains. I don't think they are going to react as they did in the 1970s."[59] Adirondack Mountain Club Executive Director Walter Medwid claimed that a proposal to cut the ranger force "reinforces the state's ambivalent attitude toward the park."[60]

"Let us stop apologizing for the wonderful way New York has protected the Adirondacks" was at the heart of testimony given at the Schenectady hearing by veteran environmentalist Paul Schaefer. At the same meeting, Maynard Baker, supervisor of the Town of Warrensburg, raised an issue that was to become a major theme in the next two years: Adirondack residents "should be treated as equals with the rest of the state, not as second-class citizens. The future of the Adirondacks is being designed only for the rich."[61] The dichotomy between rich and poor, downstate and North Country, and the feeling that locals were being put down began to emerge in many ways. Susan Allen, in an interview a decade later, told me about the way she was not accepted by her Keene Valley summer neighbors. (Allen has a park-based map company that profits directly from state land because the maps depict state trails.) She expressed the begin-nings of her resentment of affluent Adirondackers in a letter to the *Adirondack Daily Enterprise* in which she noted the wealth of eight of the commissioners by detailing their Adirondack landholdings.[62]

Maynard Baker was actually booed when he attended the New York City meeting. The entire series of hearings was notable for the amount of repeat at-tendance. Baker and others opposed to further regulations went to several meetings, but they could not top the environmental groups, most of which had representatives at every hearing. This led to a comment after the Saranac Lake meeting that "the people who have spoken at other public hearings shouldn't have been there again. They should have let others speak."[63] One observer noted that there were just as many repeats among those speaking against the agency.

Mark Scarlett of the St. Lawrence County Planning Department prepared a statement for the Saranac Lake hearing. Hindsight is wonderful, and from the perspective of a decade later it is tempting to suggest that this document out-lined the best possible agenda for the commission's work. Suggestions included addressing the link between lakefront development and the forest products in-dustry. It outlined the need for developing gateways to the park in hamlets like Old Forge, something that is just being done in 2000, mostly with the help of the Wildlife Conservation Society, formerly the New York Zoological Society, which had taken on many conservation projects worldwide and in the 1990s branched out to Adirondack projects. The statement's vision for the forestry in-dustry and land acquisition is still valid in 2000. George Davis, in his transmit-tal letter sending the document to commission members, was impressed with its proposals for outreach to local government. Scarlett's paper concluded that "the commission's process to gain public input is flawed. . . . The commission's processes can only be described as . . . closed-mindedness." He suggested a so-lution—"an assessment by the Commission, in the spirit of the SEQR Act, of all commission final recommendations."[64] I asked some of the commission mem-bers I interviewed if they had heeded this statement; none of them recalled what effect it had.[65] Ten years is a long time to remember such details.

Perhaps it was the repetition of positive themes that influenced commission members and staff, because among those I interviewed, most remember these hearings as being remarkably supportive of what the commission was doing. They have told me that they recalled few negative responses except in isolated instances.[66] They felt good about the meetings and remember almost none of the undercurrents or antagonistic comments that were strong enough to have made news in upstate papers. This certainly contributed to the belief expressed six months later that they, the commission members, were blindsided by events surrounding the April 1, 1990, date that the commission report was due.

Without question the hearings as well as the commission meetings had a strong protectionist tone. James Smith, CEO of a downstate utility and a commission member who started with little understanding of the Adirondacks, was very sympathetic to residents and their economic plight as well as to the needs of the forest products industry. However, he came away from the hearings believing that "people are extremely aware of the importance of protecting the environment." [67]

From the first, George Davis believed there would be some opposition to the commission's work, but we "thought naïvely we could do what had *not* been done by the temporary commission. This time we tried to focus on problems such as the Patten Corporation's cutting up the land within the APA zoning requirements, address questions of water quality and natural resources as well as roadside development. The main difference was that the [21st century] commission hoped to look at a larger picture that included the economic situation, they hoped to change state policy for the Adirondacks to consider these things." [68]

As the hearing schedule drew to a close, many more organizations began to be heard. Tom Tobin, retired Air Force general, spoke as president of the Adirondack North Country Association (ANCA), a not-for-profit organization concerned with the region's economy. Tobin told that group that "no policy decisions of major proportions can be successfully implemented if the implementors are excluded from the planning process." Assemblyman Chris Ortloff told an ANCA audience that, "the Adirondacks isn't a colony." The Wilderness Society urged that a new national forest be created within the park, but that drew immediate opposition from the governor's office. Assemblyman Glenn Harris told the *Hamilton County News* that "the commission is coming in to tighten the noose around the neck of the people in the Adirondacks." [69]

Sierra Club released a report entitled "The Adirondack Park 1989: A Park in Trouble." One of the principal authors for the Atlantic Chapter's report was Per Moberg, a DEC employee. His condemnation of DEC was particularly scathing: "We find the DEC has neither understood its mandate for managing the Adirondack Forest preserve nor carried out its duties on a timely basis." In addition to calling for a single agency to manage the park, the report favored eminent domain, criticized the conservation easement program as a poor substitute for fee acquisitions, and called for the formation of a huge wilderness area in the northwestern Adirondacks. As usual, Sierra's goals were more extreme than those of any other environmental group.

Many of the environmental groups weighed in with supportive comments. The Upper Hudson Environmental Action Committee emphasized the need for a "comprehensive and long-range plan that should determine the final allocation of public and private land within the park."[70] The Association for the Protection of the Adirondacks (hereafter "association") emphasized the need for adequate state funding to improve the operation of existing agencies, and Adirondack Council advocated vision with the motto to "THINK PARK." Individuals spoke of concerns for pollution, gentrification, overbuilding, low-cost housing, but mostly for the need to save the park.

Some letters to Berle were exceedingly negative. Don Sage wrote on behalf of the Schroon Lake Fish and Game Club, calling for the abolition of the APA on the grounds it was not permitting reclamation of wilderness ponds and was allowing acid rain to destroy regional lakes. (His position paper called for hikers to be banned totally from Wilderness Areas, but that the amount of such areas should be only 10 percent of state land.)[71]

Even before the last hearing, on October 26, 1989, commission member Robert Flacke addressed the Inter County Legislative Committee. "Armageddon is coming by the next state legislative session and you don't even know there is a problem. . . . All county governments have to understand the issues and react now."[72] Flacke said, "If the commission fails to foresee a legitimate, continuing role for local governments, I am afraid it will result in a fatal vision."[73] He claimed the commission's "Update had been written by 'chicken little'" and that it was "angled to create a crisis that does not necessarily exist."[74] With popular phrases and clichés such as "nutsy cuckoo right" and "voodoo statistics" Flacke tried to show that the commission was exaggerating and that "Update" actually contained false statements such as the claim that there were more than a thousand signs along the Northway.

"Update" may not warrant all of Flacke's criticisms but the report was certainly one-dimensional in depicting open space as beautiful but showing only examples of bad development. Flacke believed that only concern for preservation was driving the commission's agenda. He thought that change did not come without a crisis, and later stated that creating a crisis was exactly what environmentalists and the commission had done.[75] He claimed he had not seen "Update" before it was released. Both he and James Frenette were concerned that few of the fifty technical reports were available to town officials.

Really, there was no excuse for town officials not to pay more attention to what was happening. *Hamilton County News* reporter Virginia Jennings editorialized that "I blame them for not having the foresight to attend these meetings." She also noted that representatives of environmental groups made every meeting.[76]

The Inter County Legislative Committee
and Local Government Review Board Respond

Within days, but belatedly, Frenette, chairman of the Franklin County Board of Legislators, and others had mobilized the Inter County Legislative Committee to address the problem of lack of local representation on the commission. Frenette felt, "It is late, but not too late" to begin a dialogue with the commission.[77] Hamilton Robertson, chairman of the Warren County Board of Supervisors, arranged a meeting with Davis, Bogdanovich, and staff members. Since future meetings, at which the recommendations were to be hammered out, were scheduled to be closed to the public, there never was a full meeting between the county group and the commission. The counties' position was based on their belief that "Adirondack local governments are deeply interested in preserving the natural beauty of the Adirondack Park and should be involved in land use planning and administration."[78] The major result of the meeting was that the county planners would get a copy of the technical reports and that Frenette, Dick Purdue, and several county planners would be able to analyze them. Spurred on by Flacke, who thought that county governments getting together marked an historic moment, the group tried to form an effective lobby in the state legislature, but noted they needed a "strong leader, as the commission had in Davis."[79]

The Local Government Review Board rejected the proposal for the group of planners to meet with the Commission on the Adirondacks in the 21st Century and asked county legislators to help shape a response to the commission. But Purdue and Frenette were not deterred, and both felt "something was different. It is as if the governor has given the signal to Davis that we're to be given respect."[80] Purdue even challenged Glenn Harris, who, he said, was stating "the negative very effectively. But I hope that there is a positive case lurking somewhere behind what is going on." He said the LGRB was "fractionalized and overly antagonistic" and afraid that "the planners would not be tough enough."

As Purdue began to formalize his concept of a planning group, he extended it to call for an Adirondack Regional Planning Authority, comprised of county leaders, which would take over all Class B planning responsibilities for all towns unable to administer such plans on their own.[81]

On February 23 the Inter County Legislative Commission formally endorsed the group, calling it the Adirondack Planning Commission (APC in this book to distinguish it from the 21st Century Commission, which is usually referred to as "the commission"). Hamilton County, Purdue's home county, pledged $25,000 to fund the APC.

Representatives of other groups began to express their fears for what the commission might do. They used their own agendas to push their interests before the commission. Some of these fears were expressed at a live call-in program produced by WCFE, Plattsburgh public television. Among those appearing were sportsmen, worried by the closing of hunting leases in Lassiter lands. They also expressed concern about restrictive land classifications.[82]

George Davis envisioned preparing a skeleton draft of commission recommendations with justifications of the items on the list in February and having the recommendations printed in March. To do that, he scheduled eight commission meetings in January alone. Even though members voted on specific issues, they generally worked by consensus. Technical reports were again discussed, and if members suggested a recommendation that met with little opposition, the recommendation was quickly accepted with minimal discussion. The majority concurred on most items; only a few topics generated any real dissension.

The Commission Map

At the November 30 meeting in Saratoga, members saw for the first time the map depicting recommended state acquisitions.[83] The map had been put together from work done earlier for APA planning in the 1970s, when Clarence Petty and others had compiled real biological survey work, and from research by George Davis for council's *2020 Vision,* where he focused on protecting biological diversity and completing wilderness areas. The latter was an expression of Davis's belief that this was the last chance to realize Bob Marshall's plan from the 1930s for creating a large wilderness in the western Adirondacks. In that it represented a vision for the future, he believed it fulfilled Cuomo's desire for a blueprint for the ultimate shape of the Adirondacks. More importantly, the map would show that there was a limit to what the state would acquire.[84] However, commission members recall little or no discussion of its contents, only concern that it would fuel the argument over eminent domain. A compromise worked out by Ross Whaley called for a paragraph to be added to the back of the map stipulating that eminent domain would not be used, that all additions would be with willing sellers, willing buyers. The members approved the map with that proviso, but the paragraph was never printed on the map.[85]

Opposition to the Commission

At the same time the Commission on the Adirondacks in the 21st Century was debating its recommendations, opposition was growing. The most negative response to the commission's existence actually started late in 1989, when Donald Gerdts formed the Citizen's Council of the Adirondacks, based solely on his violent opposition to the very concept of the Commission on the Adirondacks in the 21st Century. Gerdts, a contractor who had moved to the Adirondacks from Long Island three years earlier, acted so swiftly that by February 1990 he claimed the group had one thousand members who had paid a $5 membership fee.

Profiles of Gerdts do little to explain his power over the Adirondack scene during the next two years. Raised in Queens, he attended Hobart College and New York University and had obtained degrees in marketing and finance. After leaving the army, where he said he worked in intelligence, he took over an advertising firm founded by his father. The sale of that firm in 1972 resulted in an IRS lien, which clouded the transaction for some time. After the sale he held different jobs and said he started a management consulting firm before becoming disillusioned with life in the city. He bought land in the Adirondacks, which he subdivided, in the Town of Schroon, and then, late in 1989, he surfaced in the Adirondack political arena. The *Post Star* noted that at first he was dismissed as a lunatic with a typewriter because of his unorthodox ways. His persistence gained him credibility that defies reason. Gerdts wreaked havoc throughout the park and, before he left the area in 1994, virtually everyone who knew him or knew of him repudiated his actions. But while he was on the scene he exerted a power over Adirondack people and the region's press that is incomprehensible, given his uncouth rhetoric and inflammatory behavior.

On the first day of February 1990 Gerdts began sending out a barrage of press releases under a logo of patriots in three-cornered hats. He stated that the commission report was going to appear six weeks early because the commission feared "increasing opposition from local groups." He prepared three lawsuits against the commission, one against the commission's claim that it was not subject to the open meetings law; the second, an injunction to stop the commission from issuing its report; and the last a federal suit involving taking issues.[86] (For years, opponents of the APA Act had claimed that regulations limiting the way land could be used reduced its value, hence resulting in a government taking. This "taking issue" had become a rallying call for many western anti-environmental groups,[87] and Gerdts appears to be the first in the Adirondacks to take it up in the courts. Gerdts may have read literature from the John Birch Society, but at this early date it does not appear that he had contacts with western groups.)

It is amazing how much support Gerdts garnered, given that Jack Leadley, in an early February column for the *Hamilton County News,* had found most of Gerdts's claims ludicrous. Leadley wrote that the "Citizens Council seems already to be no fussier about getting the facts than the Review Board," and that the LGRB's meetings seemed to be little more than anti-APA pep rallies.[88]

It is interesting to stop at this point and wonder if opposition to the commission could have reached the peaks it did without a few people, in particular Donald Gerdts. Just how much had opposition to the agency and regulations quieted down? Was the opposition dormant enough to create an atmosphere in which the commission could have succeeded? Or was it latent, as it appeared to be in 2000, so that it still might be difficult to introduce significant park legislation? Would it ever have been possible, in a calmer world, for Governor Cuomo to negotiate with Senator Stafford to pass Adirondack legislation?

Gerdts continued his attacks by claiming that advance copies of the commission report were being circulated to a select group of preservationist insiders screened by the Adirondack Council.[89] He published a list that did contain some elements that would actually appear in the commission report, choosing his list to make sure it would inflame concern. He announced that the report would contain a moratorium on backcountry subdivision and building permits. Gerdts was so capable of fomenting opposition that the Hamilton County Board of Supervisors voted to blast the commission, citing "disturbing indications that the commission would put forward extreme ideas."[90]

Gerdts's claim about the circulation of early copies of the report was based in fact. In mid-February, Laura Rappaport of the *Adirondack Daily Enterprise* and the Plattsburgh *Press Republican* obtained and published what the papers said were draft recommendations, considered by the commission on January 17 and 25. Davis said the recommendations were not yet final, but what appeared in the papers certainly sounded like things the commissioners had considered.[91] These leaks so upset Read Kingsbury, journalist and commission member, that he suggested, "Maybe we should release it all because part of it is already out. . . . People will jump to conclusions if we do not have the full story."[92] Thom Randall, in the *Adirondack Journal,* published a more detailed list of the leaked documents in early March. Commission members have told me that they suspected that Flacke had something to do with the leaks. Flacke denies this, but there was a basis for their suspicion—Flacke's discontent with the way the commission report was shaping up was so great that, as early as February 12, he mentioned possibly doing a minority report.[93] Members and staff remember him talking about a minority report as early as October.

George Davis's hubris may be the real source of the leaks. He gave several interviews to Charles Little, who was readying an article entitled "The Forest that Will Be Saved" for submission to *American Forest*. While Little claimed he was never given any draft recommendations, the copy of his proposed article, obtained by the *Enterprise*, was remarkably close to the commission's final report.

Governor Cuomo's program for 1990 contained the proposal for a $1.9 million 21st Century Environmental Quality Bond Act for land acquisition and solid waste management. This proposal seemed to come out of the blue and confounded the commission, which had been discussing a 1992 Adirondack Park Centennial Bond Act.[94] In March, the governor appointed Berle to be vice chairman of a committee to promote public acceptance of the act, which would come up for vote in November. That committee was co-chaired by John Bierwirth, a member of the commission, and Frances Beinecke, a trustee of National Resources Defense Council (NRDC). From this time on, the fate of the commission report and acceptance of the bond act were inexorably intertwined.

Adirondack Fairness Coalition

Opposition to the Commission on the Adirondacks in the 21st Century began to come from many different sources. Glenn Harris worried about the fiscal problems that might be created by the commission's expected "bombshell."[95] Local government officials and residents formed a second group opposed to the commission: the Adirondack Fairness Coalition became a public entity in early February, collecting "more than $15,000 in membership dues from several hundred applicants."[96] Glens Falls attorney Dennis Phillips helped organize the group. (Later on Phillips helped organize another group that arose to oppose the commission's work, the Blue Line Council.)

Fred Monroe, Chestertown lawyer, became president of the Fairness Coalition, which saw itself as a grassroots lobbying group representing people who "felt excluded from the dialog about the future of the Adirondacks." Mark Behan, public relations specialist, spoke for the coalition; later he became an important organizer of and spokesman for the Blue Line Council.

Within days, the board of directors of the Adirondack Regional Chambers of Commerce voted to join the Fairness Coalition.[97] The coalition threw its

THE COMMISSION ON THE ADIRONDACKS | 127

support to the Inter County Legislative Committee. The Fairness Coalition held several meetings with board members, talking about their inability to obtain copies of the technical reports, the influence of environmental groups on the commission, their belief that the APA Act was adequate to protect the Adirondacks, and opposition to any commission recommendation for a building moratorium on development.[98]

Even as the commission debates were continuing, Flacke spoke out against it. He told the press that "people are beginning to confuse what the [Adirondack] council says with what the commission says."[99] And, in many ways, the commission was saying what the Adirondack Council had said in the past. There is no question but that commission ideas for land acquisition came from the three volumes of *2020 Vision*, two of which George Davis had written.

The *Lake Placid News* featured an article on the Adirondack Council's growth from three thousand to fifteen thousand members in two years, a budget that doubled in a year to over a million dollars in 1989. The article's headline, "$1 million lobby flexes muscles" was paired with a headline stating, "Inter County group seeks moderation."[100] An Albany *Times Union* feature showed the emerging lineup: Adirondack Council and Adirondack Mountain Club versus Flacke, the Fairness Coalition, and Gerdts's Citizens Council.

This lineup was not entirely fair, for Dennis Phillips told the Fairness Coalition's March meeting of the need for a balance between development and preservation. There was, however, no unanimity among speakers at that meeting, and the group failed to achieve the unified voice they sought for local residents.[101] The Fairness Coalition reached out to residents of the tri-lakes area (Saranac Lake and Lake Placid) and the western Adirondacks in its efforts to recruit members, all the while questioning the commission's data and preservationist leanings, this long before the commission issued any official report.[102] At a meeting in Old Forge to generate support, speakers for the Fairness Coalition claimed the "report was worse than anticipated" and presented a study that claimed to refute any overdevelopment crisis. Their stated goal was to find a "fair balance between preserving the environment and maintaining economic growth." Speakers for the Fairness Coalition told a Saranac Lake meeting that the group would prepare an alternative report. Phillips talked of the group's environmental concerns and support for the commission's easement proposals. In succeeding weeks the coalition would pick different issues relating to the parts of the commission report and use them to generate press coverage. Fred Monroe, coalition chairman, castigated the commission for the way it used the technical reports as "the basis of the controversial findings."[103]

What to me is amazing about the sudden appearance of these opposition groups is that they arose so early in 1990, three months before the report's print date—March 28. Commission members have told me that they recalled that opposition started during the long delay (six weeks) between the time the report was to have been published and the actual date it appeared. There is no question that protests became fierce in those six weeks, but that could only happen because so many groups had a head start in organizing their opposition. And, although Flacke denied it, many suspected that he had a hand in the further leaks that fueled the uproar in that short interval.[104]

Toward Completing the Commission Report

The commission's meetings through early March were now filled with debate, but as with prior meetings, if it appeared that there was a clear majority, debate was severely curtailed. Most items were accepted with little change, leading some in the minority to recall that there was inadequate discussion. Berle said that Flacke did not participate in the final draft, that he became so distant he did not even respond to drafts as they were being generated.[105] It is clear that the majority supported strong controls on key areas such as waterfronts and roadsides.

Only the debate on backcountry regulations caused much dissension. There was no consensus for strong use zoning that would have prohibited development on timberlands. A compromise achieved an extraordinarily complex set of recommendations to protect open space. A subcommittee of commission members defined structural development rights (SDRs) for each two thousand acres in Resource Management (RM) and Rural Use (RU) areas. These SDRs could be transferred with the sale of two-thousand-acre parcels only if the land were enrolled in a forest use tax plan. This was essentially two-thousand-acre zoning. For tracts of less than two thousand acres the owner would receive one transferable development right (TDR) for each lot currently permitted by the APA Act; that is, one TDR for each 42.7 acres in RM and 8.5 acres in RU. These TDRs could be sold to decrease lot size only in areas where greater densities were permitted. The TDRs could be sold to the state at $100 an acre, creating a type of conservation easement whose only restriction would be that there could be no development on the land. These recommendations were so complicated that many commission members doubted they would be workable or even legal. Some questioned whether the state would have funds to purchase the TDRs; others questioned whether there would be a private market for them; still others doubted that they could or would be transferred between towns.

Harold Jerry and John Oakes were so dissatisfied with these recommendations for not being strong enough that their minority report was included in the commission's final set of recommendations. The two men felt the transferable development rights and structural development rights permitted too much fragmentation of backcountry, allowing over six hundred private estates. In addition they felt the proposals went too far in subsidizing the forest products industry. Ross Whaley voted to include TDRs and SDRs in the final report, but with serious reservations about how they would work over multiple jurisdictions. After the report was completed John Banta and others questioned whether TDRs might be contrary to state tax law. Even if TDRs did not require a legislative change in the tax law, Banta believed that given the scale of the park, inter-jurisdictional questions would require clarification with respect to property values and local taxing authority. (For instance, if an owner transfers development rights to another jurisdiction, are taxes owed to the new town or do they remain with the land?)[106]

The general tone of unanimity on the other recommendations in the final report suggests that Davis's initial goals were dominant. His vision, supported by Berle and Jerry, was shared by the majority of the commission members. Much was said later about the speed with which the report was prepared and the lack of funds for the work, especially the technical reports and the printing. It seems to me apparent that more time, more money, more discussion would not have resulted in a different document. The conclusions reflected Davis's vision, and as such were at least partly predetermined. In 1999 Berle told the author that giving the commission "more time would not have made the conclusions substantially different." [107]

In a note to Berle, Claire Barnett asked that the commission establish a one-day intensive background session on the report for members of the Inter County Legislative Committee,[108] to bring local government into the picture. No such meeting was held.

On March 20 George Davis told the press that the report was nearly complete, that he hoped "that it will be a pleasant surprise to people who have been saying these terrible things are going to happen." He noted also that it would not be made public without permission from Governor Cuomo. Every upstate paper filled the waiting period with articles on the Adirondacks; the *Post Star* had a front-page spread of interviews with several residents on the subject of development in the Adirondacks.[109] Organization of the Adirondack Planning Commission was completed and Mark Behan became a spokesman for it, as well as for the Fairness Coalition. Flacke was given credit in several news articles for spurring the organization of the Adirondack Planning Commission.

Berle, who saw the role of the Commission on the Adirondacks in the 21st Century as presenting the vision the governor wanted through the recommendations, thought it was "clear that what came out would go through a tremendous amount of debate. . . . There is no doubt there would be opposition. Let them shoot at it." He said, "Some in the Adirondacks have views different from the rest of the state. There is a great problem in developing shared ideas." He believed that because "the largest regulatory land use plan in the country was already in place, the commission's role was simply to make changes that would make it work better."[110]

Cuomo's environmental advisors, presumably Frank Murray and Joe Martens, told Davis on March 29 that the report would be delayed a week because of ongoing budget negotiations with the legislature. One newspaper asked the governor about the report a day or so later and the governor denied having seen it.[111] During the delay in the report's release, Gerdts's Citizen's Group (renamed from Citizen's Council) began sparring with the Adirondack Planning Commission. Purdue questioned whether Gerdts had much following and claimed that "the great majority of Adirondackers today are a lot more moderate and more sensible on how they deal with land issues."[112] Gerdts claimed thousands had called, written, or expressed interest in his group but he could only muster three active associates to attend a meeting with Purdue.

A second delay in the release of the commission report certainly benefited Gerdts, but the other groups appeared to be biding their time. On April 4 Cuomo proposed that the entire park be designated an Economic Development Zone "to continue old businesses and create new ones." Purdue said the designation might be a "smokescreen," and Gerdts called it a "bribe."[113]

Gerdts used the delay to stage a "rebellion," with thirty people confronting Gary Randorf at Adirondack Council's office in Elizabethtown on April 12, calling Council's *2020 Vision* reports "Genocide" and announcing a protest for April 16 at Ticonderoga. Gerdts brought his plans for a major protest to the Local Government Review Board's April meeting, which turned out to be a seminal event—Tony D'Elia, who had been ill for some time, announced that he would take a leave of absence and might even retire.[114]

On April 9 commission spokesman Graham Cox assigned the report's delay to printing problems. The four parts to be printed were the technical reports, the main report (twenty thousand copies), an executive summary (fifty thousand copies), and the map showing potential acquisitions. A congressional subcommittee (General Oversight and Investigations of the Committee on the Interior) had scheduled a hearing on the commission's report. That hearing was rescheduled twice, and finally held in June in Albany with Peter Kostmayer as chairman. Representative Kostmayer praised the commission report, suggested ways Congress could help by protecting key rivers, obtaining funds to assist New York with land acquisition, and assuring that federal agencies would comply with state mandates for the region.[115] When DEC Commissioner Jorling spoke for the commission, Kostmayer questioned his reluctance to say when legislation to implement the report would be submitted. (More and more Jorling was appearing as spokesman for the commission. He became a leading spokesman for the governor in later negotiations to find a middle ground with residents. I have always been suspicious that he took the lead to soften the commission's criticisms of DEC and forestall any change in its organization.)

Meanwhile, the commission staff had dispersed to their regular jobs, the office was basically closed, and no meetings were scheduled for members of the commission. Only George Davis and Graham Cox were left to speak for the commission. Finally, the governor's office scheduled the release for April 30, and Davis organized a series of meetings to discuss the report with the press and local officials. With hours to go, the governor again cancelled the release and Cox and others scurried to tell the 150 invited guests of the further delay.

The Minority Report

Flacke sent a copy of his minority report to both Frank Murray and Governor Cuomo on April 12, with the comment that he did not intend to distribute it to anyone else until the governor released the commission's report. He concluded his letter with a handwritten note asking, "What next, please let me know how you want this report to be made public."[116] He claimed he did not know of the cancellation of the governor's press conference. He had sent his minority report to the Crandall Library in Glens Falls, a mistake, he said, since he believed the governor would release the full report as planned. Berle later speculated that Flacke had considerable help in writing his minority report, but he never suspected who might have helped him. I learned that Flacke asked Dick Persico to help him and that Persico did it as a favor to his former boss. It contained basically Flacke's thoughts, which they discussed; drafts were reviewed by Tom Ulasewicz.[117]

Berle recalled that Flacke never sent a copy of his report to the commission.[118] The governor's office knew that Flacke was writing a minority report, and Frank Murray may have been given a copy of it before it was released.[119]

According to the *Adirondack Daily Enterprise,* Flacke's minority document criticized the commission's report, questioned the premise that there was a development crisis, and objected to the "massive shift to open space preservation on 90 percent of the Park's private lands."[120] Davis countered by criticizing Flacke for not sending the governor or the commission a copy of his report first and for missing twenty-one of the commission's first twenty-four meetings. (According to commission minutes, Flacke was present at eleven of twenty-six, or 42 percent of the 1989 meetings. Other members and staff recall that he often attended only a part of many meetings or that he would make a statement and leave without participating in discussions.[121]

In his report Flacke claimed that the proposals for open space protection would result in "writing out almost a billion dollars in value. . . . The paper companies are taking [this view]. I'm speaking for one paper company—Finch, Pruyn."[122] In most of the events that followed, that paper company and Flacke's hand are evident. Flacke was a member of the board of the company and continued to chair its woodlands committee through 2001. In contrast to Flacke's opposition, Bob Stegemann of Empire State Forest Products Association was generally pleased with the prospect that the easement proposals would help the industry in the long run.

Flacke wrote his report from a philosophical perspective that put him at odds with what he believed were the commission's principles—that environmental considerations must be set ahead of any other in the park. Flacke referred back to the Temporary Study Commission and guidelines for the APA, which were intended to balance "optimum overall conservation, protection, preservation, development, and use."[123] Flacke was very concerned with gentrification.

If Flacke's proposals that deal with open space protection are excluded, his ideas are generally close to those of the commission. The other differences include Flacke's opposition to shifting public lands planning from DEC to the APA; Flacke thought DEC's planning was adequate. (In light of DEC's planning inadequacies in the 1990s, especially in Region 5, it seems that Flacke really misjudged this issue.) He also thought that local planning efforts could suffice for most private land planning. In supporting the APA Act, he noted that it was the cutting edge in planning. (It was at the cutting edge thirty years ago, was not in 2001, and probably no longer was at the time of his report.) He proposed shifting compatible uses (those things that could be approved by the APA in a given area, a very inclusive list, where approval was dependent on resource factors determined by the agency) to allowable uses, a shorter list that would give much more certainty. If this shift included a way to permit exceptions in special cases, it would resemble traditional zoning and has many merits.

Flacke supported the commission in principle on shoreline controls, but quibbled on the distance in setbacks. He thought the commission's controls on travel corridors were too strong, but suggested a compromise that would encourage localities to apply the category "critical environmental area" to county roads, which in general have the greatest future need for protection.

His calling for a ceiling on land acquisition by the state had great appeal to Adirondackers. His emphasis on the use of easements, wild forest acquisitions, funds for improvement of tourist amenities, and recognition of the way tourism had and continued to change were all reasonable ideas. He pointed out how expensive the commission's recommendations for open space protection might be and criticized the lack of studies to substantiate recommendations and the failure to study the carrying capacity of water bodies. He supported a strong role for the APC in local planning and called for model ordinances. Even though there were inconsistencies in his report, even though the document lacked quality of life recommendations (perhaps he considered the commission's recommendations adequate) and ignored questions of the effect of cumulative development, it is hard to see what was wrong with having his recommendations as part of the commission's debates. But all along Flacke had so isolated himself from the process that he ended up alienated from the commission, never achieving the role Frank Murray said Cuomo hoped he would—becoming the commission's moderating influence.[124]

Growing Opposition to the Report

The commission prepared a rebuttal to Flacke's report. It was written by Read Kingsbury and berated Flacke for not offering a guiding principle for a vision for the future, for having the perspective of a businessman, and for misunderstanding the proposals for open space protection. In light of the fact that George Davis told me in 1999 that the commission's open space proposals (TDRs and SDRs) were probably too complicated to be workable, it seems in retrospect difficult to understand why Flacke's ideas were rejected peremptorily. He was castigated for absences and for not participating in the dialogue that produced the final recommendations. One wonders how much of his rebellion was attributable to the fact that he felt his ideas were not acceptable to the commission from the start, that he was not just in the minority but a minority of one.

Opposition to the commission report took center stage and remained there as a driving force for several years. Today Frank Murray believes that "75 % or more of the report was acceptable, and the whole might have been if packaged differently. . . . Some recommendations on the fringe drove people up the wall. . . . There will always be a group opposed to such a report; but the commission lost the middle ground." [125]

The opposition began in earnest on May 5 when a group of Essex County residents staged a "solidarity rally" organized by Dale French of Ticonderoga. This event marks the beginning of the Solidarity Alliance. Davis had received an anonymous letter from a group calling itself "Adirondack Liberators" that warned that the park would burn that summer, starting with state-owned land, and that homes and offices of preservationists would also burn. [126] In an editorial, the *Adirondack Daily Enterprise* described the Adirondack Liberators as a "farce" and a "pathetic group that backs terrorists." The editor bemoaned the fact that such actions detracted from a real discussion of the commission report by those like Woody Cole, who "have expressed reservations about the Commission's extreme land-use recommendations." [127] Cole went so far as to agree with Flacke and "his observations about the complete change in the direction of our understandings of the Park." [128]

13 | The Release of the Commission Report

THE RELEASE OF THE REPORT of the Commission on the Adirondacks in the 21st Century on May 8 was almost an anticlimax. According to Frank Murray, the governor agreed with the vision for the park expressed in the report. "People think the governor had a preconceived outcome in mind, but he did not. He believed in an independent commission. . . . The report was issued without being cleared with the Governor's office. Apparently the commission did not want the governor's approval, they wanted to be independent of the governor." Murray also told me, "It was unrealistic to assume that anything in the report would be enacted into law." [1]

Both Murray and Joe Martens believe that there was a positive aspect to the report: it created an opportunity for them and Commissioner Jorling to visit the park and meet with local officials. According to Martens, the governor did become truly interested in reaching out to the people in the park.* But the conflict that had started, with the force of tectonic plates colliding, doomed, as the rest of this section describes, any hope for legislative change.

Articles telling of the report's release were accompanied by discussions of Flacke's thirty-five-page report and a charge by the Fairness Coalition that legislation implementing the report had already been drafted. George Davis admitted that, "about 90% of the commission's 245 recommendations have already been drafted into [proposed] legislation." [2]

Rumors were right about one part of the report. It did call for a moratorium for one year to halt all subdivision and development in Resource Management and Rural Use areas of the park. Objection to this recommendation was the

---

* Martens had handwritten notes from the governor that detail his hopes for the Adirondacks. The author had permission to quote them in this book, but as of publication time, they have not been located.

dominant theme in the angry reaction that greeted the report. According to Tom Ulasewicz, Murray had told Berle not to produce a report with a moratorium in it, and the fact that it was included may have been part of the reason for Cuomo's delay in releasing it.[3]

The map, however, created an even stronger reaction. The problem was partly the rush with which it was put together and partly its contents. The map contained actual errors, which Davis admitted. At first it appeared that the small scale of the map and the haste of its assembly might have caused the problems. While many of the recommendations for land acquisition paralleled those of Davis's *2020 Vision,* those volumes did not contain the errors in the commission map. The question of how and when the state was to acquire the pinpointed lands was just as contentious. The Vaccaro case and the use of eminent domain were on everyone's mind. Davis told one southern Adirondack meeting, "the Vaccaro case has probably caused me more grief in the last three years than anything else."[4] The map was perceived as part of a huge land grab, not as an upper limit to the Forest Preserve.

Blue Line Confederation

Map errors in Speculator, Benson, and Caroga areas were unfortunate, but the mistakes in Bleecker spawned another opposition group, the Blue Line Confederation. The map advocated state acquisition of roadside parcels built up with homes, a church, and town buildings. A few residents, a mix of old-timers and newcomers, organized in June and July 1990 and at first tried to join up with other like-minded groups. The old-timers were more complacent than the newcomers. according to Eleanor Brooks, who still keeps the group's records.

Bleecker residents formed the nucleus but were soon joined by people from nearby Johnstown and Gloversville. At first, monthly meetings attracted from eighty to one hundred people, a number that dwindled to less than fifty after a short time. A quarterly newsletter continued until 1996, and only the organization is left, but according to Brooks, "the group is ready to take up the cause if it comes up." Members attended meetings of other groups, including the Region 5 Open Space Committee. But the local group felt itself on the fringe of the park, lacking knowledge of what was happening in the rest of the park. Initially its response to the commission report was relatively moderate: it opposed the bond act out of concern for additional state borrowing for purchase of land; it questioned whether there was a land crisis but did support most regulations, particularly those that were environmentally important. It opposed those recommendations that the group felt were based purely on aesthetics. Because the group's activities emphasized studying issues, it invited speakers from other organizations; Gary Randorf and members of the Fairness Coalition both made presentations.

What inflamed the group even more than the commission map was a DEC map showing lands in Bleecker and surroundings that the state was interested in. Commissioner Jorling had sent a portion of an Adirondack map (a copy of a hand-colored version of the state's pink and white state lands map) to the Blue Line group, probably to dispel the uproar over the commission map. This "secret map" later figured in a suit against DEC. In a letter of transmittal, Jorling said that the map "displays the lands that are closest to you which are the only ones we anticipate will be considered for state acquisition." [5] However, the map also depicted DEC interest in lands around Canada Lake and shorelines fully built up with cottages. Richard Lefebvre, who was then president of the Canada Lake Protective Association, attended a Blue Line Confederation meeting in September along with numerous people from surrounding communities. This meeting was held jointly with the Fairness Coalition. It was Lefebvre who brought along Canada Lake neighbors Harry and Doris MacIntosh to the meeting.

That meeting with the Fairness Coalition was a pivotal event in the lives of David Howard, who became Blue Line's first co-chairman, Harry MacIntosh, and a few others from the Bleecker group. Their introduction to the commission's work led them to the property rights movement. Eventually queries to Commissioner Jorling brought a letter stating that the DEC had no interest in built-up land in Bleecker, but the damage was done. Because of this threat, a few in Bleecker became extremely militant, shifting their rhetoric from confederation to militia, from study to talk of needing guns. Howard went on to become chairman of the Alliance for America in 1992 (see part 3).

Don Curtis of Johnstown replaced Howard in 1992. Although he, like most in Bleecker, was not directly involved in a national movement, Curtis was well aware of it. In one of his letters seeking funds for the Bleecker group,[6] Curtis quoted Larry H. Abraham's book *The Greening*, whose thesis was that people were losing their liberty to environmental preservation.

More Sparring

One part of the commission's report was widely misinterpreted. Shortly after its May release, opponents seized on a statement that attempted to call attention to the many positive recommendations that would help residents as well as those asking for stronger controls. The recommendations "should be considered not as separable proposals but as an inextricably interwoven unit. To tease out one thread would unravel the whole."[7] Residents interpreted this to mean that they were being asked to accept the entire report, and partly because of this view discussion of any benefits in the report were curtailed. Commission member Claire Barnett, too, was quoted as saying her "biggest fear was that the report will not be considered as a whole, but taken apart in bits and piece."[8]

While negative reactions to the report dominated for the next two years, there was much support from environmental groups, but it seems lost in the onslaught of negative press. Also, it is amazing that in all the letters addressed to Cuomo concerning the report, even those that were basically supportive had criticisms of some kind. One of the more thoughtful letters came from APA chairman Woody Cole. He concurred with the commission's list of problems to be solved, but feared that the proposals to do so would unduly curtail economic development on private lands and damage the tourist industry, especially "the non-wilderness visitors."[9] He also was afraid that the commission's emphasis on human use neglected a needed ecosystem orientation.

During the spring and into summer the Adirondack Planning Commission expanded efforts to bridge the gap between locals and environmentalists. APC called a meeting with Adirondack Council, Adirondack Mountain Club, the Association for the Protection of the Adirondacks, Adirondack Park Agency, Local Government Review Board, and the Citizen's Group to try to find common ground on the commission report, but the meeting was adjourned after an hour by APC chairman Hammond Robertson because of disruptions from Gerdts, Maynard Baker, and others.[10] It was obvious there would be no common ground.

At the same time, the Adirondack Economic Development Corporation (AEDC) released a report showing that workers were being priced out of the housing market. AEDC director Ernest Hohmeyer claimed that publicity surrounding the commission was promoting the second-home development it was trying to stop.

As residents studied the report, opposition arose from many sides on many different issues. Essex County supervisors objected to the proposed tax on sales of land whose value exceeded $150,000. Senator Stafford was "incensed" by the report and said he wanted no "legislation passed on it this year, next year or any time in the future."[11] A week later he said, "I will do everything within my power to make sure nothing will be done that dignifies the report."[12]

The Planning Commission claimed the report "would harm our communities without helping the environment." The Fairness Coalition said the recommendations were "preposterous in nature and scope."[13] Most newspapers printed a brief summary of the major recommendations, but focused on those that proposed more stringent controls. The *Chronicle* predicted the report would precipitate a slugfest with clearly drawn battle lines. The *Enterprise* gave a lengthy and fairly complete description of the recommendations concerning transferable development rights and structural development rights, but they were such a complicated way of protecting backcountry from development that it seems likely that most readers did not understand the newspaper accounts.[14]

Jack Leadley, in an editorial in the *Hamilton County News,* wondered why no one was focusing on the recommendations that would bring tax money to local schools and governments. Was it because "we are afraid our neighbors will turn against us?"[15] The *Post Star* editorialized that it was "a sad commentary [that only 11 of 105 towns have APA-approved land use plans] when applied to residents who cry out that they want to control their own future."[16]

Two protest rallies were held in May; the first, on the 12th, was "a rally on wheels" staged by Gerdts's Citizen's Group and the Adirondack Solidarity Alliance, which was then only a loose conglomerate of individuals and groups emerging from the Ticonderoga area. The rally started the day before with a meeting at the Elizabethtown school, moved to a demonstration outside Adirondack Council's office, where the participants drew swastikas and tacked up a proclamation, and then to the home of council staff member Eric Siy, where a shouting match with obscenities ensued.[17] About 175 cars participated in a traffic-slowing cavalcade on the Northway and the dozens of citations for traffic violations did not deter the group from planning an even bigger rally for Memorial Day weekend. Senator Ronald Stafford led the Memorial Day rally; it attracted four hundred cars and trucks. In 1999, when I asked about his support for the rally, Stafford said, "that was just one day out of this 34-year career."[18] (A grand jury later failed to indict Gerdts and charges brought by Siy were later dismissed. All the traffic violations against participants in the rallies were ultimately dropped as well.)

Simultaneously with the first protest, Governor Cuomo's office announced that he was considering a visit to the Adirondacks to conduct a town meeting on the park's future.[19] (This meeting occurred three months later.)

Solidarity leader Dale French rationalized the protests with a view that was to emerge very strongly in the next few years. He said they wished to "assert, declare, and protect our absolute right to ownership and the enjoyment of private real property against all attacks."[20] This appears to be among the first outright expressions in the Adirondacks of the property rights movement that had been sweeping the country. (Adirondack Fairness Coalition, which was formed earlier, had focused on the commission, not property rights.)

Within a year or two, writers such as Bill McKibben and a committee for the Wilderness Society accepted the idea that the national property rights and wise use organizations not only influenced local Adirondack groups, but supported them from the start.[21] I believe that proponents of the property rights movement in the Adirondacks took up the idea independently and then reached out to national organizations; Adirondackers actually helped found and strengthen the national group, as in the case of the Alliance for America. There is no question but that those who took up the property rights banner quickly rose to the top of the movement nationally and then used its support for their work in the Adirondacks.

Compounding the turmoil, Earth First!, a radical group, appeared on the scene. Earth First! had started in the Southwest before 1980 and was known for "monkeywrenching" (destroying equipment) to stop developers. Its first foray into the Adirondacks had been a demonstration in the fall of 1989 in favor of creating a western Adirondack Wilderness twice the size of Adirondack Council's 400,000-acre Bob Marshall proposal.[22] Earth First! was greeted warily by Adirondack conservation groups, who feared its extreme tactics. In the span of a year Earth First! held encampments at Horseshoe Lake, a protest at the proposed Gleneagles development in Lake Placid, and a three-day rally at Lewey Lake and Indian Lake Islands campgrounds.[23]

They claimed to have been responsible for the destruction of the Pharaoh Mountain fire tower. The Pharaoh Lake Unit Management Plan called for the removal of that tower. Calvin Carr of Ticonderoga and others representing Solidarity Alliance took opposition to the state's Wilderness policies one step further—they helicoptered in wire to stabilize the fire tower.[24] However, it collapsed in mid-May 1990, and Earth First! claimed it had cut the tower's guy wires but denied the group had put sand in the gas tanks of logging trucks in the eastern Adirondacks. DEC Region 5 Director Tom Monroe later stated that there were no cables on the tower to cut.[25] Supporters of the tower gathered $1,500 to offer a reward if the vandals were found, but they never were identified.

Tensions ran so high that the Warren County sheriff asked the Adirondack Mountain Club to postpone a Glens Falls meeting where George Davis was to speak.[26] Davis did give a talk at Paul Smiths in late spring, but he was met with constant heckling and catcalls. He defended the open space part of the plan, which had caused the most controversy, as "the most important part to preserving the park."[27] The heckling was "abusive, distasteful, and rude,"[28] but indicative of the feeling of Adirondackers that they were getting the report stuffed down their throats.[29]

The tensions persisted until the end of May, when Cuomo met with local government officials. At a closed-door meeting Cuomo decided to recognize the Adirondack Planning Commission as the voice of Adirondackers. He said there was no realistic chance of a year-long building moratorium. Responding to Gerdts's heckling, Cuomo told him, "Listen to what I am saying," and that caused Gerdts to threaten "hardball politics from now on." [30] Cuomo asked that the ideas of the Commission on the Adirondacks in the 21st Century be studied and debated, emphasizing that "it would be the height of arrogance to make decisions without the people." [31] The governor hoped some decisions would shortly result in legislative action. "I'd like to show progress. I would like something good done." [32]

In a letter to the Albany *Times Union* former APA chairman Theodore Ruzow questioned the commission report on the grounds that it was "too beneficial to the group of large landowners, exclusive of the forest products industry." [33] A group of town supervisors met in North Creek to ask for sweeping revisions in the report's recommendations while at the same time condemning "extreme reactions" to the report. Joe Rota, new LGRB chairman, urged Adirondackers to support the Adirondack Planning Commission. [34] Rota said he hoped the governor would see the "chaos his report has created" in the park. However, common to all the questioning responses was a call for "a meaningful role for local governments." [35]

In the fray, it is amazing how little press space the environmental groups garnered in the North Country. One article detailed a letter sent to Cuomo by Adirondack Council, Adirondack Mountain Club, National Audubon, the Association for the Protection of the Adirondacks, Sierra Club, and National Wildlife Federation urging in particular protection for shorelines and the backcountry. [36] The letter mentioned a "critical element of common ground: the need for immediate legislative action." [37] But within a month a crack appeared in that solid stance: the Association for the Protection of the Adirondacks issued a paper denying that the moratorium was justified, criticizing the use of eminent domain, and asking for more study on the structural development rights and transferable development rights. [38]

In a very short time, opponents of the commission report implemented lessons they had learned from the environmental groups; they had become masters at using the media to sway public feelings. They organized quickly and mobilized grassroots feelings. They held meetings to discuss the report. And, they made sure the press covered everything they did.

Even the *New York Times* reported the extent of local opposition. [39] Davis did not help when he responded to the concerns of people who were worried about being able to divide property to give to their children. He followed his statement that "If we keep splitting up the land we lose the park" by saying, "People do not have to leave the park; they only have to relocate elsewhere within its boundaries."[40]

The technical reports claimed that a two-thousand-acre tract was the minimum size for sustainable forestry. The commission proposed limiting development on such tracts to one building, and that upset many opponents of the report. It also upset renowned environmental attorney David Sive. He wrote George Davis asking his views on Sive's plans for mixed development and preservation of his 2,400-acre tract, and Davis replied that Sive's situation was not unique, that "fragmentation of such tracts would lead to significant impacts on natural ecosystems" and decrease wildness.[41] Ross Whaley, too, questioned the number two thousand, believing a tract of that size was too small for practical forestry. He thought it was supported only because it was a compromise that might be acceptable to the forest products industry.[42]

Carol Lagrasse

During all this time, Carol LaGrasse of Stony Creek was writing columns for the *Stony Creek News,* later for the *Warrensburg-Lake George News,* which then became the *Adirondack Journal.* Her writing style matured, but her columns continued to reflect her anti-regulation beliefs. LaGrasse is a tall, angular woman, with the bearing of a Grant Wood figure. My interview with her in October 1999 (she was in her late fifties) resulted in her providing me with a wealth of background information. She has answered my questions, directed me to elusive sources, and been most helpful. This contrasts sharply with the vision many have of her, ranting against environmentalists or throwing documents at a Northern Forest Lands Council hearing. She told me she does not like to give interviews, that she has often been misrepresented. She consented to be interviewed because she said she thought I would be fair and she added that I had always been nice to her. I don't ever remember being particularly nice, but I always greeted her with the respect I would give any other human being. While I came to respect her intelligence and found her a surprisingly sympathetic person, her positions are nevertheless incomprehensible to me because we are so far apart on property rights. Little in her background explains her fervor in that regard. Both she and her husband Peter are New York University graduates. She was a civil engineer in New York City and never felt fulfilled, wanting to live with nature. Her move in 1973 to Stony Creek was prompted by a desire to get away from regimentation. She got into politics because of a dispute over a road involving her home. From living simply and growing all her vegetables, she moved beyond teaching piano to make ends meet to becoming involved in Warren County's 1978 incinerator dispute. She shifted from believing that if she presented intelligent arguments she would succeed to finding more persuasive ways to influence people into becoming activists. She too felt circumscribed by what she believes is the elitism of some environmentalists.

Among her many articles for the *Adirondack Journal* was one that faulted the commission's claim that hamlets, such as Stony Creek, were "sharp-edged, set off from the surrounding forests and trees." She used old maps and records to show just how many smaller hamlets and farming settlements were strung out along Adirondack roadsides in the nineteenth century.[43]

In reviewing the commission report, LaGrasse took the recommendations for "one stop shopping" for permits and corrections in overlapping jurisdictions to mean the creation of a superagency.[44] She equated life in the Adirondacks with living on a reservation under the Bureau of Indian Affairs.

Adirondack Planning Commission

In the blitz of local newspaper coverage, the Adirondack Planning Commission met and put forward its request that five of the members of Adirondack Park Agency be elected local officials. In succeeding meetings, that group—which included Don McIntyre, supervisor, and Bill Johnston, planner, both from Essex County; Dick Purdue of Hamilton County; and Jim Frenette and James LaValley of Franklin County—developed several proposals as points of negotiation with a committee from the governor's office. A series of meetings followed, attended by Frank Murray and Thomas Jorling, commissioner of DEC, and by Woody Cole and Robert Glennon of APA. But the meetings were held in private at the request of the governor's representatives, and soon critics began to challenge the APC. Frenette said that he believed opponents had reasoned that if "it was secret, what's happening must be bad news."[45]

Newspapers began to report criticisms of the Adirondack Planning Commission. Murray believes "that the governor's representatives had developed trust among local officials, but that the whole atmosphere was tainted by the crazies."[46] Purdue left one of the early meetings with the feeling that a "lack of respect for local government officials and Adirondackers in general had seeped into the thinking of the executive chamber."[47] Not all counties were as supportive of the APC as Hamilton County, and that county unanimously voted to form a Hamilton County Planning Commission to negotiate with the governor should the other counties drop out. The other counties appeared fearful of what negotiation might mean. Distrust was rampant; it got so bad that by August McIntyre and Johnston were forced to resign from the APC, McIntyre because his daughter worked for Adirondack Council, Johnston because his wife was a dues-paying member of that organization.

Infighting threatened to undo the APC almost from its inception. The *Adirondack Daily Enterprise* took issue with "Purdue's call for quick passage of park bills, a suggestion to be expected from preservation groups."[48] Solidarity Alliance began to press for Purdue's recall from the APC. The *Daily Enterprise* editorialized that Purdue should "be more forthright in discussing what he hopes to achieve during [Planning Commission] meetings with Cuomo's aides."[49] Jim Curry, Hamilton County district attorney and member of the Fairness Coalition, tried to get Hamilton County residents to withdraw support from the APC. Even individual towns in Hamilton County (Benson and Wells) came out against the commission's report and APC's work.

During the "negotiations" Governor Cuomo also withdrew support for the 21st Century Commission's recommendation for a buffer zone around the park. He introduced legislation to promote an economic development zone for the park. In talks he downplayed the role of eminent domain, saying it would not be used to acquire more state lands.[50] In the midst of the torrent of opposition and waning support from the governor, it is little wonder that Davis asked to be released from work for the commission, claiming his physician had recommended that he not even serve out the remainder of his last month's appointment.[51]

Wally John, director of the assembly's Environmental Conservation Committee, indicated that no major legislation would come from the commission report in 1990.[52] Assemblyman John O'Neil weighed in against the commission and Senator Stafford vowed that nothing in the report would be adopted in the 1990 session. Finally Cuomo stated in a news conference that he would not introduce any legislation based on the report in 1990.[53]

In noting the way Cuomo was distancing himself from the commission's work, the *New York Times* recalled that the Adirondack commission was just one of many that Cuomo had formed to study major problems. "The panels have enabled the governor to offer assurances that he was addressing the situation without committing himself to a solution. . . . Cuomo has backed away from recommendations before."[54] This comment clearly upset some members of the commission. In an interview in February 2000, Berle still remembered his displeasure at the way Cuomo ignored the report in the days after its release. "The governor should have called me and said we have a problem [but] no one got in touch with me." Berle believes he called someone and said, "you have to take it and acknowledge that it was on time, someone should take responsibility for the delay," but no one ever did.[55] In spite of the snub, Berle and George Davis never let up putting pressure on the governor to respond to the report or move its recommendations forward. In a letter to Cuomo written on June 25, 1990, they outlined how he could implement 69 of the 245 recommendations with executive actions alone.[56] Cuomo did not take any of the suggested actions.

On June 12, 1990, after a *New York Times* article appeared, attributing to Frank Murray the statement that the governor questioned "the factual predicate for the Berle Commission recommendations," Berle wrote a letter to the *New York Times* stating, "Let there be no doubt about it; the Adirondack Park is facing a development crisis."* A letter to Cuomo at the same time gave detailed substantiation of the crisis in quotes from the technical reports.[57] At the same time, Berle sent a letter to the *Hamilton County News* supporting the commission report and suggesting that there be a reasoned, constructive discussion. "What the Commission would not like to see on the part of Park residents is sullen silence, or people scared into silence by some of the threats . . . made by a destructive minority that hides behind anonymity and shuns a civilized debate."[58]

Environmentalists appreciated the delay as much as the opposition appreciated it. Adirondack Council, Adirondack Mountain Club, and Robert Glennon all publicly welcomed the breather before legislation was introduced, thinking it would allow for constructive debate.[59] But throughout the spring and summer of 1990 there was little debate. Gerdts kept up a barrage of faxes addressed to Governor Cuomo, occasionally with copies to Berle, Cole, Stafford, Adirondack Council, and Gerdts's media list. He accused the governor and others of criminal behavior and cover-ups, and often used foul language.[60] George Davis continued a series of talks around the park defending the commission report. The meetings were so contentious that state police accompanied Davis.

---

* Berle to *New York Times*, June 12, 1990, Berle's Commission Files at the Adirondack Museum. Berle quoted commission research as determining that sales of subdivided property rose 704 percent between 1982 and 1988, applications for building lots between 1980 and 1990 increased 325 percent, and sales of subdivided property tripled between 1982 and 1985, and doubled again by 1988. These figures were taken from volume 2 of the Commission's Technical Report 38 by Paul N. Miller, entitled "Subdivision and Development Trends: Extent and Location." Data available to Miller were not available from a centralized source, and he was only able to count building permits for one town, Webb. Better data was analyzed by Residents' Committee to Protect the Adirondacks in 2001.

Opposition Regroups

Representatives of park local governments and some of the newly formed groups opposing the commission held a meeting in Lake Placid to promote an Adirondack task force that could speak with a united voice.[61] Gerdts saw an opening, but he needed to improve his image, so he claimed his group had already done its civil agitation and would concentrate on preparing an "economic and cultural impact statement on the commission report."[62] He still continued to foment dissension, probably to undermine a rival leader: he attacked Purdue, claiming Purdue was in collusion with George Davis. But, ever the opportunist, Gerdts announced plans for what he called "Unity" meetings.

The Adirondack Solidarity Alliance jumped on the notion of unity by staging a rally on a beach at Schroon Lake, where Solidarity's "minuteman brigade" presented one of the "stones of shame," part of the barrier with which DEC had blocked Crane Pond Road. Among the festering themes that carried the opposition forward, none was as graphic or exploited as the incidents surrounding the closing of Crane Pond Road. That road, whose closing beyond the wilderness boundary was called for in the State Land Master Plan and adopted in the Pharaoh Lake Wilderness Area Unit Management Plan, was finally barricaded in 1990 by DEC. It became the symbol of resistance to government after boulders from the barrier were removed by a group of masked men in early June. On June 19 a human chain prevented DEC from replacing the barricade, and participants distributed a flyer calling for another rally and inviting people to bring their rifles. Langdon Marsh, DEC's deputy commissioner for natural resources, met with organizers of the rally and told them that although the road was legally closed, DEC would temporarily not rebuild the barricade and would use enforcement discretion in patrolling the area.[63] Many individuals supported the rally; all but a few urged that guns be left home, so the July 4 rally was peaceful. The protesters did drive their trucks down the officially closed road.

Crane Pond Road took on a life of its own in the next few months. Over the Labor Day weekend, members of Earth First! set up camp near the beginning of the road, with the intention of blocking entrance to it. An angry group of local people confronted the Earth Firsters; Warrensburg Supervisor Maynard Baker had words with Jeff Elliot, a student from the University of New Hampshire. According to the *Post Star*, Baker hit Elliot in the face.[64] (Two years after these events, the CBS show *60-Minutes* with Leslie Stahl did a program on violence in the anti-environmental movement across America and aired the confrontation at Crane Pond Road.[65])

DEC apparently declined to deal with the potentially inflammatory events. The *Post Star* editorialized that "the folks who elected Baker must be very proud of their leader, who is a problem-solver of the Neanderthal order." [66] Two days later, Gerdts and his followers returned to the road, "taunting DEC and Earth First! to come back and settle the issue." The *Adirondack Daily Enterprise* editorialized, "How can lobbying for local government representation be viewed when a local government official is rolling on the ground hitting someone who reportedly did not fight back?" [67] Berle wrote Governor Cuomo, "The incident is one more example of threatened violence and intimidation by opponents of the commission." [68] Baker was charged with harassment, a charge that was dismissed four months later. Speaking for the Fairness Coalition, Halloran deplored the event, which "had the look of terrorism," and he objected to "the way Gerdts was setting neighbor against neighbor." [69]

Cuomo and Jorling later met with upstate editors to discuss the issue of road closings in general, and Jorling said, "No place in the Adirondacks is further than three miles from a road." That misstatement did not help Cuomo's and Jorling's justification for closing wilderness roads; in fact, if newspaper accounts are accurate, their defense of road closings was pretty weak. [70]

Adirondack Solidarity Alliance generated headlines in North Country newspapers by staging a meeting at Au Sable Forks, where Calvin Carr, who had taken a leadership role in Solidarity, proposed forming a grand jury composed of two deputies from each county who could return indictments and remove lawmakers from office. Even if his call for protection under the federal constitution was farfetched, his works were "punctuated with frequent, thunderous applause." [71] Gerdts staged a third motorcade on June 15; this one was to end at the capitol, where two Adirondack chairs were placed to accommodate him and the governor for a chat. As Gerdts left, after waiting many hours for a meeting with the governor, his parting words suggested that the governor ought to read up on the French Revolution because he was about to face one in the Adirondacks. At the same time, a group, presumably the Adirondack Liberators, placed arrows outside DEC and state police offices in Ray Brook and Schroon Lake. An arrow found at Ticonderoga had the message "King Cuomo—keep out—come at your own risk." At the end of June six chapters of the Adirondack Solidarity Alliance staged a protest at Adirondack Park Agency headquarters with signs from the past: Abolish the APA.

It is not clear what created the rift between Gerdts and Solidarity Alliance, but in early July the Alliance announced Gerdts was no longer a spokesman for the group. Gerdts was not upset by his ejection from the inner circle (French, Carr, and Red Larson) that ran the Alliance. [72] Gerdts explained that he was taking his twenty thousand followers out of the Alliance because of "problems over leadership, finances, and a planned legal battle against Gov. Cuomo." The Alliance was not worried—it doubted Gerdts's membership claims.[73] Gerdts retaliated by claiming that "it is regrettable that the extreme behavior, [such as] zealots [who would] indict Cuomo, or of the likes of outsider Red Larson and the personal political ambitions of Cal Carr have forced this split." Had Gerdts forgotten he too was an outsider?[74]

Why So Much Turmoil?

As absurd, even comical, as the events of June and July seem, there was a deadly serious and threatening undertone. It is hard to determine whether residents were responding favorably to the uproar because the histrionics caught their attention or because they felt threatened.[75] Gerdts used blatant tactics, but something else was beginning to occur. Many groups within the opposition were acting in a very sophisticated way. One staffer from Adirondack Council told me it was as if these groups had learned all the ways of using the public relations techniques that had been developed by environmentalists in the past two decades. But it was more than that. These groups were actually doing a better job than the environmental groups, who were totally unprepared for and never expected the opposition to develop as effectively as it had. The environmental groups seemed to be backing off from the fray, fearing that they would not look good in the park. The opposition groups may have been acting independently and at different levels, but their combined efforts gave the impression of a tremendous groundswell, spurred on by a classic public relations campaign, which continued to increase opposition to the report. The effectiveness of the public relations campaign can be traced in part to Mark Behan and even to Bob Flacke. Behan had a good reputation in the public relations field, and even the Adirondack Planning Commission paid Behan's firm nearly half of APC's first-year funds.[76] This payment hampered APC because it was operating without the endorsement of several counties and with funds from only four counties.

Dick Beamish feels that in addition to what was happening within the park, environmentalists were failing to make their case with newspapers around the state. As a result, the press was not supportive of the commission report, in part because the issues were very complex and difficult for the public outside the park to understand—or care about. All this opposition and lack of support undoubtedly helped convince Governor Cuomo that the issue was too explosive to deal with.

A few of the commissioners sensed the need to defend their actions. Two complained about Cuomo's response to the report: Craig Gilborn said the governor lacked leadership and John Oakes said Cuomo, like President Bush, wanted to be known as an environmentalist, but rarely acts like one.[77] The *Post Star* quoted Dick Lawrence as saying that "some commission members had tried to explain to others that the park has people in it and problems in need of urgent attention."[78] But by August, Lawrence complained that the commission did not have enough time to "understand that there are people here and they own property and they have ideas of what they want to do with that property."[79] Claire Barnett expressed concern that in the "toxic climate" that followed the report there was no debate on such real issues as water quality, property taxes, fundamental health care, and economic development.[80] She, Lawrence, Flacke, and Bob Boice told Adirondack North Country Association that there was no unanimous agreement on any of the 245 recommendations and that there should be real debate and public involvement, not just among park residents, but with all residents of the state.[81] Read Kingsbury wrote a very positive analysis of the commission's work for Adirondack Mountain Club's *Adirondac* magazine as well as editorials for the Rochester paper *Democrat and Chronicle*. That paper printed a very supportive article based on an interview with Cuomo conducted by the paper's editorial board.[82]

Meanwhile, opposition to the Commission on the Adirondacks in the 21st Century from local governments expanded. Essex County filed suit to obtain a show cause order to prevent the adoption of laws and regulations based on the recommendations. The supervisors had claimed that there had been no attempt to comply with the State Environmental Quality Review law. They were undeterred by advice that SEQR did not apply to recommendations on which no action had been taken, and the court quickly dismissed the suit. Herkimer County and the Black River-St. Lawrence Resource Conservation and Development Corp. (RC&D) came out against the commission's recommendations.[83] Washington County joined the opposition in late July, as did the Town of Warrensburg.

APC Gets Down to Work

Cuomo released a letter to Adirondack Planning Commission chairman Ham Robertson stating his goals for discussions with the APC: statutory representation of locally elected officials on Adirondack Park Agency; changes in the way local governments participate in the planning and decision-making process; protection of the backcountry and shorelines; changes in hamlet classification; improving public access to state land within the park with particular concern for the elderly and disabled; and economic, social, and educational programs that would address the special conditions of the Adirondacks.[84] Cuomo wanted the APC to develop recommendations for the 1991 legislative agenda by December 1. Temporarily, at least, these announcements forestalled attempts to remove Purdue from negotiations between APC and the governor.

At a July meeting between Jorling, Murray, and APC, the governor's staff had agreed to drop transferable development rights and to recommend that the state pursue easements rather than fee acquisitions.[85] Meetings with Jorling, Murray, and others showed that other key administrative changes had been tabled indefinitely. Further, " 'the DEC is in the driver's seat' for all negotiations now underway with all parties. . . . For obvious reasons, the DEC commissioner shows no interest in some core administrative proposals of the Commission." Jorling had the governor's ear, or at least Murray's, and there would be no changes to DEC, even those that could be made by executive order. To some observers, this failure to combine DEC's park regions and consider implementing a park service is perhaps the most tragic consequence to come from the demise of the commission's work. Those recommendations remained valid after the decade of the 1990s.

Before the state legislature closed for the summer, it had passed the bond act. Tensions seemed to be easing. Adirondack Council did something of an about-face, stating that the lack of Adirondack legislation was a good thing and would give time for substantive debate. (Council had never endorsed the bond act in its entirety.) Later in July, Adirondack Council stated that a moratorium on new construction was no longer needed. Actually, Council's distancing itself from the commission report marks a real philosophical shift.

Gary Randorf remained acting director of the Adirondack Council until August 15, 1990, and when Tim Burke took over, changes in the council became more noticeable.

Adirondack Landowners Association

The end of June marked the establishment of yet another group formed in opposition to the commission, the Adirondack Landowners Association. William Hutchens of Livingston Lake Club and Robert Hawley of Wilmurt Club convened a group of representatives from eight private clubs (Adirondack League, Brandreth, Big Wolf Lake, Grasse River, Livingston Lake, Moose Pond, North Woods, and Wilmurt clubs). That number grew quickly; in 2000 ALA's membership included twenty-eight clubs and numerous private individuals. Initially, their primary concern was the threat of eminent domain to their holdings.

Some of the clubs had been in existence for over one hundred years and some represented wealthy families whose landholdings were held by private corporations. Several had granted easements on their property to limit further development. Almost all the principals lived outside the Adirondack Park.

Meeting at different clubs on a regular basis, ALA shifted its focus to stewardship, forestry, and taxation, but for the first year or so members' major concern was the commission and the way it might affect their holdings. Among the speakers at their meeting at Brandreth Park was Robert Flacke. That meeting was also attended by descendants of the first Brandreth who jointly own that large private tract. While no one remembers exactly what Flacke said, one Brandreth member was so concerned that he was panicked into thinking that Flacke had told him the state was going to take their land. Fear of the commission was rampant.

More Furors

That summer the Adirondack's hard-core opposition discovered many other issues beside the Commission on the Adirondacks in the 21st Century to arouse the public and fan the flames of insurrection. Gerdts staged a rally to generate opposition to the 1990 bond act. Warrensburg supervisor Maynard Baker announced publication of a new edition of Tony D'Elia's *Adirondack Rebellion*. Sale of the book would provide funds to fight what Baker perceived was government's taking property without compensation.

A meeting of the committee of the "Lake Champlain Biosphere Reserve," created in 1989 under UNESCO (United Nations Educational, Scientific and Cultural Organization), presented one more opportunity for Gerdts to stage a disturbance. Again reason did not prevail, for as a spokesman for the Lake Champlain group pointed out, the "biosphere reserve was created purely for academic and scientific research and has nothing to do with regulations."[86] Carol LaGrasse's article for the *Warrensburg–Lake George News* describing the Man and the Biosphere program was a straightforward discussion of the program without criticism.[87] Still, the UNESCO program became one more perceived threat from the outside, a major flashpoint that Gerdts and others used to try to prove that Adirondackers were losing control.

To the accompaniment of cannon shot, Alliance members signed an Adirondack Bill of Rights at Crown Point in early July. Gerdts complained about DEC's inconsistent policies in handling the Olympic Regional Development Authority's illegal dumping and locating of the Essex County landfill.

Throughout the summer the Vaccaro case kept making news. Hamilton

County passed a resolution urging the state to stop pursuing eminent domain and negotiate a conservation easement for Pine Ponds property.[88]

Residents' Committee to Protect the Adirondacks

By mid-1990 the tone of protest had shifted. The phrase "property rights" appeared regularly in the speeches of those opposed to the commission. In a well-reasoned piece in the *North Creek News Enterprise* supporting the goals of the commission, North Creek resident David Moro addressed property rights arguments. "Land is fundamentally different from most other kinds of private property, because its use by an owner directly affects the well-being of others, and because its supply is strictly limited. . . . Land has characteristics of both a private good (whose use affects only the owner) and a public good (whose use affects everyone, e.g. the air). . . . No one has ever found a way to manufacture wilderness land lost to development. . . . So in this respect land falls into the category of 'unique' property, which can be owned privately, but whose use is justifiably regulated."[89]

Shortly after Moro's letter appeared a home-based environmental group joined the fray. A handful of North Creek residents formed the Residents' Committee to Protect the Adirondacks to appeal to the "silent majority" of Adirondackers who would support measures to protect the land and their way of life. Their first chairman was David Moro, whose writings attacked groups opposed to the commission. Further, he gave full support of his group to most of the recommendations of the commission.[90] He said he had hoped for debate on the report, but "strident radicals" derailed any debate "by tapping into Adirondackers' 'visceral feelings' about government interference."[91] Another RCPA supporter championed government restrictions as essential to preserving the Adirondackers' way of life.[92]

Marking Time

Under the leadership of Fred Monroe, the Fairness Coalition tried to position itself as a moderate between extremes. He did so in a way that had great appeal for Adirondackers: He wanted the "state to set a permanent limit on acquisitions, zoning densities, and other policies that have such profound impacts on Adirondackers and their plans for their land. Then we know we don't have to worry about them coming back in 5 years, in 10 years, in 20 years, to take our homes and our dreams."[93] Monroe envisioned the coalition preparing position papers on subjects that paralleled those of the technical reports prepared by the Commission on the Adirondacks in the 21st Century.[94]

Meanwhile, those reports were still not printed. The two-month delay was blamed on editing problems; further delays were attributed to printing problems. They were released on September 5, 1990, and one-third of the transmittal letter that Berle sent to Cuomo was a criticism of Flacke's minority report: "he provides no guiding principle for striking the [balance of environmental and economic activity] and thus leaves both residents and the larger park adrift."[95] Berle regretted that the reports were not available earlier, since "they would have answered many of the questions that have arisen since the report was made public" and would have buttressed the main conclusions.[96] The technical reports brought comments from Purdue that some were good, but that "taken all together, they form a shaky foundation for a bold program of land use regulation."[97]

Andy Halloran, North Creek lawyer who served as counsel to the Local Government Review Board from 1978 to 1986, became director of the Fairness Coalition. His writing and outreach stressed the group's position that there was no crisis that would warrant the commission in the first place. The group's fall 1990 report was a sophisticated publication featuring analyses of growth within the park.[98]

Cuomo's August letter/press release to park residents promoted the bond act and expressed his belief that the Adirondack Planning Commission could develop broad-based recommendations for future legislation. As the APC struggled to come up with proposals to bring to the governor's team, they felt hampered by a "serious deficiency in information." Purdue said that their research had uncovered huge gaps in data.[99] The Local Government Review Board, feeling left out of the action, sought membership on the APC, but without success.[100]

Residents' Committee to Protect the Adirondacks had been the only group in the North Country to endorse the commission report, and it was the only one making a lot of noise in favor of a vote for the 1990 bond act.[101] That group continued holding meetings around the park to enlist the "silent majority." But in seeking a middle ground, even people speaking for that group backed away from total endorsement of the commission report, while promoting its economic, health, and educational recommendations.

For some time RCPA was dogged by rumors that it was a front for several national environmental groups. RCPA finally had to admit that the mailing list it used to solicit members in the park had come from Adirondack Council, but the group obtained such lists from Sierra Club and Audubon as well.[102]

Bill McKibben, in an *Op Ed* piece in the *New York Times,* criticized the governor for not supporting the commission report but found fault with the parts of that report that did not relate to backcountry or lakeside controls: "A whole series of esthetic controls [would] transform the working Adirondacks into a sort of ultra-tasteful wilderness theme park, which might be nice for tourists, but is not needed to protect real wilderness." [103]

Fall 1990—Events Without Direction

In mid-August 1990, when Cuomo visited Westport for his town meeting with residents, he talked to many people, including representatives of Solidarity Alliance. He said he would not take seriously those who opposed the entire report. About this time Dale French and others from Solidarity Alliance were making trips to the Catskills to help residents mobilize against a proposed regional commission.

The state expanded its push for passage of the 1990 Environmental Quality Bond Act, whose fate had been inextricably tied to the commission report, at least in the minds of North Country residents. A DEC pamphlet urging a vote on the bond act was challenged by Robert Schultz of Fort Ann, working with Gerdts and LaGrasse. (LaGrasse had met Donald Gerdts in the spring of 1990, but did not work with him until they joined to challenge the DEC pamphlet.) The suit claimed that the printing (5.5 million copies) was illegal because it was promotional rather than informational. (The state's constitution forbids the use of state funds to promote partisan political activity.) The appellate division agreed with the plaintiffs, stopping distribution of pamphlet.[104] While the suit only prevented circulation of the last million copies of the pamphlet, Gerdts later claimed they stopped the bond act.

That fall, while everyone was waiting for the election, Adirondack Park Agency published a report analyzing growth in the park.[105] It showed that ten towns accounted for half the growth in the park and that those ten, mostly in the Lake George basin, had land use controls.

In stepping up support for the commission's work, Berle wrote Cuomo a second letter. It rebutted more points in the minority report, but noted that twenty-six of Flacke's forty-four alternative proposals actually paralleled commission recommendations.[106] In a speech in the North Country, Cuomo emphasized that the commission's work "signals the beginning of a process, not the end." [107]

The fall meeting of the Association for the Protection of the Adirondacks was told that "the most valuable thing we can do now is stop preaching to the choir and involve a broader group," but despite bringing varied opinions to the debate on the commission's work, the association, as usual, was not able to reach out to a larger group of park residents.[108]

Also in the fall several environmental groups met with Berle in Albany to begin formulating a legislative package for 1991. Concurrently Senator Stafford was telling a group in Lake Placid that he would not support any stricter legislation for the Adirondacks than was already in place.[109] George Davis told the Environmental Planning Lobby's conference that the governor had "walked away" from the report. The *New York Times* quoted a Cuomo spokesperson as saying that the governor's "passion for the environment is at least as strong as any of these advocates, [and] where they settle for stating goals, he is trying to achieve them, sometimes against fierce opposition." Frank Murray said that "the environmentalists shared unrealistic expectation"[110] for Cuomo's ability to lead the legislature.

The *Hamilton County News* began a series of analyses based on Cuomo's meeting with North Country editors. In a balanced discussion of the need to protect the forestry industry, one article reiterated Cuomo's hopes to use easements wherever possible. The governor gave the commission a backhanded complement, noting that it was "ungrateful for us not to acknowledge" their work.[111] He told the group that he "always intended to go to the people" with the commission's ideas.[112]

That fall Paul Donaldson tried unsuccessfully to challenge Senator Stafford in the November election. Donaldson was smart enough to decline any discussion of the commission report, stating that there were much more important issues such as the depressed local economy. He did, however, note that opposition to the report was too well orchestrated to be a purely grassroots response.[113]

In an interview with the *Post Star,* Dick Purdue said that the fighting in the Adirondacks was not about the environment, but about power. He complained that the governor's representatives would not respond to Adirondack Planning Commission's concerns, that APC was being forced to discuss issues on the agenda of environmentalists before moving on to issues of importance to APC. In addition, Purdue objected to the fact that the governor sent lower-level representatives to some meetings, people who had no power to "agree to anything." Purdue believed he had been supporting reconciliation between Adirondackers and statewide interests, but began to doubt their outcome. The talks had been for Purdue a "real learning experience"— he felt that some members of APA and representatives of environmental groups "share a self-interested distrust of Adirondackers."[114]

Hinchey's Legislation

Maurice Hinchey, Democrat from Kingston and chairman of the assembly's Environmental Conservation Committee, began to formulate Adirondack legislation by conducting a fact-finding trip through the park in late August. His talks there promoted one of the 21st Century Commission's themes: consolidating functions of DEC and APA into a single agency responsible for land-use planning.[115] He noted that "much of the criticism is coming from people who have obviously not read the report." He told residents that he was not buying the whole report and "there are portions I may not agree with. [But] a lot of it is very good, solid stuff."[116] In October Hinchey circulated his proposals for legislation. They were a blend of APC's and the 21st Century Commission's proposals: putting a representative of local government on APA, giving APC jurisdiction over Class B projects, placing a cap of 52 percent on the amount of state land in the park, creating an independent park service from existing agencies, limiting the use of eminent domain, adding shoreline restrictions, and giving tax exemptions for sale of land to the state. Before the end of the year, Hinchey modified his draft legislation to reflect criticism of his proposal for a park superagency. His revised bill would still include the formation of a park service, which would be supplemented by a board of advisors representing the interests of park residents.[117]

Response was predictable: the Fairness Coalition's Susan Allen objected; Berle welcomed much of Hinchey's ideas, with reservations. RCPA's Duane Ricketson questioned whether a superagency was workable. Ricketson also urged Hinchey to talk with such groups as Fairness Coalition and Solidarity on the grounds that it was important to involve all Adirondackers in policy decisions.

Baker and Gerdts and their followers, who had been forging relationships with Catskill people opposed to further regulation there, reached out to try to defeat Hinchey in the upcoming election.[118] They were unsuccessful. Just before the election, the same men organized another motorcade, with a truck carrying more of the "stones of shame" removed from the Crane Pond barrier and signs protesting both Hinchey and the bond act. The motorcade was billed as a tribute to Tony D'Elia, who had died on October 13. Following D'Elia's death, Gerdts applied for the job as director of Local Government Review Board but without success, even though he had the support of Cal Carr and the Solidarity Alliance.[119] Gerdts even talked of opening an Albany office for his lobbying efforts.

Urged by fellow environmentalists, George Davis tried to soften his criticism of Cuomo's handling of the commission report by saying that the governor had taken the necessary time to sort out legitimate concerns from those based on ignorance, selfishness, or greed. "I guess if I was a politician in his shoes, it would have been wiser to wait and listen." [120]

Bond Act Defeat

The November election brought the defeat of the Environmental Quality Bond Act. More than a few newspapers outside the Adirondacks had opposed it on fiscal grounds.[121] Some Adirondackers claimed that their overwhelming vote against the act had contributed significantly to its narrow defeat statewide.

Environmentalists, led by National Audubon, responded to the defeat by urging even stronger legislation to protect what the state now could not buy. Dave Miller, Audubon's northeast regional vice president, called for existing use zoning to protect forest and agricultural land.[122]

Opponents of any legislation, particularly those in Warren County, proposed that the Adirondacks join up with the state of Vermont or simply secede from New York. (They ignored the fact that Vermont's Act 250 calls for strong land use controls.) Signs calling for secession popped up on back roads.[123]

"Unity" Conferences

Buoyed by the defeat of the bond act, Gerdts seized the moment to issue invitations to the first "Unity" Conference for November 1990. Included were Adirondack Conservation Council, Fairness Coalition, Adirondack North Country Association, Local Government Review Board, Solidarity Alliance, Empire State Forest Products Association, Franklin County and Schroon Lake Fish and Game Clubs, Citizen's Council, Blue Line Confederation, Foothills Confederation, and Central Adirondack Defense Committee, but none of the environmental groups. Purdue initially endorsed plans for such a conference, believing it would be significant in presenting a united front.[124]

The Adirondack Fairness Coalition withdrew before the meeting was held, objecting to Gerdts's statement of goals for the conference.[125] Cal Carr announced that Solidarity would not attend because that group objected to Gerdts's shotgun approach to solving problems. But several additional groups did attend the first Unity Conference: Concerned Citizens and Taxpayers, Foothills Confederation, Inter County Legislative Committee, Pharaoh Mountain Sportsmen's Alliance, and the Washington-Warren County Farm Bureau. Gerdts's fifteen-point manifesto, "Declaration of Adirondack Unity,"

won the support of many groups. Dave Howard of the Blue Line Confederation said, "We agree completely." [126] But many present did not support it, stating they needed approval from the groups they represented.

Blue Line Council Appears

The first Unity meeting claimed attendance by representatives of all those opposed to the commission report, and one more such group made its appearance
just in time for the Unity Conference's second meeting. At the end of November Flacke announced the formation of the Blue Line Council, a statewide
coalition of timber companies, labor unions, banks, and conservation groups—
"a potentially powerful coalition" according to the Glens Falls *Post Star*.[127]
Some observers saw the strong hand of Finch, Pruyn, and Company behind
this group, which was co-chaired by Flacke and William C. Hennessy, former
chairman of the state Democratic party and commissioner of the Department
of Transportation.[128] Attorney Dennis Phillips, who had been hired to incorporate the Fairness Coalition and whose law firm represented Finch, Pruyn, also
represented this group.

The major achievement of the first Unity meeting was the decision to hold
the second meeting in two weeks, when those attending would address
Gerdts's proposal for a Declaration of Adirondack Unity to be submitted to the
governor. Flacke attended the second meeting in early December as representative of the Blue Line Council. According to Gerdts, representatives of fourteen
groups passed eleven resolutions. Solidarity did not attend, protesting Gerdts's
Crane Pond rally, at which thirty men carried deer rifles, albeit unloaded.[129]
Other cracks in the "unity" appeared: some of those attending reported later
that they had been manipulated by Gerdts. Flacke said Gerdts's handling of
events approached "demagoguery." [130]

Jim Frenette, representing the Inter County Legislative Committee, told
newspapers that initial accounts were not true, that the group had taken no formal votes. He was incensed at being associated with the resolution to impeach
Governor Cuomo, and he worried that those who had called the Unity Conference were using it to silence the voice of elected officials working to solve
Adirondack problems.[131] Furthermore, Gerdts's call for impeaching Governor
Cuomo was condemned by many attending groups because it made them appear radical. One critic called Gerdts "a master manipulator of the media." [132]

Even fewer groups attended the third Unity meeting, and those present
failed to reach consensus on legislation for the coming year. Representatives of
the Glens Falls Independent Living Center attended and participated in the dis-

cussion of the closing of Crane Pond and other roads. Their attendance marks the birth of the organized push for handicapped-motorized access to the Forest Preserve, an issue that would consume much of DEC's activities later in the decade.[133]

Although little appears in the press of Carol LaGrasse's work on the Unity conferences, she did much to organize them. She believes they were a total failure because the leaders had little skill in getting people to work together and because Gerdts was "the kingpin of kingpins, pursuing self-aggrandizement, and hated by too many people because he was too radical, boisterous." Further, she said, Gerdts ran meetings with an iron hand, without input from others.[134] He even tried to involve the governor's office in the Unity conferences, but Joe Martens explained the administration's refusal by stating that "any group Mr. Gerdts is involved with is tainted [by the use of] intimidation and threats."[135]

It was at this juncture that LaGrasse split from Donald Gerdts, partly because of the way he handled the unity conferences and partly because of his activities with the Adirondack Cultural Foundation she had formed. This not-for-profit group was to have no political affiliation, and according to LaGrasse was designed "to promote the rich culture of the Adirondack region."[136] (Gerdts made financial commitments for the group that he did not honor, and as a result she lost money. LaGrasse distanced herself from Gerdts two years before his 1994 departure from the area.)

Adirondack Park Centennial

Lost in all the brouhaha and struggling against park resentment of anything that suggested outside involvement was a committee trying to plan for the 1992 Adirondack Park Centennial. The committee, which I chaired, was itself on shaky ground. It had no formal authorization or funding by the governor or the legislature, although it had the backing of Assemblyman Maurice Hinchey. (Governor Cuomo did offer an executive order commemorating the centennial, but no help or funding for it.)

The committee was an ad hoc group that started with the Association for the Protection of the Adirondacks; its board members came from the Adirondack Museum; Silver Bay Association; Adirondack Life Magazine; several environmental groups; state agencies DED, APA, and DEC; Empire State Forest Products Association; Adirondack North Country Association; Niagara Mohawk Power Corporation; and representatives of several legislators. The committee was nonpolitical and, against all odds, did manage to hold a number of centennial activities: a traveling juried watercolor exhibit and a wonderful traveling quilt show that opened at Niagara Mohawk's Syracuse headquarters. The committee placed articles in several national magazines, and a special issue of *Natural History* was devoted to the centennial. The group coordinated a number of events, including the centennial kickoff event at the Adirondack Museum. Reflecting the times, the group chose as centennial motto "A Park of People and Natural Wonder." [137]

The committee involved residents of the park through many different arts venues. The Cultural Foundation quickly became a thorn in the activities of the committee for the 1992 Adirondack Park Centennial because it was seeking funds from the same sources and was trying to give the impression that it was a grassroots organization.

I remember that when the Centennial Committee launched the 1992 centennial year, we had little expectation that our diverse, yet modest and well-rounded, series of events would do as we hoped: calm the anger that gripped the Adirondacks. In fact, I think most of the members of the committee just hoped we could get through the year without inspiring confrontations. In retrospect we were successful and much credit goes to Assemblyman Hinchey.

APC Position Paper

In November 1990 the Adirondack Planning Commission circulated to twelve county boards a copy of its position paper.[138] The APC and representatives of the Cuomo administration continued to meet into December, and on December 19 the governor's proposals were presented to the group. For many reasons APC members were disappointed: Cuomo recommended stricter shoreline and backcountry regulations and that two, not five, Adirondack Park Agency members would represent local governments and even these would not have to come from a pool nominated by officials. There would be no proposals for increased road access. This was not what residents had been asking for.

About this time, PAW (Protect Adirondack/Appalachian Wilderness), an offshoot of Earth First!, stirred the conflict cauldron with proposals for wilderness protection (dismantling roads and dams, reintroducing wolves, expanding the wilderness through eminent domain to 4.45 million acres, creating human exclusion zones) that were certain to further inflame local residents.[139]

Duane Ricketson, Residents' Committee to Protect the Adirondacks's original executive director, was replaced by Dan Ling as operations director. According to the *Adirondack Daily Enterprise,* Ricketson was replaced because he had favored local representation on the park agency and because he had questioned whether RCPA was becoming a tool for outside preservationist interests.[140] He had reached out to Solidarity Alliance, offering to help that group in its study of the park's economy. Although Ricketson denied the newspaper accounts, he did resign but said he would remain active on RCPA's board. However, his replacement appears to have made him the first sacrificial lamb among those working for a rapprochement among Adirondack groups.

14 | Picking Up the Pieces
1991

IN THE "WHAT ELSE CAN GO WRONG?" DEPARTMENT, the beginning of 1991 started off with the announcement that the park might for the second time miss acquiring land in the western Adirondacks. Diamond International had sold its 96,000-acre holding in the western and northern part of the state to Lassiter Properties, Inc. in September 1988. The state was interested in purchasing part of the land, particularly the low-elevation boreal forests in the Town of Altamont, but Diamond wanted to sell all its parcels together. Lassiter Corp. stepped in and offered $177 an acre, when the state could only offer $145. Lassiter sold the state easements on part of its acquisition. The corporation later acquired an additional 7,000 acres, bringing its Adirondack portion of the holdings to 87,000 acres. Because Lassiter was being reorganized, all of its lands were put up for sale again in early 1991 under federal bankruptcy laws. This offering occurred at a point when the state had no money for land acquisition. Adirondack Council saw these properties as key to the establishment of its two much-touted wilderness areas, the Bob Marshall and the Boreal. Environmental groups, led by Adirondack Council, put enormous pressure on the state to acquire the land. In 1991 Lassiter made a $1 million profit selling 15,000 acres to the state and an easement on 40,000 acres that included the boreal lands sought by Council. The easement would limit development. The state paid $194 per acre for land that Lassiter had acquired outright for $177. The administration was pressured into completing the deal, but Governor Cuomo considered this a major boondoggle.[1]

Within days of the defeat of the 1990 Bond Act, an ad listing the 2000-acre Heurich estate, with magnificent shoreline on Lake Champlain, appeared in the *New York Times*. With the possible sale of 51,000-acre Whitney Park in the background, Adirondack Council called on the state to establish a permanent land protection fund.

The Adirondack Planning Commission met with Frank Murray and others in early January 1991, the first open meeting in a series of eight designed to finalize plans for legislation to be offered by the governor. APC presented its views in a position statement, dated January 26, 1991, as a basis for negotiations.[2] In the meetings that followed there was some progress on backcountry land preservation; APC agreed that the state should have first rights to purchase development rights of parcels of over five hundred acres where change in the use of the land was proposed. (There were 441 owners of parcels that exceeded five hundred acres.) For whatever reason, neither Cuomo nor the assembly wanted to commit substantial sums to the Adirondacks, so this proposal had little chance of being accepted.[3]

There was no progress on the most contentious topic—the state would not budge on agency membership. The issue of appointing Adirondack Park Agency members from a pool of elected local officials remained a symbol that would prove that Adirondackers were victims of big government. The matter stymied efforts to mold park legislation throughout the Cuomo administration. Purdue believes it was not the genuine issue that it appeared to be, that it was a convenient cover beyond which the political half of the Adirondack Planning Commission could hide. It was also a bargaining position that helped the parties get down to negotiation of other issues. He thinks the "larger issues were whether the political element in the Planning Commission would ever permit the other issues to be negotiated and whether the governor would go beyond using the APC negotiators as pawns in his dealings with Stafford."[4]

Flacke told a national environmental group (Wildlife Conservation Society) that he predicted there would be no legislative action that year and that within a decade the Local Government Review Board would assume its true watchdog role. (Under Joe Rota, this happened much more quickly than Flacke foresaw.) Dick Beamish, who had recently left Adirondack Council and joined National Audubon, spoke at the same early spring Wildlife Conservation Society meeting representing Audubon. He said the APC, not the environmentalists, were the true radicals in the park. Craig Gilborn's speech at the same event complained about the region's press.

The Press

The relationship between the press and the Commission on the Adirondacks in the 21st Century and the events that followed the release of its report are interesting. Claims that reporting was one-sided abound, and the issue was certainly discussed at meetings of the different environmental groups. Some of the papers, such as in Warrensburg, made no bones about speaking for one side. The *Post Star* and the *Adirondack Daily Enterprise* seemed occasionally to be slanted, but in general covered different sides of the issues. The Glens Falls *Post Star* printed several guest columns, including one by Dave Miller of Audubon.[5] All were strongly in favor of more controls. The *Hamilton County News* published many in-depth background reports. The paper covered the APA and Purdue extensively. Maybe that is the key to the problem—extensively; in general there was just a lot of coverage. No aspect of any issue was neglected. And because coverage was so complete, those opposed to the report could very easily stage events, meetings, and confrontations that the press could not ignore. So they got a lot of press. It is easy to see how people who lived close to the poverty line and whose jobs were at best part-time, jobs that depended on construction or logging, would believe the headlines and become convinced that something was wrong with the commission report, that it was the work of metropolitan outsiders, even if the newspapers never really said that. They were manipulated on a grand scale by sheer quantity, and the manipulators said one thing at every place they appeared: "you, the resident, have no voice in what is happening." No wonder that many Adirondackers really believed that.

While the press was mostly balanced, if excessive, in its coverage, some papers were more environmentally oriented than others. An *Adirondack Daily Enterprise* editorial started with the comment that "It is absolutely astounding how Adirondack rights activist Donald Gerdts continues to find ways to get his point across, regardless of how extreme that point may be. . . . Gerdts has not been elected by anybody to anything."[6]

The *North Creek News Enterprise* reported on the Residents' Committee to Protect the Adirondacks and carried several guest articles detailing that organization's support for the commission's work. The Glens Falls *Post Star* was not really slanted, but it did give a lot of space to Flacke, the Blue Line Council, and the forest industry's concerns. The *New York Times* articles were balanced, as were those of the Albany *Times Union* and the Rochester *Democrat and Chronicle*. Most people in the park did not read outside papers, and downstaters were not moved by articles on the Adirondacks. The passionate pleas for support for the Commission on the Adirondacks in the 21st Century that appeared in the newsletters of environmental groups almost never contained the real concerns of Adirondack residents.

The Blue Line Council chose Pieter Litchfield as its president in early February. Litchfield said the group was seeking a middle ground that would address the rights of landowners, balancing the needs of man and the environment.[7] The group added John Stock, former APA commissioner, and

James Biggane, former DEC commissioner, to its board, but Fred LeBrun, columnist for the Albany *Times Union,* questioned Blue Line's claim to the middle of the road because they represented the "biggest landowning interests in the Adirondacks."[8]

"As Park legislation nears, tempers rise in the Adirondacks."[9] That March 1991 headline in the Albany *Times Union* suggests that the winter had been relatively quiet, but obviously it was not—or if it was, Gerdts used the lull to stir things up again. He resurfaced with a scheme to have Adirondack property owners post their land against canoeing, hunting, fishing, and so on with the expectation that 250,000 posted signs would discourage visitors.[10] Hamilton County supervisors called the scheme self-destructive and threatening to the economy.[11] Gerdts even proposed to challenge Stafford in the 1992 election. Solidarity Alliance vice president Dale French announced he would run for supervisor of the Town of Crown Point. (He still held that office in 2000.)

Open Space Plan

As part of the bill to send the 21st Century Environmental Quality Bond Act to the voters, the legislature authorized the formation by September 1, 1990, of nine regional advisory committees to help the state plan land acquisition. These open space planning groups were to be organized independent of the passage of the bond act. Among their duties was making recommendations for policies and priorities for protection of land, for studies or assessments that would assist in the development of land acquisition policies and priorities for the region, and for developing guidelines for identifying priority parcels for land acquisition.[12] The regional recommendations would go to a seven-member state Open Space Plan Advisory Council for review. That group would pass its consensus recommendations on for final decision to the commissioners of Department of Environmental Conservation and Office of Parks, Recreation, and Historic Preservation, the two agencies that would direct expenditures of the fund statewide. It is evident that there was a difficulty in melding and comparing DEC's needs with OPRHP's, in establishing criteria that would meet the needs of parks statewide as well as the needs of the Forest Preserve parks, the Adirondack and Catskill parks. Recognizing the difference between the two kinds of park and their differing categories of acquisitions might have made the committees' work more efficient. However, the Region 5 committee, which covered the eastern Adirondacks plus lands north to the Canadian border and those south of the park through Saratoga County, faced nearly insurmountable problems anyway, most of which were related to the fight over eminent domain, the bond act itself, and the Commission on the Adirondacks in the 21st Century.

Region 5's Open Space Planning Committee got a late start, holding its first meeting in mid-December; recommendations for land acquisition were expected on January 28, 1991. The nine members appointed by the state included representatives of DEC, OPRHP, and environmental organizations, all of whom showed up at the first meeting. Of the eight members appointed by county government, only three attended, prompting Hamilton County's representative to say, "we are going to have big problems." [13] Even though Tom Monroe told the committee that the "State does not contemplate any land acquisition program based on eminent domain," [14] members of the committee believed the state might still use it. The issue of eminent domain remained a problem for the committee for the next eight months and was one of the major reasons the committee made little or very slow progress on other issues.

Individual member recommendations on acquisitions were expected at the January 8, 1991, meeting, but some members objected to any state acquisitions at all. Jean Raymond, supervisor of the Town of Edinburgh, served as a member of the Region 5 committee from its inception through 2001. At this second meeting, she requested a map showing state land, snowmobile and hiking trails, and canoe routes. At later meetings the committee requested enormous amounts of background information on policies affecting state land. It received almost all that information, but it is perplexing that a map depicting the desired information was never given the committee.* It is even more perplexing to note that no such map exists today.

From the start, Tom Monroe gave the committee much latitude and discussed issues in an elemental fashion to educate committee members about the technicalities of DEC's procedures. Several members and DEC staff told me that they felt that the committee had achieved great things over the years. Others said it was an exercise in redundancy and repetitiveness. Betsy Lowe, DEC public affairs person who took minutes for most of the life of the committee, feels very positive about the exercise because "it made everyone comfortable working together," [15] because several of the things the Region 5 group did made important contributions to open space planning in general and, in particular, to resolving the issue of eminent domain. She believed that it was important because this was DEC's first attempt at public participation. (There had been earlier attempts as earlier chapters showed, such as the first High Peaks

---

* In 1993–94, DEC did provide a map showing fee acquisitions and easements, but not the other details requested.

Advisory Committee and Norm VanValkenburgh's formation of the Forest Preserve Advisory Committee, but none of these involved local elected officials.) And at the time, when local input had become such an issue, developing an effective protocol for public participation was an important achievement.

A brief survey of DEC's work and of the committee's accomplishments and problems underscores the variety of difficulties encountered. Some of the impasse that developed after the first two meetings persisted for years, despite the fact that the committee began meeting every two weeks to try to reach consensus on land acquisition. Members associated with environmental groups offered lists of both fee acquisitions and easements. The proposals of Adirondack Mountain Club's Neil Woodworth were recreation oriented, Mike DiNunzio's list was based on Adirondack Council's *2020 Vision* series, and Helen Brody's list for Audubon included many wetland habitats. These lists were extended at the next meeting, and the group began to talk about criteria for land acquisition. The discussion was initiated with an outline presented by James C. Dawson, who also made specific recommendations for acquisition based in part on geologic and historical sites as well as natural features.

DEC prepared a map based on the individual lists, but by the fourth meeting it was obvious that there would be no consensus. After much wrangling, the group voted not to send the map that DEC had prepared to the Open Space Plan Advisory Council. Local government representatives all had reservations about any new acquisitions, about the use of eminent domain, and about the impact of acquisitions on the local tax base. The committee met the initial deadline with a letter summarizing these issues and stating that they were going to continue with an agenda to educate themselves on the process of acquisition, to establish a set of criteria for acquisitions, and to involve the public.

Arguments on several topics marked the next meeting: Jean Raymond was very upset that DEC had proposed submitting to the state Open Space Plan Advisory Council the Region 5 group's unapproved map as a DEC map. Members argued over the criteria, the process, and even the minutes. In response to the latter, future minutes contained the sentence that the meeting summary was not a verbatim transcript.

Some committee members were convinced that DEC had a master plan for land acquisition, the much-rumored "secret map," a portion of which the commissioner had sent to the Blue Line Confederation. Deputy Commissioner Robert Bendick told the group that DEC had no master map for acquisitions within the park and that DEC would not share with the committee information or maps on possible acquisitions. However, because the map showed state interest in developed lands around Canada Lake, giving credence to the belief that it was part of a secret map,* Richard Lefebvre, who later became APA chairman, attended one of the Region 5 meetings. He recalls a long table lined on one side with opponents of land acquisition and on the other with environmentalists, all of whom denied the existence of the secret map. Lefebvre then produced the portion of the map.† Afterwards, Jorling explained that the map was one drawn to allay the fears of Bleecker residents, but that it was "hastily prepared" and contained errors that misrepresented "the department's priorities on Canada Lake." [16] By then a lot of people were convinced of the existence of a secret map for the whole park.

The Region 5 committee also discussed the process DEC follows in negotiation for and purchase of land as well as DEC's draft to be submitted to the Open Space Plan Advisory Council.

At the succeeding meeting, the committee formally requested a year's extension in order to complete its work. Members argued over drafts of a letter it planned to send in lieu of a report and list of recommended acquisitions. The letter listed the issues the committee hoped to deal with and general guidelines for recommendations the committee might make in the future, but concluded, "specific guidelines had to be developed prior to discussions or submittal of specific recommendations." In other words, in a half year, the committee had made almost no progress on its principal charge, but its recalcitrance to offer specifics left the door open for DEC to do so and thus made it possible for environmental groups to influence DEC's contribution to the draft open space plan.

Throughout the spring and summer, members of the committee roundly criticized DEC's priority-rating system, a compendium of criteria from earlier bond acts. They continued to discuss criteria for acquisitions while receiving background information on APA's State Land Master Plan and Private Land Use and Development Plan, wetlands regulations, work of the High Peaks Advisory Committee, Article XIV, eminent domain procedures, land exchanges, easements, the role of not-for-profit organizations in state land acquisition, taxation and assessment of state land, economic issues, forest tax laws, and economic impacts of land acquisition. The number of pages of material circulated to and from the committee is staggering, and the historical background provided by DEC on the issues constitutes a very important tutorial. While I believe that the material was a very important resource, I have a lingering question

---

* The map showed state interest in land both east and west of the author's camp, parcels with many summer homes. This fact prompted Carol LeGrasse to add to her column on the existence of the secret map the observation that it carefully avoided coloring in my property.

† A copy of a portion of the map is in the author's files, courtesy of Richard Lefebvre.

about whether so much material at such a sophisticated level was helpful. Furthermore, I question whether this information was brought back to the county government officials and the public. How much of the discussions penetrated local people and changed minds about the values of state land acquisition? Even in 2001 I still heard elected officials say, "yes, perhaps the state needs a specific parcel, but we don't want the state to buy any more land."

In June DEC extended the committee's work for a few weeks, not a year. All along the meetings were marked not so much by posturing on issues but by perspectives that were poles apart, although members seemed to be really trying to reach agreements. Dick Purdue presented a list of criteria and processes submitted by Hamilton County. The committee discussed these recommendations in detail. They included policies on road closures and the right of towns to overrule state proposals for land purchase. In June the members were able to agree on proposals relating to taxation, easements, and sales of detached parcels, but consensus on the use of eminent domain remained elusive. Several small working groups wrestled with the issue. The discussions of a draft on eminent domain went round and round again through several meetings.

In July, after seventeen meetings in seven months, plus subcommittee meetings to deal with wording of particularly contentious issues, the committee voted on resolutions defining criteria for eleven issues and agreed to submit those recommendations to the statewide committee.[17] The committee still had no specific recommendations for land to be acquired.

However, the committee was finally able to agree on a policy on eminent domain, and members consider it a major achievement in Adirondack history. They succeeded in having the policy on eminent domain included in the statewide Open Space Plan. This policy would exclude taking any residence by eminent domain for open space protection and using eminent domain where easements will achieve the desired purpose. Eminent domain can arise only in consultation with the owner in special cases, such as when a change of use threatens a specific resource or when a property is essential to creating or maintaining public access to Forest Preserve lands.[18] The committee's recommendation that local governments be consulted with respect to land acquisition was also included in the state plan. The committee wanted to include requirements for local approval, but this was not made part of the state plan.

In August, after voting to continue working, the committee shifted focus to requiring advance copies of publication of the Draft Open Space Plan, meeting jointly with Region 6's committee, involving local governments in developing an Open Space Conservation Plan, and inventory mapping. They subsequently learned that the Region 6 committee had not only produced a list of desired state acquisitions in the western Adirondacks, but had prioritized it, thus completing most of its assignment for the statewide Preliminary Draft Plan for Open Space Conservation Plan. The reasons for the disparity between the two regions are explored in chapter 18, where Region 5's efforts are discussed as an illustration of managing public participation. The joint meeting of the two regional committees did *not* produce agreement to give consistency to the two committees' recommendations. Regarding the penultimate item, the committee could only agree that they should develop a method for consulting with towns. On the last item, an extension of the request from the second meeting, the committee enlarged the list of items to appear on the desired inventory map to include every resource category imaginable. (Contemplate this puzzling comparison: A century ago similarly informative maps were made, laboriously drawn, yet in this day of GIS and computer mapping no such map exists for the Adirondack region. Lack of focus and different systems and goals among state agencies account for part of this,* but the biggest single cause is the lack of any one agency with the leadership and resource capability to make it happen.)

By August, discussions were so contradictory that it was obvious the committee had reached a stalemate. Some members said "put nothing in the plan," yet others were proposing that "nothing be purchased unless it is in the plan."

In September the committee began a program of reaching out to Adirondack towns to encourage local officials to study potential land acquisitions. The plan would have the state prioritize land acquisition sites and give that information to the advisory committee, which would in turn consult with the towns involved. Criteria for land acquisition would include the tax impact on local communities, the amount of state-owned land in the town, and the effect on future economic growth, affordable housing, and community infrastructure.

Occasionally meeting as often as every week during 1991, the first full year of its existence, the committee had found itself so split that it is amazing any consensus was achieved. Working against a background of continued opposition to anything that smacked of the bond act or land acquisition as spelled out in the commission report, the members were barely able to allay their fears, let alone allay the fears of park residents. In addition to the very important agreement on the use of eminent domain, several other of the committee's recommendations were included in the final plan: those affecting exchange of small

---

* One member of the committee wrote that "over the decades, separate criteria for classifying state lands by the APA and DEC, difficulties in depicting features in widely varying map scales, and DEC's failure to scrupulously maintain its land acquisition files contributed to the 'information gap.' "

detached parcels, state payment of taxes on its land, and inclusion of economic considerations in the selection of future acquisitions. DEC, however, submitted a proposal of types of lands to be considered for easement or fee acquisition. Some categories would be subject to review by joint Region 5 and 6 advisory committees. They were so loosely defined that they incorporated virtually all of the recommendations made by individual committee members.[19]

Dick Purdue, Jim Frenette, and several others left the committee in 1992, and their absence significantly altered the committee's productivity. The series of meetings held by Region 5's Open Space Committee seems to follow a pattern of rise and fall that is typical of such participatory meetings: a long education curve, some results, fatigue, and gradual falling apart. The remaining discussion of the Region 5 committee's work through the rest of the 1990s— its achievements, inability to compromise, and gradual drifting from its mission—is detailed in chapter 18.

The Second Half of 1991

Several Adirondack bills were introduced during the 1991 legislative session. Assemblyman Alexander "Pete" Grannis introduced the first bill; it was based on the recommendations of the Commission on the Adirondacks in the 21st Century as a favor to its chairman, Peter Berle. The bill had no sponsor in the senate. No one thought it had a chance, and Stafford vowed to kill it if it ever got to the senate.[20] Adirondack Planning Commission stood against the bill and countered with a proposal for a joint legislative study commission to be headed by Stafford and Hinchey. Stafford quickly squelched that idea, saying, "the Adirondacks has been studied to death."[21]

Assemblyman Hinchey introduced two more Adirondack bills: one gave planning responsibilities to the Local Government Review Board and pleased LGRB's executive director, Joe Rota. The other tightened restrictions on backcountry and shoreline development and combined DEC's Region 5 and 6 responsibilities into a park service and other changes that harked back to commission recommendations. Adirondack Planning Commission, Fairness Coalition, and the Blue Line Council found only a few parts acceptable. One headline said that these bills could be "DOA as Stafford expresses opposition."[22] Assemblyman Ortloff thought they were as "dead as the more extreme Grannis bill."[23]

The state budget was delayed again in 1991. This perennial problem has had a deleterious effect on much important legislation over the years. In 1990 it had delayed the commission report. In 1991 it caused Governor Cuomo to put off introducing his legislation for the park. That postponement sparked speculation about its contents, and again rumor was the subject of numerous articles in the press. In 1991 The *New York Times* reported in depth about Cuomo's legislation, before it was announced to the public or even to the APC.[24] The *Times* said that Cuomo's "proposals dealt with some of the most critical problems identified by the commission without adopting some of the strongest measures it indicated."[25] As before, newspapers were full of speculation and anticipation and the "theoretical reactions of almost all of the 14 groups *The Times* said had been formed [in response to the commission report] represent the true views of Adirondackers."[26] The delay in producing the 1991 budget opened a window filled with two months of speculation and some wild guesses, one of which was that Cuomo would dump seven members of the park agency, all those whose terms had expired.

The Blue Line Council prepared a report entitled "A Moderate Approach to State Land Acquisition in the Adirondacks" and sent it to Governor Cuomo, hoping its ideas would make their way into legislation. The paper recommended the state curtail large land acquisitions in favor of easements or land exchanges, consult with local governments on possible acquisitions, ban eminent domain, maintain existing state-owned lands before adding more, and find means of paying for acquisition other than bond acts.[27] This report elicited a sharp response from Adirondack Council that correctly disputed the figure—60 percent—given in the report for percentage of land owned by the state.

The 1991 legislative session ended without passage of any Adirondack bills or introduction of Cuomo's legislation. The blizzard of speculative articles continued until Cuomo finally released his bill at an Adirondack North Country Association luncheon in October 1991, with the expectation that it would be introduced in the 1992 legislative session. In his speech, the governor appealed to all sides: "I do not wish to end the conflict by diminishing the Park's incomparable value to anyone as wilderness, as a recreational paradise, and as a place to live and work. I want to build consensus based on a sense of obligation to give future New Yorkers of diverse interests an Adirondack Park that they value as much as we."[28]

Cuomo's proposed bill for 1992 was accompanied by estimates for its implementation, and the largest sums were to come from a proposed environmental trust fund that would provide relief for owners of timber tracts through a sort of easement program, which initially met with approval from the forestry industry. Other funds would be used to attract businesses to the park's hamlets. Upstate newspapers carried a detailed question-and-answer news release explaining the bill. Unlike the Hinchey bill, Cuomo's would not combine DEC's

Regions 5 and 6, because "a strong case for restructuring had not been made."[29] The governor held an unprecedented meeting with the staff of the *Adirondack Daily Enterprise* to promote his legislation, saying he liked the way the commission report was put together and that it was beautiful and useful. Cuomo's bill said nothing about things that might have been beneficial to North Country residents such as health care and education. DEC deputy commissioner Bob Bendick expanded on the bill's Adirondack North Country Authority, which would bring economic benefits to the region. He hoped it would alleviate the hostility that had greeted earlier proposals. But after an initial, very brief period of tentative acceptance, legislators and upstaters pounced on the bill's proposals for strengthening zoning along waterfronts and roadsides. Assemblyman Ortloff focused on waterfront controls, saying that new building is not the problem, that existing septic systems are the root of water quality problems. (This issue has never been addressed parkwide, even with the new guidelines for septic systems prepared by the agency in 1999. They are just that—guidelines, suggestions for local codes, not regulations.) Ortloff's concerns ignored the aesthetic aspects of both Cuomo's and the commission's waterfront regulations.

Many environmental groups and former members of the commission were mildly pleased with the bill. At first the *Enterprise* editorialized that the bill was quite positive and called Cuomo's position "the true voice of moderation in the Adirondack debate."[30] But the next day that paper began to find faults—"the bill is vague."[31] The Adirondack Planning Commission reversed its initial favorable opinion of the bill. Suddenly, the Inter County Legislative Committee, which had created the Adirondack Planning Commission, took off after the APC on the grounds that APC was criticizing the legislation and speaking out without telling the Inter County group what it was doing.[32] Further, the Inter County group thought the APC was going beyond its charge to support local governments in getting land use plans and map amendments. The Inter County group said, "We aren't being represented; we have no input."[33]

Critics saw the hand of Adirondack Park Agency's executive director, Robert Glennon, in the bill. Glennon's work on earlier bills was acknowledged; he was the principal author of the 1990 legislation. Glennon spoke favorably about the most recent bill's measure "to get APA out of the settled areas of the Park."[34] He and representatives of the governor met with many different groups to help them understand Cuomo's very complicated bill.[35] At a meeting with Local Government Review Board, Glennon admitted, "more work and input on the bill is needed."[36]

Planning board representatives from the towns of North Elba, Altamont, and Harrietstown met to study the bill and agreed to band together to fight it. The APC sought concessions on four major points that were not spelled out in the bill to the APC's satisfaction: the appointment of locally selected representatives to the APA; specifics to balance APA's guidelines with respect to economic, social, and cultural considerations in the permit process; erosion of local control over permits; and giving APA responsibility for some things currently under the control of DEC.[37] Adirondack Council's publication "Windows on the Park: Scenic Vistas of the Adirondacks" was thought to have influenced the governor to designate areas within one-eighth mile of all roads except village roads as critical environmental areas as a means of controlling strip development. Local responses focused on this as one of the bigger problems with the Cuomo bill; they saw it as hurting local economies and taking away controls they thought they were entitled to. (Oddly enough, in late 1999, Senator Stafford started talking about the ugliness of some Adirondack roadsides. He even secured a million-dollar member item to assist local communities in cleaning up roadsides. Where was he in 1991?)

Peter S. Paine Jr., who has known Stafford since he came into the senate in 1966 and has been his friend much of that time, believes Stafford could have stepped back from day-to-day fights and found a way to help the Adirondacks, perhaps exchanging "benefits for local economy, schools, and necessary things for environmental controls . . . he should not have fought the environmentalists. Stafford was so busy lining up with the least common denominator of local government that he failed to serve as well as he could." Paine told me he had had long conversations with Stafford and came to believe Stafford was never going to change his stance regarding environmentalists and regulations.[38]

The tourist industry criticized the bill as not being supportive. Developers were "dismayed" by the bill. Five national environmental groups urged the governor not to knuckle under to development interests. Representatives of more than a dozen groups, all with different agendas, met four times over the fall to discuss the proposed legislation, but failed to reach any consensus, mostly because they could not agree on the local representation issue.[39] Assemblyman Ortloff gave the governor "A for effort" but said the bill needed a lot of work. The governor indicated to the APC that he would be willing to bend on some issues, but opposition was coalescing.

Finally, as 1991 was drawing to a close, Cuomo's staff told the APC that the governor had agreed in concept to change his legislation in three major areas: the land-use authority of local governments would be expanded; a procedure for picking park representatives for the Adirondack Park Agency would be spelled out; and environmental criteria use by APA would be balanced by concerns for economic, social, and cultural interests.[40]

Meanwhile, in the fall of 1991, debates continued over whether there was a development crisis in the Resource Management and Rural Use areas of the park. Certainly building had slowed because the economy was slowing. Residents' Committee to Protect the Adirondacks put together a report entitled "Subdivision and Development Trends in the Adirondack Park," using data from the 21st Century Commission and the park agency. The report indicated that growth was more widespread than other studies had indicated, mostly because so much development occurs without having either APA or local permits.

Adirondack Fairness Coalition's fall 1991 report echoed many of the issues the Region 5 committee had wrestled with: How much land is enough for the state to own? Where are the maps indicating what the state already owns? Are the needs of the disabled being met?[41] Fred Monroe, who had been most responsible for trying to place the Fairness Coalition in the middle ground in the debates, announced he would run for supervisor of the Town of Chester, and Andy Halloran sought public office in Minerva.

For months, Adirondack Solidarity Alliance had been trying to raise funds so residents could defend their property rights against state regulations. Volunteers labored to build a log cabin on donated land, using some donated materials. Their raffle sold two thousand tickets at $50 each, netting ASA about $80,000.[42]

Also in the fall of 1991, the Northern Forest Lands Council (NFLC) scheduled a meeting with local officials at Ray Brook to hear a discussion of proposed federal legislation that would create a nonregulatory body to promote "traditional use of forests in the four northeastern states." Protesters, under the impression that a federal land grab was about to occur, forced the council to delay its meeting. This was, as Gerdts predicted, the first of many protests against the NFLC. Protesters preferred to misunderstand the council's activities and powers in an effort to oppose it.

In September 1991 Adirondack Park Agency member Liz Thorndike called together more than fifty representatives of groups interested in the future of the Adirondacks in an effort to find common ground. Discussions ranged from the reasons for so much hostility and the "us-them" mentality within the park to the sources of fear with respect to the commission report. Only two groups refused the invitation to attend, the Adirondack Planning Commission and Gerdts's Citizens Council. Those attending the first Park Planning Committee's Public Issues Forum were sufficiently pleased by progress that more meetings were scheduled. Thorndike said she felt it was one of the most important things she was able to do during her tenure in the agency.

Alliance for America

Also in the early fall of 1991, a major initiative occurred among several more active members of the groups opposed to the commission report, those who saw that opposition as a part of the property rights movement. Dave Howard and Carol LaGrasse and others were recruited by "grassroots leaders from all over the United States" to attend a get-acquainted meeting in Washington organized by the Oregon Lands Coalition.[43] This meeting was followed in November by a fly-in in St. Louis. Funds for the fly-in came from several sources, notably the timber industry on the West Coast and the cattle industry in the Southwest. The West Coast people did not want it to appear that they controlled the meeting, which resulted in the formation of the Alliance for America. Bleecker's Dave Howard was elected the group's first president. Howard, a contractor who had been active in local improvement issues when he first moved to the area, later changed his perspective dramatically, strongly embracing property rights. He was recognized for his organizational abilities, but also for his home base, which fulfilled the westerners' desire for representation in the Northeast.

A year later, the Alliance for America convened a second Fly-in for Freedom at which a flag, bearing Adirondack Solidarity's red horse symbol, advertised the Adirondack Rebellion to the nationwide rally of property rights organizations.[44] In the intervening year, the national group had achieved all the goals of its first meeting: representation from grassroots organizations in all fifty states and a computer-driven communication system (this nationwide fax system, the work of Harry MacIntosh, according to Sierra Club "boggles the mind" in its sophistication.[45]). The group also wanted to be in a position to challenge the election of members of Congress whose positions were inimical to the Alliance, to achieve recognition in the national press, and to be able to reach members of Congress and state legislatures on a regular basis. Through this period, Alliance funding came from the "Moon-affiliated (Rev. Sun Myung Moon) American Freedom Coalition, American Farm Bureau Association, Cattlemens Association, American Mining Congress, Chemical Manufacturers Association, Petroleum Institute, and several other industry groups."[46]

Gerdts, too, was directing his efforts elsewhere. With Carol LaGrasse and Keith Van Buskirk, Gerdts formed a new group, the Property Rights Congress (variously Council) of America. The trio had gone to Washington the previous October to lobby against the Forest Legacy legislation, which had created the

Northern Forest Lands Council. They had the support of Representative Gerald Solomon, who had attached an amendment to the act that allowed local New York governments to opt out of the program. Emboldened by this support, Gerdts made plans to open an office in Washington.

The next year in April that group issued a position paper, "Indictment of Government." It was a statement of past achievements and a tirade against national environmental groups and the Northern Forest Lands Council. The sixty-page report, which reflects the writing style and thinking of Carol LaGrasse, addressed the environmental movement in the Adirondacks and listed twenty-nine state, federal, and United Nations programs affecting the region. Every one of these programs was described as a potential threat to the property rights of Adirondackers. The manifesto also outlined the group's "PLAN OF ATTACK" to "restore our rights" through lawsuits, a media blitz, and citizens' meetings. Its press releases were aimed at several environmental groups, but its strongest attacks were against National Audubon.[47]

Gerdts said he had taken the Property Rights Council to Washington, D.C., because he was disgusted by disunity among the "self-serving leaders of Adirondack property rights organizations"[48] and because he felt that bickering among property rights and home rule advocates in the park had made it impossible to make progress.

In just two years Gerdts had masterminded the most amazing campaign against every aspect of park regulation, but as he was preparing to leave it was becoming obvious that the groups he marshaled were never as large as he claimed.[49] Throughout this period, only a few letters to local papers criticized Gerdts and his tactics. Was he the pied piper of the park? Or, were people too afraid to oppose him?

15 | Still Trying for Legislation
1992

THE LEGISLATION CUOMO OUTLINED at the Adirondack North Country Association meeting in October 1991 entered 1992 with a new name, Cuomo's "study" bill, and with many hinted-at revisions. Cuomo delayed introducing his revised legislation through the spring of 1992 because hearings on the Open Space plan were taking center stage and because, as usual, the budget was late. As the deadline, April 7, approached for submitting bills to the legislature's rules committee, speculation increased concerning just how much it would be modified. Cuomo's spokesman said the governor would make that deadline. Parenthetically, Gerdts' Property Rights Council had announced it would issue its "Indictment of Government by the People of the Adirondacks" by the same date, April 7. Gerdts met the deadline, but Cuomo's bill missed it.

Stafford's "Abolish the APA" bill remained on the senate's calendar, reminding everyone that any legislation that would be more restrictive than the status quo had little chance of passage. Undeterred, Hinchey and Assembly Speaker Saul Weprin introduced a comprehensive park bill that was supported by all environmental groups and condemned by elected officials and property rights people as being too close to the 21st Century report.[1] A spokesperson for Stafford indicated that Hinchey's second bill would have no better chance than his first.[2]

In the first half of 1992, the interval before any legislative action on park legislation could be expected, numerous magazine and newspaper articles and editorials appeared. Not all supported Cuomo's proposals, but most gave them fair consideration. Some, as in *Adirondack Life,* reached a fairly broad audience. DEC Commissioner Jorling used the department's *Conservationist* magazine to detail a vision for the park. Simple, modestly eloquent, and concise, it should have been effective in inspiring those who cared about the park to be more receptive to new legislation.[3] Adirondack Mountain Club's director of conservation, Neil Woodworth, analyzed the bill's proposals for that club's audience and found them generally favorable.[4]

Senator Stafford introduced a bill to require DEC to keep the Crane Pond Road open permanently. This was a one-house bill, which had no chance of passage even though it achieved a 45 to 0 vote in the senate. It was typical of the practice followed by legislators who want to show constituents support for an issue while making sure it cannot happen. In noting Stafford's action, Donald Gerdts commented, "That's traditionally what Stafford has been doing for 27 years."[5] This time Gerdts was not exaggerating.

May 1992 marked the official centennial celebration, and almost every article describing the event reminded readers that the park's beginning came out of a struggle between commerce and preservation and that the struggle continues. The *New York Times* noted the beauty of the park and the fact that the park was in better shape than it was when it was established. Tempering the celebration were the remarks of the region's perennial pessimist; Glennon said, "The scheme of the present statute [the APA Act] guarantees the ultimate destruction of the Adirondack Park and anoints us to preside over it[s destruction]."[6]

Cuomo met with the Adirondack Planning Commission and local government officials to brief them on his revised legislation the day before the contents were revealed to the public and two days before Cuomo spoke at the official centennial celebration at Blue Mountain Lake. To deal with the thorny issue of agency membership, the bill proposed creating an advisory council of local and statewide representatives to advise the governor on the five in-park appointments. The bill still contained strong protection for lakeshores, roadsides, and the backcountry. Cuomo used his speech at the Adirondack Museum at Blue Mountain Lake to make a strong appeal for passage of his legislation. He also announced that NIMO was selling eighteen miles of Hudson River shoreline between Warrensburg and Hadley to the state. There were no pickets at the celebration, but so many blackflies that the audience was suffering visibly—the tent holding the attending crowd seemed to trap the insects. In introducing the governor I said I hoped the flies would keep the speeches short. Cuomo started his speech by saying "the blackflies don't have the same effect on me as on you. I have been giving speeches in Albany surrounded by 211 legislators for years and years so I can survive the blackflies."[7]

Responses to Cuomo's bill, dubbed a watered-down version of his fall draft, were predictable and immediate. Empire State Forest Products Association, possibly at the urging of Finch, Pruyn's president, R. J. Carota, found fault with it. Both the Adirondack Planning Commission and the Blue Line Council came out against the study bill because their representatives believed it fell short of its goal of striking a balance between the environment and the economy of the park. Andrew Halloran, Fairness Coalition's vice chairman, said the more he studied the bill, the more outrageous some of its proposals seemed. He expressed a sentiment that was frequently mentioned by many people whom I interviewed for this book: "The preservationists and the state are like wolves who will keep coming back to get another piece of the park."[8] Peter Allen of the Fairness Coalition articulated another theme that I kept hearing during many of my 1999 interviews: "If people are not a part of the environment, then we don't have an environment, we have exclusionism."[9] Dick Purdue suggested an alternate way to solve the problem of local representation on the Adirondack Park Agency—using the Region 5 Open Space Plan membership model (one-half local government)—but no one rushed to support his idea.

When it became obvious that this bill would have no more support from Stafford than its predecessors, nine environmental groups attacked Stafford's "record of abuse" in the park and urged Senator Majority Leader Marino to "break the legislative logjam."[10] The *New York Times* reiterated this theme in an editorial that castigated Marino for believing Adirondack issues were "regional issues, best left to local residents and their champion, Mr. Stafford."[11] In an interview with the *Post Star*'s editorial board, Stafford said he thought that existing land use regulations would one day be found excessive and overturned by the courts. "It's equity and fairness, I try to be reasonable."[12] (He used the same words in an interview with me in 1999 in answer to questions about his stance on Adirondack legislation in general.)

Indian Lake supervisor Purdue sent a letter to Stafford, which was printed in several upstate papers, lashing out at the senator's stubbornness in refusing to negotiate with Governor Cuomo.[13] Purdue also criticized Stafford for saying that it was all right for him to oppose Cuomo's legislation, but that it was unacceptable that Stafford did not use his power to speed up negotiations.[14] Local government leaders, fearful of such overt criticism of Stafford, suggested Purdue ought to resign from the APC.[15]

Time was running out for legislative passage of Cuomo's bill, but the delays only gave more time for opposition to be heard. The Adirondack Regional Tourism Council led a chorus of criticism that included Assemblyman Ortloff and seven other minority members who represented the park. By the time that Empire State Forest Products Association weighed in against the bill, as did the Fairness Coalition, its demise was sealed. The *Legislative Gazette* reported that talks between the Adirondack Planning Commission and Cuomo's staff were continuing, but Purdue saw distrust and misunderstanding between the negotiators.

In mid-June the Democratically controlled assembly passed Cuomo's bill by a margin of 104 to 35. The next day sixteen Adirondack groups sponsored a rally in Albany billed as a tribute to Stafford, honoring him as "Adirondack Man of the Year." With the exception of a minor confrontation between John Sheehan of Adirondack Council and Calvin Carr of Solidarity Alliance, the motorcade through Albany and the rally on the steps of the capitol was peaceful, if lacking in taste. Don Sage, whose dominance of Adirondack Conservation Council was to continue for almost a decade, spoke at the rally, calling Cuomo, Jorling, Purdue, and others "social retards."

In the firestorm of protest that followed assembly passage of the bill, the Adirondack Planning Commission began to break apart as Warren and Clinton counties withdrew, "partly because of the controversial leadership of its chairman, Dick Purdue," and partly because "Purdue's public criticism of Senator Stafford did not reflect the views of their county representatives." [16] Purdue responded to Clinton County's action by saying, "Adirondackers are in the habit of having primitive, ritualistic responses, rather than thinking through issues." [17] Purdue sent a more reflective letter to the *Daily Enterprise,* but even that was highly critical of Stafford; Purdue called him the pied piper of the Adirondacks for blocking all Adirondack legislation and leading elected officials who "follow the piper without a moment of independent consideration." [18] However, today, people who served on the Adirondack Planning Commission or the Inter County group remembered that the single most important reason that they were upset with Purdue had to do with his failure to keep them informed of what he was doing. [19]

Purdue sees the demise of Adirondack Planning Commission as stemming from the fact that "elected officials on the commission [APC] had no interest in a negotiated settlement. The closer we came to agreement . . . the more elected officials became fearful that a deal might be struck." At the last minute, he believes the governor's office and some of the environmentalists "bypassed the Planning Commission in favor of the Senator. . . . [And what happened] was the scorn of the Senator and the immediate and total collapse of [APC]." [20] Purdue remains bitter about Flacke's role in establishing the APC, backed by Finch, Pruyn and Mark Behan, in such a way that its establishment was "designed to subvert" its proposed role. [21] He is still angry with what he believes was Neil Woodworth's role in bringing Stafford into the final negotiations and the way it resulted in the demise of APC.

Purdue withdrew from political life shortly afterward, recalling later, "Stafford's withholding and prospective withholding of member items influenced my decision to retire. His power over member items has much to do with the slavish attention he receives from Adirondack elected officials generally." [22]

In an op-ed piece in the *New York Times,* John Oakes said, "The 100th birthday celebration of the Adirondack Park may yet be turned into a wake. . . . Yet New York voters don't have a clue about what is going on." [23]

The senate took no action on the Cuomo bill, thus killing it. Frank Murray moved on to head the State Energy Office, but recalled with chagrin the failure of the Cuomo bill, which happened, "in retrospect, because Ron Stafford didn't want it to happen." Murray also bemoaned "the evisceration of the planning commission." [24]

Even though Cuomo failed in his efforts to get his Adirondack legislation through the 1992 session, he was able to secure approval of agency appointments for John Ryder (Lake George), Barbara Sweet (Newcomb), and Jim Frenette (Tupper Lake). Frenette's evenhanded work on the Adirondack Planning Commission made him acceptable to most people. The appointment went through even though Cuomo had stated that "Republicans in the Senate have declared war on ecology." [25]

The senate's action not only defeated the Adirondack bill, it killed a bill establishing an environmental trust fund, financed through existing taxes on beer and soda containers. The fund would have been used for land conservation and solid-waste management, and its death was attributed to an amendment put forward by senators Stafford and Cook that would prohibit the fund from being used on nearly all land purchases in the Adirondacks and Catskills, purchases that had been on the list approved by the recently released Open Space Plan. [26] Neil Woodworth of Adirondack Mountain Club was quoted as saying, "They've made Swiss cheese out of the state open space plan. This is two people holding hostage the needs of the entire state." [27] Also dead were Stafford's Crane Pond Road bill, his legislation allowing residents to take downed trees from the Forest Preserve, and an assembly measure that would improve assessment practices regarding easements.

Support for a locally designed Adirondack bill brought the response from Cuomo that he would consider such a measure. Howard Aubin of Solidarity Alliance proposed an office of ombudsman to assure that residents would be treated fairly by the park agency. Dean Lefebvre of Altamont proposed an Adirondack Congress.

Association of Adirondack Towns and Villages

The Inter County Legislative Committee began to plan for a summit meeting of Adirondack town, village, and county officials.[28] First planned for November, the congress was held on December 12 at Adirondack Park Agency's visitor interpretive center at Newcomb. Out of that meeting came the formation of the Association of Adirondack Towns and Villages (AATV), a group that has met regularly to the present (2001). Led by Edinburgh supervisor Jean Raymond, Horican supervisor Jean Olson, and Newcomb supervisor George Canon, the seventy representatives at first showed a remarkable measure of unity.

Indian Lake supervisor Dick Purdue, whose work with the Adirondack Planning Commission had been so roundly criticized by some of those present, "liked the quality and spirit of the first meeting." But it soon became evident that this man who tried to find a middle ground was totally defeated. The backstage manipulations were heartbreaking to Purdue, and in later years he would become very bitter about the experience.

Meanwhile, the opposition tried other tactics. Carol LaGrasse, Gerdts, and Keith Van Buskirk of Queensbury filed two lawsuits in mid-1992. One was against Cuomo for "unconstitutional delay in appointing members of the Agency." At that point all private-citizen members were serving on expired terms, some up to eight years beyond the end date of their terms. The three litigants not only lost this suit, the decision in the case defined the law in a way that was totally opposite: The judge ruled that members could sit on the agency until they are replaced.[29]

They also sued Adirondack Park Agency members individually for damages from actions taken by the agency, alleging illegal permit and enforcement conditions in thirty-two cases. The state supreme court dismissed the latter suit because plaintiffs did not have legal standing—they were not directly affected by the APA's regulatory decisions.[30] The extraordinary amount of documentation amassed for the suit contrasts with the simple legal technicality that defeated it.

In pursuing their lawsuit in state supreme court, Gerdts, La Grasse, and Van Buskirk asked court permission to depose eighty-three individuals, including APA members and reporters for upstate papers, who would be questioned about the influence of environmental groups on news coverage.[31] Gerdts had served the suit on APA members during an APA meeting amidst lights and television cameras. At the dismissal, Glennon said he wished the "cameras were rolling" in the courtroom.[32]

Persons unknown carried out several acts of violence during the 1992 summer, including the torching of APA member Anne LaBastille's barn. Governor Cuomo directed state officials to investigate this and other events aggressively. In a letter to Stafford asking for his support in condemning acts of violence, Cuomo listed this and nine other events that had occurred in the past two years, including the firing of three shots at APA staffers and the suspicious burning of Dean Cook's office in Ticonderoga (the dentist was on Adirondack Council's board).[33] Stafford and Local Government Review Board both joined the governor in his condemnation of violent acts.

Herb London, a dean at New York University and Conservative Party candidate for governor in 1990, appeared with Gerdts at an Albany conference touting property rights. Newspapers reported that London was uncomfortable with some of the language used by Gerdts and LaGrasse (such as accusing government officials of terrorism and cultural genocide).[34]

16 | Aftermath
1993

ASSEMBLYMAN RICHARD BRODSKY'S APPOINTMENT to the Environmental Conservation Committee at the beginning of 1993, after Hinchey's election to Congress, brought expectations that Brodsky would introduce park legislation. He did, thus pleasing environmentalists. Cuomo's legislation was also expected to be reintroduced, and prospects of debate on the issue brought new hopes for Adirondack legislation.

The governor's State of the State address included an olive branch to local governments—requests for funding for the Local Government Review Board (after twenty years it was still being funded by contributions from Adirondack counties) and for local planning assistance grants. Cuomo said he had learned a great deal from the past year's negotiations and would apply his knowledge to revising legislation. He said it would focus on protecting large, privately owned backcountry landholdings. Stafford seemed to agree when he commented that "Eighty percent of the private land in the park is owned by about 15 corporations or individuals, accounting for about 2.5 million acres. If these parcels are broken up, then we stand to lose the character of the park."[1]

Despite the addition of Frenette and Sweet to the Adirondack Park Agency and John Collins's appointment as chairman, the first resolution passed by Association of Adirondack Towns and Villages (AATV) called for the governor to pick the park's five representatives from a list that the group would prepare. AATV also requested a dedicated fund to pay for state-mandated environmental actions relating to solid waste and water filtration. Support for the environmental trust fund was given only if land acquisition was omitted from the act and if any acquisitions by the state were contingent on a list of criteria (actually the one prepared by the Region 5 Open Space Committee). Another resolution asked the assembly to reconsider the recently passed Brodsky bill.

It did not take long for discontent to swirl around the AATV. Paul Maroun of Tupper Lake wanted the group to oppose any purchases of land by the state, something termed "unrealistic" by Jean Raymond: "It's impossible to stop someone from selling land to the state if they want to."[2] The work of the Open Space Committee to define a method for the state to use eminent domain and to permit approved land acquisitions had not been in vain. Raymond's statements, trying to influence the AATV, are one of the many small but very important achievements the Region 5 committee added to its major success in defining eminent domain so that it remains a tool that can be used by the state.

Hurting Adirondack Park Agency more than threats to abolish it or failure to give it more authority were the cuts that had been enacted in its staff. Some resulted from state budget tightening in general, but Stafford consistently opposed any increases.

Cuomo did put forward one more Adirondack bill, his third. It proposed allowing hamlet areas to expand while restricting development in backcountry and along shorelines. It would accomplish backcountry protection by offering a tax abatement program that would help large landowners protect their property from development. This bill was drafted by Richard Persico, with help from Tom Ulasewicz, at the request of Frank Murray and Joe Martens, who told the authors to keep it simple but to address both backcountry and shoreline protection.[3]

This new bill reached a pinnacle of disfavor. Ulasewicz thought it was constructed to offer "a graceful way for everyone to say 'no.' "[4] It did produce unanimity for the first time. The Blue Line Council and others objected on the grounds of local representation on the APA. Environmentalists thought it would not offer enough protection, although they found parts of the bill they liked. The AATV made plans for five regional meetings at which each region would nominate three names for membership on the APA; one region comprised of Franklin and Clinton counties already had a suitable representative in Frenette. The Hamilton and Fulton County meeting approved the 1993 appointment of Dick Lefebvre to the agency; he would later be appointed chairman.

A May meeting between the AATV and Glennon, Jorling, Bendick, Collins, and Martens did not change AATV's opposition to Cuomo's bill, although Hamilton County supervisors later voted to ask Stafford to initiate talks with Cuomo on the legislation.

What strikes me most when looking back at the four years of debate over legislation to improve the APA Act is that talks focused on finding a balance between protection and use. I think the fundamental question should have been

"How do people fit in the park?" Shouldn't a vision for the park define the park's ecosystem in terms that included people's presence? Despite charges to the contrary, everyone but a handful of opponents spoke of wanting to protect the park; it is just that their visions for what protection meant were so different.

In 1993 Stafford and senate Republicans proposed an Environmental Trust Fund (ETF) with one hundred million dollars to come from general state revenue. Environmentalists were opposed because it would not permit acquisitions in the Adirondack Park, except the Follensby Pond tract and the Morgan property on Lake George, which the Open Space Committee had approved. Initially Stafford gave support to a trust fund as long as it did not involve new taxes, but he was criticized by many of his supporters for being open to any fund that provided money for land acquisition.

Purdue and Long Lake supervisor John Hosley held a press conference to dispel the myth that Adirondackers are opposed to any land acquisition; they supported sales by willing sellers that were approved by the town involved.

The *New York Times* profiled Senator Stafford with the subhead "when Senator Stafford says not in my district, a whole state goes without."[5] Stafford ultimately opposed the trust fund on the grounds it would generate money for acquisitions within the park. His opposition would also prevent acquisitions of pine barren tracts on Long Island and many other purchases identified in the Open Space Plan. This inspired a *Times* op-ed piece by John Oakes, in which he blamed Senator Marino for allowing Stafford to stop acquisitions within the park and elsewhere because Marino had given "Stafford the Adirondacks as his political fiefdom."[6]

After another month of wrangling, at the very end of the 1993 session, the legislature finally approved an Environmental Protection Fund to be funded by a real estate transfer tax. The concession that brought the approval of the EPF was that the fund could be used only for the seventy-five projects listed in the Open Space Plan or for other projects where cities, town, or villages involved would have ninety days to veto such acquisitions.[7] This was the proposal that the Region 5 group had fought for almost since its inception. The fund would provide $26 million the first year and $96 million annually by 1996. The bill also required the state to pay its full share of all taxes for the conservation easements owned by the state. The number of groups upset by Stafford's apparent shift with respect to land acquisition was reduced to property rights groups and Change NY, an organization concerned with the fiscal implications of legislation. The Northern Forest Lands Council reported that between 1980 and 1991 only 4 percent of the large tracts of forestland sold in the park were slated for development.[8] The Blue Line Council said this exposed the big lie perpetuated by the Commission on the Adirondacks in the 21st Century that the park was being chopped up at an alarming rate.[9]

In an interview in early 2000, Ross Whaley spoke about the workings of the Commission on the Adirondacks in the 21st Century, which had spawned those five years of tumult. His perspective seems to best sum up what happened. Whaley, who had been on many commissions in his long career, told me that he felt more intellectually engaged by the 21st Century Commission than by any other. He now believes that the threats to backcountry, which were at the core of the rationale for having the commission, were real, but extremely exaggerated; talk of "total build-out was nonsense." However, he believes that he, along with Davis and Berle, the three having the greatest experience with the public (Davis with RARE2*) "should have known better, should have given more attention to public input." In addition to his concerns with the map, he felt that the 21st Century Commission report itself was insensitively presented. "It implied judgement of life styles. It was negative in that it was written from a premise of disaster."

Gerdts's attempts to garner support from Washington sources apparently fizzled. He faced bankruptcy in the Adirondacks and in 1994 moved to a farm in Virginia. He died in April 2000 at the age of 61, still supporting, according to his daughter, his opposition to land-use regulation. However, no evidence has been uncovered to indicate that he was active in those six years in any national land-rights organization. When he died, Adirondackers whom he had tried to lead were already disavowing his efforts. Judy Ford of Adirondack Solidarity Alliance said, "I don't feel he was a leader of the people up here. . . . Early on people realized he wasn't overly sensitive to the issues we cared about." She said Gerdts had made their work "much harder because of the rhetoric and tone he used."[10] He certainly made it impossible for people with differing views to talk about Adirondack issues.

Could the total debacle have been avoided had Peter Berle and George Davis not left the scene so quickly after the report was finished? Davis had bigger challenges and plainly wanted to get on with them. Berle clearly felt his job was finished, although many insiders including Paul Bray have told me that Berle was warned that he should be available for a continuing role or at least for

* Roadless Area Review and Evaluation, a process developed under direction by Congress and published in 1977 by the U.S. Forest Service to "identify roadless and undeveloped land in the National Forest System and to determine their general uses for both wilderness and other resource management and development."

developing a strategy that would get the report across. And, in a way he did, launching, as the next chapter shows, a program through Audubon to support the APA, if not specifically the commission's report.

Cuomo's role remains an enigma. There are those who believe that the governor was more troubled by the cost of programs that would support the commission's recommendations than he was by the controversy surrounding them. John Stock compared the goals of the Temporary Study Commission to those of the Commission on the Adirondacks in the 21st Century and noted that fully a third of the TSC's recommendations that were not carried out required legislative appropriations. A quarter, sixty, of the commission's recommendations also would need specific allocations. Stock suggested that the budgets of just two of the environmental groups pushing acceptance of the commission's work would cover those sixty items.[11]

Whether it was the state's fiscal problems or opposition in the senate, Cuomo's last years in office were reduced to marking time. He seemed to have been able to do very little for the Adirondacks.

In the aftermath of the 21st Century Commission report, the legislature never passed any specific Adirondack legislation. (The EPF covered the entire state.) The grand scheme became a great fiasco. Frank Murray believes the result was "an example of splinter politics that is more pervasive today (1999) than earlier, where any single group can stop what a group of organizations agree to bring forward." In that respect the 21st Century Commission set a terrible precedent for the future. But in the strange way of politics, the next chapter will show how many of the goals of the commission were achieved in the 1990s, even if the specific recommendations were not always followed. And it will show that it was the people in the park that made most things happen, not branches of government.

PART THREE | *Issues and Activities of the 1990s*

ISSUES OF THE 1990S *include landfills, boathouses, communication towers, the agency's model waste-water treatment regulations, DEC's regulations for snowmobiles and the use of motor vehicles in the Forest Preserve, simplification of the agency's rules and regulations, proposals to build more prisons in the Adirondacks, restoration of wolves, control of jet skis, response to the blowdown of 1995, the issuance of the High Peaks Unit Management Plan, completion of all unit management plans, access to the Forest Preserve for the disabled, easements to protect land from development, acquisition of land for the Forest Preserve, and classification of those new state lands. A few issues in this part are new to the 1990s. Quite a few are not visited in this book, some because there are just too many topics, others because they are not critical to understanding the difficulties of solving problems that confront the Adirondacks.*

The descriptions are separated into three chapters. The first two, chapters 17 and 18, concern government agencies and activities. Chapter 19—"Where Are They Now?"—brings issues or organizations from the past through the 1990s. This chapter division underscores the level of progress toward park goals as outlined both by the Temporary Study Commission and by the Commission on the Adirondacks in the 21st Century. The commission goals that needed government action have generally not been attained; the goals that involved different facets of the public are slowly happening. As you read this part, I hope you will consider the multiplicity of important issues, their complexity, and their relationship to public involvement and to the government agencies that are designated to deal with them. When people get involved things can happen, but when public participation is carried out through poorly led governmental advisory committees, successful outcomes are not assured.

17 | State Government Activities in the 1990s

Introduction to the 1990s Political Structure

GOVERNOR CUOMO CONTINUED in office through 1994. The resignation of Tom Ulasewicz as executive director of the Adirondack Park Agency brought about chief counsel Robert Glennon's appointment as executive director in 1989. John Collins became chairman, succeeding Woody Cole. Collins's appointment came at the end of 1992, but his term began at the start of 1993. The Collins-Glennon era was short, 1993–95, but, as this chapter shows, environmentalists considered it a pinnacle of environmental protection for the park.

Langdon Marsh replaced the retiring Thomas Jorling at DEC for the last six months of Cuomo's term, but Jorling had the longest term (seven years) as DEC commissioner since the DEC was formed in 1970.

George Pataki's election as governor in 1994 brought dramatic changes in both agencies. Greg Campbell, Republican faithful from Plattsburgh, became APA chairman in 1995. He was much more of a political player than any of his predecessors. Campbell instigated Glennon's replacement by Daniel Fitts, a protégé of Senator Ron Stafford. A power struggle surrounded Glennon's successor, and Karyn Richards became co-chairman with Fitts. This unstable arrangement ended in 1999 when she returned to DEC to take charge of unit management planning.

Campbell was a controversial choice for agency chairman. Adirondack Council found many of his actions to be examples of why he should be replaced and the result was a breach between the council and the agency. Campbell tried to take the agency out of regulating the Essex County Landfill. In addition to upsetting Pataki, Campbell was said to have fought with Stafford.

In January 1998, when Campbell succumbed to criticism of his ability to manage the agency and resigned as chairman, his departure was made easier by

his appointment as a special assistant to the Empire State Development Corporation. The issues that probably brought him down were accusations that he
had altered minutes of APA meetings to cover up an alleged mishandling of
steps to lessen clearcutting requirements. "His resignation ended a tumultuous
relationship with environmental advocates, legislators and even agency staff." [1]
John Sheehan of Adirondack Council said it most directly: "We've had to drag
the chairman, kicking and screaming, to enforce the legislative mandates for the
park agency." [2] Six months later the state's Inspector General's office found no
evidence against Campbell on claims of misconduct. [3] The state's inspector general later rebuked both Campbell and former APA Attorney James Marrin:
Marrin for trying to introduce a change in "shelterwood" cutting rules in 1997
through an inappropriate process and Campbell for "failure of leadership for
not correcting the situation." [4] Marrin, who had been fired, admitted that the
shelterwood proposal had been developed primarily by staff because it was
thought to be a " 'non-controversial' means of promoting a Pataki administration objective—to cut government regulation." [5]

In his first appointments to the agency, Pataki replaced two strong environmentalists, Thorndike and Paine, with Eleanor Brown and Katie Roberts. Jean
Read Knox replaced Arthur Savage, but only for a short time. It was not until
1999 that Pataki made in-park appointments: Frank Mezzano and later William
Kissell. This action did not address some Adirondackers' desire for local representation on the park agency.

In 1998 agency member Richard Lefebvre became chairman, replacing
Campbell. That appointment was greeted by most APA watchers as a positive
move, bringing "a voice of reason" to the agency. Governor Cuomo appointed
Lefebvre to the agency in 1993 (he was confirmed in 1994). When he was reappointed in 1997 by Pataki, Lefebvre received backing from the Local Government Review Board. According to John Sheehan, speaking for Adirondack
Council, Lefebvre had been "a real voice of sanity in the park agency during
three very difficult years." [6] His middle-ground stance made him almost a shoo-
in for the chairmanship. Lefebvre quickly became known for his ability to listen,
and he reached out to hear everyone. His prodigious round of meetings and
visits throughout the park demanded a daunting schedule.

Lefebvre has had the opportunity to lead the agency into rewriting rules
and regulations. He has successfully encouraged the governor to enlarge APA's
staff, and the agency finally began to play catch-up on enforcement cases. The
permit process has become more streamlined, more efficient, rarely appearing
as arbitrary as in the past. Lefebvre has done more than any previous commissioner to listen to Adirondackers and to present the agency as a partner in park

preservation and management. It is still not clear whether this will be enough to bring about a partnership between towns and the agency.

A subtle aftereffect of Campbell's tenure was still evident in the dynamics of the agency under Lefebvre. In the early days, agency members, even those with wildly differing perspectives, had a sense of camaraderie, of learning together, of supporting each other. During agency meeting weeks they often ate together, socialized, and came to respect one another. Campbell so alienated some of the agency members that even with the more relaxed atmosphere that surrounds his successor, this esprit de corps has not returned.

The agency under Lefebvre shifted noticeably with Pataki's appointment of lawyers Cecil Wray of Manhattan, Richard Kissel of Lake Placid, and James Townsend of Rochester. Two of the state representatives, Richard Hoffman, designee of the Department of State, and Gregory Cato of the Department of Economic Development, were also lawyers. In 2000 the tone of agency debate became more legalistic as a result of having five lawyers among the eleven members.

The rest of this chapter looks at APA and DEC actions in the 1990s both before and after Pataki's election, with special attention to the way they have changed under the new administration.

Adirondack Park Agency

Gleneagles

In 1989 a Canadian subsidiary of Guinness PLC purchased the deteriorating Lake Placid Club on Mirror Lake and proposed turning it into a five-star resort. The Gleneagles resort was on land classified as Hamlet except for the golf course, which would be redesigned by Jack Nicklaus. Governor Cuomo favored the project as an economic asset for the region. The corporation also planned to construct condominiums, an equestrian center, and large second homes. By the time the project was to have been completed (1993) the corporation would have invested over a hundred million dollars, which would have made it the largest single development in the park. Adirondack Council called the proposals, even with later modifications, "a whale in a bathtub."

Gleneagles had to overcome many hurdles, one of which would have required a change in the state's liquor laws. (The parent corporation was a liquor wholesaler and thus, by law, prohibited from obtaining a liquor license for the resort.) Cuomo did not want to get involved in changing the regulatory process.

The agency had jurisdiction over the golf course and required an Environmental Impact Statement for the improvements there. The detailed application filled four bound volumes, but somehow it was altered before it was given to the agency by those working for the applicant. The agency, for cause, declared that the work was not acceptable and rejected it with the longest incompletion notice ever issued by the agency.

The application process dragged on so long that lawyers for the corporation believed the agency was responsible for the delays. The agency was strongly lobbied behind the scenes by Adirondack Council and others to quash, or reduce the size of, the project. Gleneagles, faced with lost revenue, tried to figure out a way to use part of the resort to generate income. Lawyers for the corporation sought a declaratory ruling that some of the activities were grandfathered because they took place on preexisting facilities. The APA ruled against the corporation on all but two activities, and Gleneagles almost killed the project. The final blow was the bankruptcy of the owner's partner, U.S. Fidelity and Guaranty Corp. (USF&G), the insurance company.

Participants in the negotiations believe the project was torpedoed by APA counsel Glennon's anti-development stance,[7] and that Collins, Paine, and Adirondack Council helped defeat the project. Actually, the project's demise had more to do with the softening economy. (Adirondack Council later encouraged Lake Placid entrepreneurs to obtain the site and develop it much more modestly.)

Local Planning and the APA

Local planning money dried up completely in 1989–90. Local planning staff decreased to one—Jim Hotaling, who remained the sole local planning staffer for over a decade. Hotaling had been hired by Flacke and Persico specifically to save the local planning effort. Between 1977 and 1990, when appropriations for local planning were stopped, Hotaling insisted "that money be spent in towns that wanted to do planning, whether or not they submitted their programs to the agency. . . . This would build a planning base for many towns that was," he thought, "more important than the 'box score' of towns with agency approved plans. With experience more towns will seek agency approval."[8] The box score crept up slowly in the 1990s: Day in 1992, Newcomb in 1993, Willsboro and Westport in 1996, and Edinburg in 1997. The Town of Chesterfield's plan, initiated in 1997, was updated and given agency approval in 2000.

Hotaling believed that there was an upsurge in local planning that began at the end of the 1990s and that most of the later planning was based on inventory work done in earlier years. Nearly seventy-five towns and villages had inventory maps and documents that were good enough to be resurrected at the end of the 1990s. However the new interest in planning has more to do with cultural changes, education, concerns for the environment (acid rain in particular), recreation, and health than with the availability of earlier work.

Since 1990 there has been no APA staff to train or hold workshops for local planners. Hotaling believes that there has been little evolution of technical skills of local boards throughout the park. Further, almost no new municipal lawyers are moving in to the North Country to become or assist local planners, a problem that is especially notable in the smaller towns.

It is not the towns that benefit from having approved local programs as much as it is developers and the public. In fact, the reasons towns are presently reluctant to develop approvable plans are no longer political. Town boards believe they gain very little. (This is really not true; for example, in the five Lake George towns and village with approved plans, the agency even uses town standards and permit criteria for Class A projects, which are stronger than APA requires, so the locals have a great measure of control over their development.) But administering zoning codes and so on requires funding, planning boards, zoning boards, and boards of appeal. For some of the smaller towns in the Adirondacks this is a significant drain on resources and manpower. Board member recruitment is difficult, and membership continuity is also a problem. In addition, some boards find it expedient to leave decisions to the agency, believing that it is difficult politically for locals to turn down applications even if that is the correct course. Political pressures on towns to dissuade them from submitting plans to the agency decreased in the 1990s. Even so, Hotaling saw "no stampede for Class B jurisdiction."

By 2000, of a total of 103 towns and villages in the park, 60 had comprehensive plans, 55 had zoning, 60 had subdivision regulations, 70 had planning boards, but only 15 towns had agency-approved and locally approved plans. Another five towns have submitted plans to the agency but have not adopted them at the local level. Further, those approved and adopted plans are generally in the areas of the park with the greatest development, such as the towns surrounding Lake George.[9] The high percentage of towns doing planning in 2000 indicates strong local interest and need for planning; the low percentage with agency-approved plans indicates lingering disapproval of agency control of development. The fact that there are not more approved plans has had serious consequences: The agency has not been able to decrease its permitting workload, and its enforcement backlog has increased so that in 2000 there were over three thousand unresolved enforcement cases.

Butler Estates

John Collins credited Glennon with being key to many things the agency was able to accomplish in the early 1990s.[10] The proposal to develop Butler Lakes illustrates the agency's strong stances at that time. The Utica Boys Club owned a 620-acre property with two lakes and a northern border along West Canada Creek. The tract was offered for sale, and it became one of many of the state's missed land acquisition opportunities. An Old Forge group purchased the tract and proposed to develop ninety-six lots on it. The lakes were largely undeveloped, except for a cluster of camp buildings. The proposal was within agency guidelines but was more than the site deserved. The agency was successful in reducing the number of lots and defining, according to Collins, "some serious clustering."[11] As of 2001, this development has not been started. Collins sees this effort and the task force, described later, as the high points of his tenure at the agency.

Cumulative Impact

In the late 1980s and into the 1990s, APA's legal committee and Counsel Glennon had tried to utilize on a very broad scale the concept of cumulative impact in the agency's permit application. To do this, the agency questioned whether the sum of many small projects would produce adverse environmental impact and tried to view individual projects in the context of total development. They believed that the impact of many permitted individual buildings would be greater than the relatively few large developments that came before the agency. For Glennon this issue was more threatening to the park than any other. He called the effect of cumulative impact on the park as "the destruction of the park by a thousand cuts,"[12] the number "thousand" referring to the new buildings that have appeared each year.

Despite the fact that Glennon believed, rightly, that recent court decisions had given the agency little choice but to consider cumulative impact, the Local Government Review Board saw it as one more way for the agency to extend its powers. Further, because addressing cumulative impact is not spelled out in agency rules and regulations, the agency was not able to address cumulative impact effectively. Nonetheless the agency, spurred on by Glennon's forcefulness, tried to do so.*

---

* Some question the legality of the concept, believing that cumulative impact was taken into account by the legislature when it created the map and the density requirements.

APA Executive Director Robert Glennon

All of the agency's strong posture with respect to enforcing the APA Act during the early 1990s can be attributed directly to Glennon. But there was also a shadow over the agency during those years and that can also be traced to Glennon, or more precisely to his personality as well as to his convictions. He was passionate about protecting the Adirondacks, but he was always pessimistic about the agency's ability to do so. In a speech in 1997 he claimed, "From the beginning, the Adirondack Park [Agency] statute has failed to preserve the Adirondack Park, instead accepting as its organizing principle the park's rational destruction, but fervently hoping that destruction is phased, orderly, clean and well-lighted. From the beginning, the Agency has had to try to administer the unadministrable and enforce the unenforceable." [13] Not only was his pessimism about the future of the park deeply rooted, it extended to the residents. He had little faith in the ability of local people to save the park or even to manage it. During his tenure as executive director his inability to relate to people extended even to agency staff, many of whom he publicly belittled.[14] As a result, during his tenure as executive director (1989–95) staff morale declined. Many people, not just environmentalists, consider Glennon to be the expert on constitutional law affecting the park, but as a leader he was his own worst enemy, a prisoner of his dark view of the world and humanity.

Starting in 1993 when Collins became APA chairman, Glennon's frustration with the APA Act pushed him to seek new ways of getting around what he felt were inadequacies in the rules and regulations. According to Ulasewicz, Glennon found a method to go beyond regulations, to push the envelope. If someone wanted a permit and agreed to APA restrictions on the permit, he or she was asked also to agree to adding those restrictions to the deed and giving up any other development rights on the property. These restrictions would run to the benefit of the state of New York, APA, and sometimes to towns and counties. That is, like any other deed covenant, the restrictions would "run with the land," and both the state and APA would have to agree to any changes. Ulasewicz believes that such tying of restrictions to the land was contrary to the APA Act's prohibition against the agency's taking any interest in real property. Glennon also filed numerous enforcement actions against applicants whose projects he questioned. These notices of potential violations were placed in the administrative record, and the applicant could not obtain a permit unless the enforcement issue was addressed. This action was an attempt to circumvent the problems APA faced in not having adequate enforcement staff.

Public Issues Forum

Park agency member Liz Thorndike first conceived the need for a public issues forum in 1991, and it began to meet in August of that year. The fallout from the commission report had been so great that participants dubbed it the "Hostility Forum." Liz believes the "commission report offered an opportunity for long overdue dialogue, building a level of trust, making some of those who had been seen by the Agency and environmental groups as the problem [into] part of the solution, and demonstrating that civility and respect could be part of the debate process." [15]

The forum met monthly for over two years until it was gradually replaced by the Collins-appointed Task Force on Simplifying APA Regulations. Thorndike believed a major achievement of the forum was the way it opened a communication process and thus paved the way for the task force, which was a more substantive, formal effort.

Liz Thorndike based the forum on section 801 of the APA Act, which she interpreted as "focusing 'the responsibility for developing long-range park policy in a forum reflecting statewide concern,' and that while Park policy recognized a major state interest in the Park's protection, 'the Agency was required to be involved in a continuing planning process that recognizes matters of local concern' as well." [16] She was trying to solve the fundamental problem of mistrust, fear of the agency, the sense that locals were as David to Goliath before the power and seeming aloofness of the agency. "These people were railing against an institution and a system which they felt was overpowering them." [17]

Whatever success the forum achieved was founded in the ground rules for civility established by Thorndike,[18] staff assistance through Ed Hood, Thorndike's ability to direct participants to listen, and, finally, her determination to keep the discussions focused. Limits to its success were directly related to the fact that it was just a forum, without formal structure. Participants' attendance was not consistent, but given their diversity, any achievement was monumental. (Adirondack Mountain Club, the Association, League of Women Voters, Residents' Committee to Protect the Adirondacks, local officials and planners, Adirondack Planning Commission, Fairness Coalition, Blue Line Council, and at first Solidarity Alliance were regular attendees; not active were Audubon, other property rights groups, and Donald Gerdts, who did not attend at all.)

Discussions ranged from the reasons for so much hostility to the need to revive local planning assistance funds. They included fire towers as an educational vehicle, agency membership, economic development, strengthening park protection, the relationship of the agency to the public, and the complexity of the permit review process. Beyond the diffusion of hostility, achievements include a joint resolution on the need for local planning, and the opportunity for the agency to accept the involvement of the newly appointed Local Government Review Board executive director, Joe Rota, as a nonvoting participant at agency sessions. Nevertheless, consensus was very difficult to achieve.

There was an initial impasse; it took the first three meetings to air the complaints and sources of hostility in order to move on. The resolution on the need for local planning almost faltered over who was to distribute legislatively appropriated funds. Even as trust was emerging, outside events, such as the announcement of Cuomo's last park bill in 1993, reminded participants how limited their efforts were.[19]

An example of the obstacles confronting such a forum comes from one participant, sawmill owner Howard Aubin, who came initially as a representative of Adirondack Solidarity Alliance. At that time, Solidarity Alliance had a reputation for disruptive and violent activities. Aubin surprised members of the forum by his active and constructive participation and by his articulate and inventive representation of people and ideas.[20] He thought that initially much good had come from the forum. But this constructive participation ultimately backfired: members of Solidarity disapproved of his actions and withdrew from the forum, Aubin with them. However, Aubin continued to attend occasionally, representing himself.

This episode points again to one of the fundamental problems in establishing public participation in the Adirondacks. When communication is established, it is still difficult to achieve compromises. And when representatives of diverse groups move toward a common ground, they often cannot bring their groups along. As successful as the forum was in helping people work together, it could not solve these problems.

APA Task Force

In March 1993, a Task Force on the Adirondack Park Agency, chaired by Chestertown attorney Daniel T. Smith, with a broadly representative membership from around the park, began trying to formulate a report that would recommend ways of expediting agency operations and simplifying agency procedures. This much-needed study was inaugurated by John Collins as an outgrowth of Thorndike's issues forum. In the spirit of the issues forum, the task force involved the park's principal users—developers, local governments, and business people, as well as several lawyers who had experience dealing with the agency.

In May 1994 the task force released an analysis of what improvements were needed to streamline the agency. Collins says he was pleased with the task force's work and still thinks the list of recommendations was "really good."[21] The agency formally endorsed 80 percent of the task force's recommendations.

The recommendations were in three categories, those that required administrative change only, those that required legislative action, and those that required rule changes. Many of the suggested administrative changes—such as those for improving the permit application process, record keeping, mapping, giving more review responsibility to staff, streamlining operations in general—have been addressed. One recommendation that affects applicants was adopted: Agency members become involved in the preapplication process so problems can be exposed and dealt with early, before reaching the decision process. High on the list of recommendations was the need for the agency to do a comprehensive review of its Rules and Regulations, revisions that even in 2001 were proceeding at a snail's pace. No revisions had reached the legislature for approval.

Part of the reason for the slow acceptance of the forum's work relates to what has happened to their report after its release. First, the agency spent nearly a year and a half assimilating the recommendations before issuing an "Agency Response." Collins had expected things to go slowly, and they did. The agency held twenty-five public meetings to get out the message that the agency was listening on reform issues.

Progress was further impeded by the shift in leadership at the agency. Regulatory reform took a back seat under Greg Campbell. This shift occurred mostly because the governor's office was ever alert to avoid steps that might lead to controversy.

In 1997, as the agency was considering task force recommendations, the inevitable opposition began to appear. Instead of seeing that changes might "put more common sense into agency land-use rules and regulations"[22] as described by the *Press Republican,* the Essex County Board of Supervisors registered concern. Property rights groups like Solidarity Alliance (Dale French was a member of the Essex County Board of Supervisors at the time) were afraid that "changes would instead make the rules more Draconian."[23] Even the Association of Adirondack Towns and Villages was opposed to streamlining the regulations because changes would increase APA staff's power.

Under Richard Lefevbre, who succeeded Campbell, the agency has not responded overtly to task force recommendations, but they have reappeared as new initiatives, as the agency's agenda, not the task force's per se. Most important, the agency never disavowed the task force's work; it just moved ahead, not wanting the current agenda tied to something done six years before. In the summer of 1999 Ed Hood summarized agency progress with respect to the task force: Of the eighty-four recommendations with which the agency agreed, fifty-eight had been completed or were underway.[24]

I wondered if the approach to specific recommendations might lead to ignoring the larger issues. Hood, assistant director of planning for the agency, reassured me by describing the agency's current "strategic planning effort." It was only at a preliminary stage of identifying priorities and trends, trying to get a handle on key indicators that showed the health of the park. That step was a long way from addressing the regulatory changes that may be identified, but it was a beginning.

The first installment on regulatory revisions was completed in 2000, and the Final General Environmental Impact Statement for revision of parts of the agency's rules and regulations was issued in January 2001. Work on the next phase began immediately.

None of this delay meant that the agency was idle. Among its many achievements was Project 2000, in which the agency secured $1.8 million from the Federal Transportation Equity Act, that illustrates how effective the agency's planning has been. The moneys were awarded to five major and eight smaller projects, primarily directed at tourism infrastructure along Routes 73 and 28. They ranged from parking facilities to bicycle trails.

Public Participation and the Agency

For more than two decades Ed Hood has had charge of or worked with many special agency programs. Even though Liz Thorndike's issues forums were a response to specific events and problems, Hood views the forums as an outgrowth of the goals program of the 1980s. Both were attempts to reach out to the public, to establish lines of communications with Adirondack towns and residents, and to promote the message that the agency was listening. It was logical to view both the Goals Program and the forum as precursors to the Task Force on the Adirondack Park Agency.

Although some of the agency staff were often distracted by planning for the VICs (visitors' interpretive centers), a five-year task, or helping with the Adirondack Park Centennial, the agency continued to be responsive to the public. Moving with glacial speed, and cloaking response to the task force's recommendations in new terms, the basic thrust remained the same. Previous or preliminary work was not abandoned; it was simply reconstituted.

There remains another side to this situation, however. Despite Lefebvre's best efforts, only limited regulatory reform has been accomplished, while the list of new issues confronting the agency continues to grow. The environmental law section of the New York State Bar has offered to help the agency with writing new regulations, but this offer has not been acknowledged.

Public participation at the agency had always been advisory with strong leadership. It took a unique twist in the late 1990s in a program inspired by a series of people-to-people exchanges between Adirondackers and managers of Abruzzi National Park of Italy, initiated by the Association for the Protection of the Adirondacks. Abruzzi is smaller than the Adirondacks but with a similar mix of public and private interests. The people-to-people exchange, a program adopted by APA Chairman Dick Lefebvre, has provided leaders of both parks with ideas and insight on park management. Adirondack residents who have visited Abruzzi have been impressed with the effectiveness of Abruzzi's strong central governance.

Strangely, at least in comparison with the amount of public land in the Adirondacks, roughly 46 percent, the Abruzzi Park Authority only owns 1 percent of the land within that park. Strong leadership has addressed the highest conservation goals, such as sustainable wolf introduction, along with the economic development of the park's villages. And it has achieved a balance that has the support of the park's residents.

Those who have visited Abruzzi, like Inlet Supervisor J. R. Risley, have returned with new insights into park management. Risley was everywhere, working for Inlet, but also, through the Forest Preserve Advisory Committee and town organizations, pushing many parkwide projects.

The "New Agency"

Changes in the agency brought about by appointments by the Pataki administration have raised some curious questions. When Glennon was counsel and executive director, he reviewed or oversaw every regulatory decision. Agency actions and decisions were consistent and predictable. Glennon even chastised his staunchest supporters among the members of the agency, Collins, Paine, Savage, and Thorndike, for not being strong enough.

Executive Director Dan Fitts does not exercise the same oversight. Staff has been given more responsibility in making decisions, but since the beginning of the Pataki administration, agency members have only in a few instances overruled staff decisions. In 1999 and 2000, no permit decision developed by staff and presented to the agency for final approval has been overruled. Agency members have added conditions and amendments to the permits, but have not voted to deny a permit that had staff approval.

The agency has swung to the opposite pole from the Glennon days. Then agency members would occasionally discuss interminably issues that were not the essential questions in the permit process. Now, agency members rely heavily on staff and give the impression of accommodating every request brought to the agency. It will take time to ascertain whether agency staff and members are truly working at the best levels to protect the park and at the same time acting more responsively with respect to the public.

APA and the Adirondack Association of Towns and Villages

The most notable effort to involve local government and engage the public originated with APA and the Adirondack Association of Towns and Villages, in a series of annual programs called Local Government Day. It was not easy to get them started; attendance was small at the first event in 1997. APA, AATV, Department of State, New York Planning Federation, and Local Government Review Board joined to sponsor the second Local Government Day in 1998, which also had support from Adirondack North Country Association.[25] Registration was so low, partly because of a poor choice of date for the event, that APA canceled the 1998 Local Government Day. With the help of AATV, the agency went to the public to ask what the agenda should encompass, and APA restructured plans for 1999 with a new agenda. That program was a potpourri of talks, one of which discussed the relationship between towns and state lands. The most popular session was about the way revitalization of the railroads could help towns.

The spring 2000 session was upbeat and positive, with the focus on planning. The Department of State talked about the way it could help towns with their local codes. Ed McMahon from the Gateways Community Project inspired towns to rethink planning in terms of their position as gateways to parts of the park. And, as Lefevbre hoped, there was much more happening than the formal sessions. With over two hundred in attendance, it was a great opportunity for town officials to meet state agency people. Lefebvre said the session provided time for people to "meet and talk, to break down bureaucratic walls."

Lefebvre gave what he calls his typical "stump speech" on partnering, on local and state government working together to define a common good. He is very positive about the results. People in the park have begun to see themselves and their needs in terms of the park and its values. Oddly enough, the environmental groups have been slow to champion his outreach: almost no one from the environmental groups attended Local Government Day in 2000. Local Government Days have functioned to awaken local governments to concerns for the environment; environmental groups have not shown the same motivation to reach out to local governments.

Public TV filmed parts of Local Government Day 2000, especially the inspirational talks on gateway planning, and distributed tapes to Adirondack town supervisors. Lefebvre told me he was excited by the fact that a few towns are showing those tapes to constituents, using them to encourage residents to think positively about local planning.

The agenda for 2001 included workshops on funding and balancing nature and commerce, sessions on controlling junk, managing storm water, finding sites for telecommunications towers, creating zoning boards of appeal, regulating jet skis and boats, enforcing codes—every topic important to communities.

APA has also held public outreach sessions for counties. The 1999 Hamilton County session was primarily a listening session, but Chairman Lefebvre kept the supervisors focused: "We need to recognize state lands are an economic potential in themselves. I don't think we've done a good job of promoting state lands for recreational use, something every community could benefit from." [26]

APA and the State Land Master Plan

There is currently sufficient opposition to revising the State Land Master Plan that it may be not be done for many years. Environmental groups have fought hard to stop any changes, fearing that in the climate of the time any discussion would "open up a can of worms" and that there would be serious attempts to weaken the plan. Throughout the 1990s groups like Local Government Review Board and Association of Adirondack Towns and Villages pushed for a revision of the SLMP. The Inter County Legislative Committee and AATV have placed revision of the SLMP at the top of their agendas. [27] The three groups want greater motorized access and consideration given to wider snowmobile trails.

The agency appears caught in the middle. Lefebvre has said that he believes the APA should wait until the unit management plans (UMPs) are finished with their inventories "so that we will know what we have to deal with." He believes that completing the UMPs is essential, the "fulfilling of a contract, and the next logical, responsible step is revising the SLMP." [28]

There are many reasons for opening discussion beside the fact that the

SLMP is supposed to be revised every five years and the last revision occurred in 1987. A policy on trail corridors is needed in order to give conceptual approval to long trails so they can be worked into the UMP process. The cap on snow-mobile trail mileage, set at 860 miles by the SLMP, might be reconsidered in light of recent past or future state acquisitions. I believe the most important re-sult of revising the SLMP before the UMPs are completed would come from describing the potential of various units for nonmotorized recreational oppor-tunities. The past has shown that DEC only does what it has been directed to do, and that only reluctantly, and it needs to have a vision that would supersede changes in administration and give real guidance to planning.

Easements pose another question. DEC negotiates easement arrangements with sellers (and sometimes buyers) of part of the bundle of rights associated with the land. Managing easements such as the Champion agreement is a DEC prerogative, but easement lands are a category of quasi-state lands not consid-ered when the SLMP was written, and general policies for them should be spelled out in the SLMP.

New things keep appearing. Snowmobile trail groomers were never imag-ined in 1970, nor were the size and speed of snowmobiles. The pressure for ATV trails escalated at the end of the 1990s. It was obvious by 2000 that the failure to revise the State Land Master Plan had created many problems and that the only way to keep it the strong document it was intended to be was to revise it on schedule and thereby address modern recreational inventions that will keep appearing.

Department of Environmental Conservation

DEC's Structure

Even with all my exposure to the workings of the Department of Environmen-tal Conservation in the past thirty years it is not always easy to see why DEC has not functioned better with respect to the Adirondacks. And, although it may be quite difficult to see how suggested reforms will correct this deficiency, it is im-possible, based on past history, to envision any significant reforms being insti-tuted. Both the structure of DEC and individuals within the department have played a role in the way things have gone, but it seems that DEC's curious cul-ture may be an overriding force in the way the department functions. Hostility between rangers and foresters continues, perhaps as a result of the traditional independence of the ranger force or the regions.

Problems certainly increased when those responsible for natural resources were combined with those working on all manner of environmental problems. But the 1970 action creating DEC was only the first in a long line of restructurings that has made DEC less and less able to deal with the Forest Preserve. For instance, in the late 1970s, the Division of Operations was designated a separate unit, so no longer was the Division of Lands and Forests in charge of trail and bridge building and infrastructure maintenance on the Forest Preserve. Then, in the 1990s, the ranger force, the eyes and ears of the department, was lumped together with the department's police force, the conservation officers. The two groups were integrated into a separate division within DEC and even began to share a common curriculum at the academies where recruits were trained. Environmental groups had to fight to have a section on Forest Preserve management and values included in that curriculum.

Rangers should be in place to inform and assist planners as well as regional foresters, and management should educate ranger staff better. There is no longer a close rapport between Division of Lands and Forests and the ranger staff.* DEC's new system of managing rangers within districts, implemented in 1999, improved coverage in general, but it has had the potential to weaken community relations. Here is one more parallel with the federal Forest Service: In the 1960s, in order to insure top-down compliance with management, the service had a policy of "regularly reassigning rangers in order to loosen their ties to a community." [29] This policy did not work and was abandoned. Time will tell if DEC's new policy preserves the rangers' fundamental presence in both community and Forest Preserve.

The disparity between policies in the different regions persists. Further, there seems to be a gulf between the regions and the small staff in Albany. This gulf was widened by the final blow in DEC's restructuring: Management of state forests was combined with the Forest Preserve in a Bureau of Public Lands, where Wild Forests were equated with state forests. The Forest Preserve Advisory Committee protested this reorganization, which has led to many missteps by the department, including the handling of motorized use in the Forest Preserve, administrative vehicular use, and compliance with the Americans with Disabilities Act.

Cultural biases continue to exist within DEC. The department is so complex that few had thought about long-range planning or solutions to new challenges; department members do not even seem to have sufficient depth of understanding of the structural problems. (Examples of these shortcomings are

---

* Starting in 1999, the Forest Preserve Advisory Committee began to serve as the locus of needed dialogue, but some managers resented it and tried to curb it.

in the case studies in the next section.) Within the department there have been a few notable individuals who wrestled with these notions, but only one individual who sought to overcome structural biases against wilderness and preservation. Probably the strongest defender of Forest Preserve values the department has ever had was Division of Lands and Forests Director Norm VanValkenburgh. Peter Berle tried, Bob Bendick labored, often successfully, but neither changed the culture. Governor Cuomo's political policy with respect to DEC—hands off almost to the point of indifference—kept his administration from making any real impact on DEC. (It must be remembered that Cuomo's seeming paralysis with respect to the Forest Preserve had more to do with the legislature and budgets than with his caring.) All these DEC men were gone long before the end of the 1990s.

Pataki's approach has been quite different, although it has not probed DEC's structural or cultural problems. He was impelled at first by fiscal restraint to severely cut DEC's natural resources staff and budget, then by pressure from environmental groups to acquire big-ticket lands for the Forest Preserve, and finally by his belated understanding of the disarray of unit management planning, which he addressed by issuing an edict in 1999 that all unit management plans would be completed in five years—that is, requiring the department to accomplish more in five years than it had done in the past twenty-five. All these acts seem to demonstrate how little his administration understood the problems of the department's bureaucracy, downsizing, and intellectual inertia.

DEC has had trouble conforming to the State Land Master Plan. On the other hand, Adirondack Park Agency has been hard-pressed to exert influence over DEC on SLMP matters because until 2001 APA had one Forest Preserve specialist for the task of dealing with all the park's public lands.*

The gradual weakening of the management of the Forest Preserve within the Division of Lands and Forests had started in the 1970s, but under Pataki it got worse. The biggest threat to Forest Preserve management occurred when state forests and the Forest Preserve lands were combined into the new Bureau of Public Lands. The Forest Preserve no longer had an identifiable unit, just one specialist and technicians. Furthermore the bureau itself is woefully under-

---

* A second Forest Preserve specialist was added in 2001, but Chuck Scrafford, whose long tenure in this position has given him a deep understanding of state lands, is not far from retirement. His departure will deprive APA of important institutional memory with respect to the land, although Banta, Henry Savarie, and Ray Curran have contributed to APA's understanding of the Forest Preserve.

staffed. The Forest Preserve Advisory Committee protested, but weakly, as if knowing it would do no good.[30] It was immediately clear that DEC was going to downplay the differences between state lands outside the Adirondacks and Catskills and the Forest Preserve, and this has continued under Tom Wolfe through 2000. All this supposed streamlining occurred on Pataki's watch, and its consequences have appeared in every division decision from snowmobile trails to ATV use to staff motorized use.

Another set of problems, uncovered by the Forest Preserve Advisory Committee, relates to the lack of policies relating to the Forest Preserve. Missing or out-of-date policies account for most of the problems discussed in the following case studies, but even worse has been the failure to enforce existing policies across the regions. Tree cutting, motorized access, and administrative use of motors are examples of policies poorly handled. The failure to enforce department policies has cropped up in several instances in which snowmobile trails and roads have been widened beyond existing standards.

The overriding campaign theme in George Pataki's challenge of Governor Cuomo was fiscal responsibility. Pataki promised to reduce the "bloated" budgets of almost every part of state government. DEC's budget had grown over the years as the department had been given ever more responsibility for the environment, but at the same time, funding for natural resources had declined. The gradual erosion of resources and deferred maintenance that began in the mid-1970s accelerated through the 1980s and 1990s and was exacerbated by several freezes on hiring. The problems caused by thirty years of well-documented budget shortfalls will take decades to overcome.[31] The backlogs include years' worth of surveying and marking boundaries of state land and improvements to infrastructure as well as bringing staff and ranger forces up to needed levels.

Over the years, DEC has become more and more dependent on everything but the state's general fund for its budget. Much of its budget comes from dedicated funds from the federal budget or special accounts such as the Conservation Fund that receives money from hunting and fishing licenses. The problem with these dedicated sources is that their use is restricted and does not always provide for the department's needs; yet increasingly, DEC funding is being weaned from the general fund and being replaced by program-generated revenues known as SROs (Special Revenue Other). Currently [in 1991] 6 percent to 7 percent of the agency's budget emanates from various SRO accounts such as the Conservation, Environmental Enforcement, and Oil Spill funds." [32]

Adding to the woes of funding cuts and making them worse was the fact that the natural resource side of the department had to spend significant time coming up with new schemes to generate funding.*

One of the strangest aspects of DEC's budget process is the way its annual requests are handled. "The amount allocated is not much more than 10 percent of the total requested." [33] Capital projects were funded at 2 percent to 3 percent of requests, rehabilitation and improvement (trail brushing, ditching, and so forth) at 5 percent or 6 percent of total requests. This allocation happens because the Division of Lands and Forests presents a budget that would correct all its accumulated shortfalls in one year. This is always an unrealistic number, given that the department could not accomplish all the requests in one budget year, and hiring that many new people to do the work is equally unfeasible. The weird thing is that the department expects and gets only those single digit percentages of its annual requests. There is a need for incremental readjustments, a ten—or twenty-year plan to do all the deferred projects incrementally with an adequate staff, and above all, to fund continuous Forest Preserve planning. With such long-range planning, a coordinated budget would allow for new acquisitions, stewardship, and a trained and adequate staff.

In recent years attempts to solve the department's budget problems have led the state to take funds from the Environmental Protection Fund for stewardship, by using it primarily for contractual work such as for the hiring of outside experts to help write unit management plans. However, writing contracts and monitoring them is often as time-consuming for staff as doing the actual work.

All this has occurred when the amount of state land has increased. Year after year, the department's requests were more than decimated! How could that be good planning and budgeting?

The department arranged that new lands acquired under the Environmental Protection Fund or the 1996 Bond Act provided funding for planning as a percentage of the cost of acquiring land. But moneys for stewardship that came from the Clean Water/Clean Air Bond Act (1996) were not available for planning; in fact they were not even available to facilitate staff work but had to be used for outside contractors. And this Catch-22 raised the issue of whether there was enough staff to monitor the contractors.

In 2001 plans to increase funding for Forest Preserve stewardship (a

---

* In one more undercutting of Forest Preserve concerns, budgets for all state lands within a region would be lumped together as of the 1997 budget cycle. This was done "to increase the entire pot of money available for state land stewardship," but it is difficult to see how that would work.

catchall term that includes planning for and taking care of state lands and building infrastructure) ran headlong into a statewide budget crisis.

Fortunately, the state has built into payment for lands acquired in the 1990s sufficient funds to create inventories and plans for the new lands and to provide such needed public amenities as trailheads, parking, signage, and so on. This helps, but the additional moneys are still bond act moneys, mortgages on the future. The results for the Whitney and Champion acquisitions are good for the present, but do not solve budget issues and stewardship needs on existing state land.

Better funding and budgeting still will not address the problems of changing directions with new administrations. In the initial Pataki years staff cutbacks and early retirements resulted in loss of institutional memory as well as low staff morale and the apparent lack of direction. It seemed as if no one in management knew the details of managing natural resources, especially in the Adirondack Park.

When the Pataki administration finally paid attention to the Forest Preserve and the park, it listened to the loudest voices in the environmental community, voices that were becoming increasingly concerned about the prospects of sales of huge tracts of timber lands owned by corporations located outside the state. Thus the administration focused first on Whitney, which was not only the tract mentioned for state acquisition on everyone's list but one that was actually threatened by development. Then interest shifted to Champion's lands, as the governor began to create an image for himself as a conservationist. But it was not long before the public clamored for other programs as it became obvious just how neglected planning, updating of policies, and management of the Forest Preserve had become.

Because of the size of the Forest Preserve, most people only become intimately acquainted with pieces of it. Knowledge of the land is essential to planning, and the institutional memory that provided that knowledge had disappeared. I draw on my own experience to underscore this point. I started writing guidebooks in 1970 and essentially finished the series that covers the Adirondacks in 1987. Even then I had not seen everything, especially parts of the remote western and northern tracts. Since 1987, I have filled this void by visiting most of the tracts I missed the first time around and by keeping up with most of the new state acquisitions. No one at DEC in 2001 had that kind of firsthand geographical knowledge of state lands in the Adirondacks.

Until late in 2001, natural resource managers from the deputy commissioner level to the division level have come from out of state. The task confronting them has been to understand the complexities of public land management here, which are nationally unique, to fathom the culture and organization of a bureaucracy that manages the public lands, and to become acquainted with those lands. It is virtually impossible to do all this without a staff whose memory is deep.

Can an agency of DEC's complexity be truly effective if the average term of its commissioner is just over two and a half years? The turnover in commissioners has been so rapid, and natural resources problems so difficult to fathom and easy to overlook in the face of the department's complexity, that few commissioners have understood the way the natural resources components have functioned. New commissioners have usually brought in new deputies with new ideas. In many instances, rather than reaching back into what the department has done, new programs have been advanced while old ones have been trashed or ignored. There has been little continuity, with the result that department programs have been a series of reinventing solutions, with little advancement. In other words, the department has gone round and round. Combine this revolving leadership with staff's cultural inertia and it becomes obvious why so little was done in planning, unit management plan writing, developing policies, or anything but maintaining the status quo. Oddly enough this characteristic of maintaining the status quo is another parallel between the federal Forest Service and DEC.

Comparing DEC and APA

DEC's internal problems have led to conflicts between APA and DEC that in 2001 are only just beginning to be resolved. However there is a more fundamental difference between the two agencies—their unequal sizes. This inequality may explain in part the disparity in their cultures and their effectiveness. DEC is so big and so spread out that it has a difficult time responding to specialized Adirondack issues. Its staff assumes a bureaucratic way of doing things, with layers and layers of decisions. APA on the other hand is so small it is barely able to do all the things it ought to do, but staff keeps trying. As a small agency it is more flexible; decisions are more easily made.

Both agencies suffer from the same rapid changes in administrations, but their responses are quite different. DEC has taken on many initiatives that are then abandoned by new leadership with new agendas (the prime example of this is the Use and Information Plan discussed below). Many good programs have just been trashed or swept under the carpet, never to appear again. DEC's failure to build on the past is one more example of its lack of institutional memory.

APA has reacted differently. It has had a series of initiatives, but staff input has been strong enough and leadership sufficiently consistent that although it appears that some programs have been set aside, their underlying values have just reappeared in different guises. The changes are more cosmetic or semantic than real shifts in emphasis. APA's focus is still not so strong that it has been able to complete necessary regulatory reform or deal with required revisions in the State Land Master Plan in a timely fashion.

The Lingering Conflict Between APA and DEC

At the end of the 1990s, it had become obvious that DEC's management of the Forest Preserve was slipping precipitously. APA appeared to have trouble bringing DEC within compliance with the State Land Master Plan. In July 1998 a portion of the Rondaxe-Big Moose snowmobile trail had been widened and graded with a bulldozer. The resulting trail was described as being able to accommodate an eighteen-wheel truck.[34] During the building of a new snowmobile trail section between Indian Lake and Rock Lake a second illegal widening occurred. The trail from Newcomb around Vanderwhacker Mountain to NY 28N was the scene of a third such incident. That trail had been closed since the 1970s, but local crews bulldozed it to remove trees that had grown up so that they completely filled the trail.* Boulders were removed and the track was widened; APA required remediation. The activities brought up the question of how the department could issue a permit to a local group to open up a trail—which was officially closed and had received no maintenance in nearly twenty years—without a unit management plan. It was a far stretch to think this was covered by the department's Memorandum of Understanding (MOU) with APA as some in the department claimed. (Such a MOU permitted maintenance without APA's oversight, but no new work.)

Dissatisfaction with APA's response led Residents' Committee to Protect the Adirondacks to file suit against the agency on the grounds that APA's oversight only dealt with the wetlands issues, not with other violations of the State Land Master Plan and the state's constitution. RCPA charged that the agency had invented a Memorandum of Agreement (MOA) to solve the issue, not a generic process for enforcing APA's authority over DEC. (APA has never promulgated section 585 of its Rules and Regulations. That section would define APA's enforcement of the State Land Master Plan and the unit management

---

* That trail was filled with new-grown trees in the mid-1980s, and I was asked by the local ranger to remove any mention of it from my guidebook because the "trail had been closed."

plans.) RCPA's ploy was to force the administration to deal with DEC's continuing failures with respect to the State Land Master Plan. No other environmental groups joined RCPA in this suit, but the suit itself raises serious questions. Why do people feel compelled to go to court to gain APA's or the DEC's attention? Is this another sign that DEC and APA are not fulfilling their charters?

Specifically, do these failures with respect to Forest Preserve issues indicate that DEC is still fighting against the guidance of the State Land Master Plan? The answer to this reverts again to DEC's underlying culture, to the fact that there seems to be a lack of a sense of legacy for the traditions of the Adirondack Park or the Forest Preserve.

Land Acquisition: New Policies and Practices

Before 1990 acquisitions for the Forest Preserve faced many hurdles beyond the chronic lack of funds. Most notable was the complicated process designed to prevent the state from spending too much. Upward of thirty-six steps involving DEC and other agencies such as the Department of Law, Division of the Budget, and the Office of the Comptroller are required before a purchase can be completed.[35] Sellers were often unwilling to wait for the state to complete the process, and significant parcels have sold to private buyers, among them lands on Forked Lake, Kings Flow, tracts adjoining the Independence River Wild Forest and the Ha-de-ron-dah Wilderness, and Veteran Mountain Camp on Tupper Lake. Further, the state's determined "fair market value" has often been below the asking price of some tracts. In the late 1980s, DEC, under Robert H. Bathrick, then director of the Division of Lands and Forests, reformulated the process so that the *average time* required to complete an acquisition was reduced from thirty-one months to ten months.[36]

The sale of the Lassiter lands to the state in 1991, both fee and easement, marked a turning point. Governor Cuomo's office stepped into the negotiations to speed them up and to allow the state to offer what appeared to be more than market value. The governor was pressured by the environmental community to complete this sale. DEC was allowed to ignore some of the hurdles, and Cuomo proved that the state could move faster when pushed. That sale heralded the most significant change in the state's acquisition policies and led in the 1990s to an increased role by the governor's office.

As of 1990 DEC had approved for acquisition more than a thousand projects totaling 750,000 acres, for which no funds were available. Easements had been offered the state by Otterbrook Timber Company for lands north of but not adjacent to Lows Lake and by Yorkshire Timber Company for its lands

along the Grass River. (The Adirondack Nature Conservancy acquired an easement to the development and timber rights from Otterbrook, but not the
recreational rights. The land is not open to the public. The state was later able
to use funds from two different sources to acquire the development rights to
the Yorkshire tract. The tract itself was sold to John Hancock Life Insurance
Company.)

International Paper Company gave the state an easement on lands north of
Piercefield along the Raquette River in 1992 as a centennial gift. NIMO com-
pleted an agreement to convey and protect some of its lands along the Hudson
River south of Warrensburg.

Acquiring easements as a way of protecting land, primarily by limiting development, was greatly enhanced after 1990 with the passage of bills that
streamlined the process and made negotiations simpler for determining the
amount of tax relief an easement would bring. The state used conservation
easements many times in the 1990s and into the new century. They have proven
to be a valuable tool in limiting development, protecting open space, and assisting the forest products industry, but they are not without problems. Tom
Ulasewicz, former executive director of APA, predicted that in the next thirty
years the most critical problem would be trying to decide how to manage easement lands. Easement agreements are individually negotiated, and the terms
are determined by the seller. Ulasewicz notes that the terms are "all over the
place," making it difficult for DEC to find a consistent way of managing them.
Informing the public about the multiplicity of conditions under which the
lands can be used will become chaotic. Further, it may be impossible to do
some of the things included in particular agreements.[37]

The establishment of the Environmental Protection Fund (EPF) in 1993 finally gave the state funds for stewardship, acquisitions, and easements. The law
establishing the fund had prohibited the state from using those moneys for general fund expenditures, but this prohibition lasted less than two years. A budget
crisis caused Pataki to immediately raid that cache to make up the shortfall and
to add DEC salaries to items covered by the fund. Environmental organizations
convinced the legislature to restore part of the EPF money, and the next year
additional funds were earmarked for land acquisitions and easements. There
was a strong push in 2001 to increase EPF funding for stewardship.

A feature of the Environmental Protection Fund was the inclusion of purchase of "small parcels"—those less than two hundred acres with a price of less
than $250,000. However, granting each DEC region across the state the
money to acquire only one small parcel per year did little to address the tremendous backlog. At first, Region 5, because it had done so much preparatory work

on small parcels, was able to acquire more than one a year, but soon other regions caught up and competition between regions for funds became fierce. Furthermore, the process became politicized in that recommendations from elected officials could move a parcel to the top of the list. Since most small parcels in large urban areas cost more than the limit, the fund has not been able to make much of a dent in the acquisitions. The limit of one per year is especially unfortunate in the park, where access to large tracts of state land is often blocked by private land, in many instances by small parcels.

Governor Pataki, as part of a rather obvious campaign to be seen as the "environmental" governor, also proposed a $1.75 billion Clean Water/Clear Air Bond Act in 1996. Further, he put his prestige and much staff effort behind the push to get the electorate to approve that bond act. This "something for everyone" act would provide for capital expenditures for localities, create a safe drinking water program, and provide a $150 million fund for land acquisition and conservation easements aimed at protecting the quality of surface waters. An early draft for the bond act included language similar to the that of the EPF that would have given towns vetoes over projects. It was rumored that the governor did not want locals involved, so the veto was not included in the legislation, and it appears that the senate was not aware it had been omitted. (Adirondack Mountain Club's Neil Woodworth claims major credit for ensuring that a town's use of veto power over projects was limited to EPF funds.)[38]

The passage of the act released a frenzy of big and splashy acquisitions, which quickly depleted the money, long before it reached all the small parcels the state had been offered. Furthermore, negotiations for lands to be acquired under the bond act became increasingly secret, partly because of their complexity, partly to speed them up. But the end result has been an escalation in land prices during a period of low inflation, advances that could compromise the state's ability to acquire more land in the future.

For years the state had wanted to acquire the Whitney tract with its numerous ponds, lakes, and waterways. The land could become the nexus in a canoe area that would be as important as the St. Regis area. Whitney Industries had applied for a subdivision permit for two properties with existing homes on Little Tupper Lake in 1996 and barely six months later proposed to develop Little Tupper Lake, a $60 million endeavor covering forty "great camp" sites ranging from 17 to 1,000 acres in size and averaging 300 acres. Acquisition of the Whitney property met the criteria of the Open Space Plan, and the DEC saw the Whitney tract as part of a 600,000-acre protected forested area, which differed from Adirondack Council's vision of it as a part of their proposed Bob Marshall Wilderness.

Sale to the state of a portion of the Whitney tract was completed at the end of December 1997 with the help of the Adirondack Nature Conservancy. Little Tupper Lake, the largest privately held lake in the park, was hailed as the gem of the transaction; Governor Pataki called the purchase the "crown jewel of the Adirondacks." The $21 million purchase of 15,000 acres included several other lakes beside Little Tupper, but the state was unable to negotiate a permanent easement on the remaining 36,000 acres that would prohibit further development there. A Connecticut couple was negotiating for Camp Bliss, one of the three existing private homes on the lake. The Nature Conservancy raised $575,000 to buy Camp Bliss so that it could be torn down. The state decided to retain Whitney's headquarters complex for state use, a questionable wilderness intrusion.

In October 1997, with the Whitney deal nearing completion, Champion International proposed to sell the state its Adirondack parcels, almost 144,000 acres. The paper process used in Champion's mill in the Black River Valley required softwoods, largely spruce. Their logging methods had over a period of time taken almost all of the softwoods from nearly 100,000 acres of their land—this despite the fact that historically, those tracts had a much heavier proportion of softwoods than is typical of the park.

The sale, negotiated with the help of the Conservation Foundation of Arlington, Virginia, gave Champion $24.9 million for its land. With this, New York was able to place under conservation easement 110,000 acres that were sold to The Forestland Group (TFG), based in Washington, D.C.. TFG would continue to log the forests under contemporary sustainable forestry practices. The land would be open to the public. This agreement represents a new kind of easement transaction in that the new owner is backed by a not-for-profit group, the Conservation Foundation, and the agreement requires that sustainable logging be practiced.

In addition the state acquired from Champion fee title to 29,000 acres that included seventy miles of the St. Regis, Oswegatchie, and Grass Rivers and the magnificent Madawaska Bog. The much-sought-after northern canoe area was finally taking shape. The acquisition of the Grass River adjacent to Tooley Pond Road brought a string of small gems into the public domain.

The long, three-way negotiations to define a sale and easement package met with considerable opposition: Blue Line Council led "an intense lobbying effort" that convinced eight counties, fifteen municipalities, and the executive committee of the Association of Adirondack Towns and Villages to pass resolutions criticizing the state's proposal.[39] Blue Line claimed that the acquisition would jeopardize three hundred jobs. (Champion employed fifty individuals in timber harvesting and related fields.) Pieter Litchfield, speaking for Blue Line Council, opposed the Champion deal, claiming that fifteen jobs were lost in the Whitney sale. However, when asked, he never produced a list of those who lost jobs. Litchfield and Peter Bauer of Residents' Committee to Protect the Adirondacks engaged in a debate focused on the economics of the Champion proposal. Bauer asked why Blue Line Council objected to a nonmember timber company selling land to the state when the council did not object when one of its members—International Paper—did the same thing.

By the terms of the transaction, hunting clubs that leased land from Champion would lose their leases after five or fifteen years depending on whether the land was purchased by the state or The Forestland Group. The hunting clubs' loss of lease land was the most upsetting aspect of sale for leaders in surrounding counties, despite the fact that after fifteen years all the land would be open to all hunters. DEC had not obtained rights to an old railroad right-of-way, which bisects the Champion lands and is posted by its owners. This ownership limits access between the two parts of Champion land and seriously complicates future use of the tract. DEC included in the easement an agreement that would keep many of Champion's roads open and create a large network of snowmobile trails. (No one has yet determined how the state is going to pay for maintaining these additional roads.)

Lloyd Moore, St. Lawrence County supervisor, objected that supervisors were not consulted in the negotiations as they should have been. Carol La-Grasse's Property Rights Foundation sued to block the transaction on the grounds that it was unconstitutional. That suit was dismissed in July 2000. In 2001 the appellate court unanimously upheld the lower court and concluded in its decision: "We have reviewed all of the other issues raised by appellants and find them to be without merit."

Problems over the purchase were overshadowed by classification of the purchased land. DEC submitted a package to APA for classification that included not only the Champion lands bordering the Pepperbox Wilderness but also the Whitney purchase, the Lake Lila Primitive Area, the Alice Brook tract south of Star Lake, and lands previously acquired from Lassiter in Watsons East Triangle. Hearings followed predictable routes. APA staff took a carefully drawn set of recommendations to agency members for consideration. The Whitney lands and Lake Lila would become Wilderness, Alice Brook would be Wild Forest to accommodate an important snowmobile trail connector, and the Watsons East tract would be split by a road into Wilderness and Wild Forest to give access to the huge area, while preserving the eastern portion adjacent to the Five Ponds Wilderness. As with all compromises, this one left some groups very unhappy.

Adirondack Council managed to convince the agency to create a primitive corridor for the snowmobile trail at Alice Brook, one that would return to Wilderness should an alternate route for the trail be found. (Residents' Committee to
Protect the Adirondacks also favored the primitive corridor.) Adirondack
Council was upset that all of Watsons East was not designated Wilderness so
that it would be a part of the council's proposed Bob Marshall Wilderness Area.

"The state does not need any more land." It is surprising how often you
hear this in the Adirondacks. "The state does not take care of what it already
has" is heard just as often. Like mantras, such assertions come from a broad
range of residents and numerous local officials. When I hear such a remark, I try
to counter with "but your town cannot get to a particular place because that
piece of Forest Preserve is surrounded by posted land." The reply always is "Oh
yes, there are exceptions, but we still do not need more state land." I ask,
"doesn't your economy depend on the state land, the snowmobile trails, the
fishing streams, the public boat launch sites?" Again the reply is, "Oh yes, but
we don't need more state land."

How did this opposition to state ownership become so deeply ingrained?
Did it come from the early days of the Forest Preserve? Did it start in the time
just before the turn of the century when hunting regulations were imposed?
Was it fostered by the loss of logging jobs in the teens through the thirties because the private forests had been exhausted? Was it exacerbated by the destruction of tent platforms or because it was the only tangible way to oppose
APA regulations in the early 1970s? Was it because outsiders have moved in, in
such numbers as to really change the natives' way of life? Or, was it a result of
the fact that Region 5's open space planning group had only tepidly embraced
land acquisition projects?

Probably all of the above are responsible for the dogmatic opposition to
land acquisition, but that could be cured if people were able to see not just the
values of land protection but also the values of the Forest Preserve as the basis
of the local economy. That comes right back to the need for better stewardship,
for adequate trails and parking areas, for unit management plans. Since these issues are finally being addressed in 2001, perhaps Adirondackers will begin to
see land acquisition from a different perspective.

18 | Public Participation in the 1990s

 Discussion and Case Studies

THE LEGACY OF THE COMMISSION ON THE ADIRONDACKS in the 21st Century was the principal force shaping Adirondack policy in the last decade of the twentieth century. There is no question but that it left the environmental movement stunned and seeking direction, that it enlarged a wedge between environmentalists and most Adirondack residents, that it reignited the North Country's fear of government, that it alienated Adirondack Park Agency staff from environmentalists, and that it inflamed distrust. But from this scene of devastation emerged the realization that public participation was and is essential to every aspect of government, especially those aspects designed to change, control, or limit public activities. Bill McKibben wrote that, "something useful emerged from those flaming months. Environmental groups were forced to realize, for better or worse, that Adirondackers were going to participate in the Park's future. No more dictatorship."[1]

Public participation was beginning to influence the Adirondack political scene at the beginning of the twenty-first century, but, unfortunately, input was managed through the 1990s in such a way that it was effective only part of the time. Many Adirondackers continue to believe they are left out of the process.

Defining Public Participation in the 1990s

In the 1970s and 1980s the public participated mostly through town meetings and hearings at which speakers expressed a wide range of opinions and the organizers took information back and wrote a report. The Open Space Task Force (see chap. 5) was different in that it followed a design that originated with DEC. A group of representatives of Adirondack organizations and town governments met regularly and produced a report. The Forest Preserve Advisory Committee had representatives of different groups mixed with at-large members who were expected to have a broader perspective. The Citizens Advisory Committees (CACs) for unit management planning were a mix of representatives of interested groups and local government. Thus public participation in the Adirondacks became a series of meetings, sometimes over a long period, where the participants were representatives of organizations, groups, and government entities. Only at the end of the 1990s did DEC reverse this format with respect to the unit management plans, returning to a single, informal open meeting where ideas were exchanged in a nonconfrontational way.

The effect of increased use of advisory groups that occurred after issuance of the report of the Commission on the Adirondacks in the 21st Century is presented below in seven case studies. The case studies section that follows delves into the makeup of those committees and the problems of bringing them to consensus and making their efforts useful to DEC. It shows how choosing committees made up of representatives of various groups mixed with local government officials has transformed into participation by interested groups, groups with agendas, or groups whose representatives were rarely interested in compromise. By the end of the 1990s, public participation by stakeholders had become endemic. The case studies that follow detail how and why the inclusion of stakeholders, which is common to all advisory groups, has become a problem in all but one case. But because each advisory group is unique, each example also depicts other problematical facets of public participation. I trust the reader will understand why I conclude in the last chapter that the public will be able to participate effectively only with stronger leadership to maintain the focus of such groups. Further, the members of the advisory groups need to be informed individuals and experts in different fields, as well as representatives of elected officials.

Summary of the Case Studies

Efforts toward fostering public participation took root in the Region 5 Open Space Planning Committee, whose origins were described in part 2. The committee produced a huge body of recommendations, not all of which were within the committee's charter. Even after a decade, the group had difficulty in finding consensus on the issues prime to its charter, the listing of lands for state acquisition. It has never motivated towns to work with the committee or to help develop a list of small parcels, those vital in providing access to state land.

The committee, as Study 1 shows, is a prime example of the difficulties of obtaining consensus from representatives of disparate groups. While the committee achieved notable success on such difficult issues as eminent domain, its results before 2001 were mixed.

Public participation was evident in a small way in DEC's Forest Preserve Advisory Committee, which by 2000 had expanded to be truly representative of the wide spectrum of interests concerned with Forest Preserve issues. The FPAC focus has been on the structure of DEC as it relates to protecting the Forest Preserve while making it accessible to the public. Study 2 shows one of the greatest problems faced by advisory groups: DEC has found the committee all too easy to ignore. Two of the most important sub-themes that surface in this study are male dominance in the environmental movement and the fact that many of DEC's flaws have origins outside the department.

Public participation achieved near-universal acceptance in the DEC committee that looked into the effects of the 1995 blowdown and considered proposals to salvage the downed timber. The process involved professionals and strong DEC leadership. Study 3 demonstrates this positive use of public participation.

The fourth example is just the opposite, a bungled process from which the DEC has yet to recover. DEC's involvement of the public in discussions on access for the disabled is a case study in how not to use public participation. At the root of the problem was DEC's attempt to use public participation to get around the Adirondack Park Agency's State Land Master Plan. DEC misinterpreted the Americans with Disabilities Act; DEC bent to special interest groups. Instead of solving the issues, DEC ended up in court. In this case DEC's failure to adhere to the State Land Master Plan, to update its own policies, and to provide strong leadership was a recipe for disaster.

DEC used money from the federal ISTEA (Intermodal Surface Transportation Efficiency Act) program to begin a program—Use and Information—tailored to the funding source. It, too, was a largely bungled affair, partly as a result of the way it used public participation, mostly because DEC, with its changing priorities, squandered the opportunity. Study 5 documents this situation.

The Citizen's Advisory Committee (CAC) that worked for so long on the High Peaks Wilderness Area Unit Management Plan brought in a consensus draft that finally broke the logjam of completing unit management plans in Region 5. However, the final version, modified by DEC and accepted by the governor, left many on the committee displeased. The elapsed time between the committee's report and the state's approval of the plan, nearly eight years, further undercut the effectiveness of such CACs.

The long, drawn-out work of that and earlier CACs was not very efficient, but it brought consensus. But this consensus fell apart in the High Peaks plan, not because of what DEC did with the advice it received, but because of certain stakeholders trying to superimpose their positions. Studies 6 and 7 illustrate this problem.

At the end of the decade, Governor Pataki's pledge to complete unit management plans within five years posed many questions on the use of public input. Will DEC's leadership be strong enough to overcome special interests?

As the studies look at the last decade of the century from the perspective of public participation activities by analyzing their effectiveness, they find some activities inadequate and conclude with a positive appreciation of others. The final studies look with hope to the reinvigorated Unit Management Planning process as reconstituted to make public participation a reality. But the denouement is a personal conclusion that all this has still not achieved adequate mechanisms for meaningful public participation in the complex governance of the Adirondack Park, one that melds its two sets of constituents—park residents and residents in the rest of the state—with their differing concerns.

DEC's track record in playing a leadership role in the marshaling of public opinion is not good. By not focusing on the Forest Preserve, it has diluted both protection and stewardship for the park. It has had a series of statewide special-topic planning efforts, but none that looks at its management components through the perspective of the Forest Preserve. Most, but not all, department planning efforts have gone on in a bureaucratic vacuum, without adequate public input. Before the 1990s both DEC and APA found it difficult to find Adirondackers to discuss issues in public participation attempts. With the exception of the Adirondack Conservation Council, locals were not organized. DEC's move to involve representatives of various groups has unfortunately only offered a platform to the various stakeholders.

In *Losing Ground*, Mark Dowie concluded that in the early 1990s national environmental groups were "losing ground" because they had failed to overcome the cultural distrust of direct action and active members. They had lost leaders with vision and fervor.[2] At the same time leadership of Adirondack environmental groups was losing ground by becoming ever more elitist. However, Dowie failed to anticipate the next challenge, integrating public involvement in governmental decision-making. The Adirondack examples clearly demonstrate why this integration is so difficult.

CASE STUDY 1

Region 5 Open Space Planning Committee

THE ORIGINS OF THIS COMMITTEE, whose work was to be considered by the Advisory Council of the Open Space Plan, and its first year of activities, were introduced in chapter 14. As noted, the committee made no recommendations leading toward a list of acquisitions, but it did achieve consensus on eminent domain and the other criteria for local input that were adopted in the first Open Space Plan. These recommendations were a monumental achievement given the dissension within the group. The draft for the first Open Space Plan contained general criteria for land acquisition;[3] the hard-won consultative process and list of constraints for eminent domain acquisitions; and recommendations on taxation on state land, purchasing of easements, sale or exchanges of small detached parcels of existing state lands in Adirondack or Catskill parks, public access to Adirondack forest lands (preserving or enhancing motorized access for any open space acquisitions), and paying market rates for any property purchased for back taxes.

In succeeding years, working on the recommendations for the scheduled updates of the Open Space Plan, the committee produced many other small achievements, refinements of its initial package of recommendations, but few significant additions to the work of the first six months.

The most consequential step the committee took during its first year was to vote that "specific land conservation sites not be listed in the draft plan until they [the committee] had the opportunity to further their work,"[4] something the Department of Environmental Conservation honored. Comments on the draft, which was issued by the statewide committee on November 2, 1991, showed the gulf between members and the organizations they represented. The Adirondack Council sent its own maps and suggestions, recommendations that were a further expression of their *2020 Vision* volumes, and was upset when these were not included in the draft. The Council had presented ideas to the committee, but they had never been discussed in detail. The Fairness Coalition took exception to the draft because the recommendations appeared as just that, recommendations to the state committee, and not policy for the statewide draft as some had expected. In addition, the Fairness Coalition felt the issue of how much Forest Preserve land was enough was not addressed. Elle Berger, representing Adirondack Audubon, protested the cumbersome system of prior consultation as an "endless delay" tactic.

After hearings on the draft, the Region 5 committee was reappointed and continued to discuss the draft plan. DEC proposed a list of acquisitions or easements to be included in the Open Space Plan: Finch, Pruyn's Blue Ledge tract, Follensby Park, Whitney Park, the scenic vista lands along Heart Lake Road and NY 73, NIMO's Hudson River lands in Warren County, and the Heurich property. (More than half of these acquisitions were completed in the next decade.) The committee adopted twelve changes to the draft it felt were essential.

At the end of February 1992, DEC put together an executive summary of the actions taken at the thirty meetings the committee had held. In March 1992 the committee began a new phase: it put in place a program to invite towns and villages to appoint local open space advisory committees. Members of the committee met with about a third of the towns and villages; some towns declined meetings because they remained adamantly opposed to the Open Space Plan. A committee resolution calling for GIS (Geographic Information System) mapping of state holdings and easements and other attributes necessary for decision-making was added to the final plan released in June 1992.

The Region 5 committee then immersed itself in the forestry issues, especially those related to taxation. It made recommendations on wetland acquisitions and local reimbursement of taxes under 480 and 480A programs. The committee's efforts on limiting eminent domain were recognized in 1993 when the commissioners of DEC and Office of Parks, Recreation, and Historical Preservation (OPRHP) reaffirmed their commitment to the procedure and suggested that the wording in the Open Space Plan, which the Region 5 committee generated, should be put into a regulatory format. Trust between committee members began to emerge after the long harangue on eminent domain, which had required not only committee meetings, but also many subcommittee meetings. Jim Frenette and Dick Purdue earned credit for bringing about that hard-won compromise on eminent domain. Many members believe that it was one of their most important achievements. It had far-ranging implications, changing even the mission of the Adirondack Landowners Association, which owed its existence to opposing eminent domain.

Region 5 Open Space Planning Committee meetings dwindled in number from twenty-four in 1991 to ten and nine in the next two years, then down to eight in 1994, 1995, and 1996. Information trickled in from the local (town) advisory committees, but the majority of those with recommendations were outside the Blue Line.

Tom Monroe's welcome to the first of the 1994 meetings was an attempt to get the committee back on course; he asked the group to focus on conservation strategies that could lead to the consideration of priority projects in the region. (The first mention of a Champion acquisition appeared in the minutes of that meeting.) Monroe announced his retirement from DEC at that February meeting, at which a number of issues were rehashed, including the opposition of the Association of Adirondack Towns and Villages to state land acquisition unless local government review was required for other than the seventy-five parcels in the first draft.

Monroe's summary of activities sent to DEC's acting commissioner Langdon Marsh and OPRHP's commissioner Joan K. Davidson shows how broadly the committee had reached:

> The region has kept the committee up-to-date on activities of the Department, OPRHP, not-for-profits and private landowners regarding proposed and actual open space conservation activities. Other topics deliberated since adoption of the Plan include Forest Legacy, timber industry issues, the High Peaks Unit Management Plan, assessment practices on forest lands, transitional assessments, the Environmental Protection Fund Enhancement proposal, among other items. In addition, the Committee formed an Agricultural sub-committee last December in which Farm Bureau, the NYS Department of Agriculture and Markets and other agricultural representatives were invited to participate. They developed a framework for agricultural recommendations for the Open Space Conservation Plan.

In 1994 Finch, Pruyn requested that its Blue Ledge property be re-moved from the list of projects in the statewide plan. Woodlands manager Roger Dziengeleski's letter requesting this removal emphasized Finch, Pruyn's most serious objection to the Region 5 committee's work: "It is also our understanding that none of the projects listed for Region 5 [in the existing Open Space Plan] were actually recommended by the Region 5 Land Acquisition Citizen's Advisory Group [original name of the com-mittee]. Rather, they were put together by a statewide group when Re-gion 5 Advisory Committee refused to forward a list of projects agreed to by consensus."

The 1994 draft contained recommendations for ten projects, two of which were outside the Blue Line, and most of which had been added by DEC to the earlier drafts of the Open Space Plan. Note that the creation of the Environmental Protection Fund, which would make these acquisi-tions possible, was a DEC proposal and did not originate with the work on the Open Space Plan. NIMO's Hudson River project was dropped from the 1994 Open Space Plan because it was completed. It was ex-pected that the Champlain Palisades tract would be dropped from the plan because its purchase was anticipated. The National Lead property at Tahawus, properties grouped together as the Northern Flow River Cor-ridors, undeveloped Lake George shoreline, and a Working Forest Lands' category were added to the list. The Finch, Pruyn Hudson River Gorge (Blue Ledge) tract and mention of working forests were eliminated from the final 1995 draft.

Discussions during the 1994 update of the plan contained the same themes as earlier: Jean Raymond wanted the plan to require economic impact analysis on government and businesses for every parcel. Despite DEC's effort to educate committee members, there was a lot of misun-derstanding, as a roundtable discussion at the June meeting revealed. "Dave Gibson of the Association for the Protection of the Adirondacks commented that the Committee has lost some of the glue that held it to-gether. The Committee has done a terrific job on policy. It is unrealistic for a group such as this to vote up or down on individual projects. How-ever the group is poised to do local consultation to arrive at good infor-mation."[5] Was this a recognition of the fact that the committee could not perform as the Open Space Plan required?

Members generally felt good about the committee's progress on pol-icy, but notes from the roundtable indicate it was just that, another exercise in themes that go round and round. DEC Deputy Commissioner Bendick was quoted in the minutes: "the state has gained tremendously from what committees have provided. [I am] hopeful that this committee can . . . engage in discussions over the draft update and participate." Mike DiNunzio stated that he felt the committee may have lost track of its legislative mandate; Jean Raymond thought the committee "is doing what it is mandated to do and it just needs to develop a new work plan. . . . Whether we ever recommend land or not for another year or two is not material." Some members felt the state was closer to environmental groups than to locals.

In a sense, polar distances continued to separate some members. Di-Nunzio carefully adhered to Adirondack Council's principles. Several committee members told me that Jean Raymond's method appeared to be that of trying to tie up the committee with discussions. On the issue of the failure of DEC to provide adequate background maps, at least one member thought she used it as a delaying tactic. However, Raymond was absolutely right—DEC should have created such a map depicting the inventory of trails and infrastructure. Such a detailed map was essential to the committee for making decisions and it was also basic to DEC's planning efforts. It is absolutely inexcusable that in 2001 DEC still has not prepared a basic map of the one most needed component of the infrastructure—all the snowmobile trails.

DEC's inability to lead the state into a GIS-based mapping system across all executive departments is one of the great information tragedies of the 1990s. Even with enhanced mapping capabilities, DEC lacks information on both natural resources and infrastructure such as trails and bridges in the Forest Preserve from which to create inventory maps. (Adirondack Park Agency's mapping activities using GIS systems under the leadership of John Banta and Ray Curran is exemplary.)

Inlet supervisor J. R. Risley joined the committee and participated in the poorly attended final meeting of 1994, at which the members seemed to be preoccupied with soul-searching; Fred Monroe thought people were not participating in Adirondack discussions "because there is a feeling that there is a hidden agenda or goal."[6] Risley thought people just did not understand the value of the Oswegatchie great forest. (Oswegatchie is DEC's name for the "Big Bob" Wilderness that Adirondack Council proposed. Calling it a great forest recognized that it would probably always contain Wild Forest areas and commercial forests.)

Another member thought the next iteration of the plan ought to look at "open space *and* recreation needs." The minutes show a lack of understanding of what the plan was protecting, and even the key term in the plan's title—open space—remained a poorly understood concept.

To improve its ability to get things done, the committee formed three subcommittees in early 1995: Assessments and Taxation, Inventory and Committee Goals, and Biodiversity. By April, Commissioner Michael Zagata had joined DEC and Stu Buchanan had been appointed director of Region 5. At a Region 5 Open Space Plan meeting shortly after the transitions, Tim Burke reiterated Adirondack Council's viewpoint as described in *2020 Vision,* but it was obvious that not all members agreed. Buchanan suggested the need for "vision" in the committee's deliberations, the first time that word appears in the minutes. Long discussions of subjects to be depicted on DEC-prepared GIS maps resulted in an ultra-comprehensive wish list. (There is no question but that such an enhanced inventory would help both the DEC and advisory committees do a comprehensive job of long-range planning as well as planning for acquisition and easements.) To augment its request for inventory information, the committee asked several times that the Use and Information Plan be completed.

Even though few local town planning groups were responding with recommendations for acquisitions, and most that did were outside the Blue Line, Indian Lake came in with a plan and Schroon Lake had submitted a list in 1992. But other towns were still on record as opposing most, if not all, new acquisitions.

Discussions wandered so that by 1996 the minutes record such comments as "the committee has fallen apart or become fractionalized by voting." Several meetings failed to attract a quorum. DEC distributed information on purchases and easements the state was pursuing, on the announcement of Governor Pataki's Clean Water/Clean Air Bond Act to be voted on in 1996, Environmental Protection Fund monies, and the increasing number of gifts to DEC's land acquisition program.

Land acquired under the proposed bond act would include projects affecting water or access and would not require local approval as those funded under the Environmental Protection Fund. While the act states that in deciding projects, "consideration" should be given to the Open Space Plan, again locals felt excluded. The committee went so far as to complain to Gavin Donohue of the governor's staff about the announcement of the bond act. The committee commented that several environmental groups were identified in the governor's press release as participants in the press conference announcing the proposal, unlike local officials. It was obvious that environmental groups had the governor's ear, that their lobbying for land acquisition, protection of large tracts in particular, had caught Pataki's imagination. Donohue assured the committee that if local governments do not want an open space project, "that ends it." Projects, he affirmed, would be based on the Open Space Plan and committee input. However, there were indications that the committee was not as central to land acquisition in the park as it might be. Did the failure to develop a priority list contribute to this distancing? Certainly it detracted from the fragile trust that had been built up within the committee when it reached an agreement on the use of eminent domain. The failure to generate a list emphasized how little trust existed outside environmental groups for DEC's acquisition policies.

In the summer of 1996, all regional committees began work on a third revision of the Open Space Plan to be completed in 1997. In Region 5, DEC made a good presentation on the need to protect wetlands but the department never made such an analysis of lands needed for recreation access. The committee continued most of its prior recommendations, especially those affecting protection of farmland. In discussing the proposed update, the committee went round and round on familiar issues: inability to discuss specific parcels because of lack of background information and opposition to listing specific parcels even if lists were separated into those areas needing protection and those that might become available. While the committee reaffirmed most of the policy in its segment of the Open Space Plan, objections were raised to the amount of money available for small projects. Dave Gibson: "The committee's passivity about listing and making specific recommendations means loss of opportunities to involve landowners, leaves the onus on DEC to notify property owners. . . . There would be less surprise about listings if the committee were more involved in selecting priority projects." Ultimately, the committee reacted positively to several proposed acquisitions listed by DEC in earlier drafts: Floodwood, Pilot Knob, and Blue Mountain Lake Islands. Later it added the Cedarlands easement project near Long Lake and wetlands in the Lake Champlain basin to the priority list.

The 1997 minutes indicate a sharp departure in DEC's working with the committee: Rather than expecting the committee to originate discussion of possible projects, it became obvious that DEC was bringing projects to the group for approval. That was fine, except DEC had no overall plan other than what was in the Open Space Plan, and that remained marginally adequate for the park as a whole. Fish and Wildlife presented recommendations, but they asked for road or motor access in some instances, contrary to the State Land Master Plan.

The third revision of the plan, now the Open Space Conservation Plan, was finally adopted in April 1998, and the governor's announcement made it clear that much land conservation had been accomplished throughout the entire state during his term. Many new county representatives joined the committee that year. Instead of revising the plan every two years, the schedule changed to revisions every four years.

A recommendation to purchase the Bartlett Carry tract, a vital link for canoeists with shorefront on Stony Creek, Middle Saranac Lake, and Saranac River, was approved by the Region 5 committee, but not unanimously and with the understanding that even if the committee did not approve it, the purchase would go through. (The town involved—Harrietstown—did not approve, but did not oppose.) Roger Dziengeleski, woodlands manager from Finch, Pruyn, substituted for Jean Raymond at several meetings. (His letters to her reporting the meetings mention that "they had very little substance.") Mike DiNunzio protested that the committee in eight years had not put together a list for protection, and implied that the new request for economic analysis was just another roadblock. Some felt that purchases had gone beyond those needed for protection to those wanted—but I do not feel this could be true because the committee had never looked at small parcels related to recreation and access issues. Buchanan justified the repetition of discussions as helping educate new members. Among the highlights of 1998 meetings were DEC's presentation of long lists of acquisitions achieved, including many small projects that the committee had never discussed.

The year 1998 ended with the governor's announcement of the Champion lands deal. Because DEC had kept secret most of the negotiations for this complicated acquisition, the committee had little input. However, some committee members were actively involved in discussions. Neil Woodworth said that studies made under the aegis of Adirondack Mountain Club were vital to justifying and outlining the fee acquisitions of the river corridor purchases. DEC had added the North Flow River Corridors to the 1992 Open Space Plan list, taking the lead from Adirondack Mountain Club's proposals, and they were listed again in 1995 as a joint Region 5 and 6 priority. They had not originally been a Region 5 recommendation, and the committee had little direct input in listing those waters for protection. The Adirondack Nature Conservancy was also involved in studies for the project.

The next year, 1999, began with an announcement of the Blue Mountain Lake acquisition, a combined gift and purchase from the Hochschild family of shoreline and islands that included an endowment to manage and supervise use of the lands. A subcommittee under Jim Ellis began studying economic issues relating to land acquisition. He resurrected the concept of transferable development rights (TDRs) as a means for local governments to obtain development rights extinguished by state purchases. Also in that year, Buchanan presented a very long list of acquisition projects and observed that they were mostly projects offered to DEC by landowners that met DEC's (and the committee's) criteria. Individual projects were not discussed, and funding was available for only a few of them. If, as reported in a technical report for the Commission on the Adirondacks in the 21st Century, DEC had a backlog of one thousand approved projects in 1990, why were none in Region 5 presented to its Open Space Plan committee or to town subcommittees for discussion?

Up to this point, the committee had discussed major acquisitions proposed by the state, giving approval to only a few. However, in early 2001 something quite different happened. The state and the Adirondack Nature Conservancy announced an ANC purchase of three tracts from International Paper. Parts would ultimately go to the state, but the Open Space Committee had never considered any of this land.

It is difficult enough to see from the minutes what happened in the Region 5 Open Space committee deliberations; but even with the hindsight gained by delving into the committee's work, it is virtually impossible to see how the public participation process could have been made more effective. The committee was not the right forum for some issues. On the one hand, it is possible to understand the committee's desire for background information on such a wide range of issues, but it can be argued that this information and the resolutions adopted dealing with peripheral issues were misplaced. The background provided was beyond what was needed to come to grips with such issues as easements and forestry, and much of the insight gained by members had no place to go.

The committee was supposed to create part of the Open Space Plan, but that document was not designed to force legislative or DEC policy changes. What influence could the committee have on the legislature? Did DEC take the committee's recommendations to the legislature, or could it even do so? Dealing with easements was among the more difficult issues faced by the committee, mostly because of the complexity of the legislation and the failure of the state to tie payment of taxes to localities for easements from the start. The payoffs from hard discussions were positive and the committee acted as a good sounding board for some issues, but too often discussions took them away from their charge.

Some members of the committee had praised Tom Monroe for the way he ran the committee, letting it set agendas, ranging widely, and the way he provided detailed background information. Yet, as new members were appointed, especially those representing towns, some newcomers complained that they did not even know the purpose of the committee. Still, for a ten-year span, membership was quite consistent. Four representatives of environmental groups—Dave Gibson, Mike DiNunzio, Neil Woodworth, and Duane Ricketson from Residents' Committee to Protect the Adirondacks —attended regularly. George Canon and Jean Raymond were county representatives from the start. The greatest changes in members came from the county representatives.

As several members recalled, the steam just seemed to go out of the committee after the initial rounds. Some attribute it to the long process with frustratingly few results while others attribute it to the change of DEC leadership of the committee. The group approved criteria for acquisitions and the purchase of a few parcels but never reached broad consensus on a detailed program. Reading the enormous file of minutes and reports generated, I came to the hypothesis that the committee did very well examining all the issues surrounding land acquisition, but because so much of what it saw as needing changes (mostly by the legislature) was outside its charter, the committee could not sustain positive direction.

Since the committee's role was only advisory, DEC or the governor could follow the committee's recommendations or go around them; the latter was often the case. The group lost power when it did not present projects, leading to the question, Could the group as constituted ever reach consensus on that issue? When the floodgates were opened to funding in the mid-1990s by the Environmental Protection Fund and the 1996 Bond Act, the committee had no map, no direction, no priorities of its own for acquisitions, only a policy that was freely interpreted by others. More time was spent discussing real estate and economic values of land acquisition than the significance of protecting land or creating recreational opportunities.

Even the acquisition criteria, generally the work of Jim Dawson from the first draft plan, were in need of refining by the end of the decade. The criteria in the statewide Open Space Plan for assigning a numerical value to parcels under consideration were a problem from the start because of the way the Open Space Plan was constituted: criteria had to apply both to acquisitions for the Forest Preserve and those for urban and state park areas. The Region 5 committee added criteria to the statewide guidelines that reflected the Adirondack situation. Region 5's criteria included biological diversity, water quality, open space administration, critical environmental areas, recreation, historic and cultural resources, scenic resources, working landscapes, and key tracts.[7]

There were those on the committee who wished to see Region 5 and 6 combined or at least work together, but Region 6 was opposed, mostly because its leadership feared the way the political spotlight that dominated every action in Region 5 might affect Region 6. Region 6 is largely omitted from this discussion, primarily because that Open Space Plan committee worked well. It had strong leadership from DEC; regional director Tom Brown was a master at bringing the group to consensus and keeping them focused on the charge to recommend sites for state acquisition. Brown made sure agendas addressed clear land protection goals, including riparian rights and public access.

Region 5's environmentalists were largely staff from lobbying groups. Only one of Region 5's "environmental" members was a resident of the park; the majority on the Region 6 committee were local people. They included Peter O'Shea and Clarence Petty. Tod Dunham represented the Adirondack Nature Conservancy. Neither local government representatives nor residents were politicized. Lloyd Moore of St. Lawrence County took information on potential acquisitions back to his constituents; there was never a problem as long as he checked with them. Dan Tickner, who has a business built around canoeing in the Old Forge area, brought a perspective that melded preservation and business. Bruce Carpenter of New York Rivers United was able to speak to the recreation benefits and needs. The environmental groups appeared slightly more mainstream or at least willing to compromise.

From the start, the Region 6 committee proposed specific acquisitions. It created two categories that suited the region—Working Forests and Northern Rivers—and seemed to have a clear perspective of what was needed. In addition, Doug Wilson, who was Region 6's real property supervisor through part of the 1990s, brought information on acquisition projects the department had considered to every meeting. The Region 6 committee discussed them carefully as potential additions to the Open Space Plan. As in Region 5, the Region 6 committee asked for and received background material, policies, and technical details, but those were centered on specific issues of land protection and easements.

Work on the fourth revision of the Open Space Plan seemed to rejuvenate the Region 5 committee. Several resolutions were revised and new ones added in 2000. The group favored planning and maintaining long-distance trail networks. Two recommendations dealt with private forests: a study of the long-term viability of Adirondack commercial forests and endorsement of sustainable forest designations.

The environmental movement in the nineties inspired Governor Pataki to act on land acquisition on a grand scale. These acquisitions had remarkably little input from the Region 5 Open Space Committee. In the end, even the committee's recommendations for consultation were largely ignored.

Because of the crazy-quilt nature of public lands within the park, there are long boundaries of state land that are bordered by private land, which when posted blocks access to the Forest Preserve. The state does not need to acquire all the private land on the boundaries; in fact that is undesirable. But it ought to acquire key access parcels or easements along roadsides. The Open Space Committee has been unable to contribute to such a list or to elicit suggestions for the list from communities.

The Region 5 committee did not achieve success when it tried to carry its quest to the towns. And that raises one more of the problems confronting public participation efforts: Is it ever possible for representatives to return to their groups and convince them of the need to bring their own agendas into the consensus sphere developed by the committees to which they have been sent? Some of the committee votes were unanimous; most of the few resolutions were passed by majority vote. Although committee members agreed to support majority resolutions, this was not binding on the organizations or towns they represented. This to me is one of the committee's weakest aspects. Members do not truly represent in the sense that they can compromise or join in a consensus agreement, and the group or town they represent often continues to oppose the compromise or just returns to its earlier stance. Was it even possible for the committees to reach out to the Association of Adirondack Towns and Villages or to towns to bring them into discussions about land acquisition? Was this too much to expect from such participatory groups? What can be learned from the fact that the Region 6 committee was ultimately more effective?

The Environmental Protection Fund, whose funds by law are still subject to local veto, generates between 90 and 120 million dollars a year, of which between 15 and 33 million is available for land acquisition statewide. The 1996 Bond Act was either spent or almost totally committed as of 2000. In 2001 environmental groups began a big push to increase the amount of funds available through the EPF.

Adirondack Park Agency Chairman Lefevbre's 2001 Gateway Plan, still in its formative stage, is attempting to involve towns in roles as gateways to the Forest Preserve. Perhaps this initiative will prove a better place to discuss acquisitions needed to connect towns and existing Forest Preserve. Only time will tell.

CASE STUDY 2

Forest Preserve Advisory Committee

THE ORIGINS of the Forest Preserve Advisory Committee in 1980 are detailed in chapter 7. FPAC had been appointed to advise DEC, through the director of the Division of Lands and Forests, on matters affecting the Forest Preserve of both the Adirondack and Catskill parks. Gradually the committee's charge was expanded to include review of Adirondack and Catskill State Land Master Plans, review of all DEC activities in the Forest Preserve including those of the Division of Fish and Wildlife and of Operations, and easements within the park boundaries. In its early years the committee made important recommendations, but, from the mid-1980s on, its effectiveness seemed to decline.

The last four years of Governor Cuomo's term were obviously not easy times to deal with DEC's Adirondack problems. For various reasons, Catskill problems were easier to solve than those in the Adirondacks. Commissioner Jorling appeared to be completely removed from anything the FPAC recommended. Even the tenor of the FPAC meetings changed. The minutes reflect negativity; DEC staff reports became sparse; and suggestions or recommendations to DEC fell on deaf ears. Everyone was aware that calls for additional funding would go nowhere. There was a sense that nothing could be done, that DEC staff was becoming demoralized.

The FPAC continued to push for the completion of unit management plans (UMPs) and the updating of DEC policies. As the decade of the 1990s progressed, the specter of the uncompleted Adirondack Forest Preserve Public Use and Information Plan (see case study 5) kept appearing, but the committee never saw a draft. The parallel Catskill Use and Information Plan was completed after almost all the Catskill UMPs had been written. It is possible that having a completed inventory as provided for by the Catskill UMPs made writing that use and information document possible. But it is also true that most of the Catskill plans contained proposals for new trails and recreational opportunities as well as measures to rein in use where it was inappropriate. Those documents had a practical vision for the units, a more positive vision than is found in most completed Adirondack plans. The Catskill region had tackled plans where use within the units had to be restricted or where recreational opportunities within the unit were already fully developed.

The FPAC worried that each of the state agencies initiating GIS tools to map and analyze their work (Department of Transportation, Department of Environmental Conservation, Adirondack Park Agency, and so forth) was creating an independent system. A committee that was supposed to work out coordination between agencies could never agree and seems to have disappeared.

The FPAC backed the General Obligations Law, which would limit liability for landowners whose land is used by the public; Forest Preserve training for new rangers; and DEC funding for rehabilitating fire towers. The committee wrote state senators asking them to support a speed-up of the UMP process on the grounds that it would provide economic benefits to Adirondack communities.

Things must have appeared pretty bad in late 1996, for even Commissioner Zagata said that "the natural resource side of the department needs to be strengthened; it has been allowed to wither in recent years."[8] In 1995 pressure from outside had saved the Bureau of Preserve, Protection, and Management, but its demise began anyway as part of Zagata's reorganization in 1996. Apprehension about the change was heightened by the announcement that DEC was preparing a recreation policy for all state lands. Zagata saw recreation in terms of hunting and motorized use. Applauded by Adirondack Conservation Council and other sportsmen's groups, Zagata attempted to be everything for everybody. His position became untenable, and Pataki replaced him after two years.

The FPAC was unanimous in calling for a comprehensive plan for access by persons with disabilities,[9] and this recommendation was ignored as described in case study 4. The committee was also unanimous in its opposition to budget cuts proposed by the incoming Pataki administration.

In 1996 DEC forester Tom Kapelewski asked the committee to consider a revision to Norm VanValkenburgh's 1986 snowmobile policy to allow for wider trails and bridges. (In the discussion DEC referred to the trails as multiple use trails, but the committee noted that its longstanding suggestions to make them truly multiple use by avoiding wetlands, adding connectors to form loops, and providing drainage for summer use, and so forth had been ignored.) In April 1997 the committee asked that DEC and Office of Parks, Recreation, and Historic Preservation prepare a master plan with a map showing all snowmobile trails on both public and private lands in the Adirondacks and Catskills. The map was to show not just the corridor trails, but all the trails used by local clubs.

DEC asked the committee to recommend cutting of trees on corridor trails to bring them up to the existing 8-foot-width standard. The committee demurred, asking just how many trees that meant. When, nearly a year later, it learned that this meant that 87 miles out of the 306 miles of corridor trails in the Adirondacks had an average of 29 trees per mile standing in the 8-foot corridors, the committee was reluctant to recommend approval of that much cutting. The committee found that the total was not "immaterial," as defined by an attorney general's opinion that permitted limited cutting on the Forest Preserve. Without the committee's recommendation, Frank Dunstan, then director of the Division of Lands and Forests, said he would approach the question by revising the current (January 1998) snowmobile trail policy.

The width of snowmobile trails was at the heart of issues to be resolved in the snowmobile policy. DEC had been issuing permits to local clubs to do routine trail maintenance, and the understanding of what was routine seems to have expanded through the decade. Eight-foot-wide trails, the standard in the Adirondacks established by the State Land Master Plan, were considered too narrow, especially in comparison to trails in Canada and the upper Midwest and even to some trails on private lands in the Old Forge area. Passing and negotiating curves were considered difficult, and such trails allowed only moderate speeds. The newer snowmobiles, in fact the only ones being produced, were considerably wider and more powerful than older machines.

When the FPAC heard about DEC's illegal widening and bulldozing of snowmobile trails, the committee voted to advise DEC to complete a snowmobile trails policy that was in keeping with the State Land Master Plan. The committee considered a resolution calling for a moratorium on snowmobile trail work, but that was voted down. A sidelight to the public participation issue was the fact that Neil Woodworth, then a member of FPAC, was unhappy with the rejection of the moratorium and continued to lobby for it as a representative of Adirondack Mountain Club. At his insistence, DEC did issue a moratorium. Towns and snowmobile clubs became enraged, and although the ban was quickly lifted, the incident created more distrust than ever. The issue simmered, with some people (among them ADK's Woodworth) objecting to the use of motorized equipment such as groomers to maintain snowmobile trails.

There appeared to be a real division between Adirondack Park Agency's position on the issue and DEC's. In the fall of 2000, with the help of APA, Dick Lefebvre, and the governor's office, DEC finally issued a statement that interpreted what was meant by existing policy. The finished product brought DEC's policy in line with APA's State Land Master Plan, where it should have been all along. Still under discussion was a new DEC policy for snowmobiles, but the "focus group" discussing it, made up of DEC, snowmobilers, and environmentalists, began meeting with the governor's staff in 2001 so that the policy could be worked out without creating a public dispute. The map showing existing trails was still not complete in 2001.

About the same time the snowmobile trails issue flared up, the committee learned about an Americans with Disabilities (ADA) lawsuit against DEC, and for the next two years DEC staff would not/could not discuss with the committee issues of motorized access to the Forest Preserve because of the litigation. In fact, several other issues under litigation had to be removed from committee discussions. The FPAC did, however, reopen the issue of DEC staff use of motorized vehicles and staff authorization of motorized use by volunteers working on trails.

The subject of motorized use in the Forest Preserve is a glaring example of the way DEC has lost institutional memory of the struggles of the sixties that resulted in the Adirondack Park Agency. Then, environmentalists were not just alarmed by the way the old Conservation Department had constructed or designated snowmobile trails throughout the Forest Preserve; they believed that motors had no place on those lands at all. DEC's continuing resistance to embracing the State Land Master Plan brought the comment from one environmental lobbyist that DEC makes sure its policies follow the State Land Master Plan only after it has been "brought down kicking and screaming."

This stretching of what the department could legally do generated several lawsuits, and these kept staff so busy filling the requirements of discovery that what little staff was left was almost overwhelmed. In November 1998, I talked to Frank Dunstan to protest his absence from most FPAC meetings (DEC was represented by Tom Wolfe of the Bureau of Public Lands instead) and to point out to him the value of using the FPAC to diffuse contentious issues, to gather information, to make recommendations that, if used, might have averted problems confronting the department. Dunstan's attendance at FPAC meetings improved, but he remained wary of the committee.

At the April 1997 meeting, when I was elected chair, I was also appointed to attend meetings with the National Park Service to help represent DEC's wish to promote a route for the North Country National Scenic Trail (NCNST) through the southern Adirondacks. DEC had decided on a southern route after an earlier meeting when nine alternatives had been considered. Several meetings followed, including one attended by both DEC and APA, but so far no method has been devised for dealing with such long-distance trails, whose planning involves several Wilderness and Wild Forest units with their individual UMPs. Both the FPAC and the Region 5 Open Space Plan committee have passed resolutions asking APA and DEC to deal with this issue, but as of 2001 there is no progress. A solution should go beyond choosing a general route for the NCNST because a number of proposals for long-distance trails have been circulated: snowmobile corridor trails; extensions of the Long Path (it now exists from the George Washington Bridge to the Mohawk River and the extension would take it across the Adirondacks to Whiteface); rerouting of the Northville-Placid Trail to eliminate the road sections; a hilltop trail in the Hudson River Gorge; a trail over the Little Great Range that lies west of Indian Lake; canoe routes; and so on. The author believes that general location of routes spanning several units should be determined by the State Land Master Plan, not planned piecewise by the unit management plan process.

For years, the committee asked for a legal opinion on whether DEC could regulate public motorboat use on lakes whose shores had both public and private lands. It was not until the use of motorboats and airplane landings on the western (Wilderness) end of Lows Lake became an issue that a DEC attorney told the committee that DEC had the legal authority to regulate motorized use in this situation, but so far the department has not attempted to do so.*

As DEC's ability to manage the Forest Preserve continued to decline, more and more problems arose to become crises. (Motorized access for the disabled is one example.) FPAC meetings became litanies of despair. Can the decline in the quality of care and custody of the Forest Preserve be traced to DEC's downplaying it through reorganizations and funding decreases? And where were the voices of the environmental groups? They protested, but weakly, choosing instead to appeal to the governor's enthusiasm for big, splashy acquisitions, which were their primary concern anyway.

At about the same time, various members of the FPAC chose to downplay its importance, preferring to talk directly with the governor's office or with DEC Commissioner Cahill. For a while, it was as if it no longer mattered what the FPAC said or did.

The Region 5 Open Space Plan group extended its sphere far beyond land acquisition so that there has been considerable overlap with the FPAC. The two groups differ in membership: the Open Space Plan committee having county representatives as well as not-for-profits, the FPAC having environmental groups and a wide range of user groups from snowmobilers to hikers as well as selected officials. The FPAC has been as concerned with issues surrounding the workings of DEC as with policy issues and in this way differs greatly from the Region 5 Open Space Plan group.

I was able to accomplish one of my goals for the FPAC—widening the breadth of its membership to include a broad range of user groups. I was not able to change the committee's gender bias, and this issue leads to an interesting parallel between the Adirondacks and the environmental movement nationally. There have been two women beside myself on the FPAC: Peggy O'Brien represented High Peaks interests from the formation of the committee into the 1980s. Helen Chase represented the Catskills starting in the late 1990s. Until the end of 2001, every other or-

---

* There are four lakes with partial Wilderness Area shores that present similar questions: Lows Lake, the east shore of Indian Lake, a second Indian Lake on the western boundary of the Moose River Plains, and Thirteenth Lake. A related question concerns Sacandaga Lake, where a resident wanted a permit to establish a water-ski slalom course.

ganizational representative was male. Although more women have joined the boards of diverse Adirondack organizations, they are still a minority. All but a handful of the major lobbyists are male. Mark Dowie, who wrote about the national environmental movement, saw problems with the fact that both mainstream and grassroots environmental groups were dominated by men. He looked for the emergence of ecofeminism or feminist ecology to counteract the "male dominance and masculine bureaucratic structure of mainstream American Environmentalism." [10] Environmentalism in the Adirondacks may even trail behind the movement in the rest of the nation in overcoming male dominance.

I also worked hard to broaden agendas to cover as many issues relating to DEC and the Forest Preserve as possible. With everyone else on the committee, I hoped the FPAC could influence the way DEC works, but that goal has met with few successes. The reasons why are varied: the state budget; the legislature, which has not passed key laws; the governor, who has an agenda focused on acquisition, who only in 2000 began to address stewardship needs, and who appears frightened by any effort that might cause controversy. Individual members and the organizations they represent have been more effective than the FPAC in influencing the legislature or the governor's office. But, probably the biggest reason the FPAC has had so little clout lies within DEC itself. The department devotes too little effort toward overseeing the Forest Preserve and is hampered by bureaucracy fettered by inertia. The FPAC can only observe, advise, recommend, and continue to function even when ignored.

Like the Open Space Committee, the FPAC has served best as a forum at which members could learn about DEC's programs, its successes, its funding shortfalls, its staffing problems, whatever. DEC representatives did hear suggestions, advice, another side to issues, but whether this perspective ever made a difference in DEC policy is hard to discern.

There is no evidence that committee members were ever able to change the positions of the groups they represented to bring them closer to any consensus positions achieved by the FPAC. The anecdotal evidence points to the fact that individual groups pursued their own agendas without regard to broader solutions that arose through committee discussions. But then, this is true of most DEC citizens' advisory committees.

CASE STUDY 3

The Blowdown of 1995

THE WAY DEC MANAGED the aftermath of the blowdown of 1995 is a glowing example of good management of public interest. The blowdown was a major event, affecting nearly a million acres. The *derecho*, or storm with straight-line winds, leveled trees on 430,000 acres, along a series of parallel lines stretching from west-northwest to east-southeast, the broadest of which devastated parts of Brandreth Park, the commercial forests of Whitney Park, and the Five Ponds Wilderness Area with its old-growth forests. The state immediately closed the Five Ponds to prevent fires. The threat of fire was real, not, as many thought, primarily those spreading to private forests from campfires on state land but also those spreading from private lands that backed up to state land. Nevertheless, pictures showing the fire devastation started by railroads and people in the early 1900s were resurrected to bolster the arguments for salvage.

Governor Pataki and DEC Commissioner Zagata could have fallen back on the state constitution, which clearly prohibits the taking of trees, standing or fallen, from the Forest Preserve. However, that prohibition has not always been perceived to be as absolute as it sounds; it had been modified by law and by opinions of attorneys general. Further, under the guise of fire management, the old Conservation Department's response to the blowdown of 1950 had been not only to "salvage" or cut trees over a wide area but to construct numerous fire roads, most notably in the western High Peaks. (These were also permitted by an opinion by the attorney general.) At that time not all conservationists were opposed to the harvest. The New York State Conservation Council's Forest Preserve

---

Committee, led at the time by Paul Schaefer, recommended that the Conservation Department carry out the salvage (with many provisos) because it was thought "necessary to protect the Forest Preserve" as a whole.[11] Despite the protests of some environmentalists and a long and acrimonious debate, the 1950 harvest went on using trucks and large machines so that the effects—hardened roads—are visible fifty years later.

In 1995 most owners of industrial forests feared a glut on the market; there was already an oversupply of wood, especially marginal wood, in the Northeast and Canada. Despite this, the precedent of the 1950s and a fierce charge, led in 1995 by the Adirondack Conservation Council and parts of the timber industry, made it politically difficult for DEC to direct that there be no salvage. Further, the DEC was not unanimous in wanting to support the constitution. But despite the fact that there was little chance salvage would be permitted, the threat of it was enough for the Adirondack Council and other groups to counter with a warning that they would sue if DEC permitted salvage.

DEC set up a working group to recommend a solution. Staff provided the group with background information, including the legal framework for discussion. There was an adjunct committee of scientists, which analyzed what was known about the ecological effects of such a storm. The committee analyzed past blowdowns, salvage, and droughts; the aftermath of the 1950 blowdown; and the historical relationship between blowdown and fire.[12] This was included in a final report, put together by Michael Birmingham of DEC. The report also covered the ecological effects of blowdown and salvage on the regeneration of affected tree species, fish and wildlife, insects and disease, hydrology, and wilderness values, as well as methods to determine fire potential. The committee's recommendations were also based on a sophisticated DEC report dealing with fire mitigation and response. The Division of Lands and Forests' speedy preparation of a report assessing and mapping the windstorm's damage (completed in November 1995 under the direction of Bob Bathrick, division director) was essential to the committee's work and was also the reason the legislature acted so fast to provide funds to carry out the recommendations of the final report.

The high quality of the report made the job of the working group easier, but the most important part of the latter's activities was the staff who ran the group's meetings. Lois New and Karyn Richards acted as facilitators, moving the meetings along, making sure all points of view were heard, but keeping the attendees from the three p's (posturing, position-ing, and the politics of division).[13] This was no mean feat given that the group of over forty was evenly divided between representatives of envi-ronmental organizations opposed to any salvage and those who were concerned with fire prevention, utilization of downed timber, and wildlife (deer) populations. Sportsmen joined representatives of the tim-ber industry in viewing the issues from the perspective of an enormous economic resource going to waste.

The working group's recommendations, issued in March 1996, went way beyond the decision to do no salvage: small areas around camp-grounds, campsites, and trails should be cleared; remote controlled weather stations should be installed; and buffers should be cleared be-tween settled areas and state land.

In a related move, Adirondack Park Agency tried to make it easier for industry to obtain permits to clearcut privately owned tracts severely af-fected by the blowdown. Adirondack Council claimed that the initial pro-posals gave away too much APA control; Council was able to get APA to tighten the permit conditions. Forest researcher Jerry Jenkins's post-blowdown assessment of the Five Ponds Wilderness contributed signifi-cantly to the discussions.

The DEC's working group served to educate and allay the fears of lo-cals. Don Sage, then vice president of Adirondack Conservation Council and a member of the working group, was chastised by ACC for writing intemperate letters to the governor and legislators on ACC stationery, demanding salvage. Whether it was that or the really open way the work-ing group was conducted is not clear, but at the meeting announcing that there would be no general salvage, Sage said he felt the meetings had been conducted fairly—no small admission given the intensity of his statements in favor of harvest.

Most of the working group's recommendations have been carried out; two have not: DEC's protocol for closing blowdown lands when drought conditions warrant has not been effectively applied to all state lands.* Nor has DEC acted on the recommendation that a database be established listing all scientific research on the effects of the blowdown so

---

* The state was slow to close the High Peaks to campfires during the drought of 1999. As a result an unextinguished campfire spread over a ridge west of Noonmark in the High Peaks.

that such information would be available for the next such event. This recommendation is particularly relevant because the next event occurred within five years—a destructive ice storm that ravaged the northern boundary area of the state.

The process upheld the state's relevant laws, heard public concerns, and most important, served as a real educational exercise. Furthermore, there were no fires, although, as in the years after 1950, the weather in the years after 1995 did as much to prevent fires as any state actions. It rained!

CASE STUDY 4

Motorized Access to the Forest Preserve
and Access for the Disabled

DEC HAS APPEARED TO PURPOSELY misunderstand some of the legal mandates under which it should act. At times the department, under pressures from special interest groups, has taken actions contrary to the State Land Master Plan. Examples range from the delay in taking out interior cabins, continuing the phone lines to Lake Colden, keeping open the truck trail to Marcy Dam, allowing overuse of High Peaks, and excessive tree cutting on Forest Preserve land in the Catskills. The most egregious involved the issuance of temporary revocable permits for motorized use in the Forest Preserve without clear guidelines and necessary changes to the State Land Master Plan.

Use of ATVs (all-terrain vehicles) and their predecessor machines has been a problem from the late 1950s. Adirondack Council wrote APA in 1984 requesting that the agency, in cooperation with DEC, "develop a generic, articulated policy" concerning ATVs.[14] In 1985, the New York Supreme Court's ruling in the case of *Baker v. DEC* reaffirmed the State Land Master Plan's restriction of motorized access and denied that the plan discriminates against disabled persons.[15]

At the time, 1986, when the law went into effect requiring that ATVs be licensed and carry insurance, the Forest Preserve Advisory Committee was concerned that the department had not done an adequate job of informing the public that ATVs were banned from Forest Preserve trails.[16] On April 19, 1986, a DEC ranger served an appearance notice on a paraplegic for driving his three-wheel ATV to Wilcox Lake (in Wild Forest, not Wilderness) to fish, something the driver said he had done many times in the eight years since his paralyzing accident.[17] DEC tried to close all roads to ATV use.

It appears that DEC had not paid much attention to the use of ATVs until the passage of the licensing law in 1986 and that incident. The Forest Preserve Advisory Committee, concerned that DEC had made little progress on compliance with the 1986 Americans with Disabilities Act, urged that the department publish a brochure showing where there was disabled access for camping, fishing, picnicking, and so forth. DEC, under Henry Williams, did issue a brochure, "Opening the Outdoors to the Handicapped," directed at the entire state, but it was inadequate with respect to the Adirondack Park. The FPAC urged that DEC prepare a brochure showing trails suitable for wheelchair access and listing which roads through Forest Preserve lands were open to motor vehicles. The committee spent a session in 1987 discussing the federal guidelines outlined in the Americans with Disabilities Act with representatives from Office of Parks, Recreation, and Historic Preservation responsible for implementing the program. DEC should have been knowledgeable about the act's requirements, but in the department's typical bureaucratic maze, this information was lost or ignored in the next few years.

In the early 1990s, DEC, in response to concerns about access for the disabled, issued a temporary revocable permit to a disabled individual who wanted to use an ATV to hunt along an abandoned railroad right-of-way. The number of such permits granted escalated until it generated criticism of DEC's actions. DEC called a series of public meetings from late 1995 to the summer of 1996 to guide the department in resolving the issues of access for the disabled and in responding to the federal Americans with Disabilities Act. These meetings were so poorly handled (in stark contrast to the blowdown response) that issues related to motorized use continued into the new century.

This brief summary of what happened in the 1990s conceals a number of problems that DEC created for itself; details that follow reveal them. Regulations permitting use of motorized vehicles on Forest Preserve lands were at the heart of the matter. The regulations were loosely covered in the Environmental Conservation Law, ECL 190.8; however, department policy spelling out exactly how the department interpreted the regulations was vague until 1990.

The department had produced drafts of a "Non-ambulatory Access Permit Application" in early 1990. The FPAC suggested revisions and remained concerned about the loose way such policies permitted motorized access to state land. In 1993 Deputy Commissioner Robert Bendick issued a revised policy,[18] giving temporary revocable permits to "mobility impaired" individuals to use motors on state lands except Forest Preserve lands. However, a regional land manager could, if he thought motorized use would not have a deleterious effect on the road or trail, issue temporary revocable permits for such use in Intensive Use Areas and in Wild Forests. It is amazing that this very respected deputy commissioner issued such a policy, which appears in conflict with the State Land Master Plan, without clearing it with Adirondack Park Agency. Following the gubernatorial election, some of Bendick's responsibilities were shifted to Herbert Doig, although Doig was given only the title of "Assistant Commissioner for Fish and Wildlife and Marine Resources." Doig was regarded by many as ill prepared to supervise the Division of Lands and Forests, and problems under him became much more serious.

Maynard Baker, supervisor of the Town of Warrenburg, filed a complaint with the National Park Service Equal Opportunity Office in March 1995. It charged that DEC's policies for access to the Forest Preserve violated the Americans with Disabilities Act. The Park Service determined that DEC's definition of a disabled person was in violation of the Americans with Disabilities Act; by September, DEC had corrected this and the National Park Service Equal Opportunity Office wrote DEC that the definition, which included medical criteria, was in compliance.

With the Pataki administration and the appointment of Commissioner Michael D. Zagata in early 1995, temporary revocable permits were issued for ATV use by the mobility-impaired, but only in limited areas. In June 1995, DEC ticketed Ted Galusha, who had multiple sclerosis, for operating a motor vehicle on restricted trails in the Hudson River Recreation Area. In September 1995, a new policy was issued that tightened the definition of disability, added certain conditions, but still allowed the issuance of temporary revocable permits for state trails in Wild Forest areas.[19]

Herbert Doig, assistant commissioner, was assigned by Zagata to work with Baker to draft a new policy. DEC staff met with Galusha, Baker, and others in October to broaden the policy for motorized access. A report of the meeting in the *Post Star* prompted environmental groups to petition DEC to widen the discussion. The governor and DEC leaders agreed that the State Land Master Plan and DEC Rules and Regulations had not been properly cited in the closed-door meeting.

As a result Commissioner Zagata formed a "working group," near the end of 1995, to deal with motorized access and compliance with the State Land Master Plan. The plan permits snowmobiles on specified trails in Wild Forest Areas. All other public motorized access is limited to roads in the Moose River Plains and other deed-allowed roads, to town roads, and to Intensive Use Area roads; and not all of these categories are open to ATVs.

The working group was loosely composed of environmentalists, hunters, fishermen, disabled individuals, and in particular some who had previously been issued temporary revocable permits for access to state lands, including Baker and Galusha. I came to the conclusion that the different people from DEC who managed the meetings all displayed a lack of direction and common sense. The result was a fiasco. The first mistake was that DEC was trying to develop policy for all state lands, when the restrictions on the Forest Preserve are much different from those on state forests. (One staff person asserted that Wild Forests are almost like state forests, when the difference is a chasm: In Wild Forests, motor vehicle use is prohibited except as noted above and no new roads can be designated in existing Forest Preserve. On existing trails motorized access is limited to snowmobiles and administrative use. In many state forests motorized access is allowed.) Further, it was quickly obvious that most of those in attendance had a single-minded agenda, the opening of Forest Preserve roads to motorized access, cloaked in the guise of access for the disabled. The department was not prepared with background information on such issues as what roads in the Adirondacks were open to motorized access. In fact, it did not put together such a list until after a "final policy" was released in late May 1997.

Adirondack Council used what it termed "the DEC's attempt to dismantle its long-standing policy which prohibits the use of motorized vehicles in certain areas of the Forest Preserve" as a plea to its members for a special financial contribution. Several individuals on the working group who were frustrated by DEC's actions (Dave Gibson of the Association for the Protection of the Adirondacks in particular) contacted Janet Zeller, Equal Public Opportunity program manager, Eastern Region USDA Forest Service. She administered the Forest Service's compliance with the Americans with Disabilities Act and was in a position to offer DEC advice on the department's compliance. Unfortunately she could not attend the first meeting of the working group, but she sent comments on DEC's draft policy, noting that the first step would be for DEC to define the "program" that is to be accessed by this policy. Further, she wrote, "the ADA states the program is not to be fundamentally altered for access by persons with disabilities. . . . The program impact of providing a special program for persons with disabilities must be managed with the rights of all recreationists in mind."[20] DEC proceeded as if the only issue was determining how to provide motorized access for some.

The agenda for that first meeting was open-ended; those attending were asked to list issues they felt were important, and from this list came principles for policy development and a list of issues that could not be addressed by the working group; that is, they would require legislative action, new rules and regulations, or changes to the State Land Master Plan. Also put into the pot for discussion was a huge list of issues, 132, identified by written comment, all of which were grist for the mill at the second meeting. This form of public participation, which was adopted for some of the Unit Management Plan meetings as "scoping sessions," has proven misleading: once something is written down the public assumes it can be addressed by those participating even if it is outside the purview of the session.

The second meeting, which was rather chaotic, only produced a request for the DEC to prepare a map depicting all old roads in the Adirondack Forest Preserve, including those that had been closed.[21] This proposal was put forward by those wanting motor access to all the roads, including nineteenth-century logging roads that had disappeared into forest.

The assistant commissioner who chaired that meeting had to be reminded that such a roster would include places where no motorized access could possibly be authorized.* Many present felt that individuals representing DEC were clearly supportive of allowing the use of ATVs on trails and of broadening the definition of what constituted a disability.[22]

---

* I was so disturbed, as were others, by this meeting, that I faxed Doig, who chaired the meeting, a letter noting that there were two agendas at the meeting: those with disabilities who simply wanted to know what accesses were available and "a segment that wanted only to open the Forest Preserve to motorized access and they are seizing on this process as a way to that end."

I was so frustrated that I asked Deputy Commissioner Doig in advance if I could address the April 2 meeting to outline a broader agenda based on (1) dissemination of information on access for the disabled (existing sources as well as a much-needed DEC brochure); (2) a list of roads, currently driveable, with wilderness settings; (3) a list of existing wheelchair-accessible trails; (4) suggestions for trails that could be made wheelchair-accessible with minimal effort. When it was my turn to speak, Maynard Baker and others protested that I had no right to do so. They set up such a chorus of opposition that it occupied three times the fifteen minutes I had been allotted. The attack on my right to be on the agenda was so personal and devastating that it left me shaking; the facilitator and DEC staff made feeble attempts to let me talk, and in the end I did, unable to hold my notes steady enough to read. No one paid any attention, reinforcing the fact that true access for the disabled was not the agenda of the majority of the group. I was further distressed that my limited attempt to expand the scope of the working group did not even include disabilities other than mobility impairment.

Even more distressing was the fact that the group proceeded to discuss another modified draft policy that was limited to permitting motorized access. That draft focused on technicalities of definitions, but contained the phrase that the policy would permit the disabled access by motor vehicles to lands "including certain Forest Preserve lands, where use of such vehicle by the general public is not otherwise permitted." The supposedly final draft presented at the April meeting expanded definitions of disability and specified the number of companions (one, although discussions have ranged as high as six) who could accompany a disabled person. It said no permits could be issued that would be contrary to existing laws, but still did not state specifically where in the Forest Preserve vehicles could or could not be used.

Meetings were contentious, tedious, and circuitous at best, and appeared to be ducking the main issue, that the DEC could not, given existing state laws, provide motorized access to Forest Preserve land for anyone. They devolved into rancorous affairs where disgruntled Adirondackers sat around arguing over minutia of a regulation that basically could not and did not apply to the Adirondacks. The breadth of the discussion reinforced the belief some held that the state could write a general regulation permitting motorized access. The deliberations centered on the number of wheels on a permitted ATV or the number of companions who could travel with the disabled person. Drafts were discussed, re-worded, but little changed.

The agenda for the next meeting, which was postponed at least once, came with the title "WORKING GROUP ACCESS TO DEC LANDS BY PEOPLE WITH DISABILITIES USING A MOTOR VEHICLE." In limiting the scope of the working group, DEC had set a trap for itself. That May 29 meeting was the last for the working group before DEC presented its final version of the policy. In the next few months, DEC issued fifteen temporary revocable permits for motorized access to Wild Forest places and to the Siamese Ponds Wilderness as well as to Santanoni's Primitive Corridor. DEC's permits were purportedly issued subject to the working group's recommended final draft policy, but it was clear that the permits did not comply with it because some of the destinations were contrary to the State Land Master Plan and DEC rules and regulations. These permits were revoked in September.

The issue languished (festered) until the beginning of 1997, when Zagata had been replaced by Acting Commissioner John P. Cahill. A new draft was quickly released, containing one key new sentence: "In the Adirondack Park and Catskill Park, motor vehicle use is prohibited on trails and in areas [meaning the Forest Preserve], and is limited to designated and specifically marked roads (and snowmobiles on designated snowmobile trails) on lands classified as Wild Forest." Either people had been working behind the scenes to convince DEC that this was what the State Land Master Plan said or perhaps the change of leadership made staff see the inevitable. The wasted year had silently allowed those who wished increased motorized access to believe they would have it. There had been no clear message to the contrary, so that those in the working group who did not wish to accept the limitations just did not hear or absorb that information.

Comments to this new draft were mixed. The majority were supportive, although, as Peter Bauer of Residents' Committee to Protect the Adirondacks, Mike DiNunzio of Adirondack Council, and Susan Allen of Fairness Coalition pointed out, there still was no list of roads that could be used. A few letters were quite angry: Ted Galusha, who now would be denied a permit to drive his ATV to Wilcox Lake, complained that the "thousands of hours" spent by the working group had been changed "to give the disabled less rights than we had before this process started in 1995."[23]

Teena Willard, a paraplegic working at the Center for Assisted Living in Saratoga, was concerned that the new draft had been circulated before it was presented to the working group. (A reporter had called Ted Galusha in February asking for comments on the draft and on learning that Ted had not seen it, faxed him a copy, which he had presumably obtained from Adirondack Council). Willard was also upset that the working group had not been asked to comment on the draft.[24] Dave Gibson of the Association for the Protection of the Adirondacks wrote that it was unfortunate that the working group had not been extended the courtesy of receiving the draft at a meeting where it could be discussed.[25]

The final draft came out as a Commissioner's Policy, dated April 29, and on May 1 members of the working group were sent a letter thanking them for their participation. With the letter came a list of roads and trails in Wild Forest areas that were open to motorized use and not one new road was added. That policy sparked instant reaction: Maynard Baker staged a June rally at Newcomb, intending to drive ATVs down the road to Santanoni Great Camp. The flyer for the event called for an end to Wilderness designations parkwide, which Peter Bauer of Residents' Committee to Protect the Adirondacks believes was the day's real agenda.[26] Baker's group, which included a few disabled individuals, was outnumbered by those opposed to motorized access. People accompanying the disabled did remove concrete barricades, however.

In September, the National Park Service reiterated its allegation that DEC Forest Preserve policies discriminate against persons with disabilities. DEC again, this time with much documentation, denied the charge.

In June 1998, three individuals, including Galusha and Willard, filed suit in federal court alleging discrimination under the Americans with Disabilities Act. The plaintiffs and the attorney general's office, representing DEC, argued before federal judge Lawrence Kahn. In July he issued a temporary restraining order granting relief for the plaintiffs to access the Forest Preserve by ATVs. Environmental groups such as Adirondack Mountain Club, Residents' Committee to Protect the Adirondacks, Association for the Protection of the Adirondacks, Adirondack Council, and Environmental Advocates quickly communicated the danger this decision presented to the Forest Preserve. They met in August to coordinate efforts via a petition to Judge Kahn that they be allowed standing as Intervener-Defendants, arguing that the unique interests of their groups were not sufficiently represented by the State of New York.

The discovery process for this suit revealed that DEC had issued an enormous number of temporary revocable permits for special use of the Forest Preserve; many of the permits authorized use of motorized vehicles. Further, the number of such permits had risen dramatically since 1995.[27] In August, Judge Kahn granted the petition and voided his temporary restraining order, refashioning it to give plaintiffs motorized access only to places where DEC already allows motors to operate. In October Judge Kahn granted plaintiffs' motion for a preliminary injunction against the state, with limited access to eight roads, all but two of which were already open to the public. His order prohibited motor vehicle access on hiking, snowmobile, or horse trails, footpaths, or other pedestrian paths or waterways in the Adirondack Forest Preserve that are not otherwise used by non-emergency motorized vehicles. Use was limited to those with permits under Cahill's 1997 policy.

This ruling provoked questions of just how much DEC was using vehicles for administrative use. It quickly became obvious that there was a lot of such non-emergency use. Under pressure, in April, the department issued a policy for administrative use of motor vehicles on Forest Preserve roads and trails. Fearing that Judge Kahn might grant plaintiffs access to all roads/trails used by DEC, the environmental groups petitioned the appellate division to bring cross-claims against the state in relation to the Galusha case. This petition was granted, but the groups chose not to file cross-claims pending negotiations with DEC.

In December, DEC issued a final "Policy on Administrative Access to the Forest Preserve by Motorized Vehicles and Aircraft." The deficiencies in the policy prompted the environmental groups, minus Adirondack Mountain Club, to file a cross-claim in federal court in late January 2000. Also encouraging the groups to file the cross-claim was the fact that DEC continued to allow motorized use of the Forest Preserve through temporary revocable permits and that the department sanctioned and increased the use by staff and by individuals "acting for DEC." (DEC claimed that groups using ATVs for snowmobile trail maintenance were "agents of the state" and that such non-DEC administrative use was exempt from the State Land Master Plan and DEC's own guidelines.)

The attorney general's office filed a motion to dismiss the cross-claim, citing the Eleventh Amendment of the U.S. Constitution's provision granting immunity to states from such suits. (No citizen can sue a state in federal court if the state does not expressly give its permission to be sued.)

Thus the attorney general placed defense of the DEC, a state agency, above defense of the Forest Preserve. Within a month Judge Kahn granted the state's motion to dismiss the cross-claim, noting that Article XIV did not state in a sufficiently explicit manner that the state waived its immunity to suit in federal court.

The judge's dismissal of this case on the technicality had potential untoward consequences: it opened the possibility that all Article XIV suits have to be referred to state, not federal, court. It is to be noted that Adirondack Mountain Club did not join in with the other groups in this phase of the suits; the club's lawyers chose other strategies.

At the end of March, the office of the governor's counsel announced revocation of DEC's administrative use policy. It replaced it with a policy that eliminated all reference to non-DEC administrative use. The policy, strictly procedural, spells out an internal reporting system to keep track of all staff motorized use, but not such use by rangers and environmental conservation officers. The environmental groups involved issued a press release praising DEC for establishing a revised policy that was now in compliance with the State Land Master Plan, as it should have been all along (the groups seem to have ignored the fact that it was a partial victory because it did not apply to rangers and ECOs). The DEC could still issue permits for non-staff motorized use, subject to temporary revocable permits. Pending the writing of a DEC permitting policy satisfactory to the groups, the environmental groups suspended legal action against DEC "for now."[28]

A footnote to the later sequence of events is the varied responses by the environmental groups. Both Residents' Committee to Protect the Adirondacks and the Association for the Protection of the Adirondacks reported technical details of the suits in their newsletters. Adirondack Council's newsletters and releases continued to focus on acid rain and other causes, with the exception of a small press release that thanked the state for its revised policy and noted that their legal team would "take a rest for a while."[29] And this sequence underscores the way behind-the-scenes negotiations replaced public participation for many groups seeking to solve problems. The entire process has retreated behind closed doors.

The suit by Galusha et al. to open certain trails to motorized access by the disabled was settled in July 2001. After much negotiation DEC, the plaintiffs, and representatives of environmental organizations reached an agreement that called for DEC to open sixty-seven miles of trails for motorized access by the disabled. The state was to spend 4 million dollars improving those trails. The solution was again a narrow one in that it only addressed motorized access. DEC still did not have a full-fledged plan for the disabled. An early draft of the settlement required such a plan, but the final settlement required only that certain unit management plans address motorized access for the disabled. As of 2001, DEC has not begun to create a broad-based plan for recreation for the disabled.

CASE STUDY 5

DEC's Use and Information Planning and the Adirondack Access Plan

DEPUTY COMMISSIONER ROBERT BENDICK probably did more to invigorate DEC staff than any other individual. He came to New York from a similar position in Rhode Island in 1990, but, since he grew up in New York, he was already familiar with our unique Forest Preserve. He seemed from the first to understand what staff needed, and he used several sources to fund staff projects.

Bendick recognized the need for long-range planning for the Adirondack Forest Preserve, and he envisioned a way that federal funds could be applied to that end. The Intermodal Surface Transportation and Efficiency Act (ISTEA) of 1991 provided funds that could be directed through Department of Transportation and used for a study on roads, access, and the Forest Preserve. With the help of Wendy O'Neil, former council staffer, he assembled a large committee, actually one of the best and most diverse put together in the park because it had so many people active in the tourist industry and local government as well as representatives of the not-for-profit groups. It was an ideal forum for discussions of how the Forest Preserve could relate to communities and how access could be improved.

It is amazing how quickly a group's enthusiasm can be dampened. This happened when the participants realized how little of this potential work could relate to private interests. Bendick had been restricted by the funding source so that the grant focused on access to the Forest Preserves. Bendick believed that the people of the state did not understand the forests, that the agency had never matched people's needs with the Forest Preserve experiences. He envisioned an adaptive process, with information about what existed, then an effort toward new facilities, followed by new maps and new information. He believed that people do not value what they do not know and that the program he envisioned had great merit. From his perspective, knowing as he says that, "the rest of the country is trying to play catch-up because the legacy of our resources is so exceptional," he thought the Use and Information program would do as he hoped.[30]

To the distress of many local people, especially those with tourist industry interests, Bendick did not and probably could not fashion the proposal to find ways of making state lands complement private needs or to help private interests gain from their proximity to public lands. Thus, public participation for planning that Bendick saw as a component of the ISTEA program never gained any momentum.

The Forest Preserve Advisory Committee discussed the fact that there was overlap between its mission and that of the committee Bendick assembled as the first component of the Use and Information Plan. FPAC minutes point out that the Use and Information Citizen Advisory Committee was being asked to consider issues that the FPAC had studied and made recommendations on.[31] Apparently Bendick was unaware of the FPAC's work, a partial explanation of why the committee felt ignored.

For the second component of the grant, DEC channeled funds through Adirondack Mountain Club for a study of non-motorized recreation in the park. The funds could be used to hire a consultant, in this case the LA Group of Saratoga, to prepare a Non-Motorized Recreation Plan. In 1993 ADK created a committee to solicit information on where trails existed and where they were needed. The LA Group began mapping all state trails on U.S. Geological Survey quadrangle maps (something one would think the DEC had already done) and then digitizing the information. The maps quickly ran into trouble; it was an impossible task, for no one source knew what the DEC had out there. Rangers were asked to correct the maps, and this proved virtually impossible.

For the planning component of their work the LA Group solicited information on where within the park trails might be needed or desired. The LA Group produced a plan with criteria, analysis of proposals, and in the final draft, a list of priorities. By the end of 1996, the plan was virtually completed. And then, because there seemed to be no one at DEC to receive the plan and make use of it, it languished. A third component was marshaling information to create an Adirondack map that was to show trails, access points, trailheads, and so on. Preparation of the map dragged on for years. It was shown at various FPAC meetings, but never discussed in depth. The *Adirondack Forest Preserve Map and Guide* was finally completed in 2000. It is not the easiest map to read, and my DEC sources tell me that it has errors. It is not something hikers could use because the detail is not adequate. And when it was printed, there were no funds to distribute it. My principal complaint has been that this map was published before any real recreational planning had been done. Although this is the first "comprehensive" map DEC has produced, it essentially shows the Adirondack Park as it has been depicted on other informational maps for the past two decades or more.

Why so little has been realized from the grant and why there have been so many delays can be explained in part by the change of administration. The Pataki administration's fiscal goals account for lack of staff and the requirement that any new work be done by consultants, not by new staff, who at least have the potential to be trained and seasoned.

Karyn Richard's appointment at DEC to head up Pataki's push to complete the unit management plans may yet save the day. She understood immediately that there was no cohesiveness to unit management plan work, no vision of what the Forest Preserve could provide to visitors and local communities. She pushed ahead an effort to have completed the Adirondack Forest Preserve Public Access Plan, with goals similar to Benedict's for the Use and Information Plan. It would resemble the access plan written by a consultant for the Catskills. Drafts of such an Adirondack plan had been gradually accumulating information for years (it was actually more of a compilation of what information was missing), nothing more than a proposal to accumulate information, with no sense of what is important. A consultant was to be hired to complete the work, but I could only speculate that if the work already done is not thrown out so that the consultant can breathe new life into a vision for the park, it will all be another waste of time and effort.

Where was the supervision to direct work on the first drafts of that plan? How could such an awful approach have gone on for so long? DEC was truly suffering from the decline of staff and institutional memory.

Ideally, an access plan should be an inspiration, a vision, or a guide for the unit management plan process. It still could realize that goal. In retrospect, both the Use and Information Plan and the proposed access plan were complicating factors, extra layers between the State Land Master Plan and the unit management plans. If the State Land Master Plan had been more visionary, especially with respect to Wild Forest areas, an access plan might not have been needed. If the unit management plans had been completed in a timely fashion with vision, little additional use and information planning would have been needed, and producing an informational map would make a lot of sense.

I agree with Bendick; almost everyone does: the Forest Preserve resource is an established resource, but DEC never made its broad range of values known or provided access to it by a statewide constituency. I cannot help but be cynical—too much has gone wrong. We have a great resource. We are protecting it quite well. But we have never defined a role for people in the Forest Preserve, and especially in Wilderness areas, in a way that using the resource truly complements the way it is being preserved.

CASE STUDY 6

The Citizen's Advisory Committee for the High Peaks Wilderness Area Unit Management Plan

A MIXED GROUP OF REPRESENTATIVES of environmental organizations, town officials, Trout Unlimited, Boy Scouts, recreationists, and others first met in August 1990 to form DEC's Citizens Advisory Committee (CAC) for the High Peaks Wilderness Area (or Complex as it was later termed). There was enthusiasm and anticipation at the first meeting and a sense that the High Peaks Wilderness Area Unit Management Plan (HPWAUMP) could finally be written. Even the aborted attempt in the late 1970s to develop a plan did not destroy the optimism. Several more months passed before the CAC began meeting regularly, but it worked intensely through fifteen meetings and numerous subcommittee meetings held between March 1991 and June 1992. The CAC's report was printed by August 1992.

On June 30, 1993, DEC called the committee together again to provide an update. DEC had made modest progress in the intervening year because staffers key to writing the unit management plan were unavailable. Principal author Jim Papero was ill, and forester Terry Healy had died. An initial draft of the HPWAUMP was released in January 1994, and a second, slightly revised draft in December of that year. However, it was not until the end of the decade that a plan based on the CAC recommendations was accepted by the governor; even in 2000 only temporary rules and regulations were issued to implement the plan, and Johns Brook and Ampersand Primitive Areas were omitted from the temporary measures. In 1992 the dedicated members of the CAC would have found it difficult to believe that such a delay was possible, especially as approval was rolled over into an administration that claimed to be environmentally friendly.

Discussing the CAC for the HPWAUMP poses a special kind of challenge for me. I was a participant, a very active and critical one, very supportive of the process, yet ultimately disappointed by the results. Being objective is difficult, so I have tried to note the places where I believe objectivity eluded me. Further, I have emphasized what I believe were the critical and most problematical areas discussed. Others might have a different list. In any event the sheer weight of all the minutes and interim reports dictated selectivity in writing about events. I did not make all of the subcommittee meetings (Facilities, User Management), but I was pleased that so many of the ideas I expressed in letters to those groups ended up in the final reports.

DEC was eminently prepared for the beginning of the CAC's work. Staff distributed copies of inventories and background already prepared for the plan in the late 1980s. The background information followed Division of Lands and Forests Director VanValkenburgh's format for unit management plans: section I was a brief description of the area, its boundaries, and history. Under the title "Wilderness Elements," section II summarized natural resources, cultural resources, and public use. Section III covered "Managerial Elements," past and current management, an inventory of facilities, including those considered nonconforming by the State Land Master Plan. Section IV, distributed a month later, was entitled "Recreation Use Problems." This was an excellent summary of the problems DEC thought the CAC ought to address. The analysis of "Private Lands Adjacent to the High Peaks" in section V was to be the basis for the CAC's land acquisition recommendations. These sections, modified by the CAC, would constitute the same five sections of the completed unit management plan. DEC put a lot of effort into these five papers. What the CAC had to do toward completing the plan was use this information to recommend management goals, which would constitute the section at the heart of the plan.

In addition to providing the committee with the basic inventory, which had been completed in 1987, DEC presented numerous documents on wilderness planning and managing wilderness recreation, including such modern ideas as carrying capacity and the use of "Limits of

Acceptable Change," a method of evaluating management with respect to resource protection, developed by the U.S. Forest Service. Jim Papero, principal author of the HPWAUMP, talked to people all over the United States from the Forest Service and National Park Service to gather material to educate both DEC staff and members of the CAC on the management of wild lands. Several doctoral studies on use patterns in the High Peaks were circulated. Over time members of the committee shared pamphlets and information, particularly about ways to limit use, obtained from numerous popular wilderness destinations throughout the country. Adirondack Mountain Club came prepared with a statement of the club's principles for the High Peaks, and the final product occasionally reflects that paper in detail as well as philosophically.

There were still, however, problems with DEC's initial premises and, as it turns out, with the planning process itself. The CAC solved some problems, though not easily. Others were ignored and later came back to haunt DEC's management. A few became political issues whose solutions are still not complete.

The first problem to confront the committee was DEC's decision to deal with the entire region from the eastern shore of Long Lake to NY 73, including Ampersand Primitive Area and Johns Brook Primitive Corridor, and omitting the contiguous Dix area and the Giant area, whose management requirements are virtually identical with those of the eastern High Peaks (as of the end of 2000, there was still little progress on plans for these Wilderness areas). The Long Lake shoreline and the Raquette River corridor had very different conditions that needed to be addressed, and even the eastern and western High Peaks were markedly different. DEC ignored requests to rethink the boundary of the area.[32] At the CAC's insistence, however, the region was broken into three zones (Long Lake-Raquette River Corridor, Eastern High Peaks, and Western High Peaks), and special management criteria were developed for each.

The CAC's work began from DEC's summary of major issues to be considered: Carrying Capacity (which became User Management), Facilities, Fish and Wildlife, Administration, Land Acquisition, and Nonconforming Facilities. Members were assigned to subcommittees to address these topics. Facilities included trails; lean-tos and campsites (their separation and dispersal); pit privies; bridges; signs; access; visitor facilities; and dams. The committee further subdivided trails into five categories such as trunk trails or barely marked footpaths, each with different specifications. The subcommittee considered horse trails and facilities for access for the disabled. User Management dealt with group size, length of stay, campfires, mandatory registration, glass containers, pets, and both indirect and direct methods (including permits) for controlling use. Nonconforming uses included South Meadow Road, telephone wires to Marcy Dam and the ranger station there, relocation of lean-tos and tent sites situated within 150 feet of water. The committee extended the list of subcommittees to include one on education and information and one on plant life and alpine summits. An administration and management subcommittee focused on the need for a single manager for the region, fires, search and rescue, trail closures when the resource is threatened, and monitoring. Some of these subcommittees met as much as a dozen times. The list of issues to be resolved kept expanding, and the draft reports grew longer and longer.

The length of this litany of topics facing the CAC for the High Peaks points up a significant motif that runs through most public participation exercises: The issues in this modern world are far too complicated and interrelated. While parkwide issues are daunting, even such a seemingly narrow subject as creating a unit management plan for the High Peaks is mired in complexity. The committee's goal of creating a general recommendation document, one where DEC could fill in the details, required an unbelievable amount of time on the part of DEC staff and the dedicated members.

Contrary to what some committee members have said, this unit management plan does not provide a model for the other units in the park, one that will permit more streamlined work in the future. That model existed in VanValkenburgh's outline. Further, each area is different, with varying needs and problems. Each new plan will require an enormous amount of work. If the process is streamlined to limit the time required for such public participation as seen in this citizen advisory committee, DEC will still have an enormous task before it to complete the missing unit management plans. Was the extraordinary level of public participation in the High Peaks' case productive? The answer is "probably not," because in the end special interests ruled. Is there a more efficient method that still gives voice to the interested public? I have no answer to this question, but will explore it further in the section on Governor Pataki's unit management plan initiative.

When the CAC's recommendations were melded into the June/July

1992 final CAC report, the guts of some of the initial recommendations came up missing. They show up as summaries of the work of the different subcommittees and not as an integrated part of a report. The final report from the committee was a result of compromise and in some instances so nonspecific that it permitted a wide interpretation of what it involved. There were no priorities, and even though there was much discussion about what were immediate recommendations and what were horizon goals, these categories were only roughly worked out. The consensus document was little more than a plan to plan in the future.

With few exceptions, the hard recommendations in the draft had all surfaced in the earlier High Peaks Advisory Committee (HPAC), 1974–79. Furthermore some of the earlier group's recommendations had already been adopted by DEC, although never turned into rules and regulations. These earlier recommendations showed up as nine of the major recommendations of the 1996 final DEC draft.* In the years after 1979, DEC's gradual process of improving management of the region did accomplish some of these things, and if their efforts proved insufficient, they were certainly the basis for arguments circa 1990 that much more was needed.

As noted, the final report of the CAC intentionally left a lot for DEC to interpret. It did not reflect the depth or content of the debate, especially what transpired in the subcommittees. Of the several themes that emerge, one directing our thoughts toward horizon planning stands out. In rereading the document after a number of years I could not help but speculate that Bob Ringlee's insistence on our dividing goals in such a temporal way actually impeded what we were doing. Ringlee, a very thoughtful engineer and extraordinary molder and shaper of ideas, led Adirondack Mountain Club's team. (ADK had more representatives over

---

* Recognition that use is excessively concentrated in the eastern High Peaks, funding for maintenance is inadequate, summit trampling and erosion is a serious problem, campers rather than day hikers cause most pressures, groups of ten or more have greater impact on the resource, camping needs to be commensurate with the area's carrying capacity, camping should be prohibited above 3,500 feet, hiking alternatives outside the High Peaks need to be identified, winter users need to be educated to the dangers. The old High Peaks Advisory Committee recommended that camping and open fires above 4,000 feet should be eliminated (this was done); camping should be prohibited within 150 feet of any road, trail, spring, stream, pond, or other body of water (this was done); and camping permits should be required for groups of more than ten individuals (this too was done).

time than any other group, sometimes sending more than one representative to the meetings.) He had to balance the recreation orientation of
the club with the preservation goals of many on the committee. The report is less than specific on what constitutes immediate goals, what constitutes horizon goals, and what are the horizon timeframes. We left
much to DEC's discretion.

One topic illustrates a positive aspect of the CAC's group dynamics
better than any other, and it serves as a parable for future public participation efforts. It was the question of "trailless" peaks and the canisters
placed there to document the climbs of potential 46ers.[33] Early on it appeared that the CAC was leaning toward recommending not only the removal of canisters but also the marking of one route not subject to
erosion and the closing of the multiple herdpaths that had developed
over time on the so-called trailless summits. The 46ers were adamantly
opposed to both ideas, but Tony Goodwin, their representative on the
CAC, wrote a very effective article for the group's newsletter, *Adirondack Peeks*.[34] He lobbied for the CAC's position and actually turned 46er
thinking around. From there it was an easy step for the committee to
move to the discussion of what the "best route" called for in the final plan
might be.

My only complaint is that the final plan said only that the best of existing routes be marked, not, as I had hoped, that the trails would be well-
engineered routes with minimal grades using switchbacks to minimize
erosion. ADK had long opposed such major reroutes, saying that hardening existing routes was the best policy. Goodwin later proved ADK's concept wrong with his redesign of the trail up Rooster Comb, which though
not yet perfect, has gone a long way toward showing that High Peaks
trails can be constructed in a way that minimizes both erosion and future
upkeep. Nevertheless, at the time it was almost impossible to achieve a
consensus favoring rerouting problem trails.[35] Parenthetically, it is noteworthy to recognize how such a seemingly minor issue was not easy to
solve and yet so vital to moving forward toward the goals of good wilderness management that the CAC espoused.

Also in the initial (January 1994) draft of the unit management plan
for the High Peaks were seventeen analyses of and sets of recommendations for special areas from Ampersand to Wallface. During 1994 the
draft was expanded and refined, and in December 1994 a Draft HP-
WAUMP, ready to go out to hearings, was completed. However, it was

not released to the public until October 1995. Staff attributes the delay to posturing and politicizing and the fact that DEC was reluctant to tackle the question of South Meadow Road, whose closing, required by the State Land Master Plan, was opposed by locals.

From the first, the CAC recognized that this unit management plan had to pull back some of what had been allowed to happen in this wilderness area. DEC took the recommendations and issued an initial draft for in-house and advisory committee use in January 1994. Included in it was a statement of management philosophy that was wilderness-oriented and led to the observation that "if present trends continue, DEC will soon be faced with uncontrolled use as judged by comparing field and sociological conditions to the area's stated wilderness objectives. Without controlling use, it may be almost impossible for DEC to satisfy its legal mandates."[36] This led to the plan's stated objective of limiting camping by requiring permits in the eastern High Peaks zone and limiting the number of permits issued. The plan proceeded to outline what the department had to do in the five years before a scheduled revision of the plan to insure a fair and effective permit system: Before implementing such a system, the DEC was to continue using indirect methods of control and to investigate various options for allocating and issuing permits, number camping sites, study the costs of a permit system, and determine the times of the year when permits might be needed.[37]

A press release from the Association for the Protection of the Adirondacks analyzed the draft's 158 components. It noted that there was 71 percent conceptual agreement between the CAC's 1992 report and the 1994 Draft Unit Management Plan; 44 percent total agreement, including exact language; and either no comment on or variance between the two 28 percent of the time. Association executive director Dave Gibson's analysis concluded, "the origins of many recommendations and some actual language is clearly traceable to the CAC. . . . Both reports speak to issues, needs, management tools and recommendations which have received a lot of discussion by diverse persons and organizations well in advance of the release of the draft UMP."[38] Adirondack Mountain Club's analysis objected to DEC's "blanket camping permit system," limitation of parking at ADK's Loj, and elimination of canisters on trailless peaks.

My copy of the draft issued in December 1994 contains numerous pages marked "good!" or "excellent!" and only a few with notes that more was needed. The draft recommended control of audio equipment and fleshed out a plan for instituting camping permits. Overall, I was so impressed with what the draft contained that I thought it wise not to point out its shortcomings: I felt it lacked vision for a hiking experience other than one that would lead to peak-bagging. In regard to new trails, it favored the status quo, and this was especially noticeable because it could have suggested new trails such as reopening the Twin Brooks route. It only gave lip service to the need to disperse hiking throughout the park when it should have been inspirational about the methods DEC could follow as it sought to limit use in the High Peaks.

My positive response to the draft and the process was soon deflated. Public hearings were scheduled around the state for November: Schenectady, Lake Placid, Avon, and New Paltz. Adirondack Mountain Club members attended all the regional hearings. Almost every Mountain Club speaker gave a version of the same theme: overuse of the High Peaks is exaggerated and permits are not needed. I could not help but believe the responses were coordinated. Even if they were not, their effect was damaging. In a letter to the Schenectady *Gazette,* Richard V. O'Neil, who had attended the Schenectady hearing, wrote; "It was clear that the leadership of the mountain club packed this hearing with its members mouthing the same company line, 'No camping permits!' "[39] The letter also raised the question of ADK's financial interest in the region.

ADK has a financial interest in the region and has been slow to relinquish control of the major portal at Adirondak Loj, a trailhead that attracts as much as 50 percent of all registered High Peaks hikers. At an early CAC meeting, VanValkenburgh was invited to discuss land acquisition in the area. He was quoted in the *Press Republican* as stating, "ADK's activities and presence at Adirondak Loj on Heart Lake were attracting the public to a heavily used recreational area, were damaging the Forest Preserve, and should be closed down."[40] This comment prompted a response from Ringlee defending ADK's public service record, reminding that the trails past ADK's lodges were under DEC's control (this is not entirely true since the easement is for hiking only), and that DEC could at any time provide parking on state land.

In committee discussions, when Ringlee argued that ADK had been as good a steward as the DEC and that DEC could not manage the area without ADK's trail work, CAC members muttered that there would not be so many people in the High Peaks if ADK's facilities were not there. When I asked Bernard Melewski, a lobbyist for Adirondack Council, about organizations working together, he observed that "ADK as a club is interested in recreation; that is the bottom line for club members, and they will compromise on different levels of resource protection, but not where their financial interests are involved. . . . However, ADK's direct financial interests in state contracts make them compromise on some issues."[41]

As Jim Papero wrote in 1997, "Commercialism from profit and not-for-profit groups in the High Peaks certainly does not mix with the goals of preservation. . . . Many special interest groups and elected officials feel strongly that their role and influence in the planning and decision process should differ from that of the general public. We saw that and felt that during and after the High Peaks public meetings. . . . Access monopolies are usually lucrative enterprises. There should never be a private monopoly on the movement of visitors to state lands. Few areas should have more than 50% of their activities controlled by outside interests."[42]

At the same time the CAC began meeting, ADK, in recognition that the club's Heart Lake holding was "the most heavily used entrance to the HPWA," appointed a special committee to create a master plan for the property. This was submitted to Adirondack Park Agency in February 1992, revised, and resubmitted. It was intended "as a conceptual framework to guide the Club's stewardship of the property over the ten-year horizon." The plan outlined limited expansion of club facilities, "increased emphasis on all forms of education and stewardship services," and included two proposals that could assist management of the High Peaks: (1) relocation of the parking lot to the north, downsizing it to conform to the HPWAUMP (as of 2000, ADK has discussed this, but no downsizing has occurred) and providing dedicated day-use parking and limiting overnight parking; and (2) converting the High Peaks Information Center to an education center and constructing a new High Peaks Information Center at the relocated parking lot.[43] Adirondack Park Agency planning staff endorsed this proposal, with the additional requirement that all overnight users park at the South Meadows Road junction. Discussions of what to do about parking continue as this book goes to press.

In defense of Adirondack Mountain Club, DEC certainly did not fulfill its role as manager over the years, abdicating management to ADK on the grounds of insufficient funding and personnel. Many hoped that this plan would cause DEC to stop deferring to ADK, but in the past few years it has been obvious that it did not. ADK pushed for the rebuilding of the fire-destroyed interior cabin at Lake Colden, which was not only hastily rebuilt, but constructed as a "veritable Taj Mahal" (retired ranger Pete Fish's term) that seemed even more out of place in this wilderness setting than the cabin it replaced. It certainly exceeded the HPWAUMP's and the State Land Master Plan's guidelines for interior structures.

In 1999 Hurricane Floyd not only pushed trees across trails, it caused slides whose mud and rocks mixed with trees piled many meters deep on some trails. Rather than pausing for an instant to consider whether the damaged trails were in the right place or could better be relocated, ADK pushed for and reopened almost all the trails within weeks. Closing or significantly redesigning the High Peaks network has never been part of ADK's philosophy.

Finding ways of controlling or limiting use provides an example contrary to what happened to the trailless peaks issue. From the start the committee worked under the impression that our goal was bringing the area to "wilderness" standards. Indirect methods, education, other opportunities elsewhere, limits of group size, controlled parking, all focused on limiting hiker density, which varied wildly with the seasons, the day of the week, and holidays. The thought underlying the recommendations of most committee members was that we had to somehow reduce use. DEC obviously took the CAC's recommendations seriously in preparing the portions of the 1994 drafts dealing with camping permits.

Input from the hearings went into the Final Draft, issued in 1996. A few adjustments were made, but the only major changes centered on the question of permits. The 1996 Unit Management Plan talks about permits, self-registered permits that are primarily designed to provide information, not rationing or reservations. The plan states, "Data collected over the five-year span of this plan will be used to ascertain if additional user controls are needed." (Perhaps the worst part of this undermining of working toward any permit scheme is that it took four more years before the plan was approved and temporary regulations put in place. Real controls are so far in the distance they are beyond any horizon we can see.) Dave Gibson wrote Stu Buchanan concerning the silence and lack of progress that followed the release of the plan in early 1996. He said, "What I am perceiving . . . is the open, communicative process then on display turning inward and secretive."[44] Dave Gibson brought up the question of the deletion of a permit system from the 1996 draft in a letter to the Adirondack Park Agency (that agency had to approve this and all unit management plans). Gibson wrote Jim Frenette, chair of APA's Park Policy and Planning Committee: "For this Final Draft to avoid any mention of permit reservation systems, their possible future application in the High Peaks Wilderness, and their varying levels of success and acceptability elsewhere is, frankly, disingenuous." Gibson encouraged the APA to reinsert references to permit reservation systems, "clarify what 'additional user controls' meant, and speed up its evaluation of the need for a permit reservation system. . . . Such an evaluation should not occur in year five of the plan. The department should have contingency authority to begin to implement a permit system within the five years of the plan."[45]

What happened to the High Peaks Wilderness Area Unit Management Plan between the time it was released in 1996 and the governor's approval of it in 1999 is a further example of a special interest circumventing an advisory committee's consensus. Lobbying outside the public participation process reached a new high in Adirondack Mountain Club's opposition to any permit system. Gibson, like others on the committee, was right in believing that some members were moving behind the scenes and contrary to the committee's intent. A DEC staffer, who insisted on anonymity, told the author that only three copies of each of the five or six drafts prepared during this interval, between 1996 and 1999, were circulated, one each to Buchanan (DEC), Woodworth (ADK), and the governor's office. My source called this delay "trading politics for resource management."

After 1994 Neil Woodworth emerged as Adirondack Mountain Club's principal spokesman on the committee. When I questioned why ADK was not supporting positions worked out when Bob Ringlee was their chief representative, I was asked, "What makes you think Bob represents ADK?" Furthermore, some people representing ADK denied that either ADK or the committee had changed positions, something I believe the relevant documents, minutes, and reports show has happened. Further, when I challenged Woodworth on the key issues of the necessity of planning for permits, he told me that he had adopted the contrary position because he "did not trust DEC." My bias is obvious; I still believe that use of the eastern United States' premier wilderness area should be limited.

Whether or not the governor opposed permits before the barrage of lobbying to convince him or his staff that they were not needed is an open question. But when the report was finally released, the governor spoke about the inappropriateness of permits for the Adirondacks.

The governor's approved draft put the group camping size limit back from all earlier recommendations (both the CAC's and DEC's), which ranged from ten to twelve, and set it at eight, in compliance with the State Land Master Plan. Hiking groups were limited to fifteen individuals.

Recommendations to fix parking problems at The Garden were straightened out by a fluke. The Unit Management Plan would not have solved parking at The Garden without the help of Tom Both, Keene supervisor and former ADK Trails Committee chair. The town now effectively limits parking outside the small lot and provides parking near NY 73 with shuttle service to and from The Garden trailhead. Unanswered is the question of whether the solutions provide parking for more hikers than the area can withstand. Not addressed in both cases was the suggestion that day hikers, whose impact is less than campers, should be given special accommodations. This is an especially important question in the case of The Garden, where day hiking on the periphery to such destinations as the Brothers is to be encouraged.

Parking at South Meadow was never fully discussed by the committee. In the summer of 1991, CAC Chair James C. Dawson was unavailable and the DEC did not want to reconvene the committee, so the CAC never fully discussed alternative proposals. Adirondack Council offered a solution that involved parking at Van Hoevenburg, which would never be acceptable because of the distance it added for hikers. Council and others would not consider the proposal for making a major portal or entry point near the intersection of South Meadow and Loj roads, but making it possible to construct a parking area east on South Meadow Road, closer to camp sites, making a trail to Marcy about a mile longer than those from the Loj. Swept under the table was the question of whether changes to the State Land Master Plan might make it easier to solve some management issues like South Meadow Road. However, this problem will pop up again, for the final Unit Management Plan ducked the question and put off the closing of South Meadow Road for five years.

DEC convened a pair of meetings of former CAC members and other interested individuals in late 1999 and early 2000 to get input on how to inform the public about the new plan and temporary rules and regulations. Parenthetically, in the 1994 and succeeding drafts, the HP-WAUMP mentions using the Use and Information Plan as a preliminary step in public education. A program for letting people know about the new regulations was finally adopted in early 2001.

I had conversations with many members of the CAC over the years since 1992 and a majority expressed frustration with the process. Most of the frustration dealt with the delays and with what was not accomplished. This unit management plan was supposed to give us a way of pulling back, restoring, limiting, ensuring that the wilderness values, however re- duced they were in 1990, would decline no further. Jim Papero summed up his disappointment with the process thus:

> Are we willing to begin to treat this area with the respect and reverence it deserves as one of New York's great natural resources? With more people visiting the High Peaks each year under our current management scheme, we in the long run will only see more damage to the resource. We need to look at this area in the long term, perhaps decades ahead. If recreation use in the High Peaks rises much more, current problems like resource dam- age and visitor crowding will continue to rise proportionately with long- term effects.[46]

Perhaps one of the most perplexing aspects of the long delay in the High Peaks plan was the fact that Region 5 appeared not to be working on any other plans. We made jokes about the region not being able to walk and chew gum at the same time. It was not a joke. The unit man- agement plan process suffered a decade-long hiatus on top of a nearly two-decade delay. We were promised that work would begin on the back- ground for the unit management plans for the Dix and Giant wilderness areas so that their plans could be addressed immediately on the release of the High Peaks plan. That did not happen until 2001.

For all its inadequacies, the HPWAUMP is a fair management tool, one that can guide DEC in the future. It was not groundbreaking, it did not deal with future and inevitable pressures, it has not solved all the problems the CAC, DEC, and APA catalogued. It is a first step, and if the next steps—implementation, revision, and planning for permits—are taken in a timely fashion and with vision, good things might yet be ac- complished, for experience has shown that amending unit management plans can be a much swifter process than creating them.

CASE STUDY 7

Unit Management Planning and Revisions
to the State Land Master Plan

BEFORE THIS SECTION DESCRIBES PROGRESS and problems relating to unit management plans and the State Land Master Plan, it is important to understand how almost nothing has been done to integrate
the philosophical ideas of wilderness protection and human presence in
wilderness planning efforts. DEC's analysis seemed to stop with Van-
Valkenburgh's wilderness management paper. Because of this DEC
seems to be split: Sometimes the department advocates keeping people
out of wilderness, not developing recreation by hiking on any of the
large, low-elevation, virtually trailless southern wilderness areas. At the
same time, there are some within the department who advocate increasing use of motorized vehicles on Wild Forests, the almost wildernesses.

Actual wilderness experience in the Adirondacks has for too long been
the realm of an elite group of recreationists. As William Cronon asks, why
is "wilderness experience" viewed as a form of recreation enjoyed by
those whose class privileges give them the time and resources to "get
away from it all?"[47] Cronon objects to some concepts of wilderness because they make us dismissive of "humble places and experiences." That
is precisely what has happened in the park—the less dramatic wildernesses
and our wild forests have been largely overlooked. The planning process
that was supposed to have corrected this remained a failure until the end
of the 1990s, and even then the department proceeded without benefit of
a philosophical base. Furthermore, the State Land Master Plan does not

provide a philosophical base that emphasizes human activity in a wild land setting.

In all the unit management plan processes, preservationists have become adamant about not revising the State Land Master Plan for fear that even discussing a few key questions would open the door to weakening the document. When written, the SLMP was scheduled for revisions every five years, and it is now fourteen years out of date and badly in need not only of revision but also of updating to address questions of long corridor trails, greenway connectors, and methods of enhancing the economic benefits of the Forest Preserve to local communities.*

On a more pragmatic level, a review of the minutes of the Forest Preserve Advisory Committee shows just how inconsistently DEC dealt with the unit management planning process: The Catskill regions, especially Region 3 under Chief Forester Fred Gerty, have done a spectacular job. Catskill plans are almost all completed and many improvements have been made, including new trail work. Volunteers have helped restore fire towers and work on trails. Adirondack Region 6 has done remarkably well. For years DEC handed out summaries of unit management plan work at the quarterly meetings of the FPAC. None of our protests about the slow process of Region 5 were ever addressed. In 1999 after yet another depressing "progress" report, FPAC member-at-large Dawson calculated the number of years to complete all plans based on current progress—his prediction was 110 years.

When the Division of Lands and Forests officially downgraded unit management plan efforts in 1993, it had little effect since not much work was being done anyway. In 1994 the Blue Mountain Wild Forest plan appeared, with little vision for recreational opportunities in the area.[48] Bob Bathrick "voiced staff concerns regarding how far from current fiscal reality should a plan project. Forest Preserve Advisory Committee members indicated that the plan should reflect what is perceived as the ideal accommodation of human activity while protecting Forest Preserve character and resource."[49] No one at DEC was thinking about the potentials inherent in the Forest Preserve; staff could only see the immediate future. Shortsightedness of staff was not necessarily their fault; there seemed to be no leadership to inspire them to broader visions.

---

* As bad as this number seems, it pales when compared with DEC's twenty-six-year delaying tactics to prepare unit management plans.

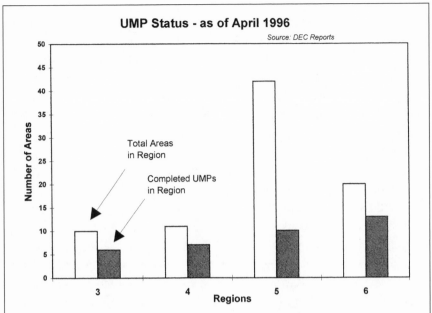

Comparison of the total Forest Preserve acreage in the four regions and the Unit Management Plans completed as of 1996.

In 1994, the Forest Preserve Advisory Committee unanimously proposed that DEC combine some units for planning purposes, such as the Hudson Gorge and Blue Mountain Lake. DEC could not see the benefit of corridor planning for the Hudson and ignored the committee. In fact, DEC went on to split units into smaller ones, thus making more work, further dimming the prospects of ever finishing the task.

With respect to the High Peaks plan, the FPAC consistently backed including similar recommendations for the Dix and Giant areas. Expanding some restrictive recommendations to wilderness areas outside the High Peaks was only just being considered in 2001.

Unit management planning finally got DEC's attention when, in 1999, the governor declared that all unit management plans should be completed within the unbelievably short time of five years. With eight major wilderness areas, ten major wild forest areas, and several primitive and canoe areas to go, this timeframe seemed impossible. It certainly seemed unlikely that the plans for wild forest areas would be done with vision for the recreational potential of these lands, most of which lack any but multiple use (read snowmobile) trails. No wilderness plan yet written has done more than stamp the status quo or eliminate nonconforming uses, so it seemed equally unlikely that the new plans would contain much in the way of discovering recreational potentials or designating new wilderness trails. If the completion of the HPWAUMP did one thing, it has made us all wary of hoping that future plans will do much more than guide DEC's bureaucracy. Their sum is unlikely to be a great plan for the park or for the communities within the park. (It was prophetic that the day I was proofing these words, Commissioner Cahill announced he was leaving DEC. His term beat the average by six months. He did get a lot started, many things whose completion became once again uncertain.)

DEC's great push in 2000 started with the hiring of several new people. The first "scoping sessions" (meetings to obtain public input) were badly done because there was not enough emphasis on what the State Land Master Plan allowed and what a unit management plan could do or not do. As Tom Martin, Region 5 forester, admitted, "vision was needed." Further, some of the new staff was only marginally familiar with the areas they were to write about. Many were preoccupied with the status of old roads and ways of accommodating ATV use, despite the fact that new ATV trails are clearly prohibited by the State Land Master Plan.

Several of the unit management plans, which were started in 2000 or were being revised as in the case of the Siamese Ponds plan, will have sections of the North Country National Scenic Trail. Planning in those units for the NCNST cannot proceed until the Adirondack Park Agency works with DEC to outline a possible route. That is not going to be easily done unless the agency amends the State Land Master Plan to include general outlines for the proposed routes and guidelines for planning across several units.

In 2001, unit management planning finally began to take off. Karyn Richards made some essential changes: having those working on the plan attend classes in managing public participation, changing the formats of public meetings, assembling a legal team to respond to questions that plague those writing the plans. It was still too early to be assured that the end was in sight, and even before the end of 2001 there were admissions that the five-year goal was unachievable. A change of administration, the prospect of a new commissioner, or budgets cuts could still derail the process.

19 | Where Are They Now?

Forestry

BY THE 1990S, the forest products industry definitely trailed tourism as the major component of the Adirondack economy, but it was not far behind even in 2000. Forestry changed so much in the 1990s that it was difficult to understand what was happening. So much depended on taxation, global markets, and corporate finances, and these conditions have caused industrial landowners to offer huge tracts for sale.

However, the desire to sell industrial forest tracts also reflected previous abuses of the land. International Paper's sale of land previously owned by Brandreth is an example of how heavily some tracts have been logged in recent years. Industrial forests have had trouble producing what the industry needed at competitive prices. The Adirondacks can never produce fiber as economically as the southern states. Roger Dziengeleski, woodlands manager for Finch, Pruyn, claimed, "silviculture in the Adirondacks is terrible. Because of taxes there is no money to be made on owning land." He added, "Companies lose money on land, only make it on mills." He estimated that when costs are computed with the minimal return on land—3 percent to 4 percent—it no longer made sense to buy land at the current prices that require at least a 10 percent return. He concluded that few companies were practicing good silviculture and that those that did, like Ward Lumber Company, had both good management and productive mills.

The number of mills processing timber has continued to shrink despite the addition of log home manufacturers and many small sawmills. Softwood saw logs are trucked to Canada to be sawn into dimension lumber and the best hardwoods are shipped to Europe for veneers. The largest furniture manufacturers are outside the park and there are only two paper mills left inside the park. New pulp or paper mills require such large investments that it is unlikely any more will be built in the park. There are serious drawbacks to investing in the mills and factories that can use the park's timber because other areas are more competitive. Furthermore, most companies in the Adirondacks are owned by national or international corporations, which require that all components of their operations are profitable. All this added to the tax problems creates an economic situation that is not favorable to the industry in the park.

In addition, Dziengeleski believes that timber harvesting is not done well in the Adirondacks, and he ascribes two reasons to it: First, forest owners can get away with bad practices. Second, the economic structure works against the industry. What upset him most is that foresters "deplete the land and still have a buyer in New York State because the pressure for land is so great."

The decline in acreage of Adirondack industrial forests has extended even to Finch, Pruyn, the second largest landowner in the park; its holdings have declined from 167 to 150 thousand acres. Dziengeleski is one of the region's strongest advocates for forestry, and his deeply held beliefs mirror Finch, Pruyn's current philosophy and have carried over into the Blue Line Council's outlook. Dziengeleski was worried about the fact that sales of land to the state have reduced land in timber production to a level that discourages manufacturing (saw logs, pulp, paper, furniture, and so forth) and already has worked against investment in new mills. "With the state buying so much, who would invest in timber-producing factories?" According to him, pressures for land acquisition from both public and private sources became so great in the 1990s that he became alarmed that future state acquisitions might not depend on "willing seller-willing buyer" situations. He was still afraid of condemnation, despite state policy adopted as a part of the Open Space Plan. (Those new restrictions on eminent domain are quite specific and would preclude its use in ways Dziengeleski fears.) This persistent fear might explain Finch, Pruyn's and Blue Line Council's positions in this regard. Dziengeleski's beliefs seem to minimize the real economic problems—cheap paper comes from many foreign sources and the paper industry always trails the general economy.

One solution, according to Dziengeleski, would be for the state to walk away from purchases of overharvested tracts. (This solution ignores the question of who will buy those lands and return them to forest production. It assumes that landowners will use better forestry practices if there is no market for severely cutover land. And it does not take into account the need to protect that open space.) Another solution he promotes would have the state examine land from an industry perspective and "declare out loud 'there's a great piece of land for the forest products industry.' "

International Paper maintains it will continue to have a presence in the Adirondacks, but the sale of land by the largest multinational corporation owning land in the park is worrisome, in part because it raises the specter of backcountry development. According to Dziengeleski, "The development issue for tracts held by timber companies is smoke." (Residents' Committee to Protect the Adirondacks's study of development certainly confirmed his belief, for it showed that little development was occurring on commercial forestry tracts.) Sales of easements also worried Dziengeleski: he suggested that easements present an economic problem because of the seller's potential loss of appreciation on his land. (This opinion ignores the fact that no owner has to sell an easement on his land.)

Assessment of forest tracts is based primarily on the quality of the forest, so that in some instances private tracts are assessed for a lower amount than Forest Preserve parcels of equal acreage. (The state pays local taxes on all Forest Preserve lands.) Because most of the industry's problems are related to land or corporate taxes, they must be addressed by state or federal governments. To this end, Adirondack landowners benefit from the work done statewide by the Empire State Forest Products Association.

People like Bob Stegemann, who was a member of the Northern Forest Lands Council and is now with International Paper, are frustrated. They see value in using economic tools for the advantage of both the environment and the economy. For instance, Stegemann believes that "a well-financed forest tax law would enable the industry to make better investments and enable it to keep its forest tracts in open space."[1] Certainly the laws should include the recommendations for improving 480-A (a local tax exemption given land owners who apply stringent forest management plans to their land), as outlined in the Whaley Task Force, which would provide reimbursements to local communities for tracts in the 480-A program. These recommendations have been with us for a long time. Stegemann feels this means of helping the forest products industry would be cheaper and just as effective as easements in protecting open space. Further, he sees such programs "as a way of creating wealth, keeping income coming in from forest tracts, and keeping private forests in private hands."[2] The weight of evidence for the benefits from recommendations central to the several forestry studies is so overwhelming that it is difficult to see how the legislature all through the 1990s has consistently failed to act. To do so the legislature must not only reimburse local governments for monies lost under 480-A, it must also provide a sustained revenue source for the reimbursements that is not dependent on state borrowing.

All this discussion of ways to insure the health of the park's forest industry presupposes the importance of that industry in open space protection. The Adirondack Conservancy and many environmentalists believe that private ownership is essential to protecting open space. They see value of private ownership as being so great as to warrant subsidizing the industry through easements or special forest tax laws. And as in every Adirondack issue, there are differing opinions: Some contend that these subsidies benefit large corporations in the long run. Others contend the state ought to buy all the large tracts where the practice of forestry is no longer economical.

The state legislature has been slow to respond in other areas affecting forestry. The legislature had not passed, as of 2000, the General Obligations Law, an "Outdoor Recreation & Landowner Liability Legislation" bill, which would open more private lands to public use by extending immunity to private landowners or public or not-for-profit corporations from lawsuits when their land is used for recreational purposes. What has happened to this legislation is indicative of the way a small minority—in this case an association of trial lawyers—can stop action in the state legislature. The proposed obligations law and legislation to fund reimbursement of 480-A from the general fund rather than with bond moneys are broadly supported actions.

While state government can improve part of the economic climate for the forestry industry, it cannot solve the industry's basic economic problems. Further, there is no consensus within the industry on solutions. Nevertheless, the use of easements to enhance open space and to protect land from development has helped some forestry companies, and it may prove to be the most important tool in the future because easements protect open space.

Northern Forest Lands Council

The final report of Governor Cuomo's task force, *Capturing the Potential of New York's Forests* (see chap. 9), was a marvel of brevity compared with later studies of the forest industry, in particular the reports done by the Commission on the Adirondacks in the 21st Century and the Northern Forest Lands Council (NFLC), the latter done with considerable public input. Almost no new information or recommendations relevant to New York appear in these and other later reports, but the paper used in these reports appears enough to keep a small paper mill in business. (The technical report for the Northern Forest Lands Council alone weighs 8.5 pounds!)

At almost the same time Governor Cuomo appointed the Whaley Task Force (1989), Senators Patrick Leahy of Vermont and Warren Rudman of New Hampshire generated the National Forest Service study of the Northern Forest

Lands. When the study was completed after eighteen months, Congress funded the Northern Forest Lands Council (NFLC) to develop long-term strategies for the forests of Vermont, New Hampshire, Maine, and northern New York. Specifically, the council was charged with preparing a report to *recommend* ways to prevent the breakup of large private forests and to stop development of such tracts. The council had no regulatory, zoning, regional planning, or land acquisition authority.

During hearings in 1994 on that draft and final report, opposition surfaced everywhere. In the Adirondacks the most visible reaction to it was opposition from property rights groups. Opposition from such groups across the Northeast held up congressional authorization and funding for further work by the council. But no opposition was as dramatic to me as the theatrics at a hearing on the draft report held in Queensbury. Property rights people sobbed stories of how the council threatened ownership of their homesteads; Carol LaGrasse, in an effort to punctuate her protest, threw down a copy of the report, grazing Barbara Sweet, a member of Adirondack Park Agency as well as the NFLC.

Senator Leahy seemed to lose interest in the council's work. Many splintered efforts appeared in the three other states.

The potential existed for the New York participants in NFLC to give more than they could receive from the studies, since none of the three other states (Maine, Vermont, New Hampshire) has anywhere near the proportion of public lands that New York has. Their logging cultures differ as well. The final report, *Finding Common Ground: Conserving the Northern Forest,* contained strong recommendations on taxation, research, education, and strengthening rural communities. It was weaker with respect to public land management, acquisition, and protecting biodiversity because of the great amount of work to be done in the other three states, especially in Maine. I found the report totally deficient because it did not analyze adequately why New York's position is different, how so much has been done here to protect forests and biodiversity, and especially how New York's mosaic of public and private lands could be a model for the rest. Further, I believed at the time that the report was deficient in its analysis of the ability of logged lands to protect natural processes as the Forest Preserve is able to do. This seemed to be tacit acknowledgment of the insurmountable task of the other states in achieving even a modicum of what New York has done.

The Northern Forest Lands Council spawned two other groups: the Northern Forest Alliance, which deals primarily with conservation issues, and the Northern Forest Center, located in New Hampshire, which deals with historical, cultural, and heritage aspects of the northern forest. The latter group is privately funded. It held a series of meetings to help communities focus on their social values and used the information to create a book on the "Wealth Index" of communities in the northern forest region. It is developing regional education projects, a part of which will be a traveling exhibit on forest and communities. The organization believes that good conservation can occur only if it helps communities.

An outgrowth of the Northern Forest Alliance is the New York Caucus of the Northern Forest Alliance, a consortium of environmental organizations comprised of most of the groups focused the Adirondacks plus several with statewide interest or state chapters of national groups. Environmental Advocates, Audubon, and New York Rivers United are in the latter categories. Sierra's Atlantic Chapter is not a member, however.

The caucus, as a statewide coalition focused on the Adirondacks and Tug Hill, still upholds the structure of the NFLC and is dedicated to seeing the NFLC recommendations enacted. It has drifted a long way from whatever public participation marked the beginnings of the NFLC, and its activities are not generally made public. In 2000 the New York caucus was attempting to launch a program aimed at land acquisition within the state (see "Working Together," below).

A journal, *The Northern Forest Forum,* published six times a year, details efforts to address forestry issues and preservation attempts. In recent years, reports by Peter Bauer of Residents' Committee to Protect the Adirondacks focused on the bright side of happenings in the Adirondacks, with articles on the state's land acquisition. Residents' Committee to Protect the Adirondacks stood out among Adirondack groups in its support of the work of NFLC, with a well-researched special report calling for funding for the Forest Legacy Program and adoption of the NFLC recommendations across the board. In 2000, RCPA added a forester to its staff to help develop a program for sustainable forestry and a method of obtaining green certification (attesting to the origin of wood in sustainable forests) for the products of New York's forests.

The New Groups

Blue Line Confederation

The confederation, formed in 1990 over concerns with the Commission on the Adirondacks in the 21st Century, became almost a thing of the past by the end of the 1990s.

By 1992, Dave Howard, the group's founding co-chair, had discovered a role for himself in the national land rights movement. Don Curtis succeeded Howard as chairman in 1992. Howard continued to bring material from the Property Rights Foundation of America, the Alliance for America, and the *Land Rights Newsletter* to the attention of confederation members.

The Bleecker group published the *Adirondack Blue Line News* through 1996. Between 1992 and 1996 that newsletter's content included more and more information from the national organizations. *Blue Line News* quoted an editorial from the *Land Rights Letter,* which Howard had taken over. The editorial is an interesting exposition of Howard's property rights philosophy: "not the disposition of land but the preservation of a bundle of rights . . . codified by the Constitution. . . . Private property ownership is the bedrock upon which the foundation of this country was laid." Howard holds the principles with which he defends his right to own and enjoy property against *compromise,* which he believes is concession; against *consensus,* whose meaning he quotes from Margaret Thatcher—"abandoning of all beliefs, principles, values and policies in search of something in which no one believes, but to which no one objects . . . avoiding the very issues that have to be solved"; and against *common ground,* by which he means that his land is his private property and can never be land that is held in common.[3]

These philosophical arguments had less appeal to the group than the 1990 threats to their property. With Howard's move to the national stage, the confederation began to shrink. Eleanor Brooks and her husband, original members of the confederation and keepers of its records, traveled west in 1994 to view the hardships caused by excessive government regulation. But their interest as well as that of most confederation members was fading. In 1999 Brooks confessed that her "zeal was waning . . . as fewer people in our area remain active in the property rights battle."

George Manchester, long-time supervisor of Bleecker and active member of the Blue Line Confederation in its early days, was named chairman of the Fulton County Board of Supervisors in 2000. For the past few years he had been representative to the Inter County Legislative Committee. Confederation member Don Curtis had served as Manchester's secretary for those monthly meetings. In 2000 Manchester told the author that he was more than ever hopeful for the future, that he was pleased that the unit management plans for the local area were being started, and that although he opposed much land acquisition, he was concerned with the few state parcels that had no public access. In 2001 Bleecker finally resumed work on a local plan with the expectation that there would shortly be a zoning code.

Adirondack Solidarity Alliance

The Adirondack Solidarity Alliance (ASA) was also born from the reaction to the 21st Century Commission. Dale French and his wife, Jeris, had attended a Fairness Coalition meeting and gave them money but did not at first try to start a grassroots organization. They joined many locals in participating with the 1990 and 1991 motorcades. French said the Adirondack group was loosely organized until the formation of national Alliance for America in 1991. The local group evolved from a core of fifty to claim an unsubstantiated membership of 2,500.

Solidarity Alliance did a study of the Adirondack Park Agency, trying to show that it was illegally constituted. Members believed that "government uses intellectual terrorism in rural areas."[4] The core remained active in 2001, fighting proposals to reintroduce the wolf, opposing the Champion land sale, and worrying about Adirondack timber going to Canada to be milled. The core group opposed Adirondack Park Agency's proposed model sanitary code on the grounds that it would be used to stop building. (The model code was prepared in conjunction with DEC and Department of Health along with code enforcement officers who needed such a model to guide town ordinances.)

ASA continued to believe that the agency was fundamentally flawed. In 1996 it was opposed to the support given the agency to restore its funding by Joe Rota and the Local Government Review Board. Howard Aubin, ASA director, was quoted as saying, "the review board has changed its function from that of a watchdog to that of a lap dog."[5]

In January 1999 at Dale French's instigation, Essex County Board of Supervisors, of which Crown Point supervisor French was a member, voted $5,000 to be matched by a wealthy Maryland supporter of property rights, Ralph Hofstetter, to hire the Washington-based foundation Defenders of Property Rights to study the Adirondack Park Agency to see if its decisions conform to state law.[6] French suggested this approach because of his contacts at Alliance for America (he was an officer of that group). The Essex County Board of Supervisors was deeply split by the proposal; opponents thought that using Defenders would produce a biased report.[7] French convinced a majority of the supervisors to approve the fund, saying they must take their case to federal court "because state courts are bought and paid for."[8] Essex County apparently did not support French's plans and although he was unable to raise the desired money from his fellow supervisors, ASA did contract with Defenders for the work. It was rumored that the report was prepared but that it was a rehash of the file French submitted and written by an intern. Whether he was embarrassed by the report or by his having gone out ahead of the Essex County board without their permission is not known, but French managed to conceal the report.

In 2001, ASA's membership remained centered in Ticonderoga and Crown Point and included among its active supporters Howard Aubin, Judy Ford, the Frenches, and several local businessmen. ASA was loosely connected to Dave Howard's group Liberty Matters, which is the successor to the Alliance for America.

Dale French remains adamantly opposed to Adirondack Park Agency: "it is an usurpation of rights . . . it is destroying the park because you cannot build outside hamlets. Public land is shut off."[9] But he no longer believes it is possible to do away with the APA or to gain legislative support to change it—"no sweeping legislation would be possible."[10]

Liberty Matters and Alliance for America

A fourth "Fly-In for Freedom" of the Alliance for America was held in 1994 (see chapter 14 for details of 1991 and 1992 fly-ins). In 1996, its founders were listed as Dan Byfield of Farm Credit Rights Foundation of Austin, Texas; Margaret Gabbard of Stewards of the Range; and Bleecker's Dave Howard. The "Grassroots Think Tank" took credit for defeating the National Heritage Areas Act, which it claimed was one of the largest federal land grabs in recent history.[11]

By 1996, Dave Howard had taken over the *Land Rights Letter,* previously published by Joan Corcoran. About this time, Byfield, Gabbard, and Howard listed themselves as founders of a group called *Liberty Matters,* a name that had been the logo of the *Land Rights Letter.* It continued as a three-part organization, with an address in Austin, Texas, also the home of the American Land Foundation; Stewards of the Range from Boise, Idaho; and phone and fax numbers from the Land Rights Foundation in Bleecker, New York.

According to CLEAR (Clearinghouse on Environmental Advocacy and Research), a Washington group, Liberty Matters has become much more radical compared with other "wise use" groups. Alliance for America lost funding from West Coast corporations and other national sources because the funders felt they could not control the organization. As the national organization lost luster, several groups remained active locally, among them Adirondack Solidarity Alliance and Howard's Bleecker-based Land Rights Foundation.

The Bleecker group, trying to go it alone, apparently suffered financial problems and restructured in order to continue. Under the letterhead *Liberty*

Matters News Service, the organization changed with new technologies. It shifted from a mailed newsletter to providing *Action Alerts* and *FAXBACKs* to grassroots organizations and interested individuals. At the end of 1999, the Land Rights Foundation still faced financial difficulties. It announced, "We have been able to reinvent the *Land Rights Letter* as an Internet Publication." Starting in 2000 the group handled most outreach on the Internet; the *Land Rights Letter* can be downloaded from the Internet. The organization still provides news releases along with a news service for smaller media, in keeping with its philosophy of "ground-up" efforts to change public policy.[12]

With the Internet format, *Land Rights Letter* expanded its national coverage of property rights issues; articles dealt with taking of wetlands, privatizing federal lands, threats from biosphere reserves, water rights, and charges that environmentalists are responsible for taking the rights of individuals. Howard's wife contributed an article on a lawsuit by a Middletown, New York, resident who claimed that the way municipalities tax residents is illegal. An article by Dave Howard claimed that the federal "Land and Water Conservation Fund would erode the private land base in America to dangerous levels." Excessive regulation undercuts the whole concept of "willing sellers," he claimed.

While the Internet version of *Land Rights Letter* has become quite sophisticated and nationally oriented, that was not always so. An article by Dale French in the printed December 1996 issue is an example. The article described a legal case that Howard took nationwide through *Liberty Matters News Service.* It involved Glenda and Kent Duell (Maynard Baker's daughter and son-in-law). According to the finding of the New York State Supreme Court, appellate division, the defendants owned a building in Minerva. "Over a five-year period, an officer for the Department of Environmental Conservation made numerous visits to the defendant's premises and discovered that defendants' sewage system as constructed was discharging raw sewage onto the surface of defendant's property in close proximity to [Minerva] Stream."

An article on the Duells by Dale French termed the DEC's and the court's actions a "regulatory abuse," stating that the case had been twice dismissed before a new case was brought before a grand jury. French claimed that the district attorney prosecuted the case only because DEC requested it. The Duells were found guilty of 164 counts of polluting, intending to pollute, and so on. The potential fines ($250,000) and jail sentences (fifteen years) for each count amounted to thousands of dollars and an astronomical number of years. In denying the Duells's appeal, the appellate court stated that "the evidence elicited disclosed that on numerous occasions raw sewage was observed flowing from defendants' property and going into the stream, that they were repeatedly directed to remedy the situation but, rather than doing so, apparently attempted to conceal it." [13] Hence the appeal was denied on the basis of incontrovertible evidence of the defendants' guilt. This decision inflamed both Howard and French, who was at the time vice president of the Adirondack Citizen Aid Fund.

The Duells lost their property for nonpayment of taxes. French described the court's finding them guilty in November 1996 as "just another effort to control property and create a revenue stream by criminalizing innocent Americans." Howard's information sheet, distributed nationally by Liberty Matters, said, "it is just another example of how environmental law is terrorizing ordinary, honest, law-abiding citizens, and destroying American families." The Duells were each sentenced to six months in jail and fined $68,000 each. According to the district attorney, they had declined a plea bargain "in which Mrs. Duell would have received no jail time and her husband would have received only a $10,000 fine and 1000 hours of community service." [14] As of completion of this book, the wife served two months of her sentence but the husband's sentence is still under appeal.

It is peculiar that the case, with such a strong legal settlement, became such a cause célèbre in the *Land Rights Newsletter*. In a 1998 issue, [15] the Duells' loss of the property was ascribed to a scheme by the town to acquire the land for a park, the foreclosure was attributed to threats made against the bank holding the mortgage, and the sewage problems were blamed on actions by the U.S. Department of Housing and Urban Development. The Duells were portrayed as people ruined financially by an unfair legal system, and their total expenses in the case were said to be $200,000.

Very few people would deny that over the years a few individuals have had "a raw deal" from Adirondack Park Agency, but it is telling that the property rights group chose to exploit this case, involving DEC, as symbolic of the downtrodden in the Adirondacks.

Property Rights

The property rights movement may be quiescent, but it remains an Adirondack force. Carol LaGrasse may have been defeated in her litigations, but she had no plans to stop litigating. The question I see is whether the movement can ever help shape, or at least not obstruct as before, attempts to improve the forms of government and agencies in the park today. Can we have streamlining without having bigger and more government?

Many environmentalists are so convinced that property rights people are a fanatical fringe that they were surprised that I talked to people like LaGrasse. It is true that a few of those opposed to government regulation have resorted to really vile name-calling in print and that most of the derogatory remarks made by environmentalists against the opposition are expressed only to fellow environmentalists. But this does not excuse those environmentalists. Many believe, as I do, that civility and understanding should prevail. But would understanding the origins of the property rights movement ever be enough? Jim Cooper, Warrensburg attorney who successfully challenged the county's support for a lawsuit against the agency, sees the property rights movement in the Adirondacks as absolutist, and he defends what has been done in the Adirondacks: "We have always had government control of private property, starting with regulation of noxious things like slaughterhouses, even in colonial times. Such regulation has its foundation in English common law. Certainly there is a big step from such controls to density zoning. Congestion breeds necessary controls, so civilization can function. The majority of those in the Adirondacks opposed to controls have fled such congestion and the extraordinary level of controls found in big cities. But no place is that uncomplicated any more." [16] Viewed simplistically, property rights defenders reflect America's early settlers' search for freedom, the desire to hold individual property that was denied most of those who emigrated from Europe. A few espoused sharing common ground, fields for grazing cattle for instance, but most sought their private piece of the seemingly boundless land that greeted them in America. The environmentalists of the past few decades do not deny individual property ownership, but they look beyond it to a shrinking land base, to a world where population has surged and where its residents have all too often fouled their land. So, the nascent environmental movement sought to rein in those excesses, to define ways of preserving both private property and common rights. But devising legislation, regulation, and controls to protect both common and individual rights is necessarily restrictive.

A majority in the Adirondacks does espouse actions that help the common good, seeing the benefits of protecting common land for all. Unfortunately fear and self-interest have sometimes clouded their views. How this can be overcome is a challenge so far not addressed.

All of the property rights people I interviewed professed concern for protecting the environment; they just place individual rights first. Ross Whaley has three criteria that sum up his empirical approach to property rights: "(1) private property rights are more important in culture than in law, and therefore should be respected; (2) when social good overrides private property rights, there should be compensation, and (3) with respect to air, water, and such common needs, regulations that protect them for everyone are necessary." It is questionable whether Whaley's guidelines can be applied to the aesthetic and philosophical goals of land preservation that permeate the values necessary to the Adirondack Park, but they may be a starting point for discussions to breach the division in the Adirondacks. However, achieving consensus is probably an insurmountable goal, even in the relative quiet of the new century.

Carol LaGrasse and a New Property Rights Foundation

Carol LaGrasse's disillusionment with Donald Gerdts only strengthened her work for property rights causes. Gerdts's behavior at the "Unity" conferences convinced her that a broad-based Adirondack property rights group was needed. She believed the formation of the Association of Adirondack Towns and Villages was a good step, but that the association has never become effective. She objected to the other Adirondack organizations, as well as the national groups such as the Alliance for America. She objected to the focus of the national wise-use groups on issues affecting use of public land. Her interests were limited to private property, so in 1993 she formed the Property Rights Foundation of America, Inc. (PRFA), which was incorporated in 1994.

LaGrasse's organization took on many issues: In 1995 she and John Salvador, a resort owner from Lake George, filed a citizen-taxpayer action against the Adirondack Conservancy and Land Trust and the state for the state's payment of $2.6 million to the conservancy for the Morgan property on Lake George. LaGrasse charged that the payment included 35 percent more than the "bloated purchase price" paid four years earlier by the conservancy. The conservancy claimed it paid $2.5 million for the land and incurred an additional nearly $900,000 in interest and carrying costs. The issue was clouded by the facts that the conservancy's purchase was at a time when real estate prices were inflated and that because of the 1990 bond act's failure there was no money for the state to acquire the land more expeditiously. The state and the conservancy were also concerned that the ridge tops with spectacular views might be developed. Further, the Bird property to the south had even greater development potential along the shoreline, so there were additional important reasons for the acquisition of the Morgan property. The state successfully defended its acquisition against LaGrasse's challenge.

PRFA's third annual conference in Albany in 1998, hosted by the Pacific Legal Foundation of Sacramento, California, was cosponsored by the American Land Rights Association; American Policy Center; Civil Rights Associates, Inc.; Competitive Enterprise Institute; Coxsackie Awareness Group; Long Island

Builders Institute; New York Farm Bureau; New York State Taxpayers Alliance; and People for the USA.

LaGrasse has funded some of her activities with her own money. She has a small following and uses the contributions from them for her lawsuits. LaGrasse writes most of the Property Rights Foundation's publications; topics range from the cost of bond acts, Northern Forest Lands Council, UNESCO's Man in the Biosphere program, and an intriguing treatise on the state's "Arbitrary and Excessive Environmental Regulation of Private Land and Resources." With some partial truths and confirming examples, the article points up the problem of having an agency, the Adirondack Park Agency or the DEC, regulate when regulations are imperfect, where discretion by the agency is possible, where regulations leave room for interpretation.

Wetland regulations and loss of property value through wetland designation were her concern in 2001. That year LaGrasse was still publishing *The New York Property Rights Clearinghouse,* a quarterly newsletter from the Property Rights Foundation of America, of which she was president. The majority of her lawsuits have failed on technicalities, the failures attributable to lack of good legal advice, but her most recent suit against the state on the Champion sale failed on the merits of the case (see Champion below).

Blue Line Council

Blue Line Council continued to grow through the decade of the nineties, but it is far from a grassroots organization. From its inception, BLC reached out to New York State officials, people with political know-how. Robert Flacke and Bill Hennessey remain active. It is not a membership organization; it takes its direction from its appointed (self-perpetuating) board, but in reality it is guided by a strong executive committee. BLC's activities are funded by directors, and its budget barely approached $100,000. From the start, Mark Behan's Glens Falls consulting firm has handled most of the group's public communications. Much of this discussion of BLC comes from an interview with Behan, who seemed to maintain a strong grip on the group's image. He said that from the start BLC focused on larger policy issues. Its philosophy was close to that of the Fairness Coalition, whose focus was always inside the park, but the two groups never really worked together. BLC has occasionally worked with Adirondack Landowners Association, but only where they have shared goals.

BLC's board has had two former APA commissioners, two former DEC commissioners, a tax commissioner, and a judge—people with experience in state government. Many individuals have claimed that BLC was a front for Finch, Pruyn, and board member Roger Dziengelewski certainly maintained Finch, Pruyn's strong influence on BLC's activities. But, as Behan pointed out, International Paper is also very active with the group and that company has been strongly represented by Joe Hanley. Representatives of the NYS Business Council, NYS Builders Association, banks, and unions serve on BLC's board. For years Pieter Litchfield served as executive director and ably represented the group at agency meetings. In 2000 that position was given to Barbara Sweet, former APA member. Litchfield became president of the board, and the full board continues to meet only once a year. Behan said that BLC depended on board members for background on issues, but it seemed obvious that Behan controlled BLC's image and outreach.

BLC has reached out for advice to numerous experts. In 1991 it commissioned Norm VanValkenburgh, who had retired from DEC, to prepare a paper on land acquisition. His paper shows how the state could establish a permanent land acquisition program by developing a permanent funding source, strategies for easements, and criteria for land acquisition. His paper is little different from ideas he expressed at DEC, but his recommendations were never adopted by the department. It is a simple and elegant outline that deserves to be followed, but there is no indication that it was taken up by the BLC, perhaps because VanValkenburgh's list of priority acquisitions included Finch, Pruyn's Blue Ledge and the Gooley Club tracts. His short list is similar to many prepared over the years, with one notable addition—Adirondack Mountain Club's inholdings in the Johns Brook Valley.

BLC has focused on regulatory reforms with respect to the park agency, issues that rose to the level of law. Concerning state land acquisition, Behan maintained that "strategic purchases should be made," but he derided the current trend of large purchases. "The big ones," he said, "have been made for political reasons; they rob the public treasury." He insisted that the state should not use public money to acquire land where motorized use is not permitted.

Behan considered easements to be all right when specific rights are purchased, but "our directors are unhappy with the amount [size and number] of fee acquisitions." Litchfield carried BLC's opposition to the Champion acquisition and easement arrangement. Behan's concern in the matter was that the "deal was done in secret, the state refused to talk, and there was no public oversight." Further, Behan was upset by the fact that selected individuals had access to the process; "The governor's office did not understand the nuances."[17]

In the interview, Behan went so far as to charge that "the public process is corrupt and policy is driven by a small number of special interest organizations. No one group should control outcomes, all should be heard, but there is distorted access by some special interest groups."[18]

Behan expressed bewilderment at the number of organizations representing different interests in the park. He thought they were maturing in that they have stopped trading derogatory and ridiculous press releases, but he still worried that groups were not working together. He did admit that Adirondack Council has done "a good job on acid rain."

However, he noted that not enough attention has been paid to the local economy, that no one in government has policy expertise; they have "political expertise, but not policy expertise," he claimed. "Policy moves from Albany to the north, not the other way around. Albany cooks it up and passes it by the locals." This comment led to a discussion of his primary concerns, which adamantly echo the concerns from the past that still haunt the Adirondack scene. Behan asserted that there was no real local representation, a statement that reverted to the old argument that the majority of Adirondack Park Agency membership should be Adirondack residents. In addition he stated that the forest products industry and tourism should be represented on the APA and that all members should have individual political will and demonstrable abilities in a field requiring technical knowledge. Behan would have "strict, vigorous enforcement of existing APA laws," regulations that make boathouses just that, not living places.

It is obvious that Behan has thought seriously about basic problems confronting the park. One solution, which he proposes, would require "addressing historical ills, by de-institutionalizing differences of opinion and institutionalizing fairness and balance." It sounds fine, but when it comes down to the bottom line of how to achieve this, the issue of local representation remains paramount; in his mind, and that of many others, there is no other way. He also added his belief that statewide interests are not properly represented with respect to park issues. Behan's comments on how to address historical ills prompted the author to challenge him to propose other solutions. He wondered if the problem might not be a social one, one of disparate class conflict. The similarities between controlling the park and dividing Jerusalem presented a not-farfetched parallel. Behan said he believed that "people need to be comfortable with history, but in the Adirondacks they can't put it behind them." Then, Behan turned the interview on the author to ask why there was still so much animosity on Adirondack issues.

Adirondack Landowners Association

From its formation, Adirondack Landowners Association has consistently held that private landowners were as important as the state in conserving open space. The organization has been at the forefront in promoting the concept that the state does not need to purchase all that it needs to protect. It has also promoted the idea that conservation organizations, not the state, should monitor easements.

After 1993 when the tumult over the Commission on the Adirondacks in the 21st Century died down, Adirondack Landowners Association continued to meet regularly, but its concern shifted from fighting the state's use of eminent domain to promoting stewardship of privately owned forest tracts. ALA's membership—twenty-eight clubs and organizations—collectively represents ownership of a quarter million acres of noncommercial Adirondack lands. ALA's emphasis on stewardship earned the praise of several conservation organizations, those that realized that state ownership and preservation are restricted by the limited amount of money the state would have for land acquisition and management. In addition, environmentalists recognized that stewardship of private lands plays a key role in preserving backcountry and open space.

At the end of the decade ALA's primary concern was taxation of forested land, in particular land that was not managed for forestry but left in its natural state. The group believes that assessments should reflect their stewardship, which members believe is comparable to the state's stewardship of public lands. They feel they deserve tax relief, and they hold this view despite the fact that none of the members' land is open to the public as is comparable state land.

The organization has become supportive of many of the park's established institutions. One of its founders, Bill Hutchens, serves on the board of Adirondack Nature Conservancy and the proposed Tupper Lake Natural History Museum. Their counsel, Franklin Clark, speaks out frequently on ALA's role and on taxation issues. In a white paper on the organization's purpose, Clark recognized the problems faced by local communities when landowners obtain tax relief under 480-A and the organization has been a leader in fighting to have the state reimburse localities for revenue loss under 480-A.* Clark believes that

---

* Forest land owners who produce an acceptable management plan for their land and forestry practices can receive a tax abatement under 480-A. Any reduction in taxes hurts the communities in which the tracts are located. In some instances, where commercial tracts constitute a significant portion of a township, companies have declined to apply for 480-A status. Everyone has worked for legislation to have the state reimburse localities for loss of revenues from 480-A. It would

"slowly, and over the long term, current tax policies offer powerful incentives to these private landowners to sell land to commercial interests. . . . We believe the State must reassess its tax policies in light of the potential impact on the Park of the continuing 'erosion' of its private land base." His appeal for tax relief argues that this help would not benefit the rich, but would maintain open wilderness.[19]

In 2001 ALA was studying one more novel approach to reducing taxes on private tracts. The group commissioned research to substantiate their claim that their members were better stewards of the land than the state because they did not permit public access. They were trying to prove that public access destroys natural resources and brings exotic flora to the forests. Jerry Jenkins, biological consultant to Adirondack Nature Conservancy and others, said he has "seen no evidence that biodiversity is obviously different on lands open to the public and those not open to the public." Even if this latest attempt to reduce ALA members' taxes fails, the group will try again.

Adirondack Fairness Coalition

The Fairness Coalition no longer meets regularly. Its nine-member board is stable, although a few of the founders are absent. Fred Monroe is now a clerk for Essex County judge Andy Halloran (Halloran had also been active with Local Government Review Board). Susan Allen remains executive director and has also served as an alternate on the LGRB. She began attending park agency meetings as an observer starting in 1990, and in April 1992 she launched the *Adirondack Park Agency Reporter,* designed to cover in detail the activities and issues of agency meetings. There is no question that in succeeding years this small monthly report has filled a gap in newspaper coverage, and it has maintained an objectivity that supersedes any of her affiliations.[20]

In 2000, Fairness Coalition's concerns were largely those from the past—how much state land is enough, reasonable access to state land with a mix that includes roads, APA reform including revisions of the State Land Master Plan, and lack of factual information on such issues as pollution, sewage problems, employment.[21]

Shy, even tentative in person, Allen has really made a serious study of Adirondack issues, but nevertheless concluded the Adirondacks is not a special place. "Calling it a special place is a trap that encourages special [and unneeded]

---

have passed in 2000 if reimbursements had come from the general fund, not the Environmental Protection Fund.

regulations." [22] She told the author that the Adirondacks should be treated like the rest of the state. She seemed unaware that land use and building are even more stringently regulated in urban areas than in the park.

My interview with her brought home to me the belief of many Adirondackers that environmentalists are an elitist crowd. The explanation of why she felt this so deeply may come from the way she felt ostracized after she moved to Keene Valley in 1981. She encountered a deep social division or class system in that community. She made me wonder how much of current divisions stems from the region's social structure. Locals sometimes do feel that outsiders, summer people, and downstaters are arrogant, and even I have felt the weight of that arrogance. Even as late as my series of interviews, I heard several members of environmental groups refer to some of those who gained their reputations opposing the 21st Century Commission as the "crazies." It is not simply that those environmentalists are being elitist, they are also sinking to the level of those who castigated the environmentalists in such despicable terms in the early 1990s.

It is strange how so many of the residents who took up opposition to regulations were recent immigrants from New York City and environs. (Contrariwise, in 2000, the majority of leaders of environmental groups had also come from downstate, but many Adirondack residents with deep roots in the park were among the staunchest protectors of public lands and protective regulations.) Some of the more recent immigrants were outsiders in the urban areas from which they fled and often remained outsiders in the park. Certainly the division between residents and outsiders became an insurmountable gulf around 1990, enhanced by the outrageous behavior of a few people. Still, a large proportion of people with deep roots in the park were only quietly opposed or resigned to the Adirondack Park Agency, although some remained willing to be led, to become more radical. Even today, as quiet as things are, as accepting as people are of APA as a way to solve problems, there is an undercurrent that continues to be expressed with the refrain: We do not have adequate representation on the Park Agency.

Adirondack Conservation Council

In losing its attempts to lime acidified ponds in wilderness areas, to keep roads open in the Siamese Ponds Wilderness area, or to keep floatplane access to Whitney Lake, the Adirondack Conservation Council became increasingly militant. In the early 1990s ACC strongly opposed the Commission report, the 1992 bond act, and the Northern Forests Lands Council along with all the underlying federal legislation. ACC's support for the National Rifle Association has never wavered.

The organization claimed 35,000 members in early 1990s, when a period of unprecedented turmoil began to grip the Adirondack Conservation Council. As a result, when the decade ended, ACC had to be completely restructured, replacing the more extreme leaders of the 1990s, before ACC returned to a more constructive role in state conservation. An outsider looking in might conclude that Don Sage was almost single-handedly responsible for the decade's disarray. This observation is substantiated by the fact that he was ACC's principal spokesman and most prolific letter and article writer in that unsettled period.

In 1990 Sage was president of the Schroon Lake Fish and Game Club. His letter to the 21st Century Commission contained a diatribe against Adirondack Park Agency for not permitting more liming of lakes, opposition to acquisition of any more land for wilderness, and improved access (including by motors) to all state lands. In ACC's newsletters, Don Sage, writing for the Conservation Council, claimed there had been misuse of the Conservation Fund, which received the fees generated by hunting, fishing, and trapping licenses.

After the Commission's report was issued, Sage called on Adirondackers to start action to secede from the state. He demanded that the legislature impeach Governor Cuomo. "If war is required, so be it."[23] In 1991, Ernie Lantiegne, executive director and editor of ACC's *Adirondack Echoes,* was much more restrained in his opposition to the commission, but he expressed pleasure in ACC's activities to defeat a public right-of-passage bill.

By 1995, Sage was first vice president of ACC and represented ACC on such statewide committees as DEC's working group on access for the disabled. By the next year, the *Adirondack Echoes* masthead listed Bud Kilmartin as editor with Sage as "Publisher-editor" and the level of rhetoric began to rise—"Assembly continues its policy of idiocy," shouted one headline. Typical of Sage's articles in *Adirondack Echoes* was one with the headline "APA celebrates 25 years of genocide and slavery of Adirondackers." Succeeding issues mixed brook trout fishing and turkey hunting with opposition to the Northern Forest Lands Council. Support for the National Rifle Association (NRA) increased as did calls to abolish the Federal Bureau of Alcohol, Tobacco, and Firearms. In 1996 ACC welcomed Mike Zagata as DEC commissioner—"Finally! A Commissioner who cares!" But Pataki did not fare so well: "genocide by 2nd floor eco-freaks" referred to Pataki's tax policies. By 1997, ACC was also railing against Pataki's budget, which would "destroy fish and wildlife programs." A special ACC mailing invited members to Maynard Baker's Flag Day Rally at Santanoni: "Bring your ATV's, 4-wheel drives, skidders, log chains, chainsaws, and axes . . . to fight for our rights . . . [against] Governor Pataki [who] has refused to comply with the ADA and allow our disabled veterans, the elderly and the handicapped access to our Forest Preserve lands."

Following issues of the newsletter interspersed reports of bear takes with opposition to wolf introduction, biosphere reserves, and the Whitney acquisition. In 1998 opposition to the proposed Champion acquisition and easement mixed with fish hatchery protection, but there was no letup in the call to support pro-gun congressmen. ACC urged a boycott of F. X. Matt Brewing Company because its Saranac brand beer was generating an annual donation to the Association for the Protection of the Adirondacks. Articles on snowmobile trail limitations appeared beside claims that the revenue from hunting and fishing licenses, both state and federal, was being improperly spent within the state. Dale French contributed an article on the suit against DEC with respect to the Americans with Disabilities Act and motorized access within the park. Don Sage listed all roads and trails that "people want to see reopened." [24] Kilmartin's articles opposing gun controls continued, and in 1999 readers of *Adirondack Echoes* were encouraged to boycott Hallmark cards because it was one of the largest contributors to the "anti-gun, anti-sportsmen group." Articles on all these issues took on a harsher tone through 1999.

Then something happened. The spring 2000 issue had a new format. It mourned the death of long-time fish and wildlife activist and influential ACC member Ed Morette. President Red Galarneau wrote that "in the last few months ACC has accomplished quiet [*sic*] a lot of restructuring to make this once fine organization be what it used to be, but we have a long way to go." [25] The issue contained reports from county fish and game clubs, a profile of Nellie Staves previously published in *Adirondack Explorer*, reports on DEC's fish and wildlife programs—in other words a return to the organization's roots.

The story of what had changed and why is an example of an organization whose spark plug goes too far. Beginning in 1998, according to Ron Rybicki, president of the Saratoga County Council of Fish and Game Clubs, ACC had tried to rein Sage in, not just for the intemperate articles in *Echoes*. Sage persisted in using ACC stationery to write vituperative letters to state officials and legislators, expressing his own opinions. "Whenever he had a pencil in hand, he began name-calling. His was a poison pen," Rybicki told the author. At one meeting, Sage embarrassed ACC members by insulting APA chairman Dick Lefebvre, but his words for Stu Buchanan were so foul that Buchanan stopped going to ACC meetings and told DEC staff they could no longer attend them either as they always had in the past. (DEC's Fish and Wildlife staff had been close to ACC and many were members.) "You could not control Sage, so we voted him out and took *Echoes* away from him," said Rybicki. "We had to do it; the ACC had lost its effectiveness, no one would listen to us anymore. We had to bring back our credibility as a sportsmen's-based organization."[26]

But, I asked, did the going back change ACC's positions? Not at all. The organization is still behind the NRA and still fighting for opening roads and trails in the Forest Preserve to motorized use. They are just doing it more quietly. Sage is still chairman of the DEC Region 5 Fish and Wildlife Board, where, Rybicki said, Sage "cannot control the minutes."

Environmental Groups

Mark Dowie's analysis of the national environmental movement made me aware of many parallels between it and environmentalism in the Adirondacks. I was impressed by his statement that nationally the movement is dominated by "mainstream hubris," the conviction that leaders of mainstream organizations display a "self-confident conviction that their strategy—a legislative/litigative initiative—is central to the environmental movement. They see grassroots activities, which receive little or no national media attention, as at best helpful, at worst an embarrassing sideshow to the main event. The main event, almost always, takes place in the national capital."[27] Change the capital to Albany, and notice as you read about the Adirondack groups just how applicable this quote is to the park's mainstream organizations.

Residents' Committee to Protect the Adirondacks

Talking about the birth of Residents' Committee to Protect the Adirondacks as an outgrowth of its support for the 21st Century Commission gives scant notice to the intrinsic strengths of the organization. It has always had a strong and very principled board, and organizationally RCPA is board-driven, with relatively little input from members, except as members have involved the group in "local" issues in several communities across the park. A prime example of the latter is RCPA's work to close the Essex County Landfill through grassroots pressure combined with bringing national attention to the issue through an article in the *New York Times.*

RCPA has been well served by its leaders over the years: David Moro, a very effective writer and speaker; Joe Mahay, very much an academic; Evelyn Greene, tireless supporter, daughter of revered conservationist Paul Schaefer; Duane Ricketson, fifth generation Adirondacker; John Collins, former chairman of APA; Peter Bauer, 21st Century Commission staffer, initially a fundraiser for RCPA and currently executive director. Bauer is a very effective writer. He originated *Adirondack Voices* in 1991, a magazine of thought pieces by residents, not necessarily parroting RCPA stands, but expressing similar ideals from personal perspectives.

Initially RCPA held so firmly to the position that it represented resident Adirondackers that it would not let nonresidents become voting members. This policy was changed in 1998, so all two thousand members, not just the fifteen hundred within the park, gained voting rights. RCPA's positions respect the rights of Adirondackers, in the context of statewide interests.

In 2000 RCPA was alive and well, but not as large as a grassroots organization should be—although membership approached three thousand. Its budget was ten times what it had been in 1993. Positions on issues quite often are close to those of Adirondack Council, but with a local perspective that emphasizes the quality of life of residents. This perspective is well expressed in its newsletters and *Voices*. RCPA documents its positions for its members. RCPA's November 1999 *Park Report* summarized both state and federal actions against acid rain, not with Council's "we must fight" approach, but with an intelligent analysis.

Further, the group has put important studies and activities behind the issues it takes on: To support clean water, RCPA is expanding to 100 lakes a program through which residents participate in water quality studies. It produced a widely available video on protecting the park's water resources, and no other Adirondack group has produced such an important educational tool. RCPA got members in Stafford's district to let him know of their support for legislation generated by Adirondack Council that would prohibit the sale of pollution credits. RCPA's mobilizing of upstaters seems to have been what made Stafford move the bill in the senate. RCPA has promoted sustainable forestry by forming a cooperative of forestry tracts and hiring a forester to obtain certification from the Forest Stewardship Council for them.

In 2000 RCPA completed an in-depth survey on the total number of building permits issued by Adirondack Park Agency and town governments, a study that, because of the complex components that need to be analyzed, had never been adequately done, even by reports put together as part of the background for the 21st Century Commission report.[28] The RCPA report confirmed that less than a thousand new structures have been added to the park annually and that most construction was occurring in the least restrictive areas, where it was supposed to occur according to the APA Act. It also showed how great a proportion of permits for new structures came from local governments and not the APA. This finding underlined the importance of local planning and of oversight of local permitting processes. The report was substantial enough to serve renewed efforts by RCPA to improve local planning in the park.

RCPA has used its membership to generate letters and phone calls on many other issues, such as jet skis. RCPA took the lead in working for legislation that would permit towns to enact jet-ski regulations. The measure passed the state senate partly because of support from Senator Stafford, and Stafford's support can be traced to RCPA's efforts to mobilize a phone, letter writing, and lobbying campaign staged by Stafford's constituents who are also RCPA members. RCPA followed up the legislation by circulating a sample town ordinance that has the support of the attorney general. Although the entire environmental community worked for passage of the jet ski legislation, RCPA was unquestionably out front.

RCPA was active in obtaining Wilderness designation for Whitney Park by encouraging DEC and APA to consider the classification of Whitney and Watsons East together for balance. Watsons East was classified a mix of Wild Forest and Wilderness, in agreement with the APA staff recommendations.

Because RCPA has taken strong stands on quality-of-life issues, such as jet skis and lake water quality, it is in a position to use these issues to mobilize both full-time and summer residents. RCPA's *Park Report* is the thinking man's newsletter in the park today. In contrast to Adirondack Council's newsletter, which encapsulates and touts that group's successes, RCPA's *Park Report* has substantial background articles that really inform on varied issues like acid rain, areas up for land classification, the acquisition of Champion lands, Forest Preserve stewardship, DEC's use of motorized vehicles, and access for the disabled.

In 2000 and 2001, RCPA was becoming the most outspoken of the environmental organizations with respect to internal problems at DEC and Adirondack Park Agency. It resorted to a lawsuit against APA, claiming the agency had acted contrary to the State Land Master Plan.

Despite the organization's strengths and perhaps because of its focus, RCPA has still not sparked widespread, enthusiastic support among residents, stirred large numbers of locals to action, or added greater numbers of park residents to its membership. This raises an interesting question: Will public debate only be carried out by a small segment of the Adirondack population? Do most park residents find that life is just fine? Or are the people of the park, like most Americans, just apathetic?

Adirondack Council

Adirondack Council may have had to fade a bit from the public eye in the aftermath of the Commission report, but it was poised to dominate the Adirondack environmental scene through the 1990s. Its membership continued to grow and its staff and budget grew with it.

Instead of completing the last three volumes of its projected *2020 Vision Series,* "River Corridors," "Travel Corridors," and "Lakes and Lakeshores," Adirondack Council, in 1991, produced a rather subtle black and white photo booklet, written by Mike DiNunzio, that talked about scenic vistas and the importance of roadside views and their protection. Council produced a booklet summarizing a conference on "Managing Growth and Development in Unique, Natural Settings," written by John Sheehan. Council also coordinated a successful legislative campaign to improve tax payments and procedures relating to conservation easements.

A summer 1991 newsletter, sent out at the time Timothy Burke took over as executive director, contained an article bemoaning the demise of the 1990 Bond Act and all the good acquisitions it might have permitted. Council was encouraging its members to oppose aerial pesticide spraying in the park, implement the Northern Forest Lands Study, back the council in its negotiations to limit low-level flights by the Air Force, join Council's activist network, fight constitutional amendments on Piseco Airport and Canal lands, and join in opposing amendments to the Clean Air Act that would weaken its restrictions on acid deposition.

In 1991 and 1992, the Adirondack Council produced several glossy booklets extolling the organization's efforts. One celebrating the Park Centennial was dedicated to Council's dream of creating the Bob Marshall Great Wilderness, "the Big Bob." This theme of creating a huge wilderness in the northwestern Adirondacks has guided Council and its public appeals throughout the 1990s. Also in 1992, Council expanded its *State of the Park* booklet by examining the hundred years of progress in park preservation, noting remaining problems, and making recommendations to solve them.

The 1993 *State of the Park* added a thumbs-up or -down analysis of APA, DEC, the governor, the legislature, and local and federal government. Council claimed its share of credit for the passage of the legislation creating the Environmental Protection Fund and applauded the efforts of others, such as International Paper for its preservation of land along the Raquette River, Adirondack Nature Conservancy for preservation of the Clinton Pine Barrens, Open Space Institute (OSI)* for help with the purchase of the Heurich Estate, DEC for acquisition of Canoe Carry West on Forked Lake, and NIMO for agreements protecting a stretch of Hudson River shoreline. Rangers, canal lands, Northern Forest Lands Council sessions, leased hunting cabins on 480-A lands, mountain bikes, and above all acid rain were subjects in 1993 and 1994 newsletters, described in such a way as to make the reader believe that only the council could take the appropriate preservation actions.

In 1995 the Adirondack Council and a coalition of other environmental organizations took credit for restoring proposed cuts in DEC's budget for natural resources. Council strongly objected to Pataki's proposed raid of Environmental Protection Fund funds for use for DEC salaries. This diversion of funds continued despite widespread objections. Council took credit for making sure the Oven Mountain subdivision protected the pond's watershed (despite the fact that other groups, RCPA in particular, acted decisively in the APA approval process.) After the 1995 blowdown, the council took its opposition to salvage on state lands and easing of restrictions on harvest on private lands to the court of public opinion through important articles in the *New York Times*. Pressing a campaign in support of the Clean Water/Clean Air Bond Act, which went to the voters in November 1996, the council was a strong factor in the act's passage. Council led environmental groups in calling for the replacement of Greg Campbell as APA chairman.

From 1997 on, Adirondack Council's most visible crusade was against acid rain by establishing a presence in Washington, creating national appeals, and encouraging members' involvement by way of retiring pollution credits. Glossy acid rain brochures led the way in encouraging memberships and donations. Council fought for Whitney tract acquisitions in terms of its contribution to the creation of a Bob Marshall Wilderness. That image is behind much of what Adirondack Council does and says, but the council never led public discussions of the Bob Marshall Wilderness or perhaps was never able to engage people of the park in such discussions. The organization never appeared to make the "Big Bob" acceptable to the people of the park; to the organization, it was incontestable. People who received the council's appeals were sup-

* OSI is a downstate organization that does fundraising and funnels moneys into land acquisition projects; it works with ANC in some acquisition projects. Trust for Public Lands is a national organization with an eastern chapter that also works to preserve land.

posed to be inspired by the pictures and glowing descriptions that accompanied that vision.

Toward the end of the decade Adirondack Council's newsletters had become less informative in their discussions of Adirondack issues. A common thread throughout articles in the newsletters and in press releases and appeals to new or old members is "look what we have done for you." The message always has a very positive and upbeat note, letting the reader know how effective the organization is, whether or not the council has been the most effective player in particular issues. Council continued to take strong stands, but rarely did the public, or even membership, know the reasons for the council's stands. Nor has the council seemed to be taking hard stands on some of the tough issues that relate to park management or to DEC's activities. It seems to hold itself above the fray where local people are involved.

Over the years, Adirondack Council has presented its Conservationist of the Year award to politicians, officials, and people who supported the council's preservationist goals. Among them have been Governors Cuomo and Pataki, Harold Jerry, Maurice Hinchey, Robert Glennon, and Clarence Petty. Many individuals have been recognized for such things as park heritage, park stewardship, environmental education, and community conservation projects.[29]

Adirondack Council remains the financial giant among the environmental groups. It has never made any pretense about being a grassroots organization. It has the strongest lobbying force representing environmental standards. John Sheehan and Bernard Melewski have had the time and independence to be everywhere in Albany. Council has been very effective in calling for emission controls to end acid rain and is the only Adirondack environmental organization that has tried to have a strong presence in Washington.

At times the council almost seemed to present two images: the quietly strong yet outward-looking image of its Albany office versus the fixed, almost rigid, image of its Elizabethtown headquarters. Was it having two offices that gave the impression of a disconnect?

Throughout the 1990s the council's board appeared subdued. Board membership comprised mainly wealthy individuals from downstate as well as individuals who might be expected to know and influence the governor. In the late 1990s, the council did not choose to find fault with the governor or to convey any dissatisfaction with his administration. The governor's land acquisition policy proved so strong that it offered no room for dissent. It can be said that for a time the governor paralyzed parts of the environmental community.

In 2000, Adirondack Council launched an unprecedented $5.8 million "Campaign for the Forever Wild Fund," under the guidance of William Boardman. He had been the fundraiser responsible for Harvard University's successful drive, which had created the largest endowment of any private university. Council's fund will provide action money for quick response to issues and "vigilance and defense" funds for a national Pure Waters Campaign and a Park Monitoring Program. A publications and research and planning portion of the fund will allow the publication of the next volume in the 2020 series, the promotion of private land stewardship. The wilderness advocacy portion will focus on the Bob Marshall and other wildernesses. The Legal Fund will allow Adirondack Council to maintain its "independence and ability to litigate as needed when wild lands are threatened by inappropriate uses or management." [30]

Sierra Club Atlantic Chapter

"Beginning in the 1890s, the public right of navigation was usurped in the Adirondacks by wealthy landowners, sporting clubs, and timber companies. They blocked public passage on rivers by posting them, erecting fences across rivers, using guards to chase people off the rivers, and influence the courts to aid and abet them in their illegal quest for 'privacy.' For most of this century, DEC and its predecessor agencies were also captives of these special interests and its staff either advised people not to go down certain rivers or simply did nothing about researching, reaffirming, publicizing, and enforcing the public right." [31] This right is upheld in almost every other state in the country, but DEC held doggedly to the belief, to the consternation of many, that acquisition of the river corridors was the only way for the public to obtain access. For years DEC held that New York State laws did not permit public right-of-passage on its rivers where both shores were owned and posted by private landowners. Landowners, who were almost universally opposed to any public access, supported the DEC's stand. Spokesman for the Adirondack Landowners Association Frank Clark summed up their opposition in his argument that "there are rivers and streams in the Adirondacks that are better off closed to the public. . . . Public access degrades the environment." [32] But one man, Paul Jamieson, the grand old man of canoeing, spent his entire career leading the fight to open up all Adirondack rivers. Jamieson, a professor of English at St. Lawrence University, championed access to the Salmon, Grass, St. Regis and other rivers. The public is indebted to his inspiration and work. And it was because of his efforts that Sierra Club was to realize one of its greatest successes.

Many individuals claim a part of the credit for winning public access to Adirondack waters, a victory which some of the participants called "one of the most important conservation stories of this century." [33] According to Charles

Morrison, DEC's director of natural resource planning in the 1970s and in the 1980s DEC's point man in state river programs, he tried to get DEC legal affairs to research the issue. When they declined, for lack of time, Morrison contacted John Humbach of Pace University Law School to research the issue of public rights, and this request was followed up by an agreement between DEC and Pace. Humbach's analysis of case law, "Public Rights in the Navigable Streams of New York," was completed in 1989.

DEC support for action came from Langdon Marsh, Robert Binniwies, Marc Gerstmen, Phil Wardell, and Ken Hamm. DEC prepared legislation to embody the right in state law, but the governor's office (the Cuomo administration) thought it was too controversial. Then DEC tried to accomplish the same thing by amending the department's dredge and fill regulations, but again the governor's office feared potential controversy with Adirondack landowners. A broadly oriented rivers conservation law, drafted for legislative approval in 1989 by Paul Bray, also failed.

Morrison took the issue to several groups, but only Per Moberg and Tom Kligerman of Sierra Club chose to set things in motion to reaffirm the public right of recreational use, particularly canoeing, on rivers that are navigable and to show that recreational navigability is today's equivalent of the lumberman's nineteenth century commercial use of rivers for floating logs. According to Morrison, "without having the state on board, in the form of both DEC and the attorney general's office and with the tacit support of the governor's office that there should be a test case, the Sierra Club could not have gone ahead" with actions to provoke a test case.[34]

In order to find a candidate river for the test case, Moberg and Kligerman made trips on the Middle Branch of the St. Regis between Keese Mills and Quebec Brook on Brandon property and on the Beaver River from Lake Lila through Nehasane Lake to Stillwater Reservoir. Sierra Club members explored Shingle Shanty Brook upstream from Lake Lila into Brandreth Park. On their last exploratory trip Kligerman and others found the river for their test case: They paddled down the Moose River from Rock Dam in the Moose River Plains to the confluence of the Middle Branch of the Moose near McKeever, traversing twelve miles through the Adirondack League Club property.

The League Club sued and the case wound slowly through the courts. Neil Woodworth said that he and John Caffrey, working for Adirondack Mountain Club, moved the suit along by researching archival opinions, in particular one relating to the Cascadilla Creek near Ithaca. ADK and the State of New York were interveners in the Sierra case; *amici curiae* included New York Rivers United; Riverkeeper, Inc.; and Adirondack Landowners Association. The New

York Court of Appeals in 1998 ruled that "the central premise of the common law rule remains the same: in order to be navigable in fact, a river must provide practical utility to the public as a means for transportation." [35] The court did not decide if the section of the Moose should be open, sending that question back to the state supreme court for trial using the above standard, which was to be applied in this case and others like it. In June 2000 all parties agreed to a court-approved Stipulation of Settlement, which allows the public to canoe and kayak the twelve miles of the Moose River under certain conditions: registration is required; access is only between May 1 and October 1, and only when the Moose has reached a certain level; swimming, fishing, and use of tubes or rafts are not permitted; and there is no entry on the bed or banks of the river except when absolutely necessary. It is assumed that with this decision in the case of the Moose River other rivers are similarly navigable unless their owners wish to challenge the question of their navigability, which is doubtful. Further, the Champion agreement included fee acquisition of many of the remaining rivers whose access had been sought.

Sierra Club's level of activity waxes and wanes according to the strengths and interests of its leaders. It was the personal interest of several members that propelled the organization into the navigation issue. It appears typical of many environmental organizations that active members shape agendas, and this is particularly true of Sierra Club's Atlantic Chapter. It was Tom Kligerman's leadership that made possible the successful challenge to the state's navigation laws. There is little question but that issues of navigability might have remained unsettled if Sierra Club had not acted as it did.

In 2000 the Atlantic Chapter decided to focus on three major themes: Long Island, the Hudson River, and expanding Adirondack Wilderness. To put itself out in front of Adirondack Council, Sierra's Adirondack Committee announced a move to promote creation of a 630,000-acre northwestern wilderness, nearly 200,000 acres larger than the council's Bob Marshall vision.

Sierra Club's lack of grassroots support has gotten the organization in trouble with Adirondackers many times in the past, and the way it is constituted makes this an ever-present possibility. For example, in 2000, the threat of ATV trails in Wild Forests prompted Sierra's Adirondack chair Roger Gray to propose a resolution prohibiting them. A New York City member, unaware of the compromises that created snowmobile trails and the political scene surrounding them, attempted to attach a prohibition on their use to Gray's motion. Gray wisely withdrew the motion.

Over the years the list of Sierra's achievements is significant, for it includes not only those described but the work to achieve state acquisitions for a grand canoe route. DEC employee and Sierra member Per Moberg labored for a long time in the late 1980s to complete the state's purchase of Hitchins Pond and parts of the Bog River for that route.

The Association for the Protection of the Adirondacks

The other "APA" has muddled along through the last decades. The attempt to reinvigorate the board and hire an executive director, to move the association forward after the years dominated by Paul Schaefer and Arthur Crocker, was mildly successful. But time after time, when the board tried to define itself and the issues it would take on, there was never a complete consensus, certainly not enough to galvanize an entire board. One exception was the renewed interest in historic preservation as manifest in the association's work for the preservation of an enlarged Great Camp Sagamore site. The only theme that seemed to surface is that the organization should focus on educational projects. The association's principal educational effort has been its fall meetings. The single-focus programs often attract good speakers and panels, but these forums are often attended by the same old crowd. Members rue the fact that the result is "speaking to the choir," but the leadership has not broken out from the narrow mold of its affluent audiences.

In hiring Dave Gibson, the organization hoped to have someone who could manage and expand the group. Although Gibson is not a particularly adept manager, he is an exceptionally effective letter writer and he has been very influential on the numerous committees on which he has served. He is a consensus builder, capable of working with other groups, often lending the association's name to the most important issues. Joe Rota (Local Government Review Board) has complimented Gibson as being the best consensus builder in the park. Gibson's letters addressing problems relating to DEC rangers or the overbuilding of snowmobile trails have been excellent presentations of the issues. But, other than supporting educational efforts, the association under Gibson has not carved out any environmental fields where it can be the leader.

Gibson has expanded the association's annual report, *The Forest Preserve,* to include a thought-provoking array of articles on stewardship and educational issues. It has featured work with other groups such as the management of Abruzzi Park in Italy and the native reindeer people of Tuva and Mongolia. Articles include comparisons between Adirondack and national issues and tributes to important members.

One of the most telling descriptions of the association in the second half of its existence has been the way individuals have used, or not used, the organization. Paul Schaefer, who had a legendary history with the group, worked hard to bring it closer to the New York State Conservation Council in the 1950s and 1960s. But every time a serious preservation issue arose, Schaefer formed another organization, the most effective of which were described in the introduction. He often took with him some of the more active members of the association. Some of the separate groups had purposes distinct from the association's charter such as the Adirondack Research Center (now Library); Couchsa-cha-gra Association, which produced films on the Adirondacks; and the Forest Preserve Committee of the NYS Conservation Council. For his other groups, such as the Friends of the Forest Preserve, it is possible that Schaefer believed that single-purpose groups could be more effective. It is also possible that he lacked faith in the association.

Conversely, different individuals have used the association as a base for creating new programs in which they were personally interested. The most positive example of this is Paul Bray's work to create a partnership between the Adirondack Park and Abruzzi National Park in Italy. Bray was able to get the program started under the aegis of the association. Adirondack Park Agency Chairman Lefebvre later expanded the cooperative effort to highlight his concern for integrating people and preservation.

Over the years, the organization has been split by many issues, most significantly over navigation rights. Several of its board members came from the Adirondack League Club or other private groups that fought the notion that the park's waters are recreationally navigable. In the late 1980s and early 1990s this issue caused a breach so severe that the legal settlement of the issue was barely able to heal the rupture.

Compounding the inability to define itself has been the problem of finding a home for the organization. Rather than taking on a small, well-located office in Albany, the group has sought to honor long-time member Paul Schaefer by acquiring his house, rehabilitating it for its offices, and building an adjacent structure to house the Adirondack Research Library. That largely volunteer-run library has several important collections worthy of preservation, but no full-time certified staff to make it a functioning research center.

The association has also been torn between those who wish to continue looking inward and parochially, but with the intent of honoring Paul Schaefer, and those who wish to see it become more effective in Adirondack politics. The focus on Schaefer is probably the reason the association does not seem to have adhered to its long-range plan as adopted in 1992. There is a real danger that honoring Schaefer will leave the organization too underfunded and too locally oriented to enlarge its effectiveness. Yet the board does not have enough enthusiastic and environmentally focused members to take on all the tasks summarized by its original motto, "Watchdog of the Forest Preserve." For this, Gibson's work has been essential.

Until the association became caught up in acquiring the Schaefer home, the organization had trouble getting a development project off the ground. They drifted from being New York City centered to becoming Schenectady focused, losing in the process much capital that exists in the New York metropolitan area.

The association's centennial luncheon and annual board meeting were held in the spring of 2001. Only thirty-six people attended the meeting; a handful more came for the lunch alone. Those recognized at the event were staff and volunteers, not emblems of the association's "Watchdog of the Forest Preserve" role. Bob Ringlee reported that it would be difficult to achieve membership goals, implying that membership was well below the 1,900 often quoted. Carl George, new board member, talked of looking to a larger and more diverse constituency for the organization as a major effort to increase support for the Forest Preserve in the future. The level of participation and enthusiasm left doubt whether the nearly moribund group could be resurrected.

A large and enthusiastic audience greeted the "Mysterious Mountains" concert at Union College in the fall of 2001. It was the centerpiece of the official celebration of the centennial of the Association for the Protection of the Adirondacks. Donors have given the organization funds to hire someone to be watchdog over DEC's unit management planning process. None of this dispels the lingering question of whether the association can recover its past strengths.

Audubon New York

Local Audubon chapters have responded to local issues, and High Peaks Audubon has been quite active in open space planning. There is no one group within National Audubon that is focused on the Adirondacks entirely, nor is there a grassroots involvement with parkwide interests.

Dick Beamish had written Peter Berle, then head of National Audubon, several times in 1989 with suggestions for the Commission on the Adirondacks in the 21st Century. In the fall of 1990 as he was about to leave the Adirondack Council, Beamish wrote Berle with a proposal to create a strong environmental coalition to support the commission's work. "For reasons I won't go into, the Adirondack Council, which should be leading the charge, has become almost moribund during the past two years. . . . Because the Council is not inclined right now to do this job, my hope is that you will let some of us do it under the auspices of the National Audubon Society and Dave Miller." [36]

In 1991 Beamish launched Audubon's Adirondack program, taking with him two important staff members from Adirondack Council: Lynne Poteau, council fundraiser, joined as staff and Eric Siy became director. Beamish's raid on the council's staff was no more egregious than his rumored taking of the council's huge membership list. Council was none too happy with Audubon's move and its incursion on Adirondack Council's turf.

The Audubon effort, called the Citizen Mobilization Campaign to Save the Adirondacks, flourished until 1994, when Miller became Audubon's executive director for New York State and proposed broadening its focus to include all of the northeastern forestlands. In 1993 Audubon, through Berle, strongly encouraged Governor Cuomo to expand Adirondack Park Agency staff. But most of Audubon's labors seemed to be directed toward fundraising for the new group. While National Audubon claimed "sole credit for developing this growing coalition of environmental, labor, religious, sporting, gardening, education, and recreation organizations," it never got off the ground. The organization, through Beamish, was successful in placing articles in papers across the state urging support for the APA, and Siy proved to be a very effective lobbyist, but both he and Beamish left when Miller expanded the program.

In succeeding years *Audubon Advocate,* the publication of Audubon New York, brought the message "advocate for birds, wildlife, and their habitats" to the entire state. The newsletter has increased coverage of Adirondack issues. Former 21st Century Commission staffer Graham Cox, forest/wetlands coordinator, zeroes in on much of Audubon's Adirondack concerns and has joined the Region 5 Open Space Committee, where he is a strong advocate for state acquisition of a handful of important parcels, such as the Follensby Pond Tract and nine thousand acres surrounding the old Tahawus mine. (Open Space Institute has been the prime mover in negotiations for the latter tracts for several years.)

Adirondack Mountain Club

Adirondack Mountain Club floundered somewhat around 1990, but was resuscitated by Bob Ringlee and in 1991, under his direction, a master plan for the Loj property at Heart Lake, the gateway to the High Peaks, was submitted to the Adirondack Park Agency. (DEC's proposal to buy the Loj property in 1979 had been turned down.)

Enormous growth of budget and staff marked the 1990s. In 2000, the mountain club, headquartered in Lake George and at Heart Lake, was stronger than ever, with thirty thousand members. In the late 1990s, ADK made a political alliance with the New York/New Jersey Trail Conference, so the joint lobbying force could claim it represented over 100,000 individuals.

ADK's concern for its largely recreation-oriented membership and its business-oriented activities was never far from the surface, but its role in conservation matters grew throughout the nineties, mostly because of the efforts of Neil Woodworth. He had joined Adirondack Mountain Club in 1979, served on its Conservation Committee, and succeeded Dave Newhouse as that committee's chair in 1985 when Newhouse began his second term as president of ADK. Then in March 1989 Woodworth left his position as a litigator with an Albany law firm and took a full-time position with ADK. Woodworth became deputy executive director for conservation in 1995. His full-fledged lobbying effort was expanded in 1998 with an office in Albany and additional staff; his title became counsel and director of conservation and advocacy.

Woodworth's very aggressive style changed the club's image, which now stands in stark contrast to the Newhouse years. Newhouse was an engineer, quiet in manner, always fighting for principles. Even winning the club's support for those principles involved many hard-fought battles. Newhouse based his principles on the state constitution, Article XIV, the APA Act, and the State Land Master Plan. With Bob Ringlee and Eleanor Brown and other strong environmentalists, Newhouse had won a conservation charter for the club that embodied the spirit of these principles.

Woodworth told the author that when he came along, with one or two exceptions, he had the foundation for what he saw as his lobbying work. He did not have to go back to the board and "work in the trenches." No longer did the club behave as if, environmentally, "it had one foot on the accelerator, one foot on the brake," a description I heard from longtime trails committee chair Jim Cooper. As strong as Adirondack Mountain Club's environmental positions have become, there remained weak spots, such as not working to extend High Peaks camping regulations to all wilderness areas.

Woodworth credited his mentors with teaching him that research was more important than rhetoric, that documentation of ideas was essential. So, he recalled, he did not have to create new bricks, new policy; he just had to implement ADK's positions. During this period there were still battles, but Woodworth fought them differently, creating working groups to hammer out issues before they got to the club's unwieldy board. This happened when ADK, through a subcommittee, created the club's principles for the High Peaks Area, which it then expected the Citizen's Advisory Committee for the High Peaks Wilderness Area Unit Management Plan to follow.

By the end of the 1990s, Woodworth had become a very strong lobbyist, with an aggressive style. He recalled with pride the way he had been influential in achieving a number of important successes of the 1990s: the creation of the Environmental Protection Fund and the use of some of those funds for stewardship. He contributed to studies of river corridors on Champion lands, which influenced the state's acquisition, and on International Paper Company's lake tracts west and south of Whitney Park. He took pride in his advocacy on rivers and the research he and John Caffrey did to uncover state archival opinions that discussed boats and canoes as part of commerce, to show that commerce includes travel and in particular recreational travel as well as business. He saw this work as central to later opinions. He worked very hard on the Northern Forest Lands Council and on the Region 5 Open Space Committee.

Woodworth believed that when environmental groups have had common agendas, they have worked well together. However, he has not hesitated to take the club in an independent direction when he thought it was important, and when he did the club became a force to be reckoned with. His legal training prompted him to take stands that occasionally were at variance with a consensus of environmental groups. In the late 1990s, Woodworth became particularly adroit at gaining the ear of people in the governor's office or at high levels at DEC. His work behind the scenes raised questions from some quarters, such as from snowmobilers. I found it curious that the amorphous organization stood so firmly behind his advocacy. Perhaps that was an illusion or perhaps it was because he does stand so firmly on the foundation Dave Newhouse built.

But, as the discussion of the High Peaks Wilderness Area Unit Management Plan shows, Adirondack Mountain Club concern for recreation and more importantly for the club's financial bottom line affected many of its stands. Woodworth's personality was always a dominant factor, as was his ever striving to place or keep ADK and himself in the forefront of environmental stands. This was seen in his extraordinarily strong opposition to use of motor vehicles of any sort to construct, maintain, or groom snowmobile trails. Woodworth relished his role in negotiating DEC's policy that limits staff use of motor vehicles. ADK's conservation budget always paled beside Adirondack Council's, but because of Woodworth the club had become an omnipresent force in the environmental movement in the Adirondacks.

Working Together—Blue Mountain Meetings

After Governor Pataki replaced the strongly environmental members of the Adirondack Park Agency they looked for ways to continue their influence. According to John Collins, he, Liz Thorndike, Peter S. Paine Jr., and Robert Glennon formed a group of "conveners" in 1996 under Thorndike's nominal leadership. The group invited David Sive, but he has remained largely on the outside of the ad hoc group. The group expanded to include representatives of organizations loosely termed "environmentalists" in this book: Adirondack Council, the Association for the Protection of the Adirondacks , Adirondack Mountain Club, Residents' Committee to Protect the Adirondacks, Audubon, Environmental Advocates (formerly Environmental Planning Lobby), Sierra, and the Adirondack Nature Conservancy.

In 1996, with support from the HKH Foundation (Harold K. Hochschild), Collins and the others invited the executive directors of all the environmental groups with interests in the Adirondacks to meet at Blue Mountain Lake to determine common ground. The first year's meeting was successful enough that the attendees wished to repeat the meeting the following year, but there were few results in the way of developing a common ground. According to Collins, the individual groups cherished their own agendas and were not yet ready to share goals. No one seemed to recognize that the groups might be stronger together. They did, however, arrive at a shopping list of lands they thought the state ought to acquire and a suggested list of possible appointees to Adirondack Park Agency (as well as a parallel list of those who would not be acceptable). The eighteen parcels of land were mostly those identified by the Open Space Plan and the Commission report and included Champion lands and key shoreline parcels on Lake George. The group sent a letter to the governor and was able to arrange a meeting between key executive directors and the governor's staff. Peter Bauer believes that as a result of their united effort, Governor Pataki was encouraged to seek the Champion lands.

At the second year's meeting, the group, increased by representatives from almost all the other environmental organizations interested in the Adirondacks, reaffirmed the land acquisition list, talked tentatively about other issues, and assigned members to study those issues that were closest to the individual groups' agendas. Collins said that the results "were not earth shaking" and that the groups still did not "see the light" on the issue of working together.

In 1998 there was a real sense that the groups would talk together and find common ground. There was agreement that Adirondack Council would take the lead on federal acid rain legislation as it had done in the past. The lawsuit challenging use of motorized vehicles in the Forest Preserve and DEC's compliance with the Americans with Disabilities Act brought unanimity to the group and made them realize that they needed to work together. Michael Clarke, the newly appointed executive director of the Adirondack Nature Conservancy, brought new insight into the land acquisition issue. The group developed the consensus that the governor would support the acquisition of land for the Forest Preserve, cater to local governments, and not do much else for the Adirondacks. No one seemed to know how to fix that.

I attended that meeting and gave a talk on my perception of DEC's problems relating to stewardship, lack of management, the unit management planning process, and so on. I was not a part of the group's deliberations, but came away believing that a remarkable number of the representatives had a rather naïve concept of dealing with the governor and government in general. I was mistaken; a follow-up meeting with Governor Pataki in January 1999 ultimately resulted in the governor's commitment to the unit management plan process and awakened his interest in stewardship for the Forest Preserve.

According to one participant, the 1999 meeting was the least productive in the series, mostly an exchange of information on the activities of the represented organizations and agreement on the need for three additional Adirondack Park Agency staff, the Residents' Committee to Protect the Adirondacks's jet-ski proposals, and not much else. The gathering in 2000 focused again on land acquisition. Several participants began talking about small parcels and a way of "packaging" a bundle of small parcels into a big splash that might appeal to the governor. There was agreement on the need to expand funds for land acquisition available from the Environmental Protection Fund. The issue of EPF funds was a dominant theme in the 2001 meeting because their use for stewardship had been omitted from that year's budget deliberations.

Not only do organizations with relatively similar goals find it not always easy to work together, but there has been little outreach from environmental groups to organizations like Adirondack Landowners Association and Blue Line Council and no attempt at rapport with property rights groups. On the question of working with those with differing perspectives, John Collins told the author, "we really don't see the world the same way at all. I am skeptical of working with other groups."

Mark Dowie, in *Losing Ground,* related the story of G-10, the leaders of ten national environmental groups, that began meeting in the 1980s in an effort to find a common agenda. His book discusses a report produced by the G-10 in 1986, entitled "An Environmental Agenda for the Future." Despite achieving that consensus agenda, the group gradually fell apart, and Dowie's analysis of the reasons it did may be prophetic for the Adirondack group: "At exactly the moment it should have moved vertically, the movement went horizontal. It played safe. Instead of reaching out to state, local, and regional grassroots organizations, it formed an exclusive Beltway Club of white and (all-but-two) male CEOs." G-10 became "almost ineffectual," according to a Sierra Club director. Outsiders renamed it "the Gang of Ten."[37]

The Adirondack group was still talking and trying to work together at the end of 2001, although its success remained unclear.

Outside Funders

The difficulty of mobilizing only the environmental groups is illustrated by a series of meetings that began in 1996 at the invitation of a number of funders, led by the Pew Charitable Trust with the Rockefeller Family Fund and others. The HKH Foundation-sponsored Adirondack Project hosted a funder-convened meeting at the Blue Mountain Center. The money that Adirondack environmental groups receive from such national funders has been paltry compared with what some western associations receive. There was a belief that the Adirondack environmental entities were not only not working together, they were bad-mouthing each other.

The funders wanted a big, appealing joint program. One of those attending the meeting told the author that there were problems on several levels. It was much more than the fact that the groups did not get along. They had vastly different organizing capabilities, and no group had experience raising capital outside of New York State. The groups did not appear to be mobilizers; even Adirondack Council seemed to be in a state of paralysis with respect to the funders' proposal. The Adirondack groups seemed to be happy the way they were, creating a political standoff.[38]

The funders hired a consultant, Jay R. Halfon, who in the fall of 1997 prepared an analysis of the Adirondack situation and created an outline for a project that would unite the various environmental groups, appeal to the funders, and generate an Adirondack campaign. Halfon interviewed over sixty representatives of Adirondack groups as well as the funders to determine their agendas. Out of it came a program whose scale—big—was expected to appeal to Governor Pataki. The report called for hiring a project director who could develop a comprehensive plan for backcountry protection; oversee a statewide campaign; skillfully deal with the media; negotiate with landholders, the governor, and the legislature; build alliances with communities; and facilitate the involvement of the existing environmental preservation community. The emphasis on a program of backcountry preservation came from the funders; it centered on the protection of privately held backcountry lands in the northwestern region of the Adirondacks from subdivision and development. This protection was to be done without creating a new organization but with a committee representing the environmental groups. To address the parallel protection of the economic base of the forest industry, the report suggested creating an Adirondack Park Conservation and Timber Trust.

The funders' choice of director favored someone with national experience in the west and Alaska, a brilliant environmentalist, but not someone who appealed to the Adirondack groups. Whether it was the choice of director or the whole proposal that required the groups to work together is not clear, but no agreement between the groups was ever reached, so the funders withdrew. It may be that the environmentalists felt that what the funders wanted was inappropriate. It may also be that they feared loss of control over their fundraising capabilities.

Chuck Clusen, former executive director of Adirondack Council who attended one of the meetings, said the funders' desire for a "big political campaign for land acquisition in the northwest part of the park, a combination of what Adirondack Council called the Big Bob and the northern boreal wilderness, the area that all the groups had identified," proved to be a major stumbling block. "What happened was a number of people went after it as a political advocacy campaign. Council feared it would end up in their losing foundation money. Council would only agree to it if there was a central pot of money which was allocated out to the groups, instead of having one core staff." [39]

Some attendees accused Adirondack Council of walking out on the funding opportunities, and when I asked Council's Bernard Melewski to respond to this charge he raised several issues. He felt that the funders themselves created problems by being patronizing, presenting a preconceived project, and handing them a project that necessitated their becoming more aggressive. The groups, he said, feared being directed from outside, especially by someone not familiar with the Adirondacks. He thought the funders were unaware of important things that were beginning to happen, such as the negotiations on Whitney and Champion. He believes organizations would have been happy taking the money and not doing what the funders wanted. Further, given the difficulties of doing what the funders wanted, Adirondack Council in particular was worried that a misstep would upset the Adirondack scene. At the time there was little opposition from communities to the proposed acquisitions, and Council feared that a big push would create a backlash.

That the funders had an agenda of their own was borne out in 2001 by the announcement by the Pew Charitable Trust that the foundation would more and more plan and fund its own environmental campaigns, rather than funding existing groups.

Nevertheless, the failure to come up with a plan the funders would approve may be nothing more than that the groups were destined not to work together on a larger scale. Melewski believed that the groups work together only when common goals already exist. It is possible that the biggest among them feared for their own ability to continue raising funds for themselves. It is more likely that the individualism that infuses Adirondackers has shown up in Adirondack preservation organizations.

Given the problems of supposedly similar-minded organizations working together, there seems to be no answer to the larger question of how to get groups on both sides of environmental issues working together. The previous chapter on public participation analyzes some of the attempts to bring disparate groups to consensus. The leadership of the Blue Mountain group illustrates only one facet of the difficulty in working to achieve consensus between similar organizations.

John Collins, with his experience with local government and as chairman of the Adirondack Park Agency, is negative on the possibilities of bringing local governments into such discussions. He does not believe that local government can solve problems because he believes local political control is in the hands of small groups in each town, groups that include developers and local business-men. When I questioned Collins on the problems of marshaling like-minded groups and asked if he thought such an effort could be made all-inclusive, he only sighed. He does not believe even this is possible.[40]

More than a hint of working together appeared in 2001. The New York Caucus of the Northern Forest Alliance, with funding from the Pew Charitable Trusts, published a glossy booklet on important future acquisitions in the park and the Tug Hill Region and sources of funding for those acquisitions.[41] The booklet reviews successful acquisitions since 1996 and notes both fee and ease-ment possibilities. All of the environmental players with interests statewide as well as in the park joined in,* but this consensus fades in importance in light of the fact that the acquisition issues are like "motherhood and apple pie" among those groups. They have yet to address the park's hard issues with a common voice.

---

* Adirondack Council, Adirondack Mountain Club, Association for the Protection of the Adirondacks, Audubon New York, Citizens Campaign for the Environment, Environmental Advocates, New York League of Conservation Voters, New York Rivers United, and Residents' Committee to Protect the Adirondacks.

National Environmental Groups and Wolves

No issue was more contentious in the 1990s than the proposed reintroduction of wolves. Although some local people and organizations such as the Association for the Protection of the Adirondacks were in favor of wolf reintroduction, the issue came to a head under prodding by a national organization, Defenders of Wildlife. It was opposed by Association of Adirondack Towns and Villages, and St. Lawrence and Essex counties passed laws banning introductions of dangerous animals.[42] Defenders of Wildlife funded a $115,000 study to determine the feasibility of wolf reintroduction; the biological aspects were to be examined by the Conservation Biology Institute of Oregon and the sociological aspects by Cornell University. Initial studies showed that the Adirondack grey wolf is closely related to the red wolf, which is a small wolf that will interbreed with coyotes. In addition, the Algonquin wolf is also related to the red wolf. It has been predicted that because of the presence of coyotes in the Adirondacks, any introduced red or gray wolf will be fully interbred with the local coyote population within a few decades.

The issue was still alive in 2001, when a new Wild Lands Project again raised the issue and proposed introducing the timber wolf. New preliminary studies from Canada indicate that the wolf present in the Adirondacks historically was not a timber wolf; thus introducing timber wolves would not be a replacement for an extirpated species.

Wildlife Conservation Society

In the late 1990s, several national environmental organizations not traditionally active in the Adirondacks have sponsored programs directed at communities and their problems, and their results have been quite successful.

The Wilderness Society sponsored meetings with towns, offering their services to help towns make hard decisions. The meetings in Indian Lake were considered successful.

The Wildlife Conservation Society (WCS), based at the Bronx Zoo, refocused on projects in the United States in 1994. Building on his desire to know more of the Adirondacks, Bill Weber, director of WCS, began the Oswegatchie Roundtable, which continues to meet yearly. With funding from the Ford Foundation, the roundtable has discussed a number of community and socioeconomic concerns, backed wolf restoration in the park, and financed studies of the 1995 blowdown and forest succession.

More recently WCS has expanded into community outreach with a pioneering effort to create mini-visitor-information centers in vacant storefronts in the area's hamlets. This project would fulfill several goals: hamlet improvement, consistent information sources on the park and local areas, and a local sense of achievement. The WCS-sponsored Adirondack Communities and Conservation Program helps local communities open these storefront information centers. They focus public outreach on the park's hamlets, provide indirect grassroots aid to these hamlets, and most importantly create an expression for public participation.

According to Heidi Kretser, director of Wildlife Conservation Society's Adirondack Communities and Conservation Program, the center at Inlet was up and running in 2001, with thanks also to Town Supervisor J. R. Risley; the center at North Creek opened in spring 2001 in conjunction with the reactivated railroad; and plans are underway for Star Lake. A Lake Champlain group has similar plans for information centers in Willsboro and Essex.

WCS has supported a program to gather data of all kinds—natural resources, educational facilities, health services, and so on. This information will be compiled in an atlas that will be available to schools, planners, and citizens. WCS hopes in this way to give people in the Adirondacks the tools with which to make the informed decisions needed for community planning.

Rocky Mountain Institute and Clifton/Fine Area Renewal

A local project on economic renewal began in 1997 in the Clifton/Fine area, which was facing such threats as the closing of the old Newton Falls Paper Company (it closed in 2001) and the cleanup of the J&L iron mine site, which is the worst oil spill in the region. With funding, half of which was generated locally with the help of their state assemblywoman and half by a grant from Cornell Cooperative Extension, the local group hired Michael Kinsley of the Rocky Mountain Institute as a consultant. In meetings over a three-day period he helped the economic renewal group learn such basics as how to meet, how to reach consensus, how to mobilize the community.

In a few short months in the second half of 2000, the group used what it learned to identify the numerous organizations in the five hamlets that have a stake in the area's economic future. Several projects materialized, almost more than the group can keep in touch with, according to Christopher Westbrook. One was a cleanup of the area to make it attractive to larger economic projects. The "Neighbors Helping Neighbors" project accomplished several restorations that began to make the main highway through Star Lake look better, and this improvement inspired individuals in the community to fix up their properties. Cranberry Lake developed its beach with a new pavilion, a cultural affairs group brought movies, and the skating arena will have activities in summer. Since no local newspaper serves the area, community bulletin boards and a weekly newsletter keep people in touch.

According to Westbrook, people in the communities began to feel much better about themselves and the economic renewal group continued reaching out, but its membership was mostly older, retired people, with a bias toward summer folk, not residents. The state stepped in to assist with a sale of the paper mill to an outfit that could keep it going, but that effort failed. Even though the communities strung out along Route 3 still have a long way to go to establish economic viability, the project generated a sense of pride and accomplishment. Initial progress began with a few individuals and the communities' ability to learn how to work together.

Lake George Association

As I pondered on the problems of public participation and how to show what might work, Dick Lefebvre reminded me that the Lake George Association (LGA) was the archetype of an environmental group working with governmental entities. The LGA has roots as old as the Forest Preserve; it was the first lake association in the state, established in 1885 by a group concerned with the lake's fisheries and with stocking the lake. By 1900 LGA extended its concerns to the lake's water quality, to pollutants that then came mostly from surrounding farms.

Today, Lake George Association claims five thousand members in two thousand families spread through nine local governments (eight towns and Lake George village) in three counties. The association has grown with the threats to the lake. Over the years, the biggest such threat was the opening of the Northway in the 1960s, which brought an explosion in use of the lake. Lake George and its shoreline was designated a state park in 1961, with a commission appointed to oversee the park. When the Department of Environmental Conservation was created from the old Conservation Department and its various governor-appointed commissions, all those commissions across the state except two were dissolved and replaced by DEC's regional offices. LGA was instrumental in keeping the Lake George Commission, but the commission was given only an advisory role, with no DEC enforcement powers, only boat patrol.

In the mid-1960s, problems of sewage began to plague the lake, known as one of the purest in the country. Its steep, rocky shorelines and thin soils made septic systems problematical. In the 1970s, LGA, working with Department of Health, DEC, and others, got a ban on the use of phosphates and began planning for improved sewage disposal. A proposal to pump sewage out of the Lake George basin to Queensbury, where the Glens Falls system would be upgraded, was to be funded by an $80 million U.S. Environmental Protection Agency grant. The project was about to start when the proposal was overturned with the requirement that an Environmental Impact Statement was needed. After three years of EPA foot-dragging, the money was gone. There was local opposition to the project; a taxpayers' group feared big development and casinos, but LGA supported the plan. Because much of the lakeshore is APA-designated Hamlet, giving locals control over its development, much building occurred anyway. Through the 1980s miles of lightly developed shoreline were turned into condominiums with local sewage treatment. Many subdivisions were created, and not all of them have been built out yet. Several towns passed zoning ordinances in the 1980s, and some of them increased shoreline protection by declaring that shorelines within 300 feet of the lake were critical environmental areas needing APA approval. Again LGA expanded, this time to monitor planning and zoning boards and to review projects at an early stage.

In the early 1980s, the Lake George Association felt that DEC had become too large and that the region needed more power, closer to home. Lake George Association and Lake George Commission encouraged a planning effort to empower the commission. In 1987, after a two-year effort led by DEC's Charlie Morrison, many workshops, and much research, a *Plan for the Future of Lake George* was published. The revitalization it brought about started slowly; at first it only had control over the construction of docks and speed and noise limits on the lake. Boat patrols were expanded. The plan had limited power on land, but it did produce a model stream water regulation for towns to adopt. It had the authority to establish wastewater regulations and set standards for operating septic systems and inspecting them every three years. This worked until stopped by a lawsuit brought by Robert Schultz on the grounds that an Environmental Impact Statement had not been done, and so nothing is being done at present. However, results from the few years the regulations were applied show that they work; many systems were upgraded. The association has encouraged the development of a water-testing program, which is now funded by a private endowment and carried out by Rensselaer Polytechnic Institute's Freshwater Institute in Bolton Landing.

Today, according to Mary Arthur Beebe, the association's sparkplug and executive director, Lake George Association does everything from streambank stabilization to education. It obtains funding for towns to build catchments for surface runoff, uses private funds to match grants from the Department of State's local waterfront revitalization program, and works with towns to use local labor to keep costs down. LGA has resorted to legal action, but rarely, to achieve its goals. It has been involved in nuisance species control: zebra mussels and weeds like milfoil have threatened the lake. Despite LGA's best efforts, water quality continues to decline.

LGA is a privately funded, public participation group. What makes all this work, besides a dedicated leader? Its staff of eight, supplemented by many volunteers, and board of twenty-four whose members bring a wide range of perspectives are essential. Dues and grants provide a million-dollar yearly budget from the private sector just to take care of the lake. LGA is not a planning organization. Its strength lies in its ability to act. Beebe works under the belief that "management is a shared responsibility between government and citizens." In 2001, the *Plan for the Future of Lake George* needed updating and the Department of State was assisting in this go-round. It has not all been smooth sailing for LGA, especially in its efforts to gain Adirondack Park Agency approval for the use of the chemical Sonar to control the milfoil threat.

"Every success is major," says Beebe, "even the many small steps like water conservation that have become second nature to Lake George's supporters." The small achievements are in many ways attributed to Beebe's demeanor, her way of asking people or towns for help, her ability to bring people together.

Can such achievements be replicated on different scales? Are other regional efforts needed? Could additional regional efforts fit within the Adirondack Park Agency structure?

Local Government Organizations

Local Government Review Board

Tony D'Elia's death on October 13, 1990, and Joe Rota's appointment as the executive director of Local Government Review Board in January 1991 brought about a fundamental change in the organization, despite the fact that some of its positions remained the same. LGRB continued to oppose Governor Cuomo's legislative program that was an outgrowth of the Commission on the Adirondacks in the 21st Century and voted to support a proposal by Senator Ron Stafford to abolish the agency and replace its jurisdiction with DEC. Regardless, LGRB's softening was obvious enough that in April 1992, Adirondack Park Agency members, at the urging of John Collins, voted unanimously to allow a review board member to sit "at the table" with them, to attend committee meetings, and to comment on projects and issues. Peter Paine Jr. said APA's changed attitude was directly related to the LGRB's changed attitude.[43] And that change was directly attributable to Joe Rota, who would have preferred that the LGRB be given status as a voting member of the agency. Rota saw his role as that of an ombudsman, and over the next few years he promoted the board's advocacy for many permit applicants and landowners. However, Rota was not allowed to attend the agency's executive sessions, something LGRB continued to protest.

LGRB's resolutions in 1993 asked that its executive director be made a voting member of Adirondack Park Agency (a similar resolution was passed in each succeeding year), that APA hire an ombudsman, and that the state fund the review board. In 1993 LGRB received state funding for the following year; this was the first time state funding was actually given to the review board although it had been promised many times in the past. The $25,000 budget has risen under Governor Pataki to $50,000 annually.[44] LGRB supported Cuomo's appointment of a task force to study and make recommendations for improving the way the park agency functions. It asked for increased funding for APA and wanted the agency to focus its resources on projects of regional impact and "cease concentrating on the minutiae of projects having only local impact."[45]

In 1994, LGRB wanted increased funding for local planning, with the fund to be made available through a general budgeting process administered by a representative of LGRB, one from Association of Adirondack Towns and Villages, and two park resident members of Adirondack Park Agency. That year, with five APA members serving unexpired terms, LGRB sent a resolution to Governor Pataki urging that he quickly make the reappointments. Further, the LGRB wanted to limit the time the senate could consider the reappointments by declaring the seats vacant and having the governor make new choices if nominees were not approved within ninety days.

Resolutions passed in 1996 indicate that the LGRB was generally supportive of APA; one in particular commended chairman Greg Campbell and acting executive director Dan Fitts for "implementing improved policies and procedures."[46] It also supported the agency's proposed general permit for clearcutting private lands damaged by the 1995 blowdown.

The review board's shift from attempting to abolish the APA to working with it did not please everyone in the Adirondacks. In March 1996 the LGRB acted to oppose Governor Pataki's proposed 20 percent cut in APA's funding and staff. Adirondack Solidarity Alliance, which had opposed Rota's appointment in 1991, favored the cuts.[47] That year, LGRB asked that DEC to reopen lakes closed to floatplanes and maintain roads within the Forest Preserve.

LGRB opposed wolf reintroduction. Despite the shifts, LGRB's activities still went way beyond the role of watchdog.

Membership on the LGRB changed at the end of 1997. Bob Purdy of Essex County, a member since the early 1970s, and Maynard Baker, who was defeated as Town of Warrensburg supervisor, both left the board.[48]

Resolutions of 1997 and 1998 followed themes similar to those of previous years. Some, however, focused on practices in which the LGRB felt the agency had overstepped. The LGRB was sufficiently upset that it was being ignored that a resolution was passed requesting the agency to respond to its recommendations.[49] Actions were not limited to advising the APA, however. One resolution asked DEC to maintain snowmobile trails to a width to accommodate grooming equipment.

As a further sign that all the outward happy smiles between LGRB and APA concealed lingering distrust, the LGRB started off 1999 with a resolution supporting "the study of the legality of the APA Act and the compliance by the Agency with the Act, to be partially funded by Essex County."[50] A second resolution asked that the agency limit the conditions it imposes in permits to regional impacts and "leave the matters of local concern to the towns and villages" of the park as intended by the legislature.[51]

Nevertheless Rota has worked hard to soften relations with the agency. The LGRB started giving out awards to people it believed have benefited their cause, and among the recipients were several agency members, Chairman Lefebvre, and even myself.

Association of Adirondack Towns and Villages
and Inter County Legislative Committee

The Association of Adirondack Towns and Villages, under the strong leadership of George Canon and Jean Olsen, meets only twice a year. All of its members are elected town or village officials, and Canon sees AATV as a communication link with state and federal officials. The issues it takes on are determined by the membership, which synthesizes them into an agenda that AATV can take to the legislature.

In an interview in early 2001, Canon was hopeful that the Forest Tax Law providing reimbursement under 480-A would finally be passed. His optimism was based on the fact that the governor put funding for the program in the general fund. He believes Assemblyman Brodsky has blocked the Forest Tax Law in the past in order to get something in return for his support—something like more backcountry constraints. Canon has told him, "You have all the blood left to get."

According to Canon, AATV's achievements in the 1990s included its role in the successful fight to obtain funding for LGRB and its opposition to wolf reintroduction. Its biggest accomplishment, he said, was heading off a proposal by the Pataki administration to establish negotiated real property taxes on state land, rather than having local assessors determine them as they had traditionally. (AATV and environmental groups were on the same side in this fight.) Canon believes AATV averted a real disaster with this victory.

Canon mentioned one stumbling block—the fact that often AATV can only respond to actions taken by others. Canon told the author in 2000 that he would welcome a role in which the AATV could generate ideas and proposals that would be considered by Adirondack Park Agency and others. So far, AATV's proposals have been mostly for wider snowmobile trails and a network of trunk trails that would tie communities together. AATV has not turned into a forum for improving local economies through expanded and permitted use of the Forest Preserve, but it is expanding its participation in unit management planning.

The Inter County Legislative Committee plays a similar role at the county level. It was very active in the early 1990s in creating the Adirondack Planning Commission. Since then it has been more concerned with common problems of governing counties. It meets nine times a year, and its members are all county supervisors or legislators. Both groups try to take issues brought up by members to resolution at the state level, if possible.

Quasi—and Non-Governmental Organizations

The Adirondack Nature Conservancy

The last (181st) recommendation in the 1970 report on the future of the Adirondacks from the Temporary Study Commission called for private interests to establish "an Adirondack Nature Conservancy (ANC) to encourage gifts in the Adirondack Park." The ANC was formed in 1971, and Tim Barnett was hired as its first executive director. This book has not introduced ANC because the organization has never tried to be a political force, but that fact only enhances ANC's importance in the park. Although the ANC has never overtly been an advocacy group, it has shared board members and occasionally land acquisition goals with Adirondack Council. ANC has always eschewed a formal political role in park matters except in regard to land acquisition. Maybe that abstinence is the reason it has been so widely accepted, such an effective fundraiser, and perhaps the most important group at work in the park at the beginning of the twenty-first century.

ANC has achieved a number of land preservation projects, from establishing special preserves like Spring Pond Bog to raising funds to acquire land and hold it until the state had the funds to add such places as the Morgan Tract, a mile of shoreline on Lake George, to the Forest Preserve. ANC has shifted from a narrow approach of preserving heritage sites and environmentally sensitive places to protecting land more valuable as human resources, such as vistas across farmlands. To do the latter, in 1988 the ANC joined with the Adirondack Land Trust, which had been formed in 1984 by George Davis with ANC's help. This trust enabled the organization to acquire land and easements outside its original charter.

ANC focused at first on the northern Adirondacks, where there was the most private land and the greatest need for resource protection. By 2001, ANC's accomplishments touched every aspect of Adirondack preservation. The organization has established conservation easements on many tracts, launched a program to protect Adirondack alpine flora, and helped owners of large tracts produce long-range plans for land management.

Beginning in 1971 ANC was active in the purchases of many valuable tracts, including Santanoni, Lake Lila, and Everton Falls on the St. Regis River, most of which have been added to the Forest Preserve. Specifically, ANC has protected over a quarter-million acres, of which 147,000 acres were added to the Forest Preserve; 2,000 acres were agricultural land; 65,000 acres were low-elevation boreal forest including a 400-acre raised peatland; and 9,400 acres were wilderness preserves. In addition ANC has preserved 105 miles of undeveloped shorelines, 16 miles of ice meadows on the Hudson River, and pitch pine and sandstone pavement barrens.

Its first acquisition in 2001 generated questions. A 24,000-acre purchase from International Paper included tracts encompassing Bog Lake, which would add significant canoeing possibilities from Lows Lake, and Round Lake, with great canoeing and the opportunity to complete a snowmobile connection between Long and Tupper lakes. The largest part, a 15,000-acre tract, had been a part of Brandreth Park before the land—but not the recreation rights—were acquired by International Paper. Therefore the public will not be able to use this area. ANC was not concerned with the lack of recreation rights, but it was aware of the degraded condition of the forest. Nevertheless, this is an important link in completing the Five Ponds Forests, as ANC chooses to call that huge patch of variously protected land in the northwestern Adirondacks.

Adirondack North Country Association

Adirondack North Country Association has worked hard in the North Country to assist the regional economies by promoting scenic byways, producing guides that bring tourists to the local crafters and artisans, sponsoring common marketing strategies, circulating maps of scenic byways, and placing informational kiosks at key sites. ANCA was founded in 1954 by Roger Tubby, and its sphere includes the Adirondacks but stretches over the whole of upstate New York. This area includes the Tug Hill and much of the agricultural lands that border the Adirondacks on the north and west.

According to Executive Director Terry Martino, the organization has always been business oriented; its five hundred members include individuals and representatives of corporations, educational institutions, local government, and small businesses. Historically ANCA focused on opportunities and policies for small businesses. Congressman John McHugh and State Senator Stafford helped ANCA obtain state money and federal monies in the 1980s. Under the leadership of Frank Augsbury, ANCA was able to extend its program of giving grants to small businesses and entrepreneurs. ANCA's reach extended to North Country agriculture, natural resources, enterprise and community development, services and culture, and tourism.

By building partnerships, obtaining more and more grants, and adding programs, ANCA had become the most dynamic private force in the economy of the North Country by 2001. While other agencies took a more traditional approach to economic development, ANCA was more creative, as exemplified by its scenic byways project. Since 1992 one of its small staff (seven people spread around the North Country) has been a forest products industry professional who has worked to bring secondary industries to the region. ANCA also paid attention to the quality of life in the region, hence its grants to Saranac Lake's Pendragon Theater.

ANCA celebrated its forty-fifth anniversary in 1999 with a panel discussion on land acquisition and easements, a well-rounded forum that reached many segments of the park. As of 2001, ANCA's board continues to engage in considerable strategic planning, but, most importantly, it has retained its reputation for getting things done.

Champlain-Adirondack Biosphere Reserve

In 1989 the Adirondack region became part of the Champlain-Adirondack Biosphere Reserve (CABR), adding one more layer of apparent governmental structure and a lot of confusion. It brought no benefits locally and served mostly as a paper tiger used by property rights advocates as a threat to local residents. How something as innocuous as this program became associated with secret black helicopters spying on residents is one of the best examples of paranoia in the Adirondacks.

The program came from the U.S. Man and Biosphere Program in 1987 to the governors of New York and Vermont, who made the formal nomination. After two years of gathering nomination materials, UNESCO formally designated CABR in 1989. By 1989, the UNESCO program had designated three hundred biosphere reserves in eighty-five countries; the CABR was the fourth largest in the world and the largest in North America.

The CABR should not be confused with the Champlain Basin Committee, which was formed in 1968 as an advocacy group to fight proposals for a lock system that would have permitted oceangoing vessels to go from the St. Lawrence through Lake Champlain to the Hudson River. That committee still functions, promoting education and recreation in the basin.

Biosphere reserves are geographic areas of unique natural environments that have been internationally recognized for their special value in conservation, education, and scientific research. It is an international designation intended to foster study and cooperation on physical, biological, and social problems. An analysis of the CABR and similar areas determined that the CABR was the most significant candidate to be a representative of the Lake-Forest Biome in a region that extends from Manitoba to Maine.

Adirondack Park Agency planners John Banta, Ray Curran, and Ed Hood were involved in the designation. According to Hood, "there was promise for CABR but unfortunately it never materialized for a host of reasons. Three more years of effort by a NY and VT Steering Committee failed to produce any agreement on an organization for the CABR. This, in combination with allegations of an international conspiracy and regulation and the land grab hysteria at the regional and national levels, put the CABR program in limbo where it has been since 1992. . . . There is currently no interest in resurrecting such a 'political hot potato.' " [52]

How Champlain-Adirondack Biosphere Reserve got to be such a hot potato says more for the paranoia in the park than for the program. I have visited several dozen international biosphere reserves and World Heritage Sites and have been most impressed with the way local people support efforts to improve their lot while protecting their surroundings. For example, the Sian Ka'an Reserve in the Yucatan protects manatees by limiting commercial fishing, but natives supported the program because the commercial limits simultaneously improved their ability to do sustainable fishing.

The Adirondack Park was included in the designation because it is an outstanding example of the integration of public and private lands and goals. In the storm of arguments over the ills of park government, everyone seems to forget that the job of protecting the environment in the Adirondacks has gone a long way toward completion. Critics of the CABR not only ignore the fact that the designation can in no way control what happens in the park, but they claim the CABR poses a loss of sovereignty. Equating the biosphere reserve concept with the Park Agency, one critic wrote: "Instead of the robust, thriving communities promised in MAB literature, the Adirondack economy has been devastated, the culture and much of the infrastructure frozen in time, and the people repressed by a communal-feudal land tenure structure where a non-elected, non-representative NGO controlled APA develops and enforces arbitrary and capricious regulations across multiple counties."[53]

Instead of being proud that we have a region that serves as an international example, those who oppose government in any form exaggerate the threat of a biosphere reserve designation for their own purposes. Would anything be different if the governors had not sought the designation? Probably not, and the property rights movement would have found another example to symbolize the threats of big government.

Economic Development

The complaints against every proposal for land acquisition, for regulations, for almost everything have been of the sort, "the economic impact of a regulation has not been considered," or "no one is helping local economies," or simply "the economy of the park is terrible." This may have been true through the 1970s and most of the 1980s, but everyone, from APA economist Steve Erman to local businessmen to realtors, noticed the real improvements in the 1990s. Undoubtedly the most significant factor of all was the fact that the nation enjoyed a period of prosperity and growth all through the 1990s, although an improved economy nationally does not necessarily mean the park will prosper proportionately.

As this section traces the upward trends, the reader must remember that they were not consistent across the park. The Department of Economic Development splits the park into two regions, and its major thrust in recent years has been the more developed heart of the park, especially those regions close to Lake Placid.

In the past, the state economic agencies often seemed to operate in a rarified sphere that failed to appreciate the variety of community offerings within the park. They looked for big projects. Communities looked for handouts, for businesses to drop on their doorsteps.

The synergism of three different events was required to bring about the changes of the 1990s. First, the state had created the Department of Economic Development in 1987 and enlarged its regional office. The state became much more realistic in its economic goals for the park. DED recognized that new large manufacturing operations, even those tied to Adirondack resources, were unlikely. It sought out small businessmen and entrepreneurs by encouraging people who wanted to live in the park. Jean Raymond, Edinburg supervisor, still wished the governor would get as excited about a business that adds two employees in the park as he does about two hundred new jobs in the capital region. DED shifted from emphasizing businesses on the fringe of or just outside the park to encouraging them in the park.

Second, many local Industrial Development Authorities (IDAs) appeared or matured and began to promote the beauty and quality of life in the park as the basis of economic development. For many years, the naysaying of opposition to Adirondack Park Agency, bolstered by a few bad stories repeated over and over, had created a climate in which businesses did not look to the park. It was not any change in regulations that improved the climate in the 1990s, it was the positive promotion of the park's values by local groups. (Essex County now advertises itself as "A Healthy Place to Grow.") The park is seen as an economic asset.

The third positive, according to Erman, is the political climate, more positive for business now under Pataki, much more positive under APA Chairman Lefebvre, who has created a more buoyant image for the park. "He has put misperceptions to rest," said Erman. Now the agency has an economic team, not just Erman, to focus on stewardship of the environment and economics.

From big to small, business is slowly growing in and around the park. Bombardier Corporation, producer of subway cars, is an anomalous heavy industry located in Plattsburgh. It has brought in many support businesses to the area. Several businesses have grown within the park simply because their owners want to live there: Lake Placid Industries, Inc. has expanded by producing close-tolerance machinery; Wilt Industries in Lake Pleasant has a specialty business producing machinery for glass production; General Composites of Westport started with ultra-light canoe paddles and expanded from other plastic sports equipment to medical applications. Bed-and-breakfasts have proliferated.

There have been setbacks, the biggest in the Newton Falls area, where Appleton Coated Papers struggled to keep the former Newton Falls Paper Company alive. It closed, and there are no prospects that it will be resuscitated. This happened despite the fact that there are all too few secondary wood products companies, manufacturers of furniture, and the like. Adirondack North Country Association is trying to stimulate this segment of the economy because the resource could support many more than currently exist.

Also helping improve the economic scene is the Adirondack Economic Development Corporation (AEDC), a not-for-profit, started in 1984. Under Ernest Hohmeyer, AEDC has funneled loans to small businesses and entrepreneurs and offered technical assistance. For a time it was an example of a large project that failed, partly because AEDC was trying to do too much, to expand too far, to be everything for everyone, and as a result the organization faltered and lost major funding. It recovered somewhat by becoming smaller and leaner, and in 2001 was focusing on training entrepreneurs.

Such entrepreneurs are dependent on high-speed communications, and making this kind of communications possible while at the same time protecting the resource is going to be a big challenge. Fiber-optic cables are expensive and the region's towns too spread out, so that placing cables along major road corridors or railroad corridors just does not reach enough people to become economically viable.

What I found most encouraging was the fact that the Forest Preserve, with its mountains, lakes, and all kinds of opportunities, was finally considered as part of the economic base of the park. People are at least talking about economic solutions in the context of the park's natural resources.

Adirondack Explorer

Dick Beamish disappeared from the forefront of Adirondack advocacy for a while in the 1990s, only to reemerge as the publisher of a ten-times-a-year magazine with a newspaper format. For years the Adirondacks has needed a single newspaper to enhance residents' image of being part of one park. Residents traditionally see themselves as part of smaller communities. There are only a few in-park papers, none with parkwide coverage. Most residents get their news from papers published just outside the park.

Beamish believes in presenting both sides of the many Adirondack issues. He maintains the paper as a nonprofit enterprise funded by some of the same wealthy individuals who support the Adirondack Museum. Beamish has not yet achieved a paper that meets the whole park's needs, but he has been trying. Starting at first with recycled articles and reviews, issue-oriented and travel pieces by staff writers, and a broad range of topics from nature to politics, he has produced something that has appealed to many Adirondackers, especially summer people.

The paper's environmental bias is obvious, but it is relatively balanced in that it usually presents both sides of issues, and although its articles are often too short to be considered adequate background, it may yet turn out to be a major voice for the whole Adirondacks. To do that it will have to look at how legislative actions affect the Adirondacks, how local economies are faring, how local governments are functioning. It has made a good start by focusing on recreation and opportunities throughout the park. Its highest potential will be as a way for Adirondackers to share information on what works for their communities. Hopefully it will be successful enough that it will ultimately become a weekly subscription and advertising-supported paper, sought by residents and visitors alike.

Adirondack Regional Tourism Council

New York State Department of Economic Development originally defined the Adirondack Region with the seven northern counties in the park. The Adirondack Regional Tourism Council (ARTC) organized in 1979 with Essex, Clinton, Franklin, Fulton, Lewis, and Warren counties and the Old Forge area of Herkimer County. The Department of Economic Development through its *I Love New York* tourism program funds 50 percent of ARTC's budget; participating counties fund the other 50 percent. All the matching fund monies are used for marketing and advertising to promote the Adirondacks as a travel destination.

The program includes promoting Adirondacks recreational opportunities and does so in a way that outshines anything DEC has done, especially DEC's Use and Information projects described earlier. While the *I Love New York* booklets often make the Adirondacks look as if it were all High Peaks, ARTC has tried to expand its coverage of the park. ARTC's booklets on hiking and canoeing opportunities are well designed and well conceived in that they recognize almost the entire park. In 2001 ARTC began working on a much-needed heritage guide, again with the goal of promoting the whole region.

Counties promote themselves as "Adirondack," confusing visitors who are mostly unaware of the size and diversity of the region. Until DED has one region covering the entire park with ARTC serving that area, efforts to promote the "park" character of the Adirondacks will fall short.[54]

Tupper Lake: Prison and Natural History Museum

In 1997 the legislature called for a maximum security, 1,500-inmate prison to be built in Franklin County. Tupper Lake residents championed the proposal for a site on Pitchfork Pond Road. Residents of the Town of Altamont were not unanimous in wanting the prison—Tupper Lake Concerned Citizens organized to fight it—and the environmental community was adamantly opposed to it.[55] Sierra Club hired Bob Glennon, who had recently been asked to leave the Adirondack Park Agency by Greg Campbell, to fight the prison (his hiring was cleared by the state ethics board, which found that there was no conflict with his previous position).

There were problems with the Tupper Lake site: opposition from wealthy residents of nearby Big Wolf Pond and the length of time that would be needed to complete the APA-required resource assessment. The corrections commissioner chose not to wait; the site was moved to Malone outside the park and construction started before the APA review could even have been completed.[56] The decision to move the site had more to do with timing than with the brief but vigorous fight against the prison, which was also assisted by Sierra Club's threat to sue to block it.

State negotiations for the Whitney property were going on at the same time, and Mary Lou Whitney announced that she would not complete the sale unless the state did something for Tupper Lake. She said this was not a threat, but a demonstration of her concern for Tupper's citizens.[57]

Residents of Tupper Lake proposed building a $21 million natural history museum on a site on the Raquette River, and the community, led by Betsy Lowe, has been very active in raising funds for it. Mary Lou Whitney became a contributor; some prominent residents of Big Wolf Pond, many of whom had been most active in the fight against the prison, were among the most generous benefactors of the museum. The promise of state money for the project was perceived as a further sop to the community for its loss of the prison.

Like a phoenix rising from the ashes of the prison project, the natural history museum has captured the imagination of many Adirondackers. Fundraising is going forward, elegant plans have been drawn, and the committee has already sponsored many events of the sort the museum will be able to host in the future.

Cultural Activities

A cultural awakening has occurred in the Adirondacks in the three end-of-century decades, and it almost exploded in the first of those decades. From the opening of the Adirondack Museum in 1957 to the beginning of the Lake Placid Film Festival, there have been almost too many cultural centers and activities created to list. Their flourishing was partly tourist-oriented, partly the work of local residents, but mostly the result of a growing recognition of the park's heritage. In these decades the park's human history became as important as its natural history. A few activities are noted:

Adirondack Life, founded in 1969, has not only won awards for the quality of its photographs and its design, but the magazine has had many valuable articles on Adirondack politics and economy. Its founding vice president, Richard Lawrence, was the first chairman of the park agency. The magazine has been a most enthusiastic supporter of the park agency from the beginning.

Adirondack Discovery, a project founded by Joan Payne of Inlet, sponsors hundreds of talks, walks, and slide shows during the summer in communities from Cranberry Lake to North Creek and beyond. The programs reach natives as well as summer people and address history, nature, and politics.

The number of museums in the park continues to grow. From Blue Mountain's Adirondack Museum with its national prominence as a local history museum to town and county history centers at Elizabethtown, Old Forge, and beyond, the museums display the park's varied heritage. The proposed natural history museum at Tupper Lake will greatly expand the educational efforts of Adirondack Park Agency's visitors centers.

Adirondack Architectural Heritage (AARCH) started out exploiting the history of Great Camps, beginning with Sagamore and Uncas. AARCH moved beyond Great Camps to leading visitors to bridges, industrial sites, prisons, and diverse communities. It is slowly working toward preservation of a broad range of architectural history.

Paul Smith's College has become a four-year institution. A new group is trying to develop an Adirondack curriculum for local schools so they can offer courses in the region's political and natural history. State funding and local initiatives have helped numerous Adirondack communities build or expand libraries.

North Country Radio now reaches almost all corners of the park; the glaring exception is the southern part of the park. Nevertheless, its programming on Adirondack background from history to nature is wonderful, and its enhanced coverage of Adirondack news is commendable. It regularly contributes stories on the Adirondacks to National Public Radio news programs.

The Adirondack Research Consortium (ARC), an organization created by academics with interest in Adirondack subjects, publishes the *Adirondack Journal of Environmental Studies*. Its articles and the papers presented at ARC's annual conference cover a wide range of studies: undergraduate, graduate, and professional. The topics range from acid rain to limnology, from aquatic species to wolves. By 2001 it had become a valuable academic institution.

From plays to chamber music, the list of new cultural activities pursued by residents is amazing. Adirondack writers have examined the region from new historical, sociological, and anthropological perspectives and joined to form a writer's organization. Arts festivals abound. The Old Forge Art Center, one of the earliest local efforts, began to sponsor a nationally recognized watercolor exhibit. Inlet hosted the Syracuse Symphony; Lake Placid started a nationally recognized film festival.

The enrichment of Adirondack life in the decade of the 1990s was spectacular. No longer was there an amorphous "they" who claimed to speak for the park, often in protest. Countless groups began doing things to improve the park. Grassroots activities led the way in many different towns and hamlets. No group had yet achieved the same intensity for the entire park with its diverse attributes. But the pieces that will define the role of people in the park were coming together.

Funding for all these activities is not easy to find. Fortunately an independent foundation, the Adirondack Community Trust (ACT) is now receiving tax-deductible contributions that can be applied to the Adirondack projects of the donor's choice. Grants have been made in several categories: arts and humanities, community development, education, health, libraries, historic preservation, social services, environment, and youth programs. The foundation's board, outreach, and grants have been predominantly northern Adirondack-oriented, but if it develops a parkwide perspective, it will be a powerful tool for the future.

Unfortunately most of the privately supported groups go after the same funding sources, and they do compete with local tourist efforts. But nonprofit groups have had to assist local programs because the state, with the exception of Adirondack Park Agency and Department of Economic Development, has, until recently, been so inefficient in reaching out to communities.

Outside groups, consultants, and small local achievements do make a tremendous difference. But they leave unanswered such questions as how to involve whole communities, how to extend local achievements and local public participation to parkwide achievements, and how to get the state and its bureaucracies involved at a level that really helps local efforts. Bureaucracies have to go through so many layers of approval; the not-for-profits just do the work, especially the little projects that have proven to be the most effective.

The third act in the drama has a slightly different ending than the first; our stage is filled with people talking in small groups, but without concerted movement and action. The discussions are deeper; more and more players have appeared on the stage. A few small scenes have been noteworthy. But taken as a metaphor for action to bring constituents into the process of protecting and managing the park, the play so far has been unsuccessful. My final thoughts may point the way to a fourth act, which might bring all the players together in a resolution satisfying to all.

Final Thoughts

A CONCLUSION, by tradition, looks at the total picture presented by the text. I think a conclusion ought to synthesize the ideas in the material, rather than summing them up. So, here are the ideas and lingering questions I have taken from the examples presented and from people I interviewed.

There is no doubt in my mind that support for Article XIV of the New York State Constitution should be paramount and its intent should guide in all we do with respect to the Adirondack Park. But translating the concept of Forever Wild into rules and regulations that reflect all the changes in the modern world has proven very difficult. The environmental groups have been very important in keeping government on track. But for all the activity of the past thirty years, for all the real accomplishments, I believe many mistakes have been made. Further, we are missing a guide for the future.

Naïvely, I once thought that focusing on just how much has been accomplished in the park, how little remains to be done in comparison, would put any discussions of what else is needed in perspective. The battles that are left are not very exciting; they are difficult to characterize, mired in bureaucracies, consumed by details, and lacking an icon around which to generate support. Peter Bauer wrote me, "On some level the park works despite the dysfunctional way it is managed." But we cannot ignore the problems that keep appearing.

I asked many of those with whom I talked what they thought would ensure a positive climate for working together in the Adirondacks. Frank Murray was one of the first people I contacted, and he struck a theme I heard over and over: "Dialogue is essential, but I do not see it in the Adirondacks unless sides get together. There are extremes on both sides and if the extremes dominate, they succeed in stopping any action." Roger Dziengeleski worried about the emotional level of the debate in the park. He faulted the different groups whom he

341

believed depend for their existence on generating emotion; "they are monsters to be fed," he said.

I think the solutions are much more subtle, and they involve bringing people together to appreciate what has been done in such a positive and uplifting way that the differences can fade and we can work together to address modern problems. And to that end, civility, humility, and mutual respect, as Liz Thorndike tried to generate, are the foundations of that cooperation.

Are we inevitably reduced to the problem of figuring out how to balance zealots in our democratic society? Polarization persists; admittedly some of it has origins in the extremes of environmentalism as well as in extremes of opposition to governmental regulation.

Why do I believe the environmentalists have been less successful than I think they should have been? In the Adirondacks there is a tremendous overlap of membership among environmental groups. While there is a commonalty of purpose, it is overshadowed by the rhetoric each group expresses in order to stake out a special role in the environmental arena. Certainly that is a way of building constituencies. James C. Dawson has commented that environmentalists have all too often *not* reached out, but have said, "we know what is right." Jim Cooper compared both poles as representatives of a kind of thinking of true believers like the Jesuits—true believers who leave no room for compromise. Environmental thought has become a "secular religion for some people," he says, and it treats every square inch of the Adirondacks as unique.

Mark Dowie, in *Losing Ground*, concludes his analysis of the environmental movement nationally by suggesting that those groups have lost their grassroots touch. That is equally true in the Adirondacks, where a few of these groups are so far from grass roots that they have become bloated, huge, and nonresponsive except to the members of their moneyed constituencies. And money plays a huge role in what they do. Each group strives to be broadly environmental, lest any other group get ahead, but outstandingly different in some respect in order to justify their ever-increasing need for funds.

For most environmental groups any outreach goes as far as a group of sycophants; leadership "talks to the choir." The failure of environmentalists to reach out to groups that do not share their views has far-reaching consequences. How can environmentalists expect to lead if they do not even talk to all the constituents of the park? And, of course this is a two-way street.

Peter Bauer believes that the environmental groups work differently because there is no clear vision of public policy toward the park. They work independently because they have separate interests and goals and varying tactics to achieve them. But their diversity is no excuse for the cacophony of their voices;

I believe they would be more successful if they worked toward a common park vision.

When environmental organizations do agree, their joint efforts and press releases are noticed and effective, but another level of cooperation is needed. The different groups have individually focused on a narrow set of problems: Adirondack Council on acid rain, Residents' Committee to Protect the Adirondacks on quality of life, the Association for the Protection of the Adirondacks on the Forest Preserve. No organization, and certainly not a group of them, is exploring the questions of what the park should be like in a way that addresses all the park's components. Adirondack Council and Residents' Committee to Protect the Adirondacks come closest, but Council's preservationist picture does not encompass local concerns, the economy, tourism, or Department of Environmental Conservation's management problems. These organizations do not seem to recognize that it is the sum of their efforts *and* of the many local projects that can define a vision for the park.

The groups tend to react to problems and governmental misdeeds rather than taking a proactive approach to planning. As Peter Bauer has said, the environmentalists are not talking together or with others about the big issues. Why are they not focusing on the big issues? A good part of the reason is that they have had to spend so much time and effort correcting governmental problems such as insufficient legislative appropriations and administrative budgets, DEC's failures to create adequate policies to reflect the State Land Master Plan or to manage the Forest Preserve according to existing policies, Adirondack Park Agency's inability to perform the required oversight with respect to DEC's activities, and DEC's inability to manage itself or lead public participation.

Could an individual or organization lead public dialogue to a vision for the park? Ross Whaley believes that none of the major players of 2000 could do it. "Consensus," he believes, "needs more subtle advocates than today's environmental leaders."

I started out believing real public participation could be the way to arrive at policy, that closed government or closed groups could not bridge the disparate views of the Adirondacks. I became convinced that the openness of the recent past decade has not been successful because it led to fragmentation and the dominance of certain interest groups. I am aware of how challenging it is to create a framework for rational public decisions. Robert Bendick came to believe that "it is very difficult to arrive at a consensus adopting major priorities and let people have a say in the process." [1]

Could an existing government agency play a leadership role in managing public participation? DEC's attempts have been deficient; the department has listened and responded favorably to all sorts of special interest groups. APA's task forces have made the agency's outreach more successful than DEC's. But APA's efforts to update its methods have been narrowly focused and occasionally without adequate follow-through. They have been largely technical responses, operational functions, too swept up in legal details, and generally inadequate for long-range planning. Having all interests represented can't happen at agency level; there is no time. The agency's permitting and enforcement activities have prevented members from engaging in true planning.

Around the time I brought this book to a close, no one was proposing anything that would really upset or mobilize different advocacy groups. Three decades ago, much of the opposition to regulation came about not simply because Adirondackers felt no one was listening, but because they believed that they had no access to government. The lack of access is symbolized in the repeated calls for Adirondackers to be able to choose representatives to the park agency. The Local Government Review Board, Association of Adirondack Towns and Villages, and others continue raising this symbol, despite current representation by Adirondack residents.

Stories and rumors of special access to the governor's staff or of closed-door negotiations have reawakened a belief that Adirondackers have no access. What they want in representation is really access to higher-ups, to decision-making. That is what most of the groups wanted that sprang up after the Commission on the Adirondacks in the 21st Century. The environmentalists had access all along. The new groups were unable to gain acceptance partly because they were unsophisticated in the ways of politics. The parochialism among residents, which can be attributed to lack of exposure to the larger world, has made groups and individuals seem to harden positions before they understand issues. Those aspects have changed, but the level of access remains unbalanced.

Environmentalists see Adirondack Park Agency representation by Adirondackers as a symbol of losing control—and today the fear of losing control in the environmental movement is so great that no one wants to revisit the State Land Master Plan, despite the fact that the plan is fourteen years beyond its scheduled revision. However, there is much more to their not wanting to update the plan: Environmentalists fear that government will compromise with those asking for widening of snowmobile trails or permitting more motorized access, for instance, just to prevent confrontation.

There are many issues that a revision of the State Land Master Plan ought to address, and these issues will continue to appear: They include what new land to add to the park; numerous new problems concerning easements; proposed long-distance trails and corridor development; questions of snowmobile trail networks; motorboat use in areas that are part private, part wilderness; DEC use of motorized vehicles; and development of real opportunities for the disabled.

The persistent deep-seated distrust points out how easy it would be to rally opposition to almost anything related to the park, and how difficult it is to bring people together. The radicals—the fringes—are quiescent, but there is no middle ground with concerns for the whole park.

The most amazing thing to come out of all the turmoil of the early 1990s is how many of the goals of the Commission on the Adirondacks in the 21st Century have been accomplished, but not necessarily by using the specific recommendations of their 1990 report. The "score card" on achieving recommendations from the 21st Century Commission includes many of those directed at nongovernmental organizations or local governments and only a few of those directed at parts of state government: roads have been improved, tourism outreach is better, sustainable forestry has been included in easement agreements, many towns are renewing local planning, community housing projects have been started, towns are really cleaning up eyesores, Residents' Committee for Protection of the Adirondacks and the agency are working on water quality issues, hamlets and villages are building local parks and tourist information centers, education has improved and there is a renewed interest in an Adirondack curriculum. The list of accomplishments is even longer. What is missing is anything that required actions by the legislature and enhanced budgets. These have been the major stumbling blocks. The achievements have come from people working together on a grassroots level.

Another reason for the relative quiet at the end of the century was that many of the groups that sprang up to fight the 21st Century Commission had reason to believe someone was listening. Richard Lefebvre has made listening a hallmark of his term as chairman of Adirondack Park Agency, and he has not responded inappropriately to special interest groups.

The Adirondack climate is so outwardly serene that it seems inappropriate to disturb it. Given the extraordinary birth of the Adirondack Forest Preserve and park, it is sad how one of the brightest preservation efforts in the United States descended into such a pandemonium of competing "supporters" near the end of its first century. Translating the governance of the park into modern terms and creating a structure that adapts to future change are necessary but very difficult steps, steps that would be impossible without leadership and public discussion focused on the larger issues.

Much could be accomplished by creating a special region within DEC to oversee the natural resources of the Adirondack Park. The regional structures of DEC, Department of Transportation, and Department of Health need to be recombined so that their boundaries coincide with that of the park. Those needs are obvious. But the way the park suffers within DEC's management has meant that the Forest Preserve has never been integrated into the economy of the region, and I predict it never will be unless DEC's structure and mission are changed.

It would be a monumental leap to go from analyzing the problems to deducing what else ought to be done in the Adirondacks. Besides, concluding specific recommendations seems like putting the cart before the horse. I would like to think for a while on *who* ought to be making recommendations for the future; what kinds of governmental structures are needed so people can be heard; how the public can participate and do so in a way that all voices are heard, yet consensus and action result. Determining who speaks and how they speak and are heard is essential because since 1970 no broad-based forum and no planning agency has addressed the issues affecting the park as a whole. Even when the commissions, task forces, planners, or thinkers have addressed issues, they have failed to move effectively from the general or ideal to be realized to the specifics of how to do it.

Could a new agency play a leadership role? Tom Ulasewicz reminded me of the role of planners in the Rockefeller era. A planning commission or agency for the Adirondacks might work. But it would have to be an independent, long-lasting, ongoing, regularly reinvigorated, charismatically led agency, practiced in civility, open, and responsive to all points of view but not subservient to any one. An Adirondack planning agency might consist of a small group of planners, based on the Rockefeller Office of Planning Coordination, made up of professionals, people with vision, full-time workers. They would not work in a vacuum, but would regularly consult all sorts of public groups. They would use what they hear to make decisions based on their knowledge and judgment in order to meld opposing views. Three to five people with long, fixed, but rotating terms and a director would suffice, if they were isolated from political whims of the legislature and changing administrations. They would have backgrounds in law, economics, forest resources, recreation planning, and above all in the values of the Forest Preserve. They would be charged with melding public and private lands, local interests and state interests; ensuring that state agencies work together; doing the impossible. Such a separate planning group needs to be independently funded, to be able to draw funds toward the park, and to oversee the work of existing agencies.

They would need a strong leader. Rockefeller focused on environmental responsibility, Pataki on fiscal responsibility. What is needed is a new leader who would be a champion for Forest Preserve and constituent responsibility. With strong leadership and a trained staff, such a group could lead to better government. Perhaps what I have envisioned is really a park service, another layer of government. It would not be an unwarranted addition if all the agencies within the park had regional boundaries that coincided with the park boundary. It would not be an intrusive layer, if it made all existing agencies and private groups more responsive, better able to integrate public participation with bureaucracies.

Experience has shown that reform has rarely made government simpler, more efficient, or effective. That has to be a goal, for Adirondack governance is mired in complexity as this history documents. I admit that there is no guarantee that any new agency can avoid bureaucratic lethargy.

Who will the planning agency listen to? Adirondack North Country Association, environmental groups, statewide concerns, the watchdogs of the Forest Preserve, towns, counties, villages, Local Government Review Board, Adirondack Park Agency, Department of Environmental Conservation, everyone. With someone listening, there will be no need for groups to pontificate because the listeners will be most responsive to constructive ideas. The listeners will define the goals for the park, and participants will need to agree on consensus building.

There will be side benefits: Giving equal footing to all voices before an unbiased planning agency would help dispel social ills, the sense of discrimination, and class divisions, which are felt by some. That should enhance a needed sense of civility among groups. As the summary of the 1990s shows, every conceivable issue has been taken up by some watchdog group. Organizations are specializing more and more. What they are studying is wonderful, but their output must be viewed as pieces of the puzzle that when completed will spell out a way to manage the park for all, to put people in a place of protected natural resources.

To make this work people will have to step back and give proposals for structural change a chance without stumbling over the details. The planning commission will only be as effective as the support it receives from all branches of government. It will take a strong executive to make sure it stays independent and that its recommendations are adopted.

Many of the good ideas that have been developed over the years faltered because they have not reached down to the people they were meant to help. Beside planning, such a planning group must use education so that all groups can encourage their members to adopt common goals. Lots of efforts have generated good ideas, but the next step, keeping them going and bringing them to fruition, is difficult, but not impossible for such a planning group.

What should the planning commission recommend or implement? I do not know. But I am willing to trust others to figure it out. I would recommend that before planners start thinking about what to do, they go back and read the thirty-foot shelf of reports, documents, drafts, analyses, recommendations, and studies that I read before I started writing this book. Many new writers and philosophers have published thoughtful books. So much is there, so many ideas have been put forth, over and over again in some instances. The planning group may find some new ways of doing things, but most of what has to be done is a balancing act that satisfies the needs of people within the context of a park with a Forest Preserve.

If there could be such a governmental structure that will use all the diverse resources of the varied groups we might have a solution for the future. The goals for such a planning group would be the consolidation of the work of the regional open space planning groups into the plans for units of the Forest Preserve. Its planning for land acquisition would consider both preservation and forestry needs. Its planning for the economy would use such private resources as Adirondack North Country Association. The planning for the development of private lands within the park would blend regional planning with local efforts by using organizations of towns such as Adirondack Association of Towns and Villages. In doing the latter, problems of existing as well as future development can be addressed.

My conclusion might have included a checklist of problems to be solved, new methods to be put in place, but that list would quickly be out of date. The task of preserving the Adirondacks, both the way of life of its people and its precious forested lands, will be faced with new challenges all the time. It is essential to find a way of meeting those challenges based on all the interests in the park. Change is inevitable, so are new problems and situations. Modern problems like acid rain will continue to appear. What will happen when residents are predominantly newcomers, what will the culture of the park be like if there is an influx of technically trained people using the Internet? What will happen if summer residents get to vote in local elections?

I believe a centralized planning agency is the best way to build on what has been done in the past. There are ways to integrate Department of Environmental Conservation management of the Forest Preserve, Adirondack Park Agency's regulation and enforcement of private lands, and local governments within such a structure, but other planners more knowledgeable than I will have to figure out the details.

NOTES

SELECTED BIBLIOGRAPHY

INDEX

Notes

All interview notes and research material for this book will be placed in the library of the Adirondack Museum at Blue Mountain Lake after remodeling of the library is completed.

1. Introduction

1. New York: Alfred A. Knopf, 1978. See also Norman J. VanValkenburgh, *The Adirondack Forest Preserve* (Blue Mountain Lake, N.Y.: The Adirondack Museum, 1979).

2. Zahniser, an Adirondack summer resident, had a cabin near Bakers Mills on the edge of the Siamese Ponds Wilderness Area.

3. William Cronon, "The Trouble With Wilderness," *Uncommon Ground* (New York: W. W. Norton, 1995), 81.

4. Thoughts gleaned from a talk by Elizabeth Thorndike at the Annual Conference of the Association for the Protection of the Adirondacks, Oct. 2000.

5. "Park of people and natural wonder" was the theme of the 1992 Adirondack Park Centennial.

2. Formation of the Department of Environmental Conservation

1. Comments from Robert Bendick, former deputy commissioner of DEC, currently executive director of The Nature Conservancy in Florida. Robert Bendick, phone interview with author, Feb. 7, 2000.

2. The old Forest Commissions had several different names between 1885 and 1912.

3. Edith Pilcher, "Watchdog of the Forest Preserve," New York State *Conservationist* (Jan.-Feb., 1984): 16.

4. Ibid.

5. See Barbara McMartin, *The Great Forest of the Adirondacks* (Burlington, Vt.: North Country Books, 1994) for background.

6. Ibid.

7. The department's *Conservationist* promoted logging in articles in 1963 and 1964. See Norman J. VanValkenburgh, *The Adirondack Forest Preserve* (Blue Mountain Lake, N.Y.: The Adirondack Museum, 1979), 283–84.

8. E-mail to author, Dec. 8, 1999.

3. Establishment of the Adirondack Park Agency

1. Section 801 of the *Laws of the State of New York,* statement of legislative findings and purposes.

2. From a letter by R. Watson Pomeroy to Paul Schaefer, dated Jan. 1964, found in Paul Schaefer's papers by his daughter Evelyn Greene.

3. Ibid.

4. Environmental Groups and the APA

1. Discussions at Canada Lake. See note 3 below.

2. Sam Sage at Canada Lake meeting.

3. In 1999 and 2000, two meetings were held at Canada Lake to help the author understand Sierra Club's role in the Adirondacks. Those attending included early members of the Adirondack Committee: Sam Sage, Paul Bray, Per Moberg, Bob Kafin, Ted Hullar, and Charlie Morrison. Margaret Moberg and Roger Gray also attended. At each meeting those attending responded to a history of the Adirondack Chapter prepared for the meetings by Per Moberg, one of the founding members of the Atlantic Chapter. All the notes on Sierra Club activities have been taken from a transcript of those two intense sessions, a copy of which is in the author's collection.

4. Ibid.

5. William Kissel, interview with author, Lake Placid, N.Y., Sept. 14, 1999.

6. Eleanor Brown, *The Forest Preserve* (Glens Falls, N.Y.: Adirondack Mountain Club, 1985), 54.

7. Spelling according to Melvil Dewey.

8. Ibid.

9. Report of ADK dinner, 1937, vertical file of the Adirondack Museum, Blue Mountain Lake, N.Y.

10. Bruce Wadsworth, *With Wilderness at Heart* (Lake George, N.Y.: Adirondack Mountain Club, 1996), 39.

11. Peter E. Van de Water, "The Voice that Cried Out in the Wilderness," *The Quarterly,* publication of the St. Lawrence County Historical Association, Oct. 1978, 22–24.

12. Ibid.

13. Philip Terrie, phone conversation with author, July 20, 2000.

14. Van de Water, "Voice That Cried Out," 22–24.

15. William Kissel, interview.

16. 33 League for Adirondack Citizens' Rights, *Hands Across the Mountains,* undated newsletter.

17. Ibid.

18. I have been told, but cannot prove, that Tony was made an example by the agency to make a point, to develop regulatory powers that were not clear in the act, and to reverse some of the changes made in the closing hours of the passage of the act that had weakened environmental protection.

5. Evolution of the Adirondack Park Agency

1. I base this statement on my work at the agency in the 1980s, when I talked with many people in an attempt to figure a simple way to present the technicalities of the PLUDP.

2. George Davis, phone interview with author, Nov. 22, 1999.

3. Technically, density does not apply in hamlet or industrial use areas.

4. Davis, interview.

5. Richard A. Liroff and G. Gordon Davis, *Protecting Open Space—Land Use Control in the Adirondack Park* (Cambridge Mass.: Ballinger Publishing Co., 1978). Davis had been counsel to the park agency.

6. Ibid., 70.

7. Ibid.

8. Peter Bauer et al., *Growth in the Adirondack Park: Analysis of Rates and Patterns of Development* (North Creek, N.Y.: The Residents' Committee to Protect the Adirondacks, 2001).

9. Richard Persico, interview with author, Lake Placid, N.Y., Sept. 14, 1999.

10. A copy of Doolittle's speech is in the files of the Adirondack Museum.

11. Ibid.

12. *Hands Across the Mountains,* undated newsletter, files of the Adirondack Museum; Ruth Newberry, letter to members of the League for Adirondack Citizens' Rights, Feb. 18, 1976.

13. *Adirondack Daily Enterprise,* Sept. 5, 1975.

14. *Hands Across the Mountains.*

15. Privately printed, Loon Lake, N.Y.: Onchiota Books, December 1979.

16. Undated clipping in the vertical files of the Adirondack Museum.

17. *Adirondack Defender* 1, no. 1 (March 1976).

18. *Adirondack Defender* 1, no. 4 (Summer 1976).

19. This and the following paragraphs were developed from author's interviews with Richard Persico, Sept. 14, 1999.

20. *Adirondack Defender,* Winter 1977.

21. Memoranda dated Jan. 18, 1974, and Feb. 25, 1974, Adirondack Museum file.

22. Vertical file on LGRB at the Adirondack Museum.

23. *Lake Placid News* (LPN), Dec. 4.

24. LGRB report, April 29, 1976.

25. *Glens Falls Post Star (GFPS),* Dec. 2, 1976.

26. Vertical file on LGRB at the Adirondack Museum.

27. Testimony before U. S. House of Representatives, drafts in files at Adirondack Museum.

28. Ibid.

29. Information from Jim Hotaling, Adirondack Park Agency Local Planning Coordinator, June 6, 1999.

30. Tom Ulasewicz, notes to author.

31. D'Elia, letter to the editor, *Lake Placid News,* undated clipping in Richard Persico's scrapbook.

32. Shirley Ryan, letter to the editor, *Lake Placid News,* undated clipping in Richard Persico's scrapbook.

33. LGRB, statement, dated Oct. 17, 1977.

34. APA, *Report of the Citizen's Advisory Task Force on Hamlet Restoration and Development,* 1978.

35. The following discussion is taken directly from the author's interview with George Nagle and from the *Open Space Task Force Report* to the APA, April 1980, which has been published by the APA and is available at the Adirondack Museum.

36. Conversation with author, Jan. 11, 2001.

37. Press release, William K. Verner, Apr. 18, 1980, author's file.

38. *Open Space Task Force Report,* Apr. 1980, 9.

6. Environmental Groups New and Old

1. This discussion was developed from the author's phone interview with David Newhouse, Oct. 2000.

2. Ibid.

3. Pilcher, "Watchdog of the Forest Preserve."

4. Crocker became chairman of the board. He was replaced as president by Bernie Smith in 1983. James C. Dawson served as president from 1987 to 1989.

7. DEC under the Adirondack Park Agency Act

1. Rosemary Nichols, "Opinion: Ogden Reid Should Resign," *New York Environmental News* 3 (April 16, 1976).

2. Ibid.

3. Peter Berle, interview with author, Albany, N.Y., Feb. 8, 2000.

4. *Hamilton County News (HCN),* Feb. 4, 1987.

5. Interview with Robert Flacke, Lake George, N.Y., Sept. 15, 1999. He talked of the internal DEC document he wrote. No copy was located.

6. Sierra Club discussions at author's home, Sept. 19 and Nov. 11, 1999.

7. DEC document, written by Norm VanValkenburgh, director, Division of Lands and Forests, 1985.

8. *Adirondack Daily Enterprise* and Plattsburgh *Press Republican,* Jan. 21, 1984.

9. *Adirondack Daily Enterprise* Mar. 29, 1984.

10. Department of Environmental Conservation, *State Land Master Plan,* (Albany, N.Y.: DEC, 1972), 5.

11. The plans are in the files of the Temporary Study Commission at the Adirondack Museum.

12. The above discussion of the SLMP and the UMPs was developed from the minutes of the Forest Preserve Advisory Committee, from personal notes on discussions at those meetings, and from DEC's UMP and policy status reports.

13. The discussion of the first High Peaks Advisory Committee was developed from the author's files, which contain all the minutes from 1974 to 1979.

14. High Peaks Advisory Committee, *Summary Findings Report,* Feb. 18, 1977. Copy in the author's files.

15. Margin notes sent to author by J. C. Dawson.

16. DEC, *First Draft, High Peaks Wilderness Area Unit Management Plan,* undated, otherwise unidentified, 161 pages, author's file.

17. Barbara McMartin, "Forest Preserve Advisory Committee," *Adirondac,* Feb. 1982, 12.

18. This and the following discussion were developed from the author's file of minutes and DEC handouts.

19. FPAC minutes, Jan. 17 and 18, 1986.

20. FPAC minutes, July 22 and 23, 1983.

21. Interview with Dave Gibson, Nov. 24, 1998, and FPAC minutes, Oct. 1984.

22. Assembly Ways and Means Committee, *The Department of Environmental Conservation: A Program and Budget History,* Jan. 1985.

23. FPAC minutes, Oct. 1984.

8. Other Issues and Events in the 1980s

1. *Adirondack Daily Enterprise* (ADE), Dec. 9, 1982.

2. Ibid.

3. Ibid.

4. *GFPS,* Dec. 10, 1983.

5. Ibid.

6. *Watertown Daily Times (WDT),* undated, AM vertical file.

7. *Press Republican,* (PR), Sept. 27, 1983.

8. WDT, Adirondack Museum clip, undated.

9. Adirondack Park Agency press release, written by Cecily Bailey, reported in the Plattsburg *Press Republican* (PR), Dec. 12 and 13, 1983.

10. *Valley News,* Sept. 28, 1983.

11. Interview with Tom Ulasewicz, Caroga, N.Y., Jan. 13, 2001. Ulasewicz served as an APA lawyer under Moore and later became APA executive director (1984–88).

12. Ed Hood, phone interview with author, Feb. 2000.

13. Ibid.

14. Ibid.

15. Adirondack Mountain Club President James C. Dawson and Conservation Committee Chairman David Newhouse wrote Governor Cuomo on December 15, 1983, questioning whether Cole had the background and credentials to lead APA.

16. PR, Dec. 12, 1983.

17. Notes to author from Tom Ulasewicz.

18. *HCN,* Mar. 2, 1988.

19. Hale had been publisher of the *Lake Placid News,* and when it was sold to the *Adirondack Daily Enterprise* he joined the *Watertown Daily Times.*

20. Undated clipping from the *Watertown Daily Times* in the Adirondack Museum's files.

21. *GFPS,* Dec. 23, 1985.

22. *ADE,* Mar. 29, 1985.

23. *ADE,* Oct. 29, 1987. It was in this period that the agency under Ulasewicz courted Doolittle in an effort to gain positive press from the *Enterprise.* Ulasewicz told the author that he offered to give Doolittle a direct pipeline on issues if Doolittle agreed to provide a fair, objective

view of the agency. The agreement was consummated with a handshake, and according to Ulasewicz, they both kept their word.

24. Chapter 292, article 49, Laws of the State of New York.

25. Dennis Conroy, "The Sportsmen's Voice," *Adirondac,* Feb./Mar. 1984, 20.

26. George Davis to NYS Department of Law, May 22, 1986.

27. Kim Elliman to NYS Conservation Council, May 1986.

28. *ADE,* Nov. 25, 1987.

29. *ADE,* Feb. 26, 1987.

30. Ulasewicz, notes to author.

31. Ibid.

32. *ADE,* Nov. 25, 1987.

33. *GFPS,* April 13, 1985.

34. Thomas M. Lawson to Harold E. Robillard, Clerk, Warren County, April 10, 1985.

35. James Cooper to Warren County Board of Supervisors, May 8, 1985. The author was loaned all of Attorney Cooper's papers relating to the suit. They have now been placed in the archives of the Adirondack Museum.

36. *Cooper v. Wertime,* 164 AD2D 221, 563 NYS2d 354.

37. Testimony, April 25, 1989.

38. Upstate papers continued to report through 1987 on the review board's intentions concerning a lawsuit against the agency on the "taking issue." Numerous clippings in Cooper file, Adirondack Museum.

39. D'Elia Deposition in the Cooper file, Adirondack Museum.

40. *HCN,* Oct. 7 and 14, 1987.

41. *HCN,* May 3, 1989.

42. *ADE,* Mar. 29, 1990.

43. *GFPS,* Feb. 25, 1988.

44. Peter Wissel, Donald Reeb and Roman Hedges, *New York's Adirondack Park: A Study of Land Price Effects from Development Restrictions* Albany, N.Y.: NYS Division of Equalization and Assessment, July 1986).

45. *ADE,* Mar. 30, 1988.

46. Author Philip Terrie obtained from DEC a packet of letters and notices pertaining to the case under FOIL, the Freedom of Information Law. He shared that packet with me.

47. *HCN,* Jan. 31, 1989.

48. *GFPS,* Oct. 15, 1990. The phrase "Crushed and nearly bankrupt" was true, but attributing it to the APA requirements may be hyperbole on the newspaper's part. Certainly D'Elia believed it. In interviews the author heard both sides: that it was an attempt by APA to establish stringent standards for the APA Act and that it was a vendetta against D'Elia.

9. Forestry in the Park

1. David S. Smith, "Forest Resources of the Adirondacks," *The Commission on the Adirondacks in the 21st Century, Technical Report,* vol. 1 (Albany, N.Y.: AC, 1990), 546; The Governor's Task Force on Forest Industry, *Capturing the Potential of New York's Forests* (Albany, N.Y., 1989), 4.

2. Foremost was Bob Stegemann, in a phone interview with author, Feb. 2001.

10. The Adirondack Council

1. Association minutes, 435th board meeting, November 1988.

12. The Commission on the Adirondacks in the 21st Century

1. *GFPS,* Sept. 6, 1988.

2. Editorial, *Syracuse Herald American,* Dec. 18, 1988.

3. Ibid.

4. Ibid.

5. Adirondack Council Newsletter, Oct. 1988.

6. *ADE,* Jan. 15, 1989.

7. *Syracuse Herald American,* 12/18/88

8. Ibid.

9. Richard Booth to Mario Cuomo, Feb. 6, 1989, CFAM. (CFAM refers to Berle's Commission files at the Adirondack Museum at Blue Mountain Lake.

10. Ulasewicz, notes to author.

11. Kafin to Berle, April 19, 1989, CFAM.

12. Frank Murray, phone interview with author, Feb. 22, 1999.

13. From Cuomo's charge to the commission, CFAM.

14. Claire Barnett, interview with author, Saratoga, N.Y., Jan. 31, 1999.

15. Memo from Davis, May 24, 1989, CFAM.

16. PR, Mar. 18, 1989.

17. *ADE,* April 5, 1989.

18. Berle, interview.

19. PR, Mar. 18, 1989.

20. Berle, interview.

21. Ibid.

22. Cuomo to Berle, Jan. 27, 1989, Berle file at AM.

23. Davis, interview.

24. Paper prepared by John Stock, dated June 22, 1990, author's file.

25. Berle, interview.

26. Berle, letter to the editor, *The New York Times,* June 12, 1990, Berle file at AM.

27. See chap. 17, for details of the RCPA report completed in March 2001.

28. Barnett, interview.

29. *ADE,* Feb. 24, 1989.

30. *GFPS,* Mar. 7, 1989.

31. Davis, phone interview with author, Dec. 7, 1999.

32. Ibid.

33. Jorling presentation, Mar. 31, 1989, 5.

34. Ibid.

35. *HCN,* April 18, 1989.

36. Ulasewicz, notes to author.

37. *ADE,* May 26, 1989.

38. *ADE,* May 30, 1989.

39. Copies and lists are in the Berle file at the AM.

40. Claire Barnett, interviews with author, Jan. 31 and May 2, 1999.

41. PR, June 30, 1989.

42. Ibid.

43. *ADE,* July 5, 1989.

44. *HCN,* July 1989.

45. Berle file at AM.

46. Letter, Aug. 21, 1989, CFAM.

47. Tim and Claire Barnett, interviews with author, Jan. 31 and May 2, 1999.

48. Jorling to Berle, Sept. 26, 1989, CFAM.

49. Thomas Shearer to Berle, Jan. 15, 1990, CFAM.

50. PR, Sept. 26, 1989.

51. *ADE,* Sept. 26, 1989.

52. *ADE,* Sept. 19, 1989.

53. Minutes of the Oct. 5, 1989, commission meeting at Elk Lake.

54. The author obtained a copy of the report from Borrelli and used it as the basis for part of a panel discussion at the Spring 2000 Adirondack Consortium Conference that focused on realigning DEC's regional boundaries.

55. *ADE,* Oct. 11, 1989.

56. *ADE,* Oct. 10, 1989.

57. Peter Bauer, note to author.

58. *ADE,* Oct. 25, 1989.

59. *Albany Times Union* (ATU), Oct. 29, 1989.

60. *LPN,* Nov. 1, 1989.

61. *ADE,* Oct. 3, 1989.

62. *ADE,* Nov. 7, 1989.

63. *HCN,* Nov. 8, 1989.

64. *St. Lawrence County Planning Board Position Paper,* Oct. 24, 1989, CFAM.

65. Flacke, interview, Sept. 15, 1999; Ross Whaley, interview with author, Syracuse, N.Y., Jan. 28, 2000; Berle, interview; Barnett interview, May 2, 1999.

66. Graham Cox, interview with author, July 8, 1999; James C. Dawson, interview with author, June 20, 1999; Davis, interview.

67. *ADE,* Nov. 7, 1989.

68. *LPN,* Jan. 3, 1990.

69. *HCN,* Jan. 2, 1990.

70. *North Creek News Enterprise,* Jan. 4, 1990.

71. Sage to Berle, Jan. 10, 1990, CFAM.

72. *GFPS,* Oct. 10, 1989; *ADE,* Oct. 28, 1989.

73. *ADE,* Nov. 9, 1989.

74. Ibid.

75. *LPN,* May 23, 1990.

76. *HCN,* Nov. 8, 1989.

77. *ADE,* Nov. 24, 1989.

78. *ADE,* Nov. 27, 1989.

79. *ADE,* Nov. 9, 1989.

80. *GFPS*, Dec. 11, 1989.

81. *North Creek News Enterprise (NCNE)*, Jan. 9, 1990, 9.

82. *ADE*, Jan. 12, 1990.

83. Commission minutes; interview with Claire Barnett.

84. This paragraph developed from notes from a phone interview with Peter Bauer, Oct. 6, 1999. Bauer was on the commission staff. He later became executive director of the Residents' Committee to Protect the Adirondacks.

85. Whaley, interview.

86. *ADE*, Feb. 1, 1990.

87. David Helvarg, *The War Against the Greens* (San Francisco: Sierra Club Books, 1994).

88. *HCN*, Feb. 6, 1990.

89. *Adirondack Journal* (AJ), Feb. 2, 1990.

90. *HCN*, Feb. 3, 1990.

91. PR, Feb. 20, 1990.

92. *ADE*, Feb. 21, 1990.

93. *ADE*, Feb. 12, 1990.

94. Notes from Peter Bauer.

95. *NCN*, Feb. 8, 1990.

96. *GFPS*, Feb. 15, 1990.

97. *GFPS*, Feb. 13, 1990.

98. *NCN*, Mar. 22, 1990.

99. *GFPS*, Feb. 3, 1990.

100. *LPN*, Feb. 7, 1990.

101. *Adirondack Journal (AJ)*, Mar. 16, 1990.

102. *LPN*, April 4, 1990.

103. *GFPS*, June 13, 1990.

104. Barnett, interview, Jan 31, 1999.

105. Berle, interview.

106. John Banta, phone interview with author, May 10, 1999.

107. Berle, interview.

108. Letter, Mar. 19, 1990, CFAM.

109. *PS*, Mar. 29, 1990.

110. Berle, interview.

111. *PS*, April 14, 1990.

112. *HCN*, April 3, 1990.

113. *PS*, April 4, 1990.

114. *ADE*, Feb. 26, 1990.

115. *PS*, June 9, 1990.

116. Flacke to Murray, April 12, 1990, author's file.

117. Ulasewicz, interview; Persico, interview.

118. Berle, interview.

119. Notes from Tom Ulasewicz.

120. *ADE*, May 4, 1990.

121. Berle, interview; Bauer, interview; Barnett, interview, May 2, 1999.

122. *ATU*, May 28, 1990.

123. Flacke, *Minority Report.*

124. Murray, interview.

125. Ibid.

126. *ADE,* May 2, 1990.

127. *ADE,* May 9, 1990.

128. *ADE,* May 8, 1990.

13. The Release of the Commission Report

1. Murray, interview.

2. PR, May 7, 1990.

3. Ulasewicz, notes to author.

4. *HCN,* May 22, 1990.

5. Jorling to Eleanor Brooks, Oct. 16, 1990, author's files, courtesy of Richard Lefebvre.

6. Letters to Rebecca Evans, Sept. 20 and Oct. 3, 1991.

7. PR, May 7, 1990.

8. *Times of Ti* (T of T), May 14, 1990.

9. Cole to Cuomo, May 14, 1990, CFAM.

10. *ADE,* May 17, 1990; PR, May 17, 1990.

11. *ADE,* May 17, 1990.

12. *PS,* May 25, 1990.

13. *LPN,* May 9, 1990.

14. *ADE,* May 9, 1990.

15. *HCN,* May 29, 1990.

16. *PS,* May 24, 1990.

17. T of T, May 14, 1990.

18. Stafford, phone interview with author, Oct. 6, 1999.

19. *ADE,* May 14, 1990.

20. *PS,* May 18, 1990.

21. Bill McKibben, "The Great Northern Forest," *Adirondack Life,* March/April 1994, 109; The Wilderness Society, *The Wise Use Movement, Strategic Analysis and Fifty State Review* (Washington, D.C.: Clearinghouse on Environmental Advocacy and Research, 1993), 206–10.

22. *ATU,* Nov. 1989.

23. *PS,* May 18, 1990.

24. *PS,* Oct. 19, 1990.

25. *HCN,* May 29, 1990.

26. *PS,* May 15, 1990.

27. *LPN,* May 30, 1990.

28. Ibid.

29. *LPN,* May 30, 1990.

30. *PS,* May 30, 1990.

31. *ADE,* May 31, 1990.

32. PR, May 30, 1990.

33. Letter to *ATU,* May 28, 1990.

34. *PS,* May 31, 1990.

35. *North Creek News,* May 31, 1990.

36. *PS,* May 24, 1990.

37. Letter to Gov. Cuomo, May 23, 1990, CFAM.

38. Gibson to Association Trustees, June 25, 1990, CFAM.

39. *New York Times* (NYT), June 10, 1990.

40. *PS,* June 13, 1990.

41. Sive to Davis, June 25, 1990; Davis to Sive, Aug. 6, 1990, CFAM.

42. Ross Whaley, interview with author, Syracuse, N.Y., March 30, 2000.

43. *Warrensburg-Lake George News* (W-LGN) and *Adirondack Journal* (AJ), May 16, 1990.

44. *AJ,* May 30, 1990.

45. Jim Frenette, phone interview with author, July 22, 2001.

46. Murray, interview.

47. *PS,* June 12, 1990.

48. *ADE,* June 12, 1990.

49. *ADE,* June 29, 1990.

50. *AJ,* June 6, 1990.

51. Fax, from Davis to DED, making sure Graham Cox was available to serve as acting director, June 5, 1990, CFAM.

52. Assemblyman Peter Grannis did introduce legislation based on the commission report in the fall of 1990 for consideration in the 1991 session.

53. *PS,* June 28, 1990.

54. *NYT,* June 28, 1990.

55. Berle, interview with author, Feb. 2000.

56. Letter to Cuomo, June 25, 1990, CFAM.

57. Berle to Cuomo, June 12, 1990, CFAM.

58. Letter, June 12, 1990, CFAM.

59. *ADE,* June 25, 1990.

60. Copies of these faxes are in Peter Berle's folder, CFAM.

61. *PS,* June 8, 1990.

62. *Tupper Lake Free Press (LFP),* June 13, 1990.

63. *PS,* July 2, 1990.

64. *PS,* Sept. 3, 4, and 5, 1990.

65. *ADE,* Sept. 22, 1992.

66. *PS,* Sept. 9, 1990.

67. *ADE,* Sept. 7, 1990.

68. *PS,* Sept. 8, 1990.

69. *North Creek News,* Dec. 6, 1990.

70. *HCN,* Sept. 25, 1990.

71. PR, June 12, 1990.

72. *PS,* July 3, 1990.

73. *PS,* July 8, 1990.

74. *ADE,* July 9, 1990.

75. A vertical file at AM contains numerous letters from residents supporting the opposition to the commission.

76. *PS,* July 16, 1990.

77. *ADE,* July 17, 1990.

78. *PS,* June 16, 1990.

79. *ADE,* Aug. 10, 1990.

80. Ibid.

81. T of T, Aug. 13, 1990.

82. Interview and article, July 12, 1990, CFAM.

83. *Booneville Herald,* July 11, 1990.

84. Cuomo to Robertson, June 26, 1990; *PS,* June 29, 1990.

85. *PS,* July 27, 1990; *LPN,* Aug. 1, 1990.

86. *ADE,* July 16, 1990.

87. *W-LGN,* July 18, 1990.

88. *Adirondack Echo,* July 18, 1990.

89. *NCNE,* July 5, 1990.

90. *ADE,* July 20, 1990.

91. *PS,* Aug. 8, 1990

92. *PS,* Aug. 9, 1990.

93. *PS,* July 22, 1990.

94. *LPN,* July 25, 1990.

95. Berle to Cuomo, CFAM.

96. Ibid.

97. *PS,* Sept. 6, 1990.

98. *Adirondack Fairness Report,* Fall 1990.

99. *PS,* Aug. 29, 1990.

100. *ADE,* Sept. 11, 1990.

101. *Adirondack Echo,* Oct. 10, 1990.

102. *ADE,* Oct. 31, 1990.

103. *NYT,* Aug. 10, 1990.

104. *ATU,* Sept. 26 and Oct. 3, 1990; *NYT,* Oct. 3, 1990; *Schenectady Daily Gazette,* Oct. 8, 1990.

105. The report was based on a 1989 evaluation of land use change prepared by John S. Banta and Edward J. Hood. APA document dated June 7, 1989.

106. *PS,* Sept. 14, 1990; Berle to Cuomo, Sept. 12, 1990, CFAM.

107. *PS,* Sept. 20, 1990.

108. *ADE,* Sept. 24, 1990.

109. *ADE,* Sept. 24, 1990.

110. *NYT,* Sept. 25, 1990.

111. *HCN,* Oct. 2, 1990.

112. Ibid.

113. *PS,* Oct. 9, 1990.

114. *PS,* Oct. 21, 1990.

115. *PS,* Aug. 30, 1990; *ADE,* Aug. 30, 1990.

116. *ADE,* Aug. 29, 1990.

117. *ADE,* Nov. 29, 1990.

118. *PS,* Oct. 25 and Nov. 1, 1990.

119. *PS,* Nov. 9, 1990.

120. *PS*, Nov. 2, 1990.

121. *New York Post,* Oct. 8, 1990.

122. *ADE*, Nov. 13, 1990.

123. *PS*, Nov. 12 and 15, 1990.

124. *PS*, Nov. 10, 1990.

125. *ADE*, Nov. 16, 1990.

126. LH, Nov. 20, 1990.

127. *PS*, Nov. 24, 1990.

128. *PS*, Nov. 24, 1990.

129. *ADE*, Dec. 6, 1990.

130. *PS*, Dec. 8, 1990.

131. *ADE*, Dec. 11, 1990.

132. *PS*, Dec. 7, 1990.

133. *PS*, Dec. 20, 1990.

134. La Grasse, interview with author, Oct. 1, 1999.

135. *AJ*, Dec. 19, 1990.

136. *PS*, Nov. 21, 1990; W-LG, Nov. 28, 1990.

137. Motto credited to Garry Ives, DEC.

138. *PS*, Nov. 16, 1990.

139. *PS*, Nov. 10, 1990.

140. *ADE*, April 9, 1991.

14. Picking Up the Pieces, 1991

1. Notes from Tom Ulasewicz were used for this paragraph.

2. Copy given to author by Dick Purdue.

3. Notes from Paul Bray.

4. Purdue, e-mail to author, Mar. 11, 2000.

5. *PS*, May 12, 1991.

6. *ADE*, Jan. 20, 1991.

7. *PS*, Feb. 19, 1991.

8. *ATU*, Mar. 3, 1991.

9. *ADE*, Mar. 7, 1991.

10. *ADE*, Mar. 7, 1991.

11. *AJ*, Mar. 20, 1991.

12. *LPN*, Aug. 29, 1990; Tom Monroe to Robert Hathaway, chairman, Saratoga County Board of Supervisors, JR file. (JR file refers to file on the meetings of the Region 5 Open Space Advisory Committee compiled by Jean Raymond, supervisor, Town of Edinburgh. The only other complete file is at the DEC office in Ray Brook.)

13. *HCN*, Dec. 18, 1990.

14. Commission minutes, Dec. 13, 1990, meeting.

15. Betsy Lowe, phone interview with author, Jan. 2001.

16. Jorling to the *Adirondack Journal,* April 24, 1991; Jorling to Richard Lefevbre, Mar. 29 and April 19, 1991.

17. Final transmittal document, Aug. 23, 1990; minutes, July 19, 1991.

18. The actual precisely worded text can be found in *Conserving Open Space In New York State* (Albany, N.Y.: New York State Department of Environmental Conservation and Office of Parks, Recreation, and Historic Preservation, 1998), 259–60.

19. Letter to the committee from Bob Bendick, Nov. 22, 1991.

20. *ADE,* June 11, 1991.

21. *PS,* April 13, 1991.

22. *ADE,* Aug. 1, 1991.

23. *ADE,* Aug. 1, 1991.

24. *NYT,* Aug. 14, 1991.

25. Ibid.

26. Ibid.

27. *PS,* Sept. 16, 1991.

28. *ADE,* Oct. 10, 1991.

29. *ADE,* Oct. 11, 1991.

30. *ADE,* Oct. 17, 1991.

31. *ADE,* Oct. 18, 1991.

32. *ADE,* Oct. 25, 1991.

33. Ibid.

34. *ADE,* Oct. 18, 1991.

35. *PS,* Oct. 30, 1991.

36. *ADE,* Oct. 31, 1991.

37. *PS,* Nov. 15, 1991.

38. Peter Paine, phone interview with author, Jan. 3, 2000.

39. *PS,* Nov. 17, 1991.

40. *PS,* Dec. 20, 1991.

41. Adirondack Fairness Report, fall 1991.

42. *PS,* July 21, 1991.

43. Carol Lagrasse, interview with author, Glens Falls, N.Y., Oct. 1, 1999.

44. Solidarity Alliance Newsletter, undated.

45. David B. Howard, "Reluctant Warriors," *The Land Rights Newsletter* (Bleecker, N.Y.: Jan./Feb. 1995).

46. David Helvarg, *The War Against the Greens* (San Francisco: Sierra Club Books, 1994), 87.

47. Berle's files at the AM contain much of this material.

48. Vertical file at AM.

49. *ADE,* Nov. 19, 1991.

15. Still Trying for Legislation, 1992

1. *LPN,* May 3, 1992; *PS,* May 12, 1992.

2. Ibid.

3. *NYS Conservationist,* May/June 1992.

4. *Adirondac,* May/June 1992.

5. *PS,* Mar. 28, 1992.

6. *NYT,* May 19, 1992.

7. *PS,* May 22, 1992.

8. *ADE,* Mar. 25, 1992.

9. *ADE,* Mar. 25, 1992.

10. *PS,* May 27, 1992.

11. *NYT,* June 16, 1992.

12. *PS,* June 3, 1992.

13. *Warrensburg-Lake George News,* June 17, 1992.

14. *Legislative Gazette* (LG), June 15, 1992.

15. Ibid.

16. *PS,* June 18, 1992.

17. Ibid.

18. *ADE,* June 18, 1992.

19. Interviews with George Canon, Jim Frenette, and others.

20. Purdue, e-mail to author, Mar. 11, 2000.

21. Dick Purdue, phone interview with author, Jan. 7, 2000.

22. Purdue, e-mail to author, Mar. 11, 2000.

23. *NYT,* June 19, 1992.

24. *ADE,* Sept. 16, 1992.

25. *ADE,* July 2, 1992; *PS,* July 2, 1992; *NYT,* July 2, 1992.

26. *NYT,* July 2, 1992.

27. Ibid.

28. *PS,* July 25, 1992.

29. New York State Supreme Court, Appellate Division, Mar. 31, 1994, 69482.

30. *PS,* July 16, 1993.

31. *PS,* Aug. 20, 1992.

32. *PS,* July 16, 1993.

33. *ADE,* Aug. 2, 1992.

34. *PS,* April 11, 1992.

16. Aftermath, 1993

1. *ADE,* Jan. 9, 1993.

2. *ADE,* Feb. 22, 1993.

3. Ulasewicz, notes to author.

4. Ibid.

5. *NYT,* June 24, 1993.

6. *NYT,* June 25, 1993.

7. *PS,* July 9, 1993.

8. *PS,* April 17, 1993.

9. Ibid.

10. PR, April 19, 2000.

11. Stock paper, dated July 5, 1990, author's file.

17. State Government Activities in the 1990s

1. LH, Jan. 10, 1998.

2. Ibid.

3. *ADE,* undated clip, LGRB file.

4. PS 10/1/98.

5. Ibid.

6. LH, Jan. 10, 1998.

7. Notes from Tom Ulasewicz, one of the lawyers representing Gleneagles.

8. Ibid.

9. The discussion of local planning was developed from discussions with and notes from Jim Hotaling and Tom Ulasewicz.

10. John Collins, phone interview with author, Oct. 24 and Nov. 9, 1998.

11. Ibid.

12. Favorite description used by Glennon in conversations and numerous speeches.

13. Glennon, Remarks to Environmental Advocates, "Environment '97," Silver Bay, N.Y., Sept. 20, 1997.

14. I witnessed two of these events during the period I was consulting at the agency.

15. Letter to author, April 22, 2000.

16. Dana Horrell, "The Hostility Forum: Analysis of an Intervention in the Adirondack Park Dispute," undated paper for the Center for the Environment at Cornell. Thorndike quoted, 11.

17. Ibid., 22.

18. Thorndike, memo to participants, Aug. 8, 1991, APA draft.

19. Horrell, "The Hostility Forum," 30–31.

20. Ibid., 27–28.

21. Conversations with author.

22. PR, Nov. 25, 1997.

23. Ibid.

24. Dan Fitts, transmittal letter to agency members, of report detailing progress with respect to the task force.

25. *ADE,* May 25, 1998.

26. *HCN,* July 13, 1999.

27. *ADE,* undated clip, LGRB file.

28. Lefebvre, phone interview with author, Jan. 8, 2001.

29. Nancy Langston, *Forest Dreams, Forest Nightmares* (Seattle: University of Washington Press, 1995), 306.

30. July 1996, FPAC minutes.

31. These shortfalls are documented in three sources: Nelson A. Rockefeller Institute of Government, *The Department of Environmental Conservation: A 25th Anniversary Review,* 1996; Assembly Ways and Means, *The Department of Environmental Conservation: A Program and Budget History,* Jan. 1985; Assembly Environmental Conservation Committee, Chairman Richard L. Brodsky, Interim Report: *Oversight Investigation and Performance Audit of the NYS DEC,* 1998.

32. Report from Ron Berhnard to the FPAC, April 1991.

33. FPAC minutes.

34. Lee M. Brenning, personal communication.

35. James C. Dawson, "Adirondack Forest Preserve Acquisitions: Policies and Procedures," *Technical Reports, Volume I, Commission on the Adirondacks in the 21st Century,* 113.

36. Ibid., 131.

37. Interview with Tom Ulasewicz. He gives as an example the Champion agreement, where it is not clear that the state can keep all the roads open that it agreed to.

38. Woodworth, in conversation with author.

39. *ADE,* Sept. 8, 1998.

18. Public Participation in the 1990s: Discussion and Case Studies

1. Bill McKibben, "The People and the Park," *Adirondack Life,* Mar./April 1994, 109.

2. Mark Dowie, *Losing Ground: American Environmentalism at the Close of the Twentieth Century* (Cambridge, Mass: MIT Press, 1996), 254–56.

3. Region 5 recommendations dated July 12, 1991, committee minutes file.

4. Commissioner Jorling as quoted in *Press Republican* (PR), Dec, 18, 1991.

5. Draft meeting summary, June 10, 1994, Warrensburg.

6. November 1994 minutes.

7. This list was adopted July 19, 1991, and is still a part of Region 5's recommendations to the Open Space Plan.

8. November 1996, Forest Preserve Advisory Committee (FPAC) minutes.

9. April 1996, FPAC minutes.

10. Mark Dowie, *Losing Ground: American Environmentalism at the Close of the Twentieth Century* (Cambridge, Mass: MIT Press, 1996), 230–31.

11. From the Paul Schaefer papers, courtesy of Dave Gibson.

12. I contributed much of the historical background that went into this part of the report.

13. President Clinton used this phrase while mediating a conference, as quoted in David Helvarg, *The War Against the Greens* (San Francisco, Sierra Club Books, 1994), p 112.

14. Noted in Glennon to Cole, May 24, 1984.

15. Docket no. 85-CV-14.5 Miner.

16. Letter to Commissioner Henry G. Williams, March 1, 1987.

17. A letter from George Davis to Art Markey of the *Knickerbocker News,* June 10, 1986, describes the event. Davis, the program director for Adirondack Council, wrote Commissioner Williams in September 1986 urging that the DEC create a handicapped (wheelchair) accessible trail to Rock Lake along the existing route, which he described as relatively level and suitable. Those who are familiar with the trail would be amazed by this description, since the trail is so full of huge boulders that it would require either a boardwalk or much clearing by a bulldozer to smooth the route.

18. NR-93–2, Aug. 19, 1993.

19. NR-95–1, Aug. 31, 1995.

20. Zeller's summary of the ADA was exactly the same as discussed by DEC and the FPAC in 1987.

21. The author and her husband attended all of the meetings.

22. Residents' Committee to Protect the Adirondacks (RCPA), *The Park Report* 6, no. 1 (April 2000), 6–8. In this issue, Peter Bauer recalls an incident in one of the meetings in which APA staff agreed with DEC in confusing trails and roads in a manner contrary to the SLMP.

23. Galusha to Ray Davis, Feb. 27, 1997.

24. Willard to Ray Davis, Mar. 15, 1997.

25. Gibson to Cahill, Feb. 21, 1997.

26. Conversation with author.

27. RCPA, *The Park Report*, 6.

28. The timeline for the discussion of the lawsuits was prepared with the help of David Gibson of the Association for the Protection of the Adirondacks and interviews with Neil Woodworth and Bernard Melewski.

29. *New York Times*, Metro, April 2, 2000.

30. Phone conversation with author, Feb. 2000.

31. Oct. 1993, FPAC minutes.

32. In July 1990, the FPAC voted to recommend that the UMPs for the High Peaks and the Dix Mountain areas be combined. The recommendation was ignored.

33. Members are those who have climbed all forty-six peaks originally thought to be over four thousand feet. Resurveys have discovered a different number.

34. Tony Goodwin, "Herdpaths and the High Peaks Management Plan," *Adirondack Peeks* Fall/Winter 1991–92, 25.

35. My margin comments on trails discussions in 1990 contained the note "ADK's trail standards are quaintly inadequate." A comparison with federal standards for wilderness trails underscores my observation.

36. DEC, Initial Draft, *HPWCUMP*, 177.

37. Ibid., 178.

38. Association press release, Nov. 13, 1995, and Dave Gibson, "A Comparative Report," Nov. 10, 1995.

39. Adirondack Museum vertical file.

40. HPWA committee minutes.

41. Bernard Melewski, phone interview with author, Mar. 13, 2000.

42. Jim Papero, private papers and correspondence, Oct. 29, 1997, "Some Lessons Learned," communicated to the author and others.

43. ADK, *Executive Summary, Heart Lake Property Master Plan*, Sept. 1992.

44. Gibson to Buchanan, June 17, 1996, cc author.

45. Gibson to Frenette, Aug. 13, 1996, cc author.

46. Jim Papero, private papers and correspondence, Oct. 29, 1997, "Some Lessons Learned," communicated to author and others.

47. Cronon, "The Trouble With Wilderness," 85.

48. McGinn Mountain, the Stark Hills, Ledge, and White Birch Ridge are among the many small hills with views, close to NY 30, that deserve trails.

49. Jan. 1994, FPAC minutes.

19. Where Are They Now?

1. Bob Stegemann, phone conversation with author.

2. Ibid.

3. *Blue Line News*, Aug. 1994.

4. Dale French, phone interview with author.

5. *ADE,* Mar. 15, 1996.

6. *PS,* Jan. 26, 1999.

7. *PS,* Feb. 2, 1999.

8. Dale French, phone interview with author, Oct. 1999.

9. Ibid.

10. Ibid.

11. Fax from Liberty Matters, Nov. 4, 1996.

12. This information was gained from the foundation's Internet site: <http://www.lan-drightsletter.com>. The author tried to interview both Dave Howard and Harry MacIntosh, without success.

13. *The People of the State of New York v. Kent T. Duell and Glenda M. Duell,* calendar date Sept. 1, 1999, # 79391.

14. LH, Jan. 8, 1997.

15. Jack Vivitsky, "Duell Update," *Land Rights Newsletter,* Jan./Feb. 1998, pp 7–8.

16. Cooper's undated note to author.

17. Mark Behan, interview with author, Glens Falls, N.Y., Oct. 1, 1999.

18. Ibid.

19. Frank A. Clark, *In the Public Interest: Private Stewardship of Adirondack Lands,* undated paper produced for the ALA.

20. The author has been a subscriber since January 1993.

21. Susan Allen, interview with author, Lake George, N.Y., Sept. 15, 1999.

22. Ibid.

23. Sage, letter to the editor, *HCN,* June 18, 1990.

24. *Adirondack Echoes,* Winter 1998, 10.

25. *Adirondack Echoes,* April-May-June 2000.

26. Ron Rubicki, phone interview with author, June 16, 2000.

27. Mark Dowie, *Losing Ground,* 5.

28. Peter Bauer, *Growth in the Adirondack Park: Analysis of Rates and Patterns of Development,* RCPA, 2001.

29. The author received two such awards, Outstanding Adirondack Communicator in 1984 and Outstanding Adirondack Heritage Award in 1992.

30. Prospectus issued in July 2000.

31. Morrison, e-mail to author, Oct. 30, 1999.

32. Frank A. Clark, *Save the Rivers by Limiting Access,* white paper prepared for ALA.

33. Per Moberg, Charles Morrison, at Sierra Meeting at author's home, Oct. 1999, and subsequent notes on the transcripts, author's files.

34. Morrison, e-mail to author, Oct. 30, 1999.

35. *NYT,* Dec. 18, 1998.

36. Beamish to Berle, Sept. 14, 1990.

37. Mark Dowie, *Losing Ground,* 68–75.

38. Written from notes from a phone conversation with Donald Ross, formerly with the Rockefeller Family Fund.

39. Chuck Clusen, phone interview with author, Dec. 17, 1999.

40. Collins, interview, Oct. 24, 1999.

41. *Investing in New York's Northern Forest; An Agenda for Land Conservation in the Adiron-*

dack Park and Tug Hill Region (Montpelier, Vt.: New York Caucus of the Northern Forest Alliance, 2001).

42. *ADE,* Dec. 8, 1998.

43. *PS,* April 23, 1992.

44. *ADE,* Sept. 27, 1993.

45. LGRB resolution 93–3.

46. LGRB resolution 1995–13.

47. *ADE,* Mar. 15, 1996.

48. LH, Dec. 18, 1997.

49. LGRB resolution 1998–3.

50. LGRB resolution 1999–2.

51. LGRB resolution 1999–1.

52. Ed Hood, phone interview with author, Feb. 2000.

53. Michael S. Coffman, executive director of Sovereignty International, Inc., as quoted on *Liberty Matters* web site, http://www.Libertymatters.org.

54. Paul Bray, notes to author.

55. *ADE,* Oct. 23, 1997.

56. Notes to author from Tom Ulasewicz, who was counsel for Tupper Lake residents who wanted the prison.

57. *ADE,* Jan. 6, 1998.

Final Thoughts

1. Robert Bendick, interview with author, Feb. 7, 2000.

Selected Bibliography

Primary Sources

Publications

Adirondack Council. *Windows on the Park: Scenic Vistas of the Adirondacks.* Elizabethtown, N.Y.: AC, 1991.

Bauer, Peter. *Growth in the Adirondack Park: Analysis of Rates and Patterns of Development.* North Creek, N.Y.: The Residents' Committee to Protect the Adirondacks, 2001.

Commission on the Adirondacks in the 21st Century. *The Adirondack Park in the Twenty-first Century,* vol. 1, and *The Technical Reports,* vol. 2. Albany, N.Y.: Commission on the Adirondacks in the 21st Century,1990.

Davis, G. Gordon, and Richard A. Liroff. *Protecting Open Space: Land Use Control in the Adirondack Park.* Cambridge, Mass.: Ballinger Publishing Co., 1979.

Empire State Forest Products Association. *New York Forest Policy Summary.* Albany, N.Y.: ESFPA, 1988.

Holmes, Timothy P. *The Future of the Adirondacks: A Survey of Attitudes.* Saranac Lake, N.Y.: Holmes & Associates, 1990.

Holmes, Timothy P., and Bryan Higgins. *Tourism Business, Community and Environment in the Adirondacks.* Saranac Lake, N.Y.: Holmes & Associates, 1999.

Nelson A. Rockefeller Institute of Government. *The Department of Environmental Conservation: A 25th Anniversary Review.* Albany, N.Y.: NARIG,1996.

New York Caucus of the Northern Forest Alliance. *Investing in New York's Northern Forest, An Agenda for Land Conservation in the Adirondack Park and Tug Hill Region.* Montpelier, Vt.: NYCNFA, 2001.

Northern Forest Center. *Northern Forest Wealth Index.* Concord, N.H.: NFC, 2000.

Northern Forest Lands Council. *Finding Common Ground* and *Technical Appendix.* Concord, N.H.: NFLC, 1994.

Residents' Committee to Protect the Adirondacks. *Subdivision and Development Trends in the Adirondack Park.* North Creek, N.Y.: RCPA, 1991.

Roth, Alexander J., and Thomas Carr. "The Economics of Land Preservation and Zoning in the Adirondack Park; An Empirical Analysis." Unpublished copy in author's files, 1993.

Spencer, R. Philips. *The Northern Forest Strategies for Sustainability.* Washington, D.C.: The Wilderness Society, 1993.

Temporary Study Commission on the Future of the Adirondacks. *The Future of the Adirondack Park,* vol. 1, and *The Technical Reports,* vol. 2. Albany, N.Y.: TSC, 1970.

Trancik, Roger. *Hamlets of the Adirondacks: Development Strategies.* Ithaca, N.Y.: Trancik, Urban Design Consultant, 1985.

———. *Hamlets of the Adirondacks: History, Preservation and Investment.* Ithaca, N.Y.: Trancik, Urban Design Consultant, 1983.

New York Legislative Commissions and Committee Reports

Assembly Ways and Means. *The Department of Environmental Conservation: A Program and Budget History.* Albany, N.Y.: Jan. 1985.

Environmental Conservation. Interim Report: *Oversight Investigation and Performance Audit of the NYS DEC.* Albany, N.Y.: 1998.

Expenditure and Review. *Adirondack Park Planning and Regulation.* Program Audit, Albany, N.Y.: 1978.

Rural Resources. *Land Use Planning and Regulations.* Albany, N.Y.: 1999.

———. *Reform of the Forest Tax Law.* Albany, N.Y.: April 1999.

Adirondack Park Agency Documents and Reports to the Agency

Adirondack Goals Program. *Final Summary.* 1984.

Adirondack Park Agency Act: Amended. 1981.

Adirondack Park Agency Rules and Regulations. Draft. Nov. 1973.

Adirondack Park Agency Rules and Regulations: Draft Revision, 1978; Revision, 1982.

Adirondack Park Private Land Use and Development Plan: Draft for Public Hearings, undated, and Recommendations for Implementation. Mar. 1973.

Adirondack Park State Land Master Plan. June 1972; April 1979; Forest Preserve Centennial Edition, 1985; second revision, November 1987, printed 1989.

Citizen's Advisory Task Force on Adirondack Hamlet Restoration and Development. *Report.* 1978.

Citizens' Advisory Task Force on Open Space, Chairman William K Verner. *Report.* April 1980.

Classification of Land: Town Private Lands, Data Base. 1984.

Joint Government-Industry Committee. *Clearcutting in the Adirondack Park.* 1981.

Joint Government-Industry Conference. *Intensive Timber Harvest in Private Adirondack Forests.* 1980, published 1982.

Local Planning and Land Use Controls. 1975.

Long Range Planning; An Evaluation of Selected Land Use Change, 1967–87. Memorandum, 1989.

McMartin, Barbara, with agency staff. Citizen's Guides Series: Adirondack Land Use Requirements, 1980; Forest Preserve; Wetlands; Forestry; Rivers and Roads; Lakes; Community Planning.

Reports of the Adirondack Park Agency, in particular volumes 1 and 2. 1973–75, and succeeding reports.

Response to the May 1994 Recommendations of the Task Force on Expediting APA Operations and Simplifying Procedures. 1996.

Task Force on Expediting Adirondack Park Agency Operations and Simplifying its Procedures. *Report.* May 1994.

Warren County Shoreline of Lake George, A Study of Existing Land Use. 1987.

Department of Environmental Conservation Documents

Adirondack Forest Preserve Public Use and Information Plan.

Citizen Advisory Committee. Minutes of meetings, handouts, membership. Author's collection.

Draft, Public Use and Information Plan Interpretive and Information System. May 1994.

Draft, Recreation and Tourism Participation and Demand in the Adirondacks Park. Prepared by State University of New York Syracuse College of Environmental Science and Forestry for DEC, April 1994.

Environment 2000 Issues Forum. August 1986.

File on Navigation Question, including proposed legislation.

Response to the Adirondack Windstorm of July 15, 1995, March 1996, and draft report, 1995; minutes of Task Force.

Richards, Karyn B., ed. Strategic Plan for Forest Resources in New York State. 1985.

Task Force on Access for the Disabled, all minutes, handouts, and iterations of policy.

Task Force on the Lake George Park. *A Plan for the Future of the Lake George Park.* July 1984; Plan Summary, July 1985.

VanValkenburgh, Norm. *Unit Planning for Wilderness Management,* December 31, 1982.

From the Executive Chamber

21st Century Environmental Quality Bond Act, 1990.

Conserving Open Space in New York State: Preliminary Draft Plan, April 1991; Draft Plan and Draft GEIS, 1991; Plan and Final GEIS, 1992; A Summary of the Plan, 1992; Executive Summary; reprint from *The Conservationist,* April 1993; Draft Plan and Draft GEIS, 1994; *Conserving Open Space In New York State,* 1995; *State Open Space Plan and Final Generic Environmental Impact Statement,* 1998.

Governor's Program Bill, #254, 1992.

Governor's Task Force on Forest Industry. *Capturing the Potential of New York's Forests,* R. S. Whaley, et al., 1989

Periodicals

Adirondack Park Agency Reporter, Susan Allen, editor, Keene Valley, N.Y.
NYEN, New York Environmental News, Rosemary Nichols, editor, Albany, N.Y.
Connections, Northern Forest Center, Concord, N.H.

Private Papers

Berle, Peter A. A. Papers from the Commission on the Adirondacks in the 21st Century. Adirondack Museum.

Cooper, James. Papers on Warren County Lawsuit. Adirondack Museum.

Davis, George. Papers in the Adirondack Museum and the Adirondack Research Library.

Crocker, Arthur. Papers in the Adirondack Museum and the Adirondack Research Library.

McMartin, Barbara. Minutes and handouts, High Peaks Advisory Committee, 1974–79; *Final Report High Peaks Advisory Committee,* 1979; Forest Preserve Advisory Committee, 1979–2001. Files on Land Acquisition and Classification, DEC Policies, Unit Management Planning, Trespass, TRPs, personal letters on many subjects.

Miller, Erwin. Archive at the Adirondack Research Library.

Persico, Richard. Scrapbook of clippings from his time at APA.

Raymond, Jean. Minutes of Region 5 Open Space Plan Meetings.

Vertical Files of the Adirondack Museum

The Commission on the Adirondacks in the 21st Century.
Land Acquisition.
Ton-de-lay.
D'Elia.
Local Government Review Board.
Property Rights Foundation of America.
Blue Line Council.
League of Adirondack Citizen's Rights.
Adirondack Mountain Club.

Organizational Histories, Newsletters, and Flyers

Adirondack Mountain Club, New York State Archives.
Association for the Protection of the Adirondacks, Adirondack Research Library.

Author's Private Collection

Adirondack Council newsletters.
Adirondack Conservation Council newsletters.
Blue Line Confederation, papers from Eleanor Brooks.
Local Government Review Board file provided by LGRB Secretary Carol Monroe.
Property Rights Foundation of America, material from Carol LaGrasse.
Residents' Committee to Protect the Adirondacks, including notes from Evelyn Greene.
Upper Hudson Environmental Action Committee file provided by Lou Curth.

Secondary Sources

Publications

Brown, Eleanor. *The Forest Preserve: A Handbook for Conservationists.* Glens Falls, N.Y.: Adirondack Mountain Club, 1985.

Cronon, William. "The Trouble With Wilderness; or, Getting Back to the Wrong Nature." In *Uncommon Ground, Toward Reinventing Nature.* New York: W. W. Norton & Company, 1995.

Davis, G. Gordon, and Richard A. Liroff. *Protecting Open Space—Land Use Control in the Adirondack Park.* Cambridge, Mass.: Ballinger Publishing Co., 1978.

D'Elia, Anthony N. *The Adirondack Rebellion: A Political and Social Exposé of the Adirondack State Park.* Loon Lake, N.Y.: privately printed, 1979.

Dowie, Mark. *Losing Ground: American Environmentalism at the Close of the Twentieth Century.* Cambridge, Mass.: The MIT Press, 1995.

Helvarg, David. *The War against the Greens: The "Wise-Use" Movement, the New Right, and Anti-Environmental Violence.* San Francisco: Sierra Club Books, 1994.

Hirt, Paul W. *A Conspiracy of Optimism: Management of the National Forests since World War II.* Lincoln: University of Nebraska Press, 1994.

Langston, Nancy. *Forest Dreams, Forest Nightmares: The Paradox of Old Growth in the Inland West.* Seattle: University of Washington Press, 1995.

Plunz, Richard, ed. *Two Adirondack Hamlets in History, Keene and Keene Valley.* Keene, N.Y.: Keene Valley Library Association, 1999.

VanValkenburgh, Norman J. *The Adirondack Forest Preserve.* Blue Mountain Lake, N.Y.: The Adirondack Museum, 1979.

Papers and Articles in Journals and Periodicals

Glennon, Robert C. *The Constitution and the Courts: A Review of Forest Preserve Litigation*. Schenectady, Union College, Forest Preserve Centennial Symposium, 1985.

Humbach, John A. *Law and A New Land Ethic,* paper, 1989, author's file.

Kissel, William H. "Permissible Uses of New York's Forest Preserve under 'Forever Wild.' " *Syracuse Law Review* 19 (1968): 969–96.

———. "The Adirondack Park: Two Decades of Innovative Land Use Planning." *New York State Bar Association, Real Property Law Section Newsletter* 20, no. 4 (Oct. 1992): 36–40.

Nelson, Holly, and Alan J. Hahn. *State Policy and Local Influence in the Adirondacks.* Cornell University, 1980.

Program in Environmental Studies. *Working Toward Sustainable Economic Development and Resource Conservation in the Adirondack Park: Analysis and Case Studies.* Middlebury, Vt.: Middlebury College, 1992.

Sabatier, Paul, John Loomis, and Catherine McCarthy. "Policy Attitudes and Decisions within the Forest Service," *Journal of Forestry,* Jan. 1996.

Verner, William. "Wilderness and the Adirondacks—An Historical View." *The Living Wilderness* 33, no. 108 (Winter 1969): 27.

Wissel, Peter A., Donald A. Reeb, and Roman B. Heges. *New York's Adirondack Park: A Study of Land Price Effects from Development Restrictions.* Division of Equalization and Assessment, 1986.

Index

Barbara McMartin has been active in numerous environmental groups and citizens' advisory committees, including the New York State Department of Environmental Conservation's Forest Preserve Advisory Committee. She is author or coauthor of more than twenty books and guidebooks on the Adirondacks, including *The Adirondack Park: A Wildlands Quilt*, also published by Syracuse University Press.